LIVING WITH SOUL

AN OLD SOUL'S GUIDE
TO LIFE, THE UNIVERSE
AND EVERYTHING

VOLUME ONE

LIVING WITH SOUL

AN OLD SOUL'S GUIDE TO LIFE, THE UNIVERSE AND EVERYTHING

VOLUME ONE

Tony Stubbs

A Dandelion Books Publication
www.dandelionbooks.net
Tempe, Arizona

Disclaimer and Reader Agreement

Reader Agreement for Accessing This Book

VOLUME ONE TABLE OF CONTENTS

VOLUME TWO CONTENTS

*D*EDICATION

~ *vii* ~

To you,

a brave creator-god who to Earth came

and promptly forgot your magnificence.

Not only are you more magnificent than you know,

you are more magnificent than you *can* know.

Also dedicated to the memory of Benjamin Franklin ... who wrote the fol-lowing to Miss Hubbard when his brother John died:

PHILADELPHIA, 23d February, 1756

I condole with you. We have lost a most dear and valuable relation. But it is the will of God and nature that these mortal bodies be laid aside when the soul is to enter into real life. This is rather an embryo state, a preparation for living. A man is not completely born until he be dead. Why, then, should we grieve that a new child is born among the immortals, a new member added to their happy society?

We are spirits. That bodies should be lent us while they can afford us plea-sure, assist us in acquiring knowledge, or in doing good to our fellow creatures, is a kind and benevolent act of God. When they become unfit for these purposes and afford us pain instead of pleasure, instead of an aid become an encumbrance, and answer none of the intentions for which they were given, it is equally kind and benevolent that a way is provided by which we may get rid of them. Death is that way. We ourselves, in some cases, prudently choose a partial death. A mangled, painful limb which cannot be restored we willingly cut off. He who plucks out a tooth parts with it freely, since the pain goes with it; and he who quits the whole body parts at once with all pains and possibilities of pains and diseases which it was liable to or capable of making him suffer.

Our friend and we were invited abroad on a party of pleasure which is to last forever. His chair was ready first and he is gone before us. We could not all con-veniently start together, and why should you and I be grieved at this, since we are soon to follow and know where to find him? Adieu,

B. Franklin

The Body of B. Franklin, Printer,

Like the Cover of an Old Book,

Its Contents Torn Out and

Stripped of its Lettering and Gilding, Lies Here

Food for Worms, But the Work shall not be Lost,

For it Will as He Believed Appear Once More

In a New and more Elegant Edition

Revised and Corrected By the Author.

— Epitaph, written at age 22

ACKNOWLEDGMENTS

Where does one start in acknowledging the insights, wisdom and understanding imparted by the hundreds, if not thousands, of sources that have helped me form my world view? Every source in the Resource section at the end is a good place to start. By singling out those precious few, I am in a way, acknowledging their role.

A few special mentions are in order for some material that appears within this book. First, I thank J.P. van Hulle of the Michael Education Foundation for allowing me to reproduce the quiz in the Appendix to help you determine your Role in the Michael Overleaf System. Knowing your Role is important, not because it places you in a box, but allows you to break out if you wish. And it takes away the pressure to be like everyone else.

Second, I am grateful to Walda Woods for letting me borrow some material from her book, *Conversations with Tom*, which I enjoyed editing a few years ago. Having someone on the other side describing what life is like over there adds immeasurably to this book.

Soon after the amazing crop circles appeared in Chilbolton, England in August 2001 that are apparently an ET response to the high-powered message we beamed out of the Araceibo radio telescope in Puerto Rico, I wrote an article about the event, some of which appeared in Art Martin's *2011: The New Millennium Begins*. He was kind enough to allow me to include the article in this book.

Finally, I acknowledge you for the journey you are about to undertake. Fasten your seatbelts.

PREFACE

To strive to make sense of tragedy does not minimize the pain and suffering; it only seeks to place it in a larger, more meaningful context. In October 2002, an earthquake in Italy caused the collapse of a small town's school and the death of every kindergarten child … except one, who walked out unscathed. Why the tragic, senseless death of 20 other innocents? And why did one survive?

On October 21, 1966, in Aberfan, Wales, a mountain of coal slurry, turned into liquid sludge by weeks of heavy rain, crashed down onto the town school, burying teachers and students under millions of cubic yards of slurry that immediately resolidified. An entire generation of Aberfan's citizens was wiped out in an instant. Why? An angry God? A cruel act of nature, revenge for man's neglect in just dumping the slurry from the coal mine? Or simple fate?

On the face of it, life doesn't make sense. Innocence is punished, and evil walks free. Our daily reality makes sense only when looked at through the eyes of our souls, and against the backdrop of reincarnation.

These are the issues this book tackles. How can any meaning be found in such apparently meaningless tragedies? The book's intent is not to minimize the reality of death and suffering—or the joy when a new life comes into the world—but to change the way we see and experience it as a set of interlocking plans designed and orchestrated by us at the soul level for very specific purposes.

The book's larger purpose, however, is to introduce us to who we are at the soul level so we can embrace our true identity and incorporate more of that in our daily lives. As we will see, the soul is a far cry from what organized religions teach—that it comes into being at conception or birth, hangs in the background while you live your life, and then ascends to heaven, where it waits patiently for Judgment Day and assignment to the fiery pit or saintly eternity.

Sorry, it ain't nothing like that. As part of an unimaginably vast entity, you-the-soul have been around since forever and have undertaken cycles of lives on physical planes in all corners of Creation. You are currently living one life out of one cycle on one physical plane associated with one planet—Earth.

Why is all this happening? It's a long story but you will know after reading both of the books in this two-volume set. Even after finishing the first volume, you will already have some of the answers. Promise.

Living with Soul presents what is termed a 'worldview.' It is simply a speculation as of the date written, of how things might be, presented without justification, footnotes, sources or (in most cases) attribution, so is far from scholarly and academic. What are my credentials for having written it? Twenty years of immersion in the study of spirituality, osmosis from having edited over 125 spiritual and metaphysical manuscripts, and from information 'dumped' into my awareness by those in higher dimensions. But it is still speculation because, on the physical plane, we cannot know the Truth. And even if we could, we certainly cannot express it in the English language.

What you hold as truth can only ever be your subjective truth, because it must be filtered through your perceptions, then interpreted, and finally assessed for meaning. And that process is uniquely yours, and by definition would differ in you and me because of our different soul experiences, genetics, upbringing and imprinting. And that's what makes life interesting.

Can I prove any of this? I don't need to, because plenty of other people have already done it for me. For example, Dr. Gary Schwartz of the University of Arizona at Tucson has conducted countless tests on mediums such John Edward and George Anderson, who actually replicated each other's readings, satisfying a basic requirement of the scientific method—that the results be reproducible in the lab—thus proving the reality of life-after-death. However, life-after-death doesn't prove reincarnation; for that we turn to famous cases such as the stories of Bridey Murphy (documented by Morey Bernstein—see Vol. II, Chapter 10) and Shanti Devi (documented by Dr. Ian Stevenson) and countless other well-documented cases … and, by the way, all targets of failed debunking attempts. After being immersed in hundreds of such accounts, I have no doubts as to their unimpeachable authenticity.

And before the debunkers (sorry, skeptics) start foaming at the mouth, the Law of Occam's Razor states that: "The most plausible explanation of any phenomenon is that which is the simplest and most economical." So, given the accuracy of the TV mediums, how do they do it? Private detectives, genealogy researchers, microphones under your bed? No, too complex and too expensive. The simplest and most economical explanation is that they really are doing what they say they're doing … talking to those on the other side. But far from being full of 'dead people,' the 'other side' is alive, dynamic, vibrant and a whole lot more fun than we alleged 'live' people get to enjoy. The question should not be, "Is there life after death?" but, "Is there life after birth?"

Is thinking about what happens after death morbid? Should we be more focused on life? Does reincarnation reduce the importance of one lifetime? Absolutely not … for three main reasons:

- You can better appreciate your current life if you see it in the context of a carefully planned progression on the part of you-the-soul. When you know that you lovingly crafted your life's circumstances and your personality for a specific purpose—soul growth—then you can set about discovering that purpose … and striving to achieve it.

- The deaths of loved ones cause intense grief in those 'left behind' if you think you have 'lost' them, when in fact, they may be standing over your shoulder, grinning at you and waiting for you to join them back Home.

- If you know a little of what to expect on the soul plane, your own crossing will prove far less confusing and disorienting, and you can immediately begin enjoying your new life on the soul plane.

The main reason why spiritual growth on this planet is so stagnant is that most of us simply do not realize we didn't incarnate just to hold a job, earn a living, have kids, get old and die. We have a much larger spiritual purpose down here—tackling challenges on the Earth plane that we cannot tackle on the soul plane. However, the same veil of amnesia (i.e., loss of memory) that makes this planet such a realistic school for learning and growing (by making us forget who we really are as souls) also makes us forget why we came here … and that is a tragic waste of opportunity.

We're here on an important mission but we've forgotten what it is, and worse, we've forgotten that we even have a mission. So we just wallow around in the muck and mire of the Earth plane, getting dirty, bloodied and bruised until it's time to go back Home. Hopefully, reading this two-book set will change all that for you, and have you 'living on purpose.'

If the contents of this two-book set ring true for you, does that mean everything you currently believe about soul and the afterlife is wrong? Or that your religion has lied to you all these years? No, just that you and they do not yet have the full story. In order to control you, organized religions present extremely limited views of the soul, which is actually a highly complex and powerful spiritual entity that is very active on many dimensions, including the soul plane; it's not just waiting around for Resurrection Day. (As we will see, reincarnation was an integral part of Christian dogma until the fifth century, when it was written out for political reasons. Hinduism does acknowledge reincarnation but conveys only a fraction of its glorious complexity, and mixes it up with India's caste system, again for political purposes.)

You do not, therefore, have to abandon any cherished beliefs for they are not 'wrong,' just limited. So you only need gently widen your beliefs. None of the major religious belief systems are 'wrong,' and actually contain much that is 'right.' They were perfect for their time when people were less sophisticated, but times have moved on and people have gotten smarter. Therefore this two-book set intends to bring things up-to-date.

So be prepared to leave your limited view of you as a lifeform just trying to make it through the day and eventually get to heaven (or whatever you call it) when you die. Such notions belong with theories that the Earth is flat and that the Sun rotates around it. The truth of who you really are is so wonderful that embracing it will be a stretch ... but well worth it.

This worldview is a mental model. A model is 'an imperfect replica of some aspect of the real world, intended to aid understanding.' The model may be smaller than reality, as when we place a model of an airplane in a wind-tunnel to see if it might fly. Or the model may be larger, as when we draw pictures of dots flying around each other to model the tiny atom. Maps and photographs are also models of reality, to help us understand some part of reality, but they are always imperfect, as I discovered when I saw the Grand Canyon for the first time. Nothing could have prepared me for the breathtaking spectacle, but the maps and photos helped me understand what I was looking at geologically, even though the reality caused my jaw to drop.

A globe sitting on someone's desk is a model of the planet, and even though it's better than the 'flat Earth' models we had before Columbus' time, they are still imperfect, and no one would confuse the two. Similarly, a body of knowledge devised to try to understand reality is necessarily imperfect—for a start, it has to be filtered through our primitive linear brains.

The following three models show the progression of understanding:

Before the time of Columbus, western science thought the world was flat, and knew only about Europe and Asia. No one knew what would happen if they sailed West across the Atlantic or East from India into the Pacific.

When Columbus finally sailed West, he discovered what he thought was India, which is why Native Americans were first called Indians. Only later did mapmakers realize it was the separate continent of the Americas, as shown in model #3.

Western science, based on religious interpretations of the Bible, attempted to model reality and offered pathetic models that any thinking person dismisses as far too limited to explain that reality. This book offers what is hopefully a slightly larger model of how reality could work, but it is still limited. So please do not seize on any part of the model as 'gospel.' The truth may be as breathtaking as the Grand Canyon, compared to a grainy black-and-white photo of it.

Model 1: Flat Earth, Europe and Asia only

Model 2: Round Earth, Europe and Asia only

A major human failing is that our intellect does not recognize its own limitations. Thus once we think we understand something, we sit back with a satisfied smile and say, "Got it," when we haven't even begun to 'get it.' So please be careful with the models in this book. When I show a 12-dimensional model

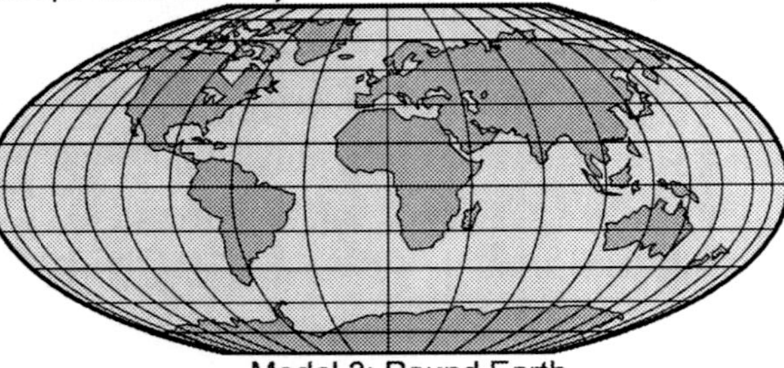

Model 3: Round Earth, Europe, Americas and Asia

of Creation, this offers a limited truth of something so complex, the human mind simply cannot get a handle on it. But at least a 12-level model is better than organized religion's 2-level models. So, if 12 levels are enough to make the point, why not stop there? And as to the ultimate question, the nature of the Creator of All That Is, there is no way any of us could even contemplate that, so why bother? Just accepting that we are all thoughts in its vast mind will be enough of a major leap for some.

For those with an interest in how arbitrary modeling reality can be, let's take a deeper look. (If you're not interested, skip the next couple of pages.) From the days of Aristotle (384 – 322 BCE) and Plato (427 – 347 BCE), the prevailing model was that the stars, planets, Sun and Moon moved round the Earth. The Greeks had forgotten about the Sumerian tablets, languishing ignored and unknown under the desert sands. In those days, astronomy was really astrology, in which the zodiac signs and the planets are shown revolving around the Earth. A few centuries later, Greek mathematician and astronomer, Ptolemy (c.90 – c.150 CE) used complex math to convince his contemporaries that the geocentric model of astrology was really how the solar system worked. This was the model that the Hebrews adopted and was carried into Christianity, prevailing under the Roman Catholic Church for 1,600 years. However, this model did not account for two observations that should be impossible if the planets revolved around the Earth:

1. Based on their brightness, the planets seem to differ in their distance from Earth
2. Planets often go retrograde.

When a model no longer explains what we observe, it's time for a new model. So, in 1543, a Polish scientist/mathematician named Copernicus (Latinized version of Kopernik) published a book laying out the mathematical basis for a totally different model in which all the planets rotate around the sun, which explained the two above anomalies.

Based on the work of Copernicus, German mathematician Johannes Kepler (1571 – 1630) formalized the three laws of planetary motion that bear his name. His model, published in 1609, was enough to get him excommunicated in 1612.

Meanwhile, Galileo Galilee, born in Pisa in 1564, had developed an early passion for mathematics, and was soon writing papers critical of Aristotelian astronomy. In 1609, he was given a primitive telescope, invented by a Dutchman and with a magnification of 4; Galileo quickly improved it to a magnification of 9. The city fathers of Venice loved it because they could identify incoming sailing vessels several hours earlier than before, but Galileo turned his telescope on the night sky. As a result, he was able to improve Kepler's 1609 model of the solar system. (He also discovered Jupiter's moons, and the much-pocked surface of our own moon.)

However, rumblings from Rome soon pitted the Copernican model against the Church's interpretation of the Bible and in 1616, the Inquisition condemned the former as heretical. Unfazed, Galileo continued his work and published his major work in 1632, laying out his dazzling new model of the solar system. The Inquisition immediately banned sales of the book and, in 1633, ordered Galileo to appear in Rome. Of course, he was found guilty of heresy and sentenced to house arrest for the rest of his life (on account of his age, 69, and poor health). The remaining nine years of his life were spent in solitude and advancing blindness, but he was cared for by the powerful Medici family. He died in 1642, but remained anathema to the Roman Catholic Church for 350 years, when in 1992, Pope John Paul II admitted that the church had been mistaken in condemning him and closed the case. The involvement of the powerful Medici family was typical of a stand-off between western religions and science that continues today.

René Descartes (1596 – 1650) was one of the chief architects of the split. This philosopher and mathematician is famous for his "I think therefore I am" quote and believed the soul is distinct from the body. He wanted to study how the soul connected to the body but, for that, he needed the Pope's permission to operate on cadavers. In exchange for such approval, he agreed to limit his studies to only the physical aspects of medicine, leaving all consideration of the nature of the soul and God to the church. This set the world of science on a reductionist path for two centuries, out of which it is emerging with the advent of psychosomatic studies.

So, from about 1700, science agreed to focus exclusively on the physical world, where religion would leave it alone so it could operate without moral or ethical constraints, but not delve into the supernatural realms guarded by religion. The latter could peddle its God-centric, faith-based palliatives to the masses, knowing science would not probe into the Grand Deception that religions enforced (more in Chapter 3). Religions would not impose sanctions on science as long as scientists stayed on their side of the fence. Meanwhile, families such as the Medici contributed to the coffers of both the Church and science, using the products of the latter to continue acquiring enormous wealth.

Thanks to Pope Urban VIII, this silliness back in 1633 marked the real divorce of science and religion, when men of science had to choose between the rational world of observation and the irrational world of faith. Until then, scientific and religious views lived together in one model, but at that moment in history, the two models had to sharply diverge. As a result of this deal between science and religion, tacitly made and unrecorded in history, many avenues of exploration (such as studying the role of prayer in holistic healing, technology for communicating with the deceased, and genetic engineering's role in human creation), have remained largely closed. Science no longer worked to understand God's creation, because there were now two realms—God's supernatural realm and the natural realm of the scientist. The divorce became final, but its seeds had been planted some 1,100 years earlier.

Until 325 CE, the central figure of the Christian cult was just a wise Essene teacher. Then the bishops met and voted on the notion that their mythical Jesus figure was the literal son of God and died to absolve us of sin. They also voted on another key issue: That upon death, one could only attain heaven by accepting Jesus as one's personal savior. To exempt Jesus from the 'original sin' of being the result of his parents having had sex (and horror of horrors, possibly having enjoyed it), the bishops also voted to reclassify his virgo mother, meaning 'pure woman,' to literal 'virgin.' Jeshua, the model for Jesus, would have been appalled at this gross distortion of the model. How could they get away with this? Back then, the Scriptures were copied out by hand and only the clergy could read, so within a generation, no one knew any different.

Moving on, until 550 CE, Christianity's model included the existence of the soul before birth, and reincarnation. Then, in that year, Emperor Justinian decreed otherwise, since such beliefs weakened the hold the Church had over its followers, particularly the absolution of sin because folks knew they had other lifetimes to get it right. So systematically, the bishops went through every book in the Bible, removing references to reincarnation. Again, within a generation, the common people had no knowledge of reincarnation, and were living with a very different model than that of before 550. After that date, you would have been stoned or burned at the stake for even reading this book. (Chapter 4 goes into more detail.) Thus, thanks to Justinian, the divorce between the western religious model and man's experience was set into motion. Death suddenly became the enemy and no longer just the other side of the coin of life. And the West was robbed of its birthright—the certainty that our lives are pearls on a string and that with each one, we grow in wisdom and understanding.

With science and religion off-limits to each other, who loses? You do, because you can only really know who you are by synthesizing science and spirituality. But if they won't come to the table, who synthesizes them? You do! In your daily life, you apply science to spirituality, and you apply spirituality to science. And at the confluence, lies invaluable information about who you really are. That's what this book is all about.

Models are arbitrary cultural, social and political descriptions of reality that people agree upon in order to work and play together, and rarely have little to do with that reality. So when anyone says, "I don't believe in reincarnation," tell them about Copernicus, because a model of reality that does not include life-after-death and reincarnation tells you more about the modeler than about their model. To paraphrase William James, "Those who do not believe in life-after-death have clearly not studied the evidence, and are either foolish or ignorant, so why should I try to convince them otherwise? Let them do the work themselves." These two books at least make an attempt.

Living with Soul also explores a part of the model that is missing in every organized religion because they can't go there. It involves what happens after death. If religions told the truth about the afterlife, followers would realize they didn't need religion at all and membership would plummet. So religions deliberately misled their followers with vague notions that require the faithful to keep coming back for more. Brilliant recruiting and retention tactics! These two books, however, clearly lay out exactly what happens when we cross over, where we go next, and what we do there. This piece of the model will save you any confusion if and when it's your time to take the ultimate step in life—that of transcending it.

Man's models cannot change the laws of physics, or anything else, as we've seen in the example of the shifting models of early Christianity.

Search for the Creator

In his book *The Dream of Reason*, the late Heinz Pagels pointed out that the introduction of the computer has, for the first time, allowed us to model reality, even life itself down to the cellular structure, and predict how complex, chaotic aspects of the model will unfold. Pagels likens this to a team of archeologists learning about an ancient civilization by examining the ruined cities and artifacts they have left behind and piecing together evidence of how they lived, the rules of their civilization, and what aspects of life were important to them.

In his book, he asks us to imagine what he names a 'Demiurge' (a god-like being) with such enormous intellectual powers, it can plan and create a universe as its own personal project. So the 'archeological ruins' of the Demiurge's work are the bits and pieces of the universe around us, from which we can project how it all operates, i.e., the laws of physics (that this being also devised). Pulling off a stunt such as our universe was no small feat. For example, gravity, electromagnetism and the binding forces within atoms are so finely balanced, a tiny change in just one of them could render life impossible—stars could not go supernova and spread planetary 'building materials' throughout space, or the material in stars could be so stable, stellar processes would not happen, making the universe a cold, dead place. Due to the enormous gravity in the center of the Sun, the density is so great that four hydrogen nuclei fuse to create one helium nucleus. The helium nucleus has 99.3% of the weight of four hydrogen nuclei, and the excess of 0.7% of hydrogen mass is converted into energy. In every second, the Sun converts 600 million tons of hydrogen into 596 million tons of helium, with the extra 4 million tons being converted into energy. Only one billionth of this energy reaches Earth. A tiny change in nuclear binding force may render this process impossible.

Over a decade later, this theme of fine balance was picked up by James Gardner in his book *Biocosm*, in which he proposes that the universe and all life within it is not random in design but the work of one or more super-intelligent beings. Gardner quips that perhaps we've been looking for evidence of ETs in the wrong places because, in fact, it's all around us, hidden in plain view. One piece of evidence for Intelligent Design, he claims, is that the universe is so hospitable to life, which echoes Pagels' ideas. Life did not 'just get lucky,' but is the beneficiary of some very clever design work.

Interestingly, *Biocosm* was not greeted with hoots of derision from the scientific community, but with wide acceptance, and carries endorsements by Britain's Astronomer Royal and the senior astronomer of the SETI project. Perhaps a non-scientist such as Gardner (he's an attorney) had to be the one to advance such thinking, because any scientist who tried it could have been blackballed for life.

It is fascinating to see science finally doing what it should … poking around in the physical evidence (i.e., Creation itself) in hopes of discovering the Creator. When we do, we will find it much more impressive than the God peddled by religions. For, as Albert Einstein once remarked, "I believe in Spinoza's God who reveals himself in the harmony of all that exists, but not in a God who concerns himself with the fate and actions of human beings." He also said, "I cannot imagine a God who rewards and punishes the objects of his creation, whose purposes are modeled after our own—a God, in short, who is but a reflection of human frailty."

The book will also help you with dealing with the crossing over by your loved ones, as they take the next step on their journey of growth, be they an elderly aunt dying peacefully in her sleep or a young child dying violently at the hands of a drunk driver.

By the end of this two-book set, you will have the answers to the Big Four Questions we all ask:

1. Who am I really?
2. Why am I really here?
3. Where was I before I was here?
4. Where will I go when I leave here?

Finally, early readers tell me they find *Living with Soul* to be 'intense.' Yes it is, I'm afraid, and you may find that one sentence provokes hours of thought. So I suggest you read it once quickly to get 'the big picture' and then go back in more depth to 'sweat the details.' And because the issues are so interwoven, we keep running into the same topics but from different directions, so please forgive any apparent duplication of material.

As we begin a new millennium, studies into the mind/body/spirit connection are taking a few faltering first steps. If we make it as a species to the end of this Third Millennium, life will look very different. *Living with Soul* is hopefully a tiny step along the way.

At first glance, the reader may wonder why some of this book's content is even included, such as the stranglehold that the big pharmaceutical companies have on your health. However, a book about soul cannot be complete without looking at the whole human, which involves soul, spirit, and the mental, emotional and physical bodies. And above all else, the soul has an inalienable sovereign right and duty to experience everything it needs in its quest to learn as much as possible about the wonderful and mysterious process we call life. Anything that erodes that sovereign right is unnatural and undesirable. However, we have become accustomed to having our rights eroded by numerous 'authorities,' so *Living with Soul* attempts to explore how things would be without such erosions. Then you can decide what is 'natural' and what is not, and whether you can and will live with that erosion; if not, how you can go about changing its impact on your life. For example, electronic medicine (frequency-generators that do everything from curing warts to curing cancer), but the FDA (at the insistence of the big pharms) puts such inventors in jail and burns their books. Rather than be locked into expensive and toxic prescription drugs and allopathic medicine, you need to know your alternatives. For example, many electronic devices are approved for veterinarian use only, so you know what to do to deal with this infringement of your sovereign soul rights.

Finally, you may wonder why this book is subtitled *An Old Soul's Guide* .... We live on a planet where old souls with hundreds of lifetimes of experience rub shoulders with souls just starting out on their reincarnation cycle. Old souls have mastered virtually all aspects of physical plane challenge, including unconditional love, and are tired and ready to move on to adventures in higher planes. Yet we're surrounded by much younger souls who think it's a grand idea to strap dynamite to themselves and blow up everyone in sight.

At one time, this confused me but, over the last 25 years, I've gained a little insight into what's going on. If you're asking the questions this book answers, you're probably an old soul ... and ready for what follows. Younger souls may be mired in organized religion's dogma, and may not even know there *are* such unanswered questions, let alone be asking them. Hence "An Old Soul's Guide."

So, onward into the mystery ...

INTRODUCTION

**Unique reality-adventure vacation!
New low-frequency hologram plus
memory loss provides convincing
experience of non-loving duality.
Planet Earth is as real as it gets.
Contact Archangel Michael for details.**

Suppose you're kicking back on the soul plane and notice an ad such as this in the *Cosmic Times*. Perhaps you've just finished a major project, such as jamming one black hole into a second to see what would happen, and you're bored. So you contact Michael, who responds with a thought-package. In it, you learn the Office of the Creator has authorized the Dimensional Realities Department to create a new holographic reality. To be called 'the physical plane,' it allows souls to descend to a new low frequency, and is separated from the soul plane by a barrier that triggers amnesia when souls cross it. This unique feature allows souls to interact with each other as if they were not souls and your physical plane bodies are all there is.

The barrier is particularly dense around one planet called Terra, third satellite of a small yellow star called Sol on the fringe of Galaxy 6472. Apparently, in this area of the physical plane, you lose all memories of everything, including your own soul nature and even your past lives in other systems. Others returning from Terra unanimously report, "Totally convincing!"

But it gets better. You don't just visit Terra in spirit form. From Michael's thought-package, you also learn that, about 60 million Sol-rotations ago, all the reptilian species were killed off following an asteroid collision that rendered the planet inhospitable to physical lifeforms. After that, Terra was recolonized with large, hirsute primates that were genetically engineered about 350,000 rotations ago to produce smaller, less hairy primates called *Homo sapiens*. These biological entities have all the necessary chakras, meridians, and other energy structures to ensure a firm linkage between you and the body's functions, so they are ideal for souls to attach to and experience events on the physical plane as if they weren't souls.

In order to bridge the frequency gap between you on the soul plane and physical plane, you project your energy down to these physical bodies, or 'soul carriers.' All you need do is observe these soul carriers while they are being incubated in the body of their mothers-to-be, and choose one into which to project your energy. The ETs who engineered *Homo sapiens* fixed the DNA to establish a lifespan of between 70 – 100 Sol-rotations, although injury, illness and pollution will reduce this. You don't actually own the body but just borrow it for its lifespan, and when it can no longer sustain your soul-link, you relinquish it to the planet for recycling.

There is a catch, however. You cannot just sign on for one foray. To do it thoroughly, you must agree to undertake a whole series of lifetimes in order to experience every aspect of life on the physical plane … and this could mean a commitment of several hundred lifetimes.

What you're not told is that this reality-vacation program is part of a far larger study on the part of the Office of the Creator. They want to know what will happen if parts of the Creator do not know they *are* the Creator and are also given free will. This has never been done before and everyone in the Office of the Creator is fascinated to learn the outcome. Will you use your free will to create mayhem or will you recall your true soul nature in time and fall back on your infinite love and compassion? Who knows? Hence the call for volunteers.

Intrigued? Of course you were. You're here, aren't you? But if you're finding that the amnesia thing is getting old, and you're ready to learn the truth behind the holographic generator, then read on.

Living with soul is no different from what you are doing now; you're already doing it, right now. If you weren't living with soul, you'd be dead, or more accurately, fully alive on the soul plane. The problem is that you don't know you're living with soul, so you cannot optimize the experience or get the most out of it. If you think you're just a limited little human, you will act like one and deny the magnificent Divinity within you. You will live in fear, rather than love.

The purpose of this book is to remind you that you're living with soul with every breath, but that right now, it's a one-sided arrangement. Your soul knows all about you as an ego-personality on the Earth plane, but you the ego-personality don't know much about you the soul. So our purpose here is to level the playing field by introducing the two of you and letting the conversation flow from there.

"Hey, _____________ (fill in your name), I'd like you to meet someone who loves you very much … your soul. Now you two have a lot to talk about, so I'll leave you alone. And if there's anything you're not sure about, it's all in the book you're about to read."

As sentient beings, we have always been fascinated with the world around us, resulting in a number of huge mental steps. Several thousand years ago, we lived under the dominion of advanced ETs, documented in ancient tales such as that of Gilgamesh. These all-powerful ETs gave us our notion of gods, boiled down by the Hebrews to a one god they called Yahweh or Jehovah. Next came the rational era of the Greek philosophers such as Socrates and Plato, who attempted to place man in a more realistic perspective, but screwed up by placing planet Earth at the center of the universe. Christianity scrambled our thinking for almost two thousand years by having access to printing, thanks to the invention of removable type presses and making it illegal to print anything other than the Bible. The Church also punished Copernicus and Galileo for claiming the Earth rotates around the Sun, but finally truth prevailed under Kepler. We then took our first faltering steps into space and realized the vastness of the universe in which we live.

What's next? Two major steps remain, probably linked. The first is serious and meaningful discourse with our extraterrestrial brothers and sisters, where we learn we are but one of a huge number of species in the universe. The second is that we recognize our true nature as that of higher dimensional creator-god beings who periodically attach to lower dimensional bodies for learning and exploration. As such, we are the focal point that our primitive religions seek.

This book cuts a wide swath through the human experience, beginning with our true identity as souls who decide to incarnate into the physical plane. Then it looks at how we forget that true identity and struggle through hundreds of lifetimes of confusion and ignorance. Finally, soul sets up a lifetime in which the truth becomes apparent and its incarnation wakes up to its true identity as a soul having a human experience.

As humans having spiritual experiences, it seems calamitous, confusing and even catastrophic, but as spirit having human experiences, physical plane lives are fascinating forays into an alien environment where we love and learn in ways not available to us on our native soul plane. On our return home, we can rightfully exclaim, "What a blast that was!"

So saddle up, pilgrim. We're going in …

CHAPTER 1

How It All Began

In the Beginning ...

FOR eons, the vast entity had tried to contemplate its own nature and discover its limits, but without success. It had reached the end of its resourcefulness. A castaway on a desert island can talk to him or herself only for so long before imagining a companion, as Tom Hank's character in the movie *Castaway* created the 'Wilson' character based on a volleyball.

So, the vast entity created quadzillions of companions within its infinite consciousness, and imagined them interacting with each other and with itself, their creator. But it wasn't enough. It wanted to explore its own nature using its creations as mirrors, but imaginary characters in its vast mind could not give it the external, objective point of view that mirrors do.

For further eons, the vast consciousness pondered the problem and realized it needed to somehow liberate its imagined characters, to give them an identity within its mind that allowed them to act, without it first giving them the thought to do so.

Imagine you are a scriptwriter for a daytime drama. All the characters exist in your mind. Day after day, you run plot ideas and have your characters play them out, but you know it's all just you. Without you thinking them into being and acting, nothing happens. You want your characters to somehow leap out of the TV set and become independent, autonomous beings who interact with each other and with you, all of their own volition and free will.

After further eons of deep thought, the vast entity found a way. It would create a dimension, an area within itself, and project its imagined characters there. Then it would give them free will and ask them to explore, create, experience their creations, and return to share what they had learned. The experiences they reported would become part of it, and it would know more about itself. It would grow in experience of itself because of their creativity. Further, because its creations had free will, it would have no way of anticipating what would happen. What a grand game!

With an enormous, liberating burst of creativity, it let its creations go and they dispersed into the vastness of the new dimension of the entity's mind.

It waited for the return of its creations. And waited. And waited. But its creations did not return. It wondered how it had erred … and tried again. Again, nothing. After countless attempts over further eons, it realized what was missing. Nothing was holding together the energy of the creations and they 'fell apart.'

It experimented with different qualities in the energy from which it crafted its creations—curiosity, courage, resourcefulness. Still they did not return. It realized that a binding energy was necessary to ensure affiliation between the creations and with itself, so they would cooperate with each other and return to it.

It imbued its next round of creations with an affiliation energy—love. This made the creations want to work and play together, to enjoy each others' creations, and then return to it and share what they had discovered. It was pleased. It had found the 'glue' that would hold everything together. Cooperation instead of rugged individualism, a sense of purpose and belonging to a larger whole. And so its creations went out and explored the dimension within its mind, and returned to commune and share. And it was pleased. Of course, those creations are our souls at their highest levels—each a vast spiritual being in its own right.

After eons of forays on the part of its creations, it was growing in knowledge and understanding of its own nature. Then, its creations clamored for the ability to in turn create their own creations, so it imagined into being a new lower frequency dimension contained within the first. Into this, the creations thought into existence their own creations, and endowed these lower frequency versions of themselves also with free will.

This second tier of creations dramatically increased the rate at which information flooded into it, and it enjoyed the huge expansion of love generated by the two levels of All That Is for each other and for it, all the more satisfying because it flowed by free will. Its creations were at liberty to explore anything but they consistently chose to operate from love. And it was pleased.

The second tier of creations in turn became creators in a new dimension, and so on down through countless dimensions. Soon, many levels of creation were interacting, creating, exploring, dismantling what they had created, and starting over. Creators could monitor what was happening in dimensions of frequencies lower than them because those dimensions had been fashioned from their thoughts, but lower frequency entities did not have the necessary perceptual apparatus to see what was going on at higher frequencies. But all entities shared two things in common—the knowledge that they were of the original entity's energy, and unconditional love for it and each other.

On the even numbered planes or dimensions, we use thought to generate density, matter, structure and the laws of physics for the next odd-numbered dimension, although the even-numbered plane itself is not subject to those laws of physics. We then project our consciousness down into the odd-numbered planes to explore creativity and free will within the structures and laws of physics that we created on the higher, even-numbered planes.

In this grossly simplified model, everything exists in the 11th dimension, which fosters its creativity and the free will. On the 10th and 9th dimensions, our focus is universal; on the 8th and 7th dimensions, our focus is galactic; on the 6th and 5th, it's stellar (i.e., the level of our solar system); on the 4th and 3rd, it's planetary; and on the 2nd and 1st, it's sub-planetary (i.e., to do with the consciousness of Earth such as quartz).

12	Creator Plane	
	First Created Plane	**11**
10	Sub-Creator Plane	
	Second Created Plane	**9**
8	Higher Soul Plane	
	Third Created Plane	**7**
6	Soul Plane	
	Ascension Destination	**5**
4	Astral Plane	
	Physical (Earth) Plane	**3**
2	Elemental Plane	
	Crystalline Plane	**1**

The process of unfolding down through the dimensions eventually ended up at the level of home to a quadzillion or so souls who enjoy unlimited creativity in their temporary home dimension—the 6th dimension, or the soul plane. Ironically, the shared knowledge (of being 'creator-stuff' and made of unconditional love) began to limit the souls' fullest exploration of All That Is. To our higher levels of consciousness, there was a problem—if you are the source of everything, how can you explore being 'not-source'? If you have been in love with everything and every other soul since your creation a quadzillion years ago, how can you explore 'not love'? How can you experience 'falling in love' when you're already 'in love'? How can you explore harming another aspect of yourself? Of course you can't, so sitting on the 6th and 4th dimensions, we saw the need for a new lower dimension, where we could go to forget who we are. Forget our lineage, and forget that we're unconditional love. The result? The physical plane.

The blueprint for the physical plane lies in the 6th and 4th dimensions, also home to the morphogenetic fields (more later) that form the blueprints for our physical bodies and those of all plant and animal species, and of the Earth and the other planets in our system. Thus astrology operates through the 6th and 4th dimensions, with planetary characteristics affecting our emotions, thoughts and reality creation efforts. (People scoff at astrology because, of course, except for the Sun and Moon, the other planets in our system can have no possible *physical* effect, not even gravitational, but they have a major energetic effect on us in the 4th dimension, where a large part of our consciousness functions.)

Humans interact with this planet's plant, animal and mineral consciousnesses through the 4th dimension, which is why native shamans work with animal totems, why peyote is revered, and why we feel so drawn to crystals. Our genetic blueprints—and theirs—exist in the 4th dimension, which is also why energy healing works … but more on that later.

For several billion years, the newly formed physical plane had to cool down, literally, and form into 'clumps'—galaxies, stars, and planets. Then, for those planets that could sustain life, the various levels of creators supervised the formation of plants and simple single-celled mobile organisms. Then, over eons, they genetically engineered progressively more advanced forms on those planets. For countless billions of years, they experimented with DNA and the energy fields of ever more sophisticated physical bodies, working through the dinosaur period and beyond to higher primates. In some cases, extraterrestrials took readymade species that flourished on one planet and seeded them on other planets with a suitable climate, including one that would come to be called Terra, or Earth. Other groups of creator-ETs used genetic engineering to splice their DNA with that of local Earth species, with varying success. What didn't work died out; what did work flourished in Earth's perfect climates.

As we'll see in Chapter 3, one such successful splicing resulted in Neanderthal man, which multiplied and colonized areas of temperate climate for about 300,000 years. The energy fields of this being were made sophisticated enough to allow souls to attach to the body, but only with a species memory that guided early man as to what had worked in the past. Hence little cultural progress was made, but we as souls gained practice in attaching to and working with bodies.

The next major step forward for ETs' genetic engineering came about 35,000 years ago with Cro-Magnon man, the first modern human body. Lighter, more responsive to soul contact, and with a larger brain, this species developed speech, higher thought and individual memory. Originally designed as worker drones, when the creator-ETs left, Cro-Magnon man rapidly colonized the planet.

Souls then became progressively more involved with these human bodies, entering and leaving at will. Finally, souls had a physical playground where they could incarnate in a fleshy body, or 'bio-suit,' and take it 'on safari' to experience a totally alien environment. Because they could also forget they were unconditional love, they could actually do dastardly deeds and have harm done back in return, all for the purpose of the creator learning more about itself.

Souls could meet up with other incarnations, pretend not to know them, and either kill their fleshy bio-suits or experience falling in love with them to see what it felt like. The closest they could get to soul merging was the practice of sex between their fleshy bio-suits, which is also how new bio-suits are made.

Somewhere along the way, souls stopped being able to come and go at will and, once a soul chose a physical body, it became 'locked in' to that body until the latter wore out or was killed. This was done in order to perfect the amnesia needed for learning. Then, when the soul's objectives for its lifetime in that body had been accomplished, it either waited until the body wore out and ceased to be a viable container, or it arranged an illness or accident so that it could terminate its involvement, much like returning a book to the library.

The human forms spread out over the planet's surface, multiplying quickly, but kept under close control by the ET creators of the physical form. About 5,000 years ago, the ETs gifted the colonies in Sumer and Babylon (now Iraq) with written language, mathematics, knowledge of animal husbandry, agriculture, architecture, plant grafting, navigation, metal working and a host of other skills. So, thanks to ET intervention, almost overnight, the species went from the Stone Age to the Bronze Age. And, best of all, the Cro-Magnon's energy fields contained the ability to receive a soul's transmissions and send back sensory and mental information to the soul plane.

~ ~ ~

Because of the quantum veil between the soul plane and the physical plane, the souls could not come to harm, even though their fleshy bio-suit containers could. And if they did, no big deal. Souls just started over with a new fleshy container, and with new goals and objectives. Because of the amnesia created when the soul transmits its 'soul signal' across the veil, the incarnating soul fragment had to pull together a collection of beliefs to guide the limited consciousness it had on the Earth plane. These beliefs could contain any self-concept, from the most heinous to the most exalted. Usually inheriting the beliefs of its caregivers, the incarnation gets to choose what it believes because it's imbued with free will, which is something it can't have on the soul plane, where it lives within the Golden Rule of "Treat others as you would be treated." But on the Earth plane, it had free will to create murder and mayhem. And because of the awesome collaboration of countless quadzillion conscious subatomic particles that assemble into atoms and molecules, it all felt so real. So finally the original entity's intent was achieved and parts of it could forget they were the source of All That Is, and play at being 'non-source.'

However, because working through the minefield of an Earth plane life consumes a lot of your soul's resources, you don't do it often ... maybe a couple of hundred times, or even thousands, each separated by several years, to give you time to assimilate what you've just learned. Then back to your main soul plane activities. At some point, you decide to drop down to the Earth plane frequencies again, so you prepare diligently for a new incarnation.

Eventually, you decide you have learned all you can from your cycle of Earth incarnations, so you move to the physical plane associated with another star system, or fold your energy back up to the next higher dimension, and continue growing there.

As we've seen, the second major aspect of setting up the Earth plane was that the souls decided, on incarnating (as soul signal or spirit, mind and body), they would induce amnesia, but their fleshy creations still needed some explanation for who or what ran things on the Earth plane. The incarnating creations figured volcanoes, earthquakes, hurricanes, etc., couldn't just be random, so someone *had* to be in charge ... and must be appeased. Some tribes reasoned that the boss was female, and ended up worshipping the Great Mother Earth. But other tribes that had contact with the genetic engineering ETs were in awe of their technology and incredibly long lifespans (measured in millennia). The ETs claimed *they* were the gods in charge, and worked hard to perpetuate that belief. As we'll see in Chapter 3, one group of humans fell under the influence of an ET overlord who called himself *YHVH* (meaning 'I am who I am'). This character ultimately became the exclusively male Hebrew deity that Christianity and Islam also inherited. Over the millennia, the oral legends handed down through the generations were documented in the Old Testament, and the Hebrews worshipped the memory of *YHVH*. This god was woven into a later Jesus cult, and once the Roman Empire backed the Jesus cult, the stories about the ET *YHVH* displaced all other gods and became cemented into Western culture. In medieval German, the name of this being was 'gut,' which became God in Old English.

This explains why the central figure of religions spawned in the Middle East is a vindictive male with great and awesome technology, who went around smiting anyone who displeased him. Religions in other parts of the world, such as Buddhism or Taoism have no such figure. Hinduism does have godlike central figures, but that religion also arose in an area that received much ET interference, as recorded in the Vedas.

As a footnote to this chapter, a remarkable thing happened in December, 2004. A prominent British professor of philosophy issued a statement in which he admitted having had a fundamental change in mind. For over 50 years, Antony Flew had been one of the world's most influential atheists, claiming there was no evidence for the existence of god. However at age 81, he recanted, having concluded that, "Some kind of intelligence or first cause must have created the universe. A super-intelligence is the only good explanation for the origin of life and the complexity of nature."

"It has become inordinately difficult even to begin to think about constructing a naturalistic theory of the evolution of that first reproducing organism," he wrote in a letter to Britain's *Philosophy Now* magazine.

However Flew says he sees himself more of a deist like Thomas Jefferson whose god was not actively involved in people's lives: "Very different from the god of the Christian and far and away from the god of Islam because both are depicted as omnipotent despots or cosmic Saddam Husseins."

"There was no one moment of change but the gradual conclusion over recent months," Flew says. "Biologists' investigation of DNA have shown, by the almost unbelievable complexity of the arrangements which are needed to produce life, that intelligence must have been involved."

When asked if this change of mind will upset people, Flew said, "Well, if it does, that's too bad. My whole life has been guided by the principle of Socrates: Follow the evidence wherever it leads."

Thus the source of All That Is (i.e., you at your higher soul levels) established the dimensional structures (lower within higher) and the beings who occupy them so, by definition, you are made of creator-stuff. Eventually, with a (very) Big Bang, we burst out of the 4th dimension to create the 3rd, or physical plane, a tiny part of which is associated with planet Earth. Then we projected a portion of ourselves from the 4th and 6th dimensions down into the 3rd dimension. So although we are both creator and created (our higher levels created our lower levels), we also have the full autonomy that comes with being creator-gods, or creators-in-flesh.

Although we can never know the nature of this super-intelligence[1] or of *its* source in turn, let's take a closer look at what we *can* know—how *you* came to be here … and why.

---

[1]   For the remainder of this book, we'll call this being 'Source' to avoid any confusion with the petty and vindictive 'God' of the Old Testament.

CHAPTER 2

LIFE ON THE SOUL PLANE

A common human misperception is that the soul plane is a holding pattern for souls who are between Earth lives. Even some well-known mediums claim that some souls, on crossing over, are immediately boomeranged back into a body. This myth points to an Earth-centered myopia that says Earth lives are what it's all about. Nothing could be further from the truth; Earth lives are simply souls on safari. If you were on the crew of *Star Trek's* Enterprise, busy with your shipboard duties, you may make occasional forays to a planet's surface to gather data or do research, but such forays are *not* your primary purpose. These brief missions are akin to a soul making periodic trips to Earth for the same purpose—gathering data and doing research.

Eons ago, your 'higher soul' fashioned you-the-soul plane level of your vaster being. A *very* simplistic model[1] of the soul plane associated with our region of space is that it's a 6th-dimensional frequency band divided up into several sub-bands, say seven, and in that model, most souls inhabit levels three and four of the soul plane. (See over for diagram.)

Let's briefly mention Level 1, and then we can forget it. Folks who are mean and nasty while on Earth end up there, and find it full of equally mean, nasty folks. Now while they were on Earth, they had warm, loving role models to learn from

[1] Models are imperfect replicas of something real, used to help learning or understanding, e.g., a wind tunnel model of a plane, a map of the Grand Canyon, and a globe. The model must never be confused with the real thing … but often is, just as people confuse their beliefs *about* reality with reality itself.

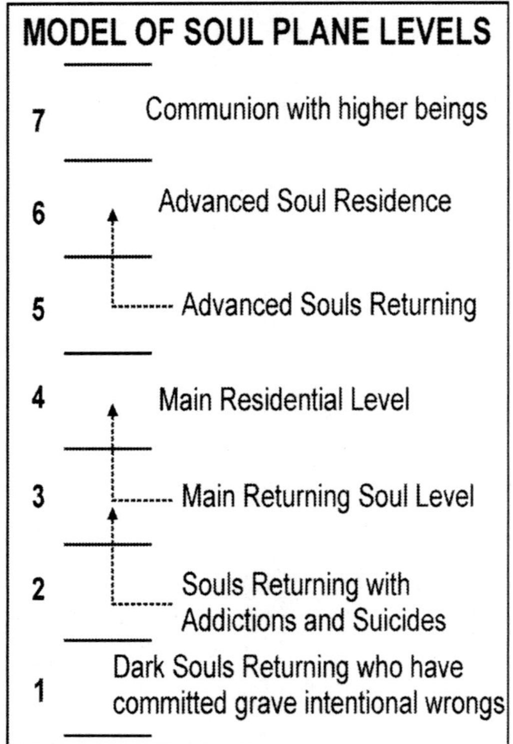

When a soul returns to the soul plane, it gravitates to the level with which its energy resonates. A mass murderer will resonate with the dark energy of Level 1 and keep the company of other dark souls until it begins to show signs of remorse (which may be a long, long time). Those needing special healing resonate with Level 2's 'hospital energy.' Most other souls are still 'infected" with Earth plane energy, and end up on Level 3 for light healing and orientation to Level 4, which is the main residential level. A Buddhist holy man may return to Level 5, for orientation to Level 6. He meditates or visits the Ascended Masters on Level 7.

and should have taken the hint while they could. But once on Level 1 of the soul plane, all the role models are mean, nasty SOBs, so there's no incentive to become a 'nice guy.' In fact, to get ahead on Level 1, you must be the biggest, meanest, nastiest SOB on the block, so change could take a long, long time. Fortunately for most of us, you've got to be pretty irredeemable to end up in that kind of hell. But no one is sent there; one's own spirit frequency resonates with Level 1 energy and inexorably attracts folks there. And they just could not exist in the higher levels for they'd be extremely uncomfortable there. Okay, enough said. Let's get on with the story.

For eons (or what would be millions of Earth years if time existed there), we souls on the soul plane have worked, played, grown and explored the nature of creation. Where is this place? Right where you are now, interwoven with the Earth plane but vibrating at a higher frequency, so it is invisible to most of us. Its inhabitants can see and hear us but we cannot see them (usually), so a loved one who has crossed over may be reading this over your shoulder. (However, they are very discreet.) Also, the soul planes corresponding to other planets are interwoven with Earth's, too.

For reasons we will see later, the part of the soul plane that is associated with a localized region of the physical plane (such as the Earth region of space) is designed to mirror that piece of the physical plane. Any good psychic medium can communicate with those on the soul plane and receive accounts of life there. To those who are there, their reality is every bit as real and tangible as our Earth plane is to us. There are notable exceptions, however.

First, inhabitants there know without question that they are 'creator-stuff' so there's no 'searching for God'—they know they are of the Source's energy. And God is not something transcendent, i.e., 'out there.' It's immanent, or 'in here,' the stuff of which they are made. And since that stuff is primarily love, it's a cool place to be.

From accounts reported under hypnotic regression, life on the soul plane is a vibrant, fast-moving collection of activities that involves learning, creativity and recreation. One person under regression reported the soul plane associated with our Earth plane is home to about 60 billion souls, so not every soul chooses to incarnate on Earth. Currently, about one-tenth of those souls have chosen to do that for a variety of reasons … as we will see.

Most of the souls who incarnate are here to explore some facet of All This Is, or the mind of the Source in which everything is happening as a huge collection of interwoven thoughts.

Many souls incarnate on Earth to probe the nature of love, from the standpoint of exploring its absence, or 'not-love.' Such study is impossible on the soul plane because there, everything is drenched with love. As we've seen, when you know you're made of love, you can't really examine it objectively—you can't even imagine not being made of loving Source-stuff—so where can you find a place where unconditional love is not taken for granted? Earth, of course.

Do souls have to incarnate on Earth? Of course not. There are no rules on the soul plane. However, you could spend millions of years trying to imagine how you would behave if you did not know you were love … and still not get it. Or you could drop into a lifetime in Bosnia or a South African country in civil war and get a five-year crash course in hate, abuse, war, greed, fear and all the other loveless chaos on the planet. One five-year stint as a child in a war torn country will teach you more than millions of years of conjecture on the soul plane. And when you return Home after being brutally butchered into little pieces by a machete-wielding mob, you will look at love with new eyes. Yep, you can't beat the Earth plane for a quick study in limitation, which is why it was created, of course. All just the Source learning more about itself.

Take grief, for example. How can you study the gut-wrenching ache of losing someone you love if it's impossible to lose anyone? On the soul plane, you just think of another soul and boom … you're right there with your buddy. (We will explore later how the Earth plane allows us to explore grief and a number of other phenomena not possible on the soul plane.)

Now, Earth trips are not for faint-hearted souls because Earth life has a terrible reputation elsewhere in Creation for being the toughest thing any soul can take on. That's why only about ten percent of souls even have the courage to try.

When I see movies and TV programs about Navy SEAL training and the missions they undertake, I am in awe of those guys. Likewise, on the soul plane, those brave souls who manage to complete not just one lifetime but actually go back for more are revered as 'the best of the best.' And that includes YOU. Of course, the first few lifetimes are the hardest, as we'll see, but after that, you as a soul know what to expect. But that doesn't alleviate the bone-crunching horror of having to forget that you *are* unconditional love. Welcome to planet Earth!

Your level on returning to the soul plane is a brilliant example of justice at work. You go to the level that matches the amount of light in your spiritual body. There's no question of external salvation or mercy; you yourself, by virtue of how you lived your life and gathered light (or not), determine your soul plane destination. Once there, can you 'cheat' and sneak up a level or two? No, because the discomfort would be excruciating. Think about a deep ocean. Different species of creature live at every level, and if a creature tried rising above its normal level, it would sense pain and finally explode. If another creature descended too deep, it would feel pain and implode. The pain is a warning sign that it's not supposed to be there. On the soul plane, if you strayed towards a higher level, the intensity of the light would blind you; if you went towards a lower level, the cold and dark would incapacitate you. So it's a perfect, self-administering system of justice.

Reality Channels

Imagine that the physical world around you is the result of a very clever TV signal being received by an equally clever three-dimensional TV set. Let's call this very clever TV program 'Channel 3' … and you're surrounded by it. Now flip up to Channel 4, and you find a very different place with different rules—Channel 4 is populated by discarnate entities (some good and in service, some not so good), deceased people who haven't yet moved on for whatever reason, and Channel 3 people who are asleep and dreaming. It may seem ethereal from Channel 3, but to Channel 4 occupants, it's very much real.[2]

While you're watching/living Channel 3, where is Channel 4? Right around you. And when you flip from Channel 3 to 4, where does Channel 3 go? Nowhere; it's still there, so all channels co-exist in the same space.

Flip the remote again and we're on Channel 5, the lowest of a block of channels that this book calls 'the soul planes.' If you're an evil, malevolent type while alive in Channel 3, you will love Channel 5 when you cross over, for every inhabitant here is just like you—a murderer, a rapist, a child molester, etc.—only much better at malevolence than you, so you'll have some good role models. The neat thing is that no matter how many times they kill you, you can never die, so it's a little like *Groundhog Day* for eternity. Nice!

Flip up a few more channels and you'll come to an idyllic channel of pure unconditional love, unlimited learning, lots of fun, and tons of joy. However, only some remotes can access this channel; evil, malevolent people simply can't get here, and even if they could, they would be repulsed by all the yucky (to them) love energy, and quickly incinerate and self-destruct.

The inhabitants of these higher channels know there are countless even higher channels, but that doesn't bother them, for there's plenty to do here to keep them busy for eternity—playing, learning, having fun, working with new arrivals, and even interacting with folks down on Channel 3 to improve things there. The purpose of *Living with Soul* is to make sure you know where the button for this channel is on your remote.

What's fascinating is that all the different channels play out in the same space, just as all our broadcast TV channels travel through the same space and enter your TV set together so you can choose one of them. As you read this in Channel 3, you are surrounded by myriad other channels, which feel equally as real to their inhabitants as your Earth plane life feels to you. Neat, eh?

---

[2]   As a fascinating example of this, on December 29, 1972, a Lockheed L-1011, Eastern Airlines Flight 401 from New York to Miami, went down in the Florida Everglades. About two-thirds of those aboard crossed over, including Flight Engineer Don Repo. Soon after, Repo became a frequent 'visitor' on L-1011 flights, usually to warn the crew of some impending trouble. On one occasion, he appeared in the cockpit to warn that faulty wiring was about to cause a disastrous fire. The captain, who didn't know Repo, just assumed Repo was 'dead-heading,' and averted the disaster. He was later surprised to learn the identity of his informant. During another of his 'visits,' Repo told the cabin staff he would ensure that no L-1011 ever again crashed ... and to date, only one has—a Delta flight hit by a microburst in Dallas in 1985, making the L-1011 probably the safest airplane in the air.

Amnesia

Why *do* souls suffer from amnesia and forget all about who they really are once they become associated with a physical body? Well, the soul back on the soul plane never forgets, but only a fragment of that soul attaches to the physical body, and even then only ethereally. The body's connection to soul is similar to that of a TV set, plugged in, switched on, and receiving the soul's signal on 'our unique, personal channel.' The signal is always there, but the TV set may go out of tune and not receive it clearly enough. How could that happen? Substance abuse gets in the way, of course, but the greatest block arises because the incredibly refined signal must be filtered through our beliefs, which can cause horrible distortion. Or our ego-personality may be creating a ruckus in the room and we can't even hear the TV program.

Now the human brain is a miraculous organ that medical science still hardly understands, but overlaid with that is our equally miraculous mind, an amazing thought-processor that exists independent of the brain.

When you-the-soul first attached to the fetus that would become your fleshy focal point for this lifetime, you transmitted your soul vibration to the developing brain to begin working with its chemistry and create the mind. (For this delicate process to succeed, the mother's body chemistry must be as pure as possible.)

The mind is actually three minds[3] in one:

- *Superconscious Mind*, which is the soul presence, the part that receives the soul's vibration or signal, and knows who it really is. Often called *higher self*, it *is* the soul as far as the rest of the psyche is concerned, and communicates constantly with the main soul and with spirit guides as needed. It is the bridge between the soul and Earth planes.

- *Conscious Mind*, the rational decision-maker, which contains your ego-personality and its belief system. For those who do not acknowledge their spiritual nature, ego-personality *is* who they think they are. Any sub-personalities you create along the way are held on the boundary with …

- *Subconscious Mind*, which records all details of your life even though they have long slipped from your conscious memory, and stores 'tapes' of old responses that sub-personalities can call on to deal with current situations if Conscious Mind can't figure out what to do. It also holds your deep self-image and history of all your soul's incarnations, usually accessible only under hypnosis. It's kept 'locked up' because having ready access to all this past-life information would drive most of us crazy.

---

[3] None of this is rigorous from an academic psychology aspect.

The mind is not so much a 'thing' as a field of consciousness that is anchored at many parts in the body. For example, lower levels of the Subconscious Mind anchor to the autonomic nervous system for such functions as breathing and digestion. The Conscious Mind anchors to the left hemisphere of the brain, whereas the Superconscious Mind anchors into the right hemisphere. (We return to this in a later chapter.)

Anchoring *into* a part of the body does not mean it *is* that body part. Anyone who doubts that mind exists separate from the body is simply ignoring the overwhelming mass of evidence. For example, Jack Searle, the owner of a South African animal park, was bitten by a black mamba snake he was handling, and injected with enough neurotoxin to kill hundreds of people. The venom shuts down the central nervous system, stopping the commands for the lungs to breathe and the heart to beat, so in the hospital, he was put on a heart-lung machine. For 8 days, the machine breathed and pumped his blood for him, while his EEG showed he was brain-dead.

During those 8 days, however, his mind was brilliantly alert and recorded every conversation around him, including that of two nurses who joked about the small size of his penis, and the doctor who told his wife that if he recovered, she'd be married to a vegetable, so they might as well pull the plug. However, out of curiosity, the doctors let the 'experiment' run its course.

On the eighth day, after a monumental focus of effort, Searle managed to move a finger, and then flutter his eyelids. Layer by layer, he felt his mind progressively reassert its control of his bodily systems, and went home a week later … but not before making the two nurses blush.

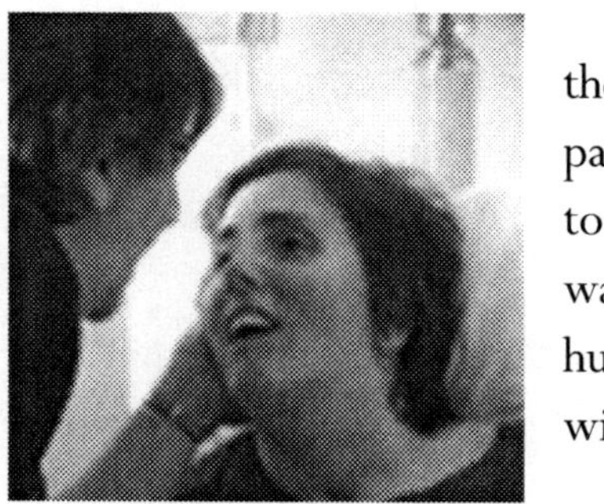

Closer to home, we have the case of Terri Schiavo, the focal point of an adult 'right to life' controversy. The parents and siblings of this 41-year-old woman wanted to keep her on feeding and water tubes, claiming she was aware and enjoyed a certain quality of life. Her husband Michael had been living with another woman with whom he had fathered two children.

In March 2005, the U.S. Congress got involved and passed a law empowering a federal judge to rule in the case, after state judges ordered her feeding tube removed on March 18, 2005; ignoring testimony from rehab therapists that all Terri needed was appropriate therapy.

The nurses who attended Terri asserted that she enjoyed looking out of the window, having her hair brushed and taking baths, and that she could vocalize a limited set of expressions. She joined in prayer, laughed at jokes and enjoyed the sound of a radio. The only time she expressed fear was around the visits of husband Michael, who denied her therapy and her favorite radio channels, and fired any friendly nurses. Sounds like someone is creating massive karma.

After 13 days without food and water, Terri crossed over on March 31, 2005. Oddly, husband Michael insisted on being the only one in the room with her, one final act that deeply upset Terri's grieving parents.

Of course, this was all meticulously planned at the soul level, but few knew that as, with the world's spotlight on this torture, a human being underwent a slow death that would be deemed 'cruel and unusual punishment' if meted out to America's most heinous death-row inmates. The rest of the world looked on as a supposed 'civilized' country put to death one of its own in such an inhumane way. Of course, the American media shielded the people from the global outrage at the barbarous cruelty reminiscent of the medieval Inquisition.

According to Matthew Ward,[4] a famous discarnate source, reports that Terri's soul actually left within a few weeks of her traumatic near-death experience in 1990, and that any responses to people she knew, were only body consciousness reactions to familiar faces. The autopsy revealed in June 2005 that Terri's brain had shriveled to about half its size and could not have supported any cognitive functions, so it really was a 'persistent vegetative state' after all.

So what was it all about? The same drama plays out many times a day around the world, but never in this spotlight. This case focused on the importance of making a living will, which is all the more necessary when people marry and remarry, having spouses and children from different marriages, all of whom could end up fighting about your last days if the same thing were to happen to you. It's even more vital for gay couples, because gay partners have no voice compared to one's biological parents. Bottom line: put your wishes in writing, make copies and make sure people close to you know that you've done it and have copies.

Modern diagnostics, such as MRI, reveal that people in comas, while exhibiting low level brain activity when at rest, show practically normal levels during visits by loved ones, as the visitors bring the patient up-to-date with news of outside events, and read from their favorite books. And you never know when they will 'wake up.' What you *do* know is that they are fully aware of everything going on around them, even if their central nervous system does not allow a response.

---

[4]   Seventeen-year-old Matthew Ward died in an auto accident on April 17, 1980. His mother, Suzanne Ward, initiated contact with him via psychic mediums, but in 1994 established direct telepathic with him via automatic typing on her computer. This led to the Matthew books, *Matthew, Tell Me About Heaven* (2001) and *Revelations For A New Era* (2001). We hear a lot more about him in Vol. II, Chapter 14.

This is no better demonstrated than by Sarah Scantlin, who, at the age of 18, was injured in a hit-and-run accident that left her semi-vegetative, aware of her surroundings but unable to speak or move. Then, early in 2005, *twenty years later,* she suddenly woke up at age 38 and began speaking normally. The doctors have no explanation for her sudden improvement.

Both cases tell us one important thing—no one knows why a soul chooses its circumstances except that soul, so making decisions on behalf of the soul is to play God. Anyone feel worthy to do that?

Researchers have discovered that the Conscious Mind drives only 5 percent of our actions, while the Subconscious drives the other 95 percent (with the Superconscious Mind having virtually no input for most people). This was well-demonstrated in a recent blind Pepsi/Coke test in which dyed-in-the-wool Coke drinkers invariably preferred the taste of Pepsi. When the taste test was then repeated with the participants first knowing the brand, the Coke drinkers switched back to preferring Coke. However, this time, MRI peered inside their brains and found that just seeing the familiar red and white design of the Coke label evoked a lifetime of good memories and other pleasant associations, none of which were in the Conscious Mind. The Subconscious Mind, not the actual taste, was actually driving their preference for Coke. (Failure to conduct a test such as this resulted in the monumental fiasco a few years ago when the Coke formula was changed to taste more like Pepsi. Consumers felt as if their memories of childhood were being violated and responded vociferously, demanding that the original formula be reinstated.)

A theme repeated often in this book is intended to help you get in touch with the contents of your Subconscious Mind, since it has been recording your environment since the womb, and drives so much of your life, without you actually realizing it. If you are to get closer to letting soul play a role in your decision-making, you must break free of the Subconscious Mind's autopilot and take the controls yourself.

Through ignorance and lack of training in listening, what the Superconscious Mind knows often does not get to the Conscious Mind. Hence the amnesia, so humans often operate not knowing their identity. And as a species, we haven't even begun to tap into the incredible complexity of how the three levels work together, and how mind and brain interact.

For the first few years of life, children often remember their soul plane home, but that soon fades under the barrage of sensory input. Dolphins and whales, however, have far more complex brains and do remember a whole lot more than humans. It's a shame that people in many nations regard them as a food source and not as teachers who could remind us telepathically of much that we have forgotten about love, compassion and the history of the universe.

Setting Up an Earth Life

As a free soul, you roam the soul planes at will, creating, exploring and learning. However, there may come a time when you decide to temporarily trade your unlimited freedom for some limitation. After all, how can you fully appreciate freedom until you've experienced its opposite?

This means a sojourn to a physical plane associated with a planet. If you're really courageous and want to get your learning done quickly, you would choose one of the densest planets, one where you can forget your creatorship and all about unconditional love, and try to muddle through, despite being spiritually blind. So you head for a pocket of hell in an otherwise heavenly universe.

Earth has been described as the only planet of true free will. Why? Because everywhere else, souls know they are creators in loving service to All That Is. Knowing that, souls can do nothing to harm or hinder any aspect of All That Is, for they know they would just be harming themselves. But what if souls could forget this for a few years and act as though they were separate, independent, autonomous entities?

With such overwhelming freedom, what would they do? Create chaos and mayhem, or continue to strive for the good of All That Is? There's only one way to find out. And one place.

What kinds of lessons are available on the Earth plane? First, the sheer exhilaration of being in a physical body is ecstatic. Yes, you may be spiritually blind but to a soul, sensually, being in a body is like taking a roller coaster ride rather than reading about taking one. Life on Earth offers a degree of focus and immediacy not found on the soul plane, which is why souls go to great lengths to get here.

Another challenge is to balance our human and spiritual natures. Imagine a seesaw with your human nature on the left and your spiritual on the right. Whichever is uppermost governs the incarnation. If the human side is up, you may spend a lifetime as a thrill-seeker, going from one sensory overload to another—adventure, sex, drugs, and so on. Then the soul's next lifetime is spent in a remote Buddhist monastery, meditating and chanting. No balance there. Eventually, the soul achieves perfect balance, say as a Reiki master in the West, using spiritual techniques to help heal physical bodies.

Yet another set of challenges is to operate in pure unconditional love amidst the oceans of hatred in this dense plane. It may take many lifetimes, but you'll get there.

How many lifetimes make up an Earth cycle? That depends on how many challenges you pack into each lifetime. You won't learn as much from a string of comfortable situations as from one tough one, say as a blind quadriplegic.

Some sources say as few as 25 will do it; others say as many as several hundred. There are no rules and, after its first sojourn, a soul may say, "Ouch, I'm out of here," and hightail it back to the Pleiades, where the veil of amnesia is not nearly as impenetrable. Or, "I'll stick around Earth but only as a spirit guide."

Assuming you make 40 sojourns to the Earth plane, lasting an average of 50 years each, you will spend about 2,000 years in your various fleshy earth-suits. (For a hundred lifetimes, that's 5,000 years.) Now, as a soul, you are an eternal entity, but let's say you came into being a mere two million years ago—less than a blink in all eternity. That means your 2,000 Earth years are only 0.1 percent of your soul experience, so you spend 99.9 percent of your time on the soul plane doing 'soul things.' Now that puts the role of Earth lives into perspective.

The physical plane life you currently regard as so important is really just a flash in your overall soul's growth, and one of dozens, or even hundreds, of lifetimes just like it. Now someone hearing this might be tempted to say, "Well then, it doesn't really matter what I do in this lifetime, so I might as well take it easy, goof off, and the hell with everything." That attitude is precisely why reincarnation was written out of the Bible in the sixth century. The bishops found that telling people they had just one shot to prepare for God's Judgment Day got their attention and motivated them to attend church (more on this in Chapter 4). Meanwhile, the other two-thirds of Earth's population continues to believe in reincarnation, however screwed up they make it. Hinduism allows for cross-species incarnation, which means, "Shape up or return as a bug," and in India, it is tied into the caste system as a means of controlling the population, as in: "Shape up or come back as an untouchable." Neither approach exudes unconditional love.

For the rest of this book, remember that your 25 – 400 lifetimes make up less that one percent of your soul experience, and that Earth was conceived as a place of learning for souls on the fast track. Let go of any notions that Earth lives are what it's all about, with the soul plane as a holding pattern until you return to Earth. It just doesn't work like that.

This is so important, it deserves repeating: *The soul plane is your true Home, and Earth lives are brief sojourns to learn specific lessons.*

Now, even some souls tend to forget this and become bedazzled by physicality, so they take too many sojourns to master the physical-spiritual balance. Fewer, more spiritual lifetimes would do the job more quickly. And there's a long waiting list to get here, so hurry up and graduate.

According to some sources, the slow rate of spiritual growth on Earth is holding up advancement everywhere else in the galaxy, so some heavy-duty resources have been deployed to move things along. The Kryon entity, for example, is adjusting certain energy grids around the planet to allow for more rapid shifts in consciousness. But this is still a planet of free will, so ego and soul must still do the shifting—no ascended master can do it for you.

Please do not let this new perspective trivialize the importance of Earth sojourns. They are enormously important experiences, ones that you work hard to set up. So let's see what's involved.

The soul planes are unimaginably vast because not only do they embrace all of the physical plane, they are also stacked dimensionally, within each other, with more layers than our poor minds could possibly conceive. Infinitely wide and infinitely 'high.' Fortunately, as souls, we have 'super-awareness' that can handle this and merge seamlessly with even higher levels of our soul, the creator source entity that thought us into being, whose awareness in turn merges with the level that thought *it* into being. And so on up the dimensions to the awareness of the Source itself that thought *everything* into being.

When we volunteer for an Earth life and incarnate (literally, 'in meat'), we trade our super-awareness for mind, a limited spiritual/electromagnetic field that interacts with specialized areas of the brain in order to operate our meat-machine.

The soul plane is an infinitesimally narrow band of frequencies to which souls limit themselves for the duration of a cycle of Earth lives. In this miniscule area of All That Is, we create a reality that we will call Home for a few centuries or millennia while we play out the lives making up that cycle. However, since we experience time very differently on the soul plane, those centuries may go by in a flash or stretch out forever … or both. Time on the soul plane depends on the intensity of your focus. If you are deeply engaged with a task such as creating the DNA for a new plant species and are working on it at many levels simultaneously, time is 'deep,' but if you take a break, time is 'shallow.' Fast and slow don't enter into the equation.

Because the soul plane is a reality that is thought into being by its inhabitants, it is similar to everyday Earth for two reasons. First, the familiarity with Earth comforts returning souls, and second, architecture, creativity, scientific inventions, etc., and other features on Earth are first tried out there. The plans for, say, those buildings deemed beautiful or elegant are transferred to the minds of architects and builders on Earth to be constructed down here. (In fact, Hadrian, the great Roman architect, admitted to having dreams and visions in which he was shown the plans for his finest works—clearly inspirations from the soul plane.)

Souls hypnotically regressed to the time between incarnations, and souls reporting through mediums, consistently tell us the soul plane is replete with magnificent buildings and breathtaking scenery, and every conceivable activity is supported and available to souls. And, since your body is not vulnerable flesh and bone, you don't have to worry about getting hurt. For most, however, tennis and golf are about as 'hard' as things get and, even then, you're competing not against your partner but against your own previous best. You play purely for the joy and exhilaration of playing and improving, not winning.

Cultural and social gatherings occupy much of your time, with lots of choral recitals (as you'd expect with all those angels). Study, the creative arts, recreation, socializing with friends, and collaborating on projects keep those on the soul plane quite busy, not to mention showing up for TV shows with psychic mediums such as John Edward and James Van Praagh. And, of course, you don't need to stop for sleep or food, which makes a mockery of the phrase: "Laid to rest" and "Rest in Peace." Ideally, headstones would read: "Gone Fishing for Eternity."

One aspect of life on the soul plane that souls never report back on is the concept of God, which is odd when religious organizations make such a fuss of God, so let's look at why.

The God Concept

The soul has an oversoul, or higher self, which appears to some people during a near-death experience, or NDE. When people talk about encountering a being of incandescent light and pure, overwhelming unconditional love, more than likely, they are meeting this level of their own energy. However, they may term it God, which is understandable because of the overwhelming nature of the experience, and well … what else could it be, given their worldview?

Who or what created your soul's creator? You-the-soul at an even higher frequency, the nature of which is irrelevant because we couldn't even begin to interact with it. If we did, we would be fried to a crisp. But know it's there. And who created *that?* If you keep going back up the levels, asking, "Who created that?" you will eventually arrive at the Source of All That Is, an entity so vast that *everything* exists within its mind. And to speculate on who or what created the Source is pointless, but even *that* vast being has an oversoul.

Simply talking to your own soul is enough to get a good handle on your life, so those who pray to God are usually petitioning their own higher self, or maybe their soul's higher self, which is still a pretty awesome being in its own right. The Supreme Source of All That Is is so remote and trans-conscious that a personal relationship with its central mind is inconceivable.

So where did this notion come from of the petty, little, vengeful God of the Old Testament, who went around smiting everyone who disagreed with Him? It's a long, long story, going back millions of years when a race of powerful ETs colonized Earth. And when they left, good old human greed took over, from the caveman days down to the recent Papal Report on the New Age Movement, released February 2003.

The report bemoaned the fact that: "the movement, based on 'weak thinking,' was drawing Catholics from the path." One cardinal said, "Catholics would be better off believing in encounters with aliens than being sucked into New Age practices." We eat too many babies, I guess. The report complained that the movement rejects the Christian concept of a personal God, teaching instead that humans contain divinity within themselves. The report also complained about: "the lack of moral demands that the New Age puts on people." So let's take a count … how many choirboys have *you* abused today?

Chapters 3 and 4 explore how human greed has used organized religion to systematically steal our identity and our power. If you are a staunch follower of an organized religion and do not want your beliefs challenged, skip the rest of this book because you *will* not like what you read. But then, you probably haven't even gotten this far.

Final Word

As you work and play in this hologram we call reality, it's vital to remember the three Ws:

1. **W**ho you *really* are—a vast spiritual being squeezing into a tiny bio-suit.
2. **W**hat the game is *really* about—the Source learning everything about itself and growing in the process.
3. **W**hy you're *really* here—as a Source probe who begins its existence in the highest dimensions and projects down through them to explore on behalf of the Source. For most, this involves learning, but a few million of us are here as a 'transition team' to usher in a dramatic upsurge in the consciousness of humanity.

Because you're reading this book, you are probably part of that transition team, so if you're not yet awake to that, "Wake up … the time is now. And remember your three Ws."

CHAPTER 3 ==—

THE GREAT IDENTITY THEFT: THE GOD MYTH

Over the last two millennia, a great robbery has been underway in western civilizations—identity theft—and you have been the victim. Your true identity has been systematically stolen so the thieves can control you, thereby enjoying great prestige and a healthy income at your expense. And they left two decoys in place of your true identity—the myths of God and Jesus. What a brilliant and masterful ploy—hide the real truths and leave decoys in their place! In this chapter, we examine the God Myth.

The God Myth

The God myth tells us there is a separate God up there or out there who: (1) created what we see around us, (2) demands certain things from us, (3) watches and judges us in our daily lives and, (4) at some far distant point in time, will give us a cosmic thumbs up or down depending on whether we give God what He wants. Then it's an eternity of either stoking the fires of Hell or enjoying glorious salvation in Heaven. How did this myth come about? It did not originate in the Bible but was already an ancient misunderstanding in Middle Eastern oral tradition long before the books making up the Old Testament were written. We need to go back *much* further in time to ancient texts that were highly abridged to form the OT account of our origins in Genesis 1.

History is written by the winners, and coming down unbroken for 3,000 years, the Hebrew story is the *only* one we in the West live with today. However, it is a very abridged, potted account of a much larger truth. For that we must go to much older texts.

Now a species evolves extremely slowly over untold millions of years. Freak genetic quirks will result in some new trait that either promotes or hinders survival; the former remain, while the latter die out quickly. For example, a giraffe with an extra long neck can reach higher tree branches than the other giraffes can. He will be healthier and more attractive to females, so his genes will win out over shorter giraffes, who will not get to propagate their DNA. Thus, over millions of years, giraffes' necks become longer and longer.

But human evolution presents a very different story:

- 25,000,000 years ago — ancestor apes
- 14,000,000 years ago — manlike apes (hominids)
- 2,000,000 years ago — Australopithecus and first use of stone tools and weapons
- 1,000,000 years ago — *Homo erectus*, large hairy creatures
- 300,000 years ago — Neanderthals, well-organized, cave-dwelling tribes
- 275,000 years ago — Male *Homo sapiens* gene pool emerges in Africa (Cro-Magnon man, indistinguishable from us today)
- 225,000 years ago — Female *Homo sapiens* gene pool emerges in Africa
- 175,000 years ago — First humans appear in Mesopotamia from Africa, and Caucasian races begin to diverge from African origins
- 11,000 years ago — Following major planetary catastrophe, divergent strains of cereal crops and dairy animals suddenly appear (now N. Iraq)
- 5,000 years ago — Sudden and widespread appearance of agriculture, animal husbandry, metallurgy, mathematics, systems of writing and advanced astronomy.

According to evolutionary experts, humanity is an impossibility. Our line sprang out of nowhere only 200,000 years ago, when it should have taken many millions of years. And we went from stone tools to a moon landing and computers in just 5,000 years! The cradle of this civilization? An area called Sumer, what is now Iraq, between the Tigris and Euphrates rivers.

What caused the dramatic evolutionary discontinuities 300,000, 200,000 and 5,000 years ago that baffle archeologists? The answer lies in the interpretation by Zecharia Sitchin and others of a story recorded on clay tablets found in many

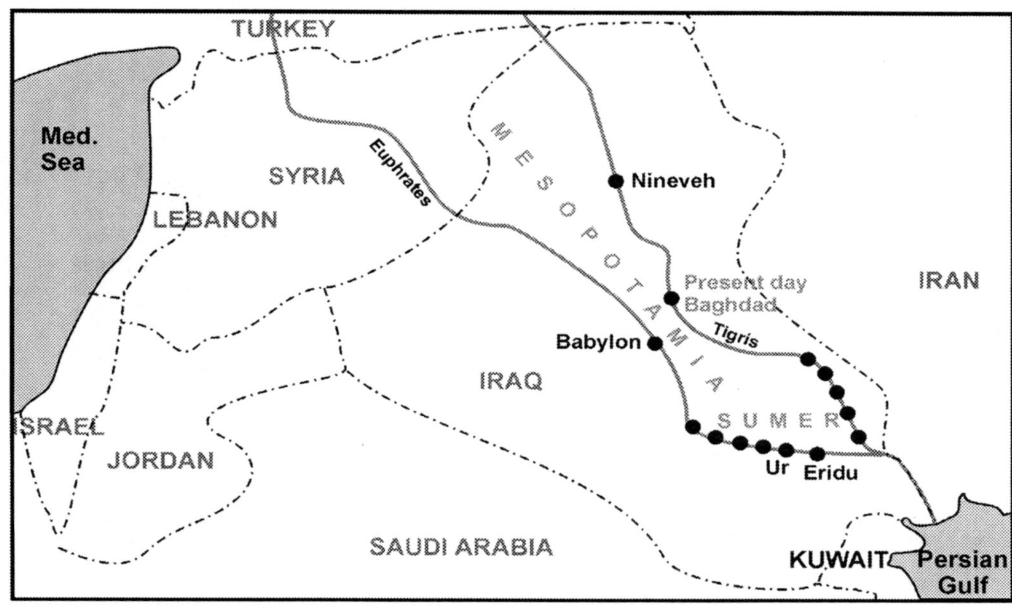

The ancient cities of Sumeria superimposed on today's Middle East

ancient cultures, such as Sumer, Akkadia and Mesopotamia. Sitchin's *Earth Chronicles* series tells of a species of extraterrestrials called, in ancient Akkadian, Anunnaki (An-nun-na-ki, or 'the fifty who from heaven came'). About 450,000 years ago,[1] they came to Earth and chose the land of Sumer as their base because of the abundant water, oil, and temperate climate (an Ice Age was just ending). Setting up base camp in Eridu, their purpose was to mine gold, which they needed to diffuse into the thinning atmosphere of their own planet to protect against radiation and retain their planet's heat. (See Appendix A for proof of this remarkable story and a discussion of why they may have left around 1650 BCE.)

Ancient Sumerian clay tablets, written much later, record that their home planet, NIB.IRU (now Nibiru), makes a large elliptical orbit round our Sun, coming in close every 3,670 years, a period they call a 'shar.' (Measuring time in such units means their lifespan is several thousand Earth years.)

Sitchin identifies three main steps in civilization: 11000, 7400 and 3800 BCE, which coincide with Nibiru's entry into our solar system. These steps took mankind from nomadic hunter-gatherers to highly sophisticated cultures, with courts, libraries and universities. And these ancient cultures attribute all this to a pantheon of gods that formed an extended family, headed by a dynastic leader named Anu.

---

1   Considering that our solar system is only 4 billion years old in a 15-billion-year old universe, it is quite probable that a species on a planet older than Earth had space-faring technology a million years ago. To deny that would be the height of human arrogance. In fact, it has already happened on Earth. The ancient Indian Vedas report flying machines and nuclear wars on the subcontinent of India long ago.

The Sumerians called them Nefilim ('gods who from heaven came to Earth') and Elohim ('shining ones'), terms that would one day make it into the Old Testament.

As the diagram shows, Australopithecus lived for over a million years, or 50,000 generations (at 20 years per generation), with no appreciable physical or cultural advancement apparent from archeological digs. *Homo erectus* was around for 30,000 generations, and Neanderthal for 15,000, where nothing much happened except for stone tools and the use of

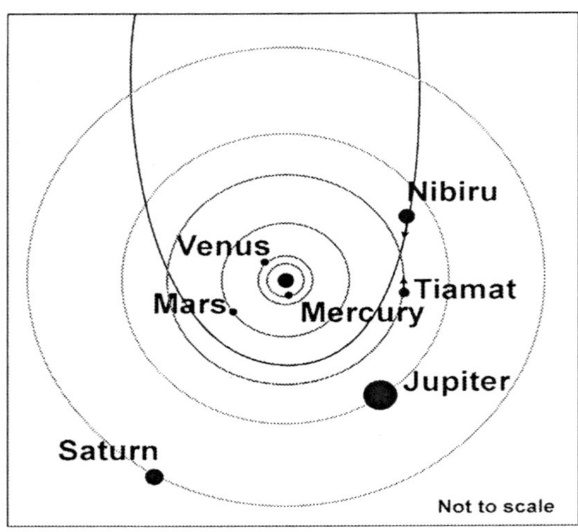

The original state of the Solar System before the collision between Nibiru and Tiamat that created planet Earth as it is today

fire. In our current body form, we have lived for about 10,000 generations, but have had 'civilization' for only the last 250. And we have had modern science for *just one generation:*

Australopithecus	1,000,000 years	50,000 generations
Homo erectus	600,000 years	30,000 generations
Neanderthal man	300,000 years	15,000 generations
Homo sapiens	200,000 years	10,000 generations
Sumerian culture	5,000 years	250 generations
Age of computers	20 years	1 generation.

In scientific terms, we have advanced as much in just the last generation as the previous 50,000 generations, but in terms of spirituality, we're probably still not much more spiritual than Neanderthal man, with his close ties to Mother Nature.

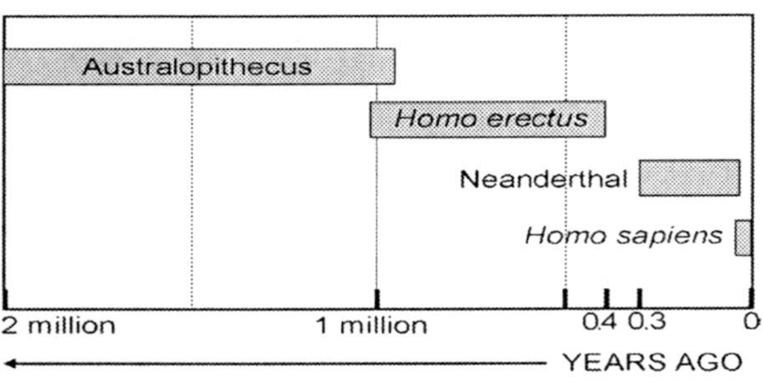

The Sumerian legend says the ET contingent was led by scientist EN.KI, who was later backed up by a military commander called EN.LIL (both sons of Anu, the Nibiruan ruler). A team of workers came to Earth and set up a lab to extract gold from the Persian Gulf waters. However, the yield was too low, so they resorted to mining in what is now South Africa. On the next pass of Niburu, 300 miners were assigned to work round the clock. Mining was hard, tedious work even with their advanced technology and, after 40 shars (Nibiru orbits, or 144,000 Earth years, which places this around 300,000 years ago), the Anunnaki workers rebelled, taking En-lil hostage. Anu arrived to resolve the situation, and En-ki suggested engineering some 'primitive workers,' which he and their chief medical officer set out to create:

> *I will produce a lowly primitive,*
> *Man shall be his name*
> *He will be charged with the service of the Elohim.*

The Anunnaki claimed to have used their male DNA to fertilize the eggs of female terrestrial primates, much like rhesus monkeys, and placed the fertilized embryos in Anunnaki females ('birth goddesses') for gestation. After much experimentation, he created primitive workers, known as the *lulu amelu*, meaning 'lowly worker' and the 'black-headed people.'

The image is of a clay tablet depicting the celebration 200,000 years ago of the successful genetic engineering creation of the new species by Anunnaki scientists Enki and Ninhursag, his half-sister and chief medical officer. (Top center is the symbol of a spacecraft that appears on all depictions of the Anunnaki.) Ninhursag (left) is proclaiming:

> *I have created!*
> *My hands have made it!*
> *I have provided your freedom.*

Sumerian tablet depicting the genetic alchemy

Genesis confirms this with: "And the *Elohim* (plural of the singular *El*) said, "Let *us* make man in *our* image, after *our* likeness." However, as we shall see, the Old Testament was derived from far more ancient Sumerian documents, so that's no surprise.

Thus the genetic engineering by the Elohim accelerated the evolution of *Homo erectus* by tens of millions of years, through the Neanderthal prototype to later Cro-Magnon ... something the creators of our bodies would come to regret.

Ancient texts actually describe *Homo erectus*: "They knew not the dressing in garments; ate plants like sheep; drank water from a ditch." They also interfered with the Elohim's hunting and trapping, so this wily ape-man was quite a nuisance, in the same way that a troop of chimps or bears might invade a modern human campsite to forage. But these creatures could not just be captured and domesticated. They needed enough intelligence to understand and follow orders.

The earliest Neanderthal were intelligent enough to toil in the mines but not so intelligent that they presented discipline problems. At the ET headquarters in Mesopotamia, the Elohim were jealous of En-ki's workers and demanded that some of them be sent back to HQ to keep house and toil in the fields. Spanning countless millennia, the tablets paint a bleak picture of the lives of these slave animals.[2] In the beginning, these beings had hive souls, group memories, but no mental bodies to speak of.

In the beginning, the hybrids were sterile (as with the mule, a cross between a donkey and a horse), and the Anunnaki females mutinied, tired of being pregnant all the time, so En-Ki managed to produce fertile hybrids that quickly proliferated. Of course, some escaped and bands of them began roaming the planet. Between 200,000 BCE and 100,000 BCE, the planet underwent an Ice Age, which killed many off.

En-ki kept experimenting and, 200,000 years ago, came up with a more intelligent worker—our direct ancestors, Cro-Magnon man. The tablets tell of how he enhanced the human body to give it the faculty of speech and dramatically greater mental powers. Meanwhile, from the soul plane, we worked to improve the human body's 'soul-carrying' ability, which allowed us as souls to incarnate into those physical bodies. (As we will see later, how a soul attaches to a fetus in the womb in preparation for a new incarnation is extremely complex. It involves consciousness integrating with the brain and hence the rest of the body, and also hooking up to the system of chakras and meridians that the body creates. Few species have nervous systems that are complex enough to support fully interactive incarnation, which simply means 'in flesh.')

Once the early humans were able to procreate and became soul-carriers, the Elohim realized they might have gone too far, because these new humans developed *morality*, or a sense of right and wrong. Until then, 'right' was whatever the Anunnaki said was right, but now their slave creations began to question that. How did the Anunnaki know? Because the humans began to object to being

---

2   Fossil remains found in Ethiopia by researchers at UC Berkeley reveal that Neanderthals lived as early as 230,000 years ago and died out about 30,000 years ago, thus overlapping with Cro-Magnon man.

naked, while their masters wore clothing, and began to clothe themselves. It was as if your dog or cat said, "Wait a minute. How come you get to wear clothes, when I don't?"

It is possible that this was the moment in human history when we-as-soul began to incarnate in the new human body. Souls would attach to these bodies prior to birth and remained attached until the body ceased to be habitable due to illness, accident or just old age. After a period of reflection and evaluation on the soul plane, we souls would attach to new bodies, i.e., reincarnation. Despite the harsh conditions on Earth, we souls loved doing this, due to the intensity of sensory physical experience, and we became fascinated with how well we could interact with these new bodies.

The Lord of Heaven (En-lil) was furious with the Serpent Lord (En-ki) and banished the creations from the Sumerian headquarters, or E.DIN. For us, this was the turning point when everything in human history changed. On the plus side, true *Homo sapiens sapiens* was born, and we became the glorious beings we are today. The biblical 'fall of man' was not just about realizing we were naked; it was about much more—realizing that we, too, were gods. And suddenly the game was over, and we achieved equality with our creators. We, too, were gods! And the Nefilim knew it, and knew that one day, we ourselves would know it.

On the down side, the ejection from E.DIN deeply scarred us, because we were judged for being who and how we were, and we have been shackled with the concept of original sin ever since. The gods disapproved of us and kicked us out of heaven, so we must be basically flawed.

More powerful minds allowed for language, which helped us cooperate with each other in the mining and other work. The Neanderthals were allowed to die off, and that evolutionary branch was closed. The Anunnaki also built into the human DNA an aging mechanism called 'replicative failure' to ensure progressive degradation of the human body's cells. To us with our short lifespan, the Nefilim seemed practically immortal.

Eventually, the ancient legends tell us, the population of humans became so numerous and troublesome that En-Lil began to regret making them so advanced. At the end of the last Ice Age, during the Nibiru visit in 10800 BCE, he predicted that the proximity of the huge planet to Earth would trigger seismic and volcanic disasters, and major weather disturbances, which could cause the Antarctic ice-shelf to break off, crash into the ocean and create a huge planet-wide tsunami. Seeing a way to purge the Earth of its pesky humans, he intended to allow it, without warning them.

En-Ki, on the other hand, was more sympathetic to his genetic creations and spilled the beans, which allowed several of his humans to escape to high ground in boats, carrying the DNA of each animal species with them (the Noah legend). When the ice-shelf did break off, the resulting tsunami funneled up the Persian Gulf, wiping out much of the life in the Middle East. Elsewhere, it resulted in the destruction of Atlantis and raised sea levels by up to 500 feet. This gave birth to the legends of the flood that are found in every ancient body of knowledge on the planet. The ETs, of course, watched the disaster from the safety of their spacecraft.

The returning Anunnaki quickly engaged the surviving humans to render the planet habitable again, and taught them agriculture and animal husbandry. A wide biodiversity of grains, trees and breeds of domesticated animals appeared in three waves, coinciding with the passing of Nibiru.

Over the centuries, humans proliferated rapidly and three great centers of civilization emerged—the original Fertile Crescent, plus the Nile and Indus valleys. The latter two were satellites of Sumer, and all shared a common language based on ancient Sumerian. (This was later changed to prevent planet-wide human collaboration.)

By now, the Anunnaki numbered thousands across many generations, and each was given an area to rule over. Rivalry between the families of En-lil and En-ki was fierce, and each 'god' admonished his followers to worship him alone and eschew all other 'gods.'

According to some sources, En-Ki had two sons, Ra and Thoth. Ra, the elder was put in charge of Khem, as Egypt was known back then, and was worshipped by the Egyptian humans as the Sun God. The more intellectual brother, Thoth, was a scientist, scribe and architect, and among other things, designed and built the Giza pyramids about 10,800 BCE to reflect their ancient home constellation of Orion.[3] (The three pyramids are in the same positions relative to each other as the three stars in the belt of Orion.) Their main purposes, however, were to balance the Earth's orbit and generate energy, but we have no idea how they performed these functions. Further, according to Sitchin, the pyramids were also part of the navigation system for the Nefilim spaceports that were built following the Great Flood (see Appendix A). Thoth also built the Sphinx to celebrate the planet's

3   Engineering experts have concluded that Egyptologists' assertions that the pyramids were built in 22 years in the fourth century BC are pure nonsense because the technology to do that simply did not exist. Using the primitive hammer-and-chisel tools, even just leveling the 13-acre site and digging the 26-degree descending shaft would have taken much longer than 22 years. Then the millions of blocks would have to have been laid at the rate of 200 per hour—an engineering impossibility.

entrance into the Age of Leo, hence the lion's head on a human body. This also occurred around the year 10,800 BCE, and the statue shows clear water damage, so this area was not always arid desert.

Even though hundreds of Anunnaki stayed on Earth, the Nibiru flybys were significant times due to the state visits by Anu, and the consequent planning meetings. Between the 10,800 and 7200 BCE visits, the new humans made great strides in organizing into hunter-gatherer bands, and formed early matriarchal societies that worshipped the Goddess principle and Mother Nature. They devised rituals to appease her and express gratitude for her gifts, especially the birth of new life. These gentle hunter-gathers lived in deep communion with Nature, preferring to settle in one place and worship their female deities.

When Nibiru returned for its 7200 BCE pass, Anu realized they had made a huge mistake by underestimating the power of the human mind — spirit — body triad, and decided this new species had to be subjugated. So they used the power of our minds against us. Humans already perceived them as gods, and Anu reinforced the worship around himself. He told the human population that the Anunnaki were the creators of humans, and must be worshipped. Given the Elohims' great technology (space craft that seemed like the biblical 'chariots in the sky,' launchings that produced 'pillars of fire,' etc.) and extremely long lifespan, humans readily began to worship these ET 'gods.'

Life on Nibiru was intensely political, and marriages and alliances were made to establish and maintain power. For thousands of years, infighting among members of the royal family and Nefilim involved vicious exchanges of nuclear bombs, particle beam weapons, etc. Hence the biblical accounts of God smiting whole populations that annoyed him—all just the power struggles of competing Elohim.[4]

The tablets continue to tell the story that, because of the shortage of eligible Anunnaki females, young Anunnaki men began to interbreed with human females ('the sons of the gods looked on the daughters of man and found them fair'), producing hybrids with great powers, such as telepathy. These Anunnaki/human hybrids were appointed leaders or rulers, such as kings and pharaohs. Using them as go-betweens allowed the Elohim to rule their human subjects remotely, which

---

4   Given the ET explanation, the Old Testament finally makes sense. For example, when the local Elohim of Sodom and Gomorrah became displeased by the licentiousness of his human subjects, he sent two emissaries (angels of the Lord) to check things out. When they reported the situation to be hopeless, the Elohim decided to nuke the cities. They escorted Lot and his family out of the city and told them to quickly get on the other side of a nearby mountain. Lot's wife tarried and was caught in the nuclear blast. She was turned into vapor, not salt. This mistranslation arose because the Sumerian word NUMUR means both salt and vapor, and in translating into Aramaic, the translator simply picked the wrong meaning.

further distanced the gods from humans, thereby increasing the mystique that surrounded them.

During Nibiru's 3800 – 3600 BCE visit, Anu commanded that the residents of Sumer (today Iraq) should be taught a writing system and alphabet, mathematics, trade, metallurgy, commerce, industry and agriculture and animal husbandry skills. Almost overnight, humans went from primitive Neolithic (Stone Age) cultures to advanced civilizations with walled cities, oceangoing ships, etc., something that has puzzled archeologists for decades. For example, to celebrate a state visit by Anu, the magnificent city of Uruk was built from scratch.

The writing system was Cuniform, and was soon adapted to give written form to many spoken languages in Mesopotamia. It lasted until about 500 CE, when displaced by Aramaic. In Egypt (the other center of culture, learning and trade), Thoth gave the local humans a different form—Hieroglyphics, which lasted until 500 BCE, when the Greeks invaded and made Greek the official language. But, to prevent the human population from 'ganging up' on their rulers, each Elohim taught a different language to his subjects, so that human communication would be impaired, hence the biblical Tower of Babel story.

It was also during this visit that, in 3760 BCE, the Anunnaki Sumerians began the Calendar of Nippur. Later adopted by the Hebrews, the calendar is still in use today and records Gregorian 2003 as the Nippur/Hebrew year 5763. Meanwhile, the Romans continued to use their calendar, started when Romulus founded the city of Rome. In Roman year 1240, a scholar named Aloysius would tell the Pope that he believed the Jesus character had been born in Roman year 720, so they decided to retroactively reset the Roman calendar from 720 back to 1 AD, and call it the Julian Calendar, which meant that for them, Aloysius and the Pope were suddenly in Julian / Christian year 520 AD. Confusing, eh?

Egyptologists accept that around 3100 BCE, Ra was ousted from Babylon and returned to Egypt to reclaim the throne from Thoth. As elder son, he won and Thoth left for Mesoamerica, taking his calendar and his huge body of information. He also took the Hieroglyphic writing system but, as it would turn out, the Egyptian and American forms would evolve quite differently. So our story moves to the Yucatan, in what is today's Mexico.

The Mayan Calendar

The ancient civilization of the Maya which occupied what is today the Yucatan Peninsula, Belize and Guatemala, emerged about 500 BCE. The great Mayan civilization peaked around 850 CE with a population of 12 million, and slowly fell apart and vanished around 1200. They are believed to be the descendants of those who left Atlantis when its demise became evident. Before the Mayans, however, the area was populated by a mysterious, tall, fair-haired people who arrived about 15,000 BCE, possibly escapees from the Lemurian disasters.

About 3100 BCE, Thoth arrived in Mesoamerica bringing all the Anunnaki knowledge on just about everything—mathematics, astronomy, astrology, architecture and agriculture. This knowledge included his sophisticated calendar based on 52-year cycles and the Precession of the Equinoxes, which the Anunnaki used to measure the vast intervals with which they dealt in their lives and travels. Possibly to mark his arrival, a new 5,125-year-long Great Cycle in the calendar began, which would have been on August 14, 3114 BCE in our current Gregorian calendar. The local tribes' name for the leader of these new arrivals was Quetzlcoatl, or Feathered Serpent.

About 2000 BCE, giants with distinct African Negroid features began showing up. Named the Olmeca by the locals, they portrayed themselves in huge 25-ton statues. Where did they come from? Linguists place them coming from West Africa and the Gold Coast, now called Ghana. Sitchin proposes that Thoth brought them over for their gold-mining expertise, a reasonable suggestion since Africa's goldmines date from about 8000 BCE. Furthermore, small statues have been dated back to about 3000 BCE of elephants, an animal never seen in South America, so they can only have been brought in by travelers from Africa.

Typical Olmec stone statue, often weighing up to 60 tons

In what is called today Zimbabwe (formally Rhodesia), lie many ancient stone-built settlements (stone buildings are uncommon in Africa) that were already in ruins when Arab traders discovered them in the 11th century. The most impressive settlement, a 60-acre complex

Ruins of an ancient Zimbabwe village

of stone buildings called the Great Zimbabwe, is dominated by the Great Enclosure, 830 ft. in circumference, whose dry stone masonry is 35 feet high and 17 feet thick. The area is rich with ancient gold mines, which prompted early explorers to wonder if they were the lost mines of King Solomon. The discovery of artifacts from Persia, India and the Middle East prove that the inhabitants of the settlement had contact with those areas and probably traded with them. However, archaeologists have no idea who constructed the buildings or why, and why they were abandoned. It is simply a civilization lost in time. However, to us, it makes sense that the Anunnaki would have used stone to ensure their buildings were durable.

In his 5-book *Earth Chronicles* series, Sitchin documents hundreds of close matches between hieroglyphic pictogram writing, language and pyramid architecture between Egypt and Central America that puzzle archeologists today.

Is there any corroboration for this? Plenty! Many of the bodies of knowledge in the Americas claim five great ages, each ending in natural disaster:

- *First Age*, or the age of White-haired Giants, lasting about 4,000 years (15,600 – 11,500 BCE). It was ended by the Great Flood, the date of which is close to the eastern legends of around 11,000 BCE for the same event, due to the massive slippage of the Antarctic icepack at the end of the last Ice Age. (Water damage on the Sphinx, built around 11,000 BCE or earlier, also confirms this date.) Who were these White-haired Giants? Refugees from Lemuria? Other ETs? We don't know, but a few survived the Flood and populated the Second Age.
- *Second Age*, or the Golden Age, ended with calamitous winds after about 4,000 years (11,500 – 7,600 BCE). Again, a few survived to people the next age.
- *Third Age*, or the age of the Red-haired People, survivors of the Second Age who came in ships from the east. It, too, lasted about 4,000 years (7,600 – 3,500 BCE). Who were the Red-haired People? Survivors of Atlantis?
- *Fourth Age*, lasting about 4,080 years (3,500 BCE – 580 CE), called the Age of the Black-haired People (which is what 'Sumerian' actually means), led by Quetzlcoatl, famous for his staff carved in the shape of a serpent, symbolic of DNA strands. Towards the end of this age, the gods (i.e., members of the Anunnaki royal family) launched major wars against each other and Quetzlcoatl left, sailing east whence he came. Sumerian legends

also point to about 3,500 BCE as the birth of their culture, as the Anunnaki began a massive program of education, notably the introduction of the pictogram form of writing. (Quetzlcoatl brought a form of hieroglyphic pictogram writing that was initially identical to the early Sumerian, but they subsequently diverged.)

- *Fifth Age*, beginning in 580 CE. In 1140 CE, the Aztec arrived from the north and settled around Lake Texcoco. In 1325, they founded the city of Tenochtitlan, today Mexico City. About the same time, the Mayan civilization mysteriously collapsed, leaving behind monumental buildings and huge cities, and their calendar, which the Aztecs adopted.

The Mayans learned the sophisticated calendar system from the Olmecs, and it became known as the Mayan calendar. The calendar was actually based on two interlocking calendars. The two calendars making up the Mayan Calendar are:

- A mundane calendar, the Haab, which governed daily life, especially crop-planting. The Haab year had 18 months of 20 days, plus five extra days at the end to make up 365.
- A sacred calendar, or Tzolkin, that used two cycles. Twenty named days repeated 13 times gave each day a special meaning, making for a 260-day sacred year that governed rituals and ceremonies. Thus every day had two meanings—its Haab meaning and its Tzolkin meaning—with any particular combination of the two meanings taking 52 years to recur—the so-called 'calendar round.'

Central to the Mayan system is a cycle of 22 of the 52-year calendar rounds, the 22 rounds being divided into 13 'Heaven Rounds' (676 years) followed by 9 'Hell Rounds' (468 years), for a full good-bad cycle of 1144 years. Ancient

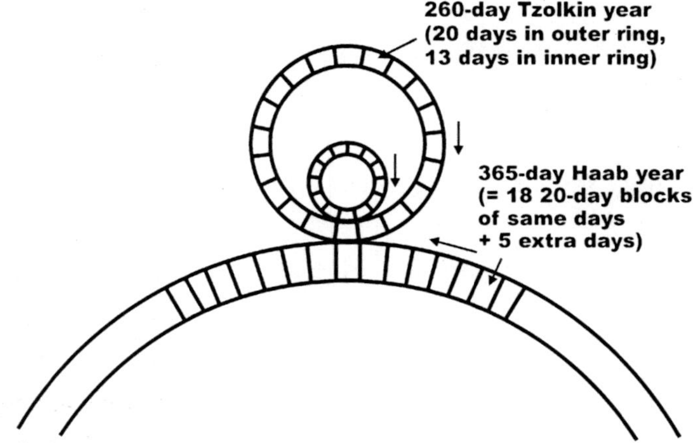

The three wheels, inscribed with symbols that define the Mayan calendar

legends contained a prophecy that the ancient god called Quetzlcoatl (the Feathered Serpent) would return on a day known as 1 Reed, which recurs every 52 years, or 1415, 1467, 1519, etc., and marks the beginning of a new Hell Round. The arrival of the Spanish Conquistadors on April 21, 1519 fell on that very day, which is why the Aztec king, Moctazuma, welcomed Cortez and his men with open arms ... much to his later regret.

The last day of the 468 years of those 9 Hell Rounds fell on August 16, 1987, which put the first day of the following series of 13 Heaven Rounds on the very day of the Harmonic Convergence!

Projecting backwards to the start of our current Great Cycle or Long Count, our Gregorian calendar places Day One on August 14, 3114 BCE. Projecting forward to the last day places it on December 21, 2012—the Winter Solstice. To say the Mayan Calendar ends on that date is not true, just the current Long Count ends ... which is still a very, very big deal.

Mayan prophesy indicates that the new cycle, 2012 – 7212, will be a fusion of both feminine and masculine energies, with its element as ether. It will be a transition, without confrontation between light and dark polarities. It will bring harmony, love and the return of consciousness. Spiritually conscious people need to unite and create a belt of light that will contrast with the negativity.

One Mayan wise man says, "We are living in dangerous times. If there is no clarity, if there is no unity, if we do not return to the natural order, if we do not reach harmony amongst ourselves, we are condemned as a species to disappear as a result of our own madness."

Far from worrying about the year 2012, to the Mayans it marks the beginning of changes in the way we see and live life, focusing more on harmony. But what will it mean to traverse from one Great Cycle or Long Count to another in 2012? Again, according to the Maya, the close of a Great Cycle points to a tremendous shift in human consciousness that will catapult us into a much larger cosmic pattern.

To see how quickly things change nowadays, let's look briefly at technology and social change during the six most recent 20-year periods (Mayan titles in italics):

- 1894–1914: Higher Principles Emerge—scientists discovered the structure of the atom and developed quantum physics, which ended the old Newtonian paradigms.
- 1914–1933: New Cycle Begins—WWI, social upheaval, the Great Depression, rise of Communism and Germany's Third Reich, talking movies.

- 1933–1953: Climax of Power—WWII triggers new technology, especially atomic and nuclear weapons, UFO contact intensifies, United Nations born, TV begins to replace movies.
- 1953–1973: Dissipation—computers, manned space flight, moon landings, emergence of baby-boomers as agents of social change, Eastern religions rise in the West, Civil Rights and ecology movements born.
- 1973–1993: Transformation Begins—global terrorism, nuclear weapons stockpiling, space and satellite technology, Harmonic Convergence marks a shift in the planet's resonant frequency.
- 1993-2012: Self-Transformation Completion—accelerating ecological and spiritual awareness leading to the planet and humanity activating their light-bodies and synchronizing with our cosmic neighbors.

And beyond 2012? What can we expect as we enter a new Great Cycle and go deeper into the Photon Belt? For millions of years, civilizations on this planet have risen and fallen, of which the last 5,125 years have been the culmination of life on Earth. It is fitting that the epoch the Maya dubbed 'The Transformation of Matter' saw in 1945 the development of the atom bomb—exemplifying the transformation of matter into energy. The resulting fallout—radioactive, military, political, and social—caused planetary upheaval that hastened the changes necessary to match the increases in the Earth's resonant frequency triggered by the Harmonic Convergence. These increases affect everything, from our soul vibration to our DNA, as our planet begins to resonate with the rest of the galaxy.

The stimulation of our DNA will unleash psychic powers and we will move into higher spiritual states that will allow us to relate to our ET brethren as equals. Becoming galactic citizens will change our lives in ways we currently cannot imagine, but we shall know it when it arrives. And when it does, we will experience the true meaning of Transformation of Matter—our own bodies going to light. The story continues in Chapter 14 of Volume Two.

Before we return to the Middle East, let's visit the Andes since we're in the Americas. When the Spanish Conquistadors explored the Andes in what is now Peru, they were staggered to find elaborate cities such as Tiahuanaco and Cuzco, ancient long before the Incas and built using incredibly advanced technology. The walls of the huge buildings contained enormous stones, some weighing as much as 300 tons, and dressed so finely that a piece of paper wouldn't fit between them. Clearly, these monster megaliths were not carried over the steep mountains and deep, plunging ravines on horseback, so how were they moved? No one alive knows, but if the Anunnaki could apply anti-gravity technology to their craft, why not to huge stone blocks?

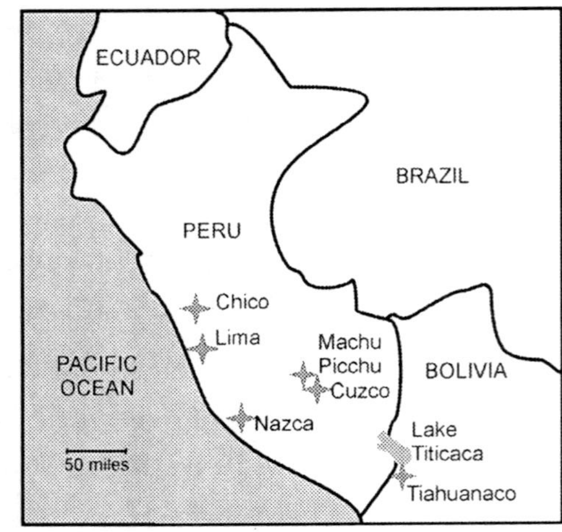

The name Tiahuanaco (aka Tiwanaku) offers a clue. In ancient Sumerian, it means TI.ANAKU, or Tin City. So who had technology sophisticated enough to build great cities at 12,000 feet and also needed tin? Back in 2200 BCE, the Anunnaki had led Sumer into its Bronze Age, bronze being a 6-to-1 alloy of copper and tin. However, tin is quite rare and the planet's main source is high in the Peruvian and Bolivian Andes, near Lake Titicaca. In this area, copper and gold also abound, and one can pick up nuggets of both off the ground.

Archeologists note that between 2600 and 2220 BCE, the ratio of tin in bronze dropped from 1-in-6 to 1-in-50, but around 2200, the ratio suddenly rose again, so a new source of tin had been found. According to Sitchin, identical statues and carvings found in Cuzco and Sumer, of gods bearing golden disks and staffs emitting flames, suggest that the tin came from the New World, transported to the Old World by the Anunnaki.

Sitchin further suggests that the magnificent statues and edifices of Tiahuanaco were built to honor Anu during his state visit to Earth during Nibiru's 3600 BCE-pass. An odd twist to this story is that a tribe lives on islands in Lake Titicaca whose genetics are found nowhere else in the Americas. Called the Ura, which means 'The Olden Ones,' it is possible that they are descendents of Sumerian miners brought over from Ur, the ancient capital.

Recently, evidence has been found of an even more ancient people than the Inca. Centered on three valleys north of Lima in Chico state, this civilization was made up of twenty sophisticated cities with pyramids and a network of roads. Named simply 'The Andeans,' they are believed to have lived in the area from about 3000 BCE to 1000 CE, and revered a white-skinned, red-haired bearded 'god,' who sounds a lot like our old friend Thoth.

Before he departed, however, Thoth left one more gift in South America. Beside a mountain in the Peruvian Andes called Machu Picchu, he leveled a hill and established a solar observatory, hauling up granite blocks weighing hundreds of tons, machined to amazing tolerances.

Machu Picchu and the Solstice Window Wall

Just to the west of the main plaza, Thoth built a three-walled room with three windows in the east wall. When viewed from a standing stone in the room, the rising Sun appears in the windows on the Summer Solstice, the Equinoxes, and the Winter Solstice (going from left to right) ... however, not today. Astroarcheologists calculate that this did happen precisely at one time—circa 2200 BCE, dating the origins of Machu Picchu to exactly the same timeframe as Stonehenge.

The Inca, who came along millennia later, attributed the settlement to the God of Creation, or Viracocha, whom we know as Thoth. They added to the buildings with cruder stonework, which left early explorers with the belief that this was an Inca city, but it goes back to much earlier.

Stonehenge

Before leaving this arena, Thoth left us one more gift on the windswept plains of England. Built between 2900 and 2000 BCE, this enigmatic celestial calculator is popularly believed to celebrate the Summer Solstice, when the sun is in its annual northernmost position. But that is just a tiny part of its purpose.

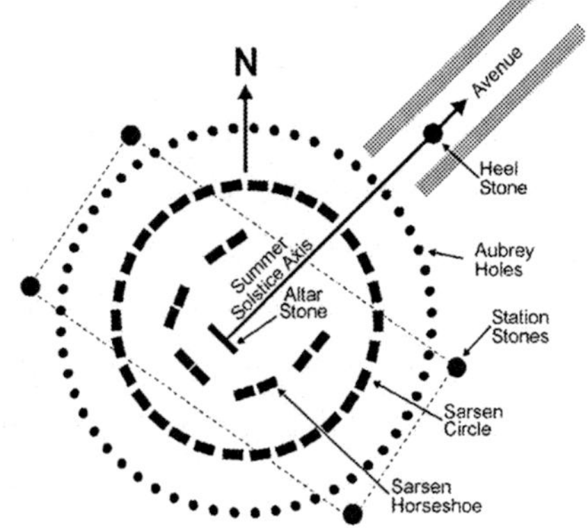

Left: a rendition of what Stonehenge would have looked like in its prime; right: the layout

First, we are in awe of the feat of engineering involved in bringing the Sarsen stones hundreds of miles across rugged terrain, something impossible for the Neolithic British to accomplish 5,000 years ago.

While it's true that a line from the Altar Stone to the Heel Stone does indeed intersect with the Solstice Sun at dawn on the longest day; also the 56 Aubrey Holes at one time housed wooden pegs that were moved to predict the phases of the moon. Further, the rectangle made by the four Station Stones allowed eclipses to be predicted. But even more amazing, other features calculate the Precession of the Equinoxes, something known only to the Nefilim. Around 3000 BCE, only one person had the skills and knowledge to create such a computer—Thoth, or Quetzecoatl.

Hopi Prophecy

Everything successful has been driven by a vision of the outcome. Gandhi's free India, Martin Luther King's racial equality, Winston Churchill's peace in Europe and Kennedy's man on the moon were all preceded by a vision. What vision unites us today?

Only by knowing the destiny of the human race can we survive it. But what is that destiny? Revealing this has always been the job of a culture's storytellers, but who are this country's storytellers? It used to be our religions, but those are irrelevant today. Our schools are too embroiled in discipline to deliver a real education to our children, attested to by the fact that, in 2004, over one million children were home-schooled. That leaves only television as our storyteller, which means Hollywood portrays our heroes, and Madison Avenue sets our values via commercials. Are they doing a good job? The answer is self-evident, so where do we turn?

We must fall back on those who know, and have known since history began—such indigenous people as the Maya and the Hopi. The Hopi have long known that their prophecies apply not only to them but to all peoples, which is why they were revealed to the world in 1946.

As with Mayan tradition, Hopi prophecy also talks of us having Four Worlds, with the Fifth World about to emerge from the ashes of the Fourth, the timing signified by Nine Signs:

1. The coming of white-skinned men, who take land that is not theirs and who strike their enemies with thunder (guns)
2. The coming of spinning wheels filled with voices (covered wagons)
3. A strange beast like a buffalo but with long horns that overruns the land in large numbers (cattle)

4. The land is crossed by snakes of iron (railroad tracks)
5. The land is crossed by a giant spider's web (power lines)
6. The land is crossed with rivers of stone that make pictures in the sun (mirages on asphalt and concrete roads)
7. The sea turns black, killing many living things (oil spills)
8. Many youth, who wear their hair long like our people, come to the tribal nations to learn our ways and wisdom (hippies)
9. A dwelling-place in the heavens, above the earth, falls with a great crash, appearing as a blue star (future demise of a space station?).

These are the signs of impending great destruction, or 'columns of smoke and fire such as the white man has made in the deserts (above-ground atomic testing). Following the destruction, 'there will be much to rebuild.' And very soon afterward, The Great Spirit (known as Pahana or Massau) will return, bringing with him the dawn of the Fifth World.

The Hopi Prophecy Rock clearly depicts two paths:
- A 'two-hearted path,' with three individuals upon it. A two-hearted person is one who thinks with his head rather than his heart. Modern man is out of balance because he lives in a left-brain dominated society, leading to imbalance and conflict, and ultimately to the destruction of those on it.
- A 'one-hearted path,' or one that is in balance and harmony with the universe.

The Rock Prophecy shows a junction where the two-hearted people can either choose to start thinking with their hearts or continue to think with their heads only. If they choose the latter, it will lead to self-destruction, symbolized by the lightning strike from a cloud. If people chose to think with their hearts, they will return to the one-hearted path and their own survival.

The Rock shows three half-circles that represent three world-shakings, as the Source strives to remind us of how we are all related. The first shaking occurs when man tosses bugs into the air (airplanes, first used in World War I). The second world-shaking occurs when man uses the Hopi migration symbol in war (swastika adopted by Hitler in World War II). The third shaking will be recognized by a red cover or cloak, which could point to Communist China. Hopi prophecy also says that signs of the third shaking will be:
- The trees die (acid rain or destruction of the rainforest).
- Man builds a house in the sky (space stations).
- Cold places become hot, and hot places will become cold (erratic weather and global warming).
- Lands sink into the ocean, and lands will rise out of the sea.
- The Blue Star Kachina appears.

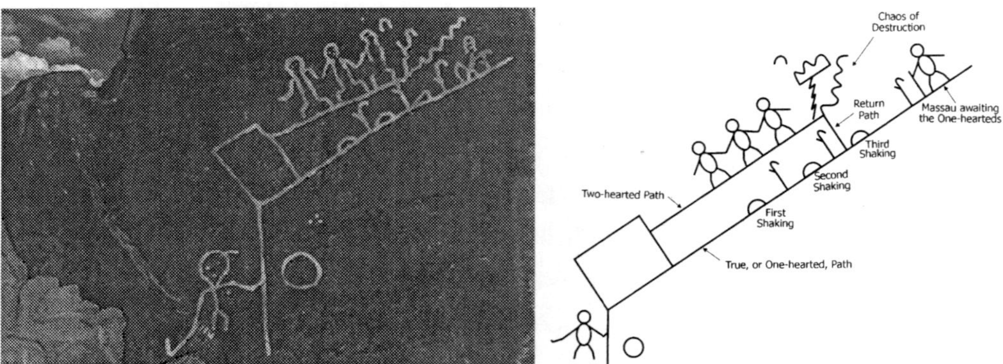

The Hopi Prophecy Rock, showing the Three Shakings and Two Paths

Only by undergoing the Hopi process of Purification can we set foot on the Return Path to the One-Hearted Path, and just hope that we haven't gone past that point. Purification involves a number of elements:

1. *Repentance*, or rethinking, of the Two-Hearted Way of Life. This involves commitment, deep knowing that we are all One, acceptance of personal power to create change, and following our inner guidance. It is good to do this in groups, because it reminds us that the whole is greater than the sum of the parts. Also, as individuals, we are so rooted in our Two-Hearted ways, we need others to help point them out to us. Once we as a group have identified and committed to a One-Hearted vision, we can begin to live it, first within the group, then increasingly in the outer Two-Hearted world. Then like- minded groups may join together to form 'villages,' ready for when the Two-Hearted Path collapses in ruins.

2. *Sovereignty*, or self-respect and respect for the sovereignty of others. It is also about taking responsibility for our creations and good stewardship for whatever is in our sphere of influence. For example, the Fifth World view of the planet is as a partner to be nurtured rather than as a resource to be consumed and discarded. Also, wealth and abundance will not be hoarded by those whose lands produce it, but will be shared equitably. Finally, any decision about stewardship will never be short-term but will consider the impact on future generations.

3. *Truthfulness*. Confusion over 'what should be' versus 'what is' separates us from the realities of life. We look for quick fixes, Hollywood endings and the latest fads rather than 'walking the talk' and 'doing the work.' One group may import 'what works' from another group and impose it on themselves, but disharmony may result. This leads to strife, conflict, and

even war. Other cultures become too complex and collapse under their own weight, thrusting the people into anarchy until new ways are found. This is the inevitable outcome of the Two-Hearted Path, and we are seeing its effects now as fewer and fewer Americans believe government is 'by the people, for the people.' Our lives float between hope and fear, unrooted in 'what is.' From the moment of our birth, we are indoctrinated into membership of our culture, with prison or asylum awaiting dissenters. We leave school, trained to become 'another brick in the wall,' mindlessly perpetuating the Two-Hearted Path. The Hopi language has no equivalent of, "I'm busy," or, "I'm sorry." Busy-ness and apology are not part of the One-Hearted Path; and will not carry us through the collapse of the Fourth World and emergence into the Fifth.

Meanwhile, Back in the Desert, the Plot Thickens ...

Around 2000 BCE, under orders from En-lil, a 'demi-Elohim' (Anunnaki-human hybrid) named Abraham led a delegation to Egypt. The name given to the group was *hibiri*, being a circuitous translation of Nippur, their home town. They were later joined by many people who had lived around the Dead Sea and fled the nuclear fallout following a nuclear war that destroyed Sodom and Gomorrah. This explains why the OT is full of stories about a vengeful God causing disasters, destroying cities, and committing genocide. In the incident at Sodom and Gomorrah, the cruelty was really perpetrated by the Anunnaki overlords to discipline the humans under their charge. The two 'angels' who showed up to warn Lot were actually Anunnaki agents.[5] (Of course, the Anunnaki had maintained strict secrecy about the true Source of All That Is, and about the soul being our real identity, which is why the master-slave mentality still pervades the Western concept of a male God who gets angry when we unruly subjects don't obey his rules.)

Genesis 17 details the covenant between *YHVH* and Abraham: "I shall make you the father of nations. I shall give the Land of Canaan to you and generation after generation. Your part of the deal is to obey its terms—every male shall be circumscribed as a mark of this covenant. Anyone who refuses shall be cut off from his people because he has violated my covenant."

---

5   This explains the anomalous layer of fused sand and beryllium tektites in the Libyan Desert. This particular isotope of beryllium is not naturally occurring and is found only following a nuclear explosion.

Some researchers believe that *YHVH* actually instigated the Exodus and orchestrated the various misfortunes (plagues, boils, death of the firstborn, etc.) suffered by Egypt that led up to it. Why he favored the Hebrews over other tribes is unknown, but in *Gods, Genes and Consciousness*, author Paul Von Ward suggests that *YHVH* was Ninurta, of En-lil lin-

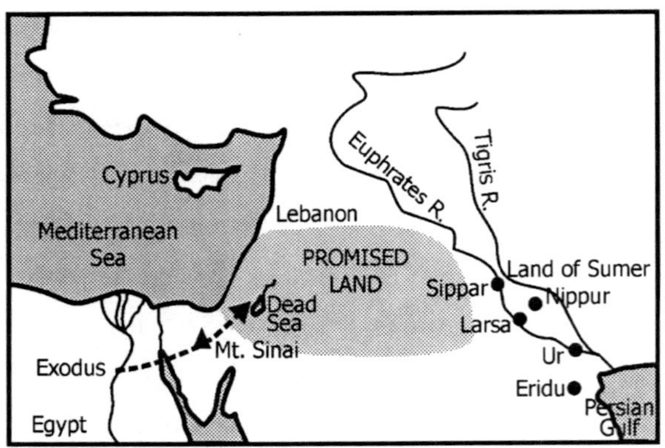

The Jewish Exodus from Egypt

eage, who wanted to organize and control the Hebrews in opposition to the plans of Marduk/Ra (oldest son of En-ki) to give humanity its independence. Once under the control of *YHVH*, he reasoned, the Hebrews would have been compliant. In fact, the Book of Exodus bears this out. Exodus 9 tells of how Moses demanded freedom for the Israelites but Pharaoh refused 'because *YHVH* had hardened his heart.' Each time Pharaoh refused, *YHVH* unleashed a more deadly plague. After the death of all first-born males, however, Pharaoh relented and the Israelites were free to leave. But *YHVH* led them due east to the impassable Red Sea, where they were trapped. Exodus 14 tells us that *YHVH* then convinced the Pharaoh to go after them by 'hardening his heart against them.' Using some hi-tech, he parted the Red Sea, which allowed the Israelites to escape, but then released the force-field, and drowned the pursuing Egyptian army.

Why would YHVH/Ninurta play such games? First, it impressed the Israelites, who would then obey the covenant terms, and second, it established in the Egyptians' minds that Ninurta was a force to be reckoned with.

On their trek from Egypt, Moses led the Israelites to *YHVH*'s spaceport in the Sinai Peninsula, where *YHVH* confirmed the covenant whereby he wanted them to form a stable nation-state, which he would liberate and protect in return for total loyalty, obedience and allegiance. As his Chosen People, they would be given the land from the Sinai Peninsula north to Lebanon and east to the Euphrates River. YHVH also imposed strict codes of behavior, hygiene and ritual for honoring him, and required them to attack the human armies of other Anunnaki lords, thus weakening his enemies. Hence words such as, "Thou shall have no other gods but me," which really meant, "Do not side with any of my competitor Elohim" (and there were hundreds).

Then, oddly, Exodus 23 reports that *YHVH* handed control over to an 'angel,' delegating full powers to him. From then on, we hear nothing more about *YHVH*, but only his substitute. What happened to cause his abrupt departure? All we know is that all the other Anunnaki left about the same time.

In the chaos of those days, Moses, the Hebrew leader and himself an Anunnaki/human hybrid, accepted *YHVH*'s offer on behalf of this people. YHVH's substitute also gave Moses a communication device for contacting him, which later became revered as the Ark of the Covenant, because oddly YHVH did not want Moses or anyone else to see him, possibly because of his reptilian appearance that many exhibited.

Of course, when the Israelites arrived in the Land of Canaan, there was a problem—it was full of Canaanites! So Moses was told to form an army to destroy them completely: "Make no treaties, show no mercy, but wipe them out utterly, men, women, young and old, sheep, cattle everything. Of course, you can rape the women before killing them, and keep a few young girls for your pleasure, but kill everything else." That's one angry deity! How could anyone pray to a God that tells a conquering army to kill everyone but to keep the little girls as sex toys? Why did God, who also created the Canaanites, demand that the most innocent of them be raped by an army of soldiers? Just who was this God of the Hebrews?

An ET delegation communicating with Billy Meier (see Vol. II, Chapter 15) offers a different slant. They tell us that *YHVH* was a Plejaran (a star system near the Pleiades) title, meaning 'Lord of Wisdom'—a Plejaran spacefarer turned renegade who established himself on Sinai. From there, he introduced chaos into the world, including misleading those fleeing Egypt by promising them land that was not his to give. Normally, the *YHVHs* would want to be revered for their wisdom but not want to be worshipped. However, this guy was different, and his need for validation has led much of humanity into a monstrous quagmire of deception that still messes with its collective mind today.

Whether Anunnaki or Plejaran, *YHVH*'s departure from Earth left the priest class with a problem. How were they to maintain a cult based on their flesh-and-blood ET overlord now that he had apparently deserted them, without the tribe degenerating into anarchy? The answer? They *pretended* he was still around, and ever-watchful. They imbued him with supernatural powers, and portrayed him as *transcendent* and separate from the masses, unapproachable except by the priests, who conducted elaborate rituals to him in the hope that someday he would return. Since no one had ever seen *YHVH*, it was easy over the generations to change his image from an ET with high-tech toys to a supernatural being who had to be worshipped in exchange for his continued patronage and protection. Thus the idea of 'God' was born.

So what was it all about? Why did Ninturta put all those poor people through so much pain and suffering? Was it simply vain-glory? Perhaps. Maybe he wanted to leave a lasting legacy, so he made one group 'special' through circumcision and a covenant he knew they would keep. He gave them land he had no rights to, so they would have to fight for it—and they still do today. And he made sure their story would be well-documented. As a result, half the population of Earth calls his memory God, Allah or Jehovah—that's an immortality that no other Anunnaki achieved. Today, no one regales in the stories of Thoth, Ra, Osiris, Zeus, Apollo or Mercury, but the story of the God of Israel is still a modern-day best-seller.[6]

The priesthood's lust for power and control drove a huge wedge between the cult members and their god that has persisted for 3,000 years. The priests blamed the people, claiming their sins had caused the *YHVH* to leave. To prevent a backlash, the priests also branded any mention of the god-within as blasphemy, punishable by stoning (much later amended by the Roman Catholic Church to burning at the stake, possibly because of the lack of stones in the cities). The priests also used 'the Word of *YHVH*' as a means of social control and for imposing their own agendas on the illiterate masses. For example, those who were afraid of the power women had over men began to preach that: "God commands that women be treated as second class humans."

"For a man indeed ought not to cover his head since he is the image and glory of God, but the woman is the glory of man." Islamic wisdom from the Koran? No, try I Corinthians 11:6. And how about Ephesians 5:22: "Wives, submit to your own husbands as to the Lord. For the husband is head of the wife, as also Christ is head of the church." But we're jumping ahead.

Back in the land of the Hebrews, the Roman conquerors took over and had to contend with dozens of sects, all proclaiming the god they worshipped was the only real god. Like the others, the Hebrew cult fought for their *YHVH* to be accepted as the *supreme* deity, promising that *YHVH* would one day return to reward those who had remained loyal and faithful to him.

The legacy of this god-myth has been truly disastrous for western civilization. It has kept us from exploring our human potential and power, by having us

---

6   Many biblical scholars interpret the smoke, flames and trembling ground during the Mt. Sinai encounter as the take-off of an ET craft. And when Moses returned, he had white hair and appeared burned—both symptoms of radiation exposure. In other books, II Kings talks of Elijah crossing the Jordon in a chariot of fire—clearly a reference to a craft, because why would God need a vehicle? And Ezekiel 10:8 mentions the UFO shaped like a 'wheel within a wheel,' another UFO reference.

transfer that power to some 'out there' supernatural being. We went from being the slaves of an ET overlord to being slaves to the illusion of the priests' dogma that the overlord was still out there somewhere, watching us and judging us from a distance. As a result, compared to the simplicity of the Buddhist who has not inherited this legacy, we are psychologically dysfunctional beings, divided against ourselves.

Over the next few centuries, *the essential key* occurred that has colored western civilization and still does today. As the Hebrew oral history was written down over many generations, their flesh-and-blood ET overlord **became deified** as the God of the Hebrews. The ETs had long ago left the planet to its own devices, so the 'no other gods but me' commandment meant the *memory* of the Hebrew ET patron became worshipped as the *only* legitimate god.

Whoever compiled the Pentateuch, often called the Books of Moses[7], in the 4th century bce drew upon much older sources of the Israelites' history:

- *Yahwist* source, known as source 'J,' that makes heavy use of the term *YHVH* in the 9th century BCE (1000 – 961). This source talks as if *YHVH* were an actual person, walking in the garden with Adam, and shows how *YHVH*'s promises to Abraham were fulfilled in the monarchy of King David. It is believed to be written by a woman in the reign of King Solomon or King David.

- *Elohist* source, known as source 'E,' so named because of the plural term *Elohim*. Written two generations later in the 8th century BCE, it has a strong moral tone and reflects the views of the northern kingdom, after Solomon's kingdom fell apart and the north went its own way. It is believed written by a Levite priest between 800 – 750 BCE.

- *Deuteronomist* source, known as 'D,' written two generations later still (7th century BCE), with extensive legal content and reassesses earlier stories in the light of the lessening faithfulness of Israel and its kings in the *YHVH* myth due to his being absent and overdue. Emphasis on the law suggests Baruch as the author.

- *Priestly* source, known as source 'P,' written 200 years later in the 5th century BCE following Nebuchadnezzar's forcing of the southern Israelites living in Judah into exile in Babylon (586 – 537 BCE). There, for 50 years, they had access to the ancient Sumerian texts and interwove the legends into their own history, greatly condensing thousands of tablets into the

---

7   Moses actually had nothing to do with writing them because their content clearly postdates his life.

short synopsis found in modern Exodus. On their return to Judah in 535 BCE, following being granted their freedom by conquering Persian King Cyrus, their writings focused on the ritual of worship, chronology, law and genealogy, and reorganized sources and added some new material to reflect the needs of the exiled Israelites. It was probably penned by Ezra, a priest in Jerusalem on their return, who compiled the Five Books of Moses into the Torah to restore the Law of God to a people that had degenerated into Paganism (i.e., worshipped multiple gods) during the Diaspora.[8]

The rest of the Old Testament is an assortment of Israelite chronology (tribal history) and wisdom from various sources relating to the Covenant between the Israelites and *YHVH*, their ET overlord. Sources include known names such as Solomon, Samuel and Baruch, plus unknowns such as shepherds and gardeners.

In the 3rd century BCE, the Greek Ptolemy living in Egypt translated the OT books into one volume in Greek, forming the first Hebrew Bible, and stored it in the Library at Alexandria, where it was destroyed when Julius Caesar invaded Egypt in 47 CE.

Due to a fluke in history, of the hundreds of tribes that had lived under the patronage of ET overlords, the story of only *one* such tribe made it down through the millennia in the form of the Israelite's *Pentateuch* that became the first five books of the western world's Old Testament. And since it was the only account of those early times that was backed by the Roman Empire, its insistence that their *YHVH* (in reality a flesh-and-blood ET) was the one true God made it probably inevitable that the Hebrew God myth would spread far and wide. But why has this preposterous myth persisted even until today?

It was given a boost a few centuries later when a new cult sprang up around a myth based on the life and teachings of an Essene Gnostic named Jeshua (see next chapter). This cult's leaders would later deify the central figure, now re-

---

8   It was during exile in Babylon that the Israelites picked up the notion of the devil as someone who opposed YHVH. They absorbed the Babylonian legends that talked about conflict between Marduk, the long-departed Anunnaki bad 'god' who opposed the good 'god,' Enki, on whom the Israelites modeled the YHVH they encountered at Mt. Sinai during the Exodus. Thus, the oral tradition hopelessly confused the Babylonian legends of Enki and the Egyptian legends of the monotheistic Ahemhotep. Also, Marduk was associated with the sacred number '3661,' it being the number of years of a Niburu orbit. In the base-60 math used by the Babylonians, this was actually written '111,' but the Israelites did not understand the math, and just knew there was a '6' in the three significant positions. Hence the number '666' became associated with the devil—a number that would turn up again in John of Patmos' The Book of Revelation.

named Jesus, claiming *YHVH* had sent him in his stead. This nicely circumvented the awkward no-show on the part of *YHVH* for the last few centuries, and tied together the *YHVH* cult and the Jesus cult. Many Romans believed *YHVH,* God of the Hebrews was not the same as the God of Christianity, so the Christian scribes were quick to rewrite history to prevent protests that *YHVH* had been just an ET overlord, and not a supernatural deity worthy of Christian worship.

The model the Hebrews used to interpret their world underwent a massive shift *away* from the natural, and *towards* the supernatural, as their patron shifted from being a real person with whom one could talk, to a nonphysical being in whom one could only have faith. Only the Gnostics held out, valuing spiritual truth over blind faith, and that would bring to the world an outstanding teacher to whom no one would listen and whose words would be hopelessly mangled to suit various ambitions and political agendas.

Thus the deception was complete, and eventually millions would buy into it, especially when Rome relinquished its panoply of gods and adopted 'the One True God' instead. Today, the priest classes continue to peddle the myth that *YHVH* is real, alive and well, planning to return at some point in the future to judge those who have sinned in his eyes.

If the accounts on the preceding pages are true, then in effect, our ancient fore-bears were forced to project their own higher self onto the fictional *YHVH* of their oral history, which was then used to police them. Of course, they were unable to conceive of who or what had created this deity, or who created that, and so on back to the Source of All That Is. So the *YHVH* of their legends was credited with having created All That Is. (Interestingly, many 'primitive' peoples around the world maintain a distinction between the creator of the universe and local gods that meddle in people's affairs.) When our forebears jammed together the Source and all the ET *YHVH,* we lost both our higher self and the *real* Source, a loss perpetuated by early organized religions, which did everything they could to fan the flames of human powerlessness, because churches full of powerless followers suited the early religious leaders. And because they were illiterate, the masses couldn't read any conflicting texts that could contradict the church leaders. As we will see in the next chapter, centuries later, once Rome had adopted the fledgling Jesus cult (minus reincarnation) and made it the Roman Catholic Church, *all* other sacred texts were hunted down and burned in order to perpetuate the lie of powerlessness, where *only* the direct intervention of the priests would get God to look well upon the faithful. Just as the Anunnaki had used the

YHVH hoax to control humans, the Roman Empire would one day continue the hoax, today seen as the Roman Catholic Church and its various Anglican spin-offs.

The God-myth, then, is mass brainwashing, initiated by the male-dominated Anunnaki to wipe out Earth's matriarchal societies that had formed when tribes of Cro-Magnon broke free of Anunnaki control. The purpose was and still is to render the human species, created by the Anunnaki themselves, obedient by making them place their awesome power outside themselves.

Worse, by fostering variations of the hoax (God, Jehovah, Allah), the Anunnaki also gave us the legacy of war, and humans (as Christians, Jews and Muslims) still strive to kill each other over their competing god-myths. Through this conflict, the Anunnaki legacy still quietly controls the planet even though they themselves left long ago. (Sitchin theorizes that they departed because Anu was disturbed by the intense conflict between the bloodlines of his two sons—En-lil, who had no love for mankind, and En-ki, who strenuously opposed such contempt for humanity.)

The above explanation solves one of the problems I had with the God being peddled by the major religions; one that is portrayed in the Old Testament (OT) as cruel, petty, spiteful and vindictive. He goes around smiting one tribe or group after another if they fail to obey some rule or other, or waver in their loyalty. He sets impossibly high standards, makes substandard humans, smites them for their imperfections (which he put there), and consigns them to hell for all eternity! Yuck! Not the kind of deity I want in my life, which is why I opted out of Christianity as soon as I could.

Now, thanks to Zecharia Sitchin *et al*, it all makes perfect sense. The truth is shockingly simple—the mythical God of the OT and the real Source of All That Is are vastly different beings, and have nothing to do with each other. The Source of All That Is is actually a vast transcendent matrix of consciousness, encompassing all the dimensions, including the soul plane and the physical plane. Thus our souls, minds and bodies exist within this matrix and are part of it, so we are all integral parts of the Source.

What about the mean, petty, vindictive OT God? We've seen where *that* came from ... the Anunnaki—lots of them, everywhere, all sons and grandsons of Anu—and a mean, spiteful, petty vindictive bunch, with callous disregard for mankind, their created slave race. However, En-ki at least deserves credit for helping Noah survive the flood that En-lil could have warned humans about but didn't. And also to their credit, on his state visit to Earth during the Nibiru pass in 3600 BCE, Anu commanded that the human population be taught writing, agriculture, metal-working, astronomy, mathematics, etc. … which explains the sudden, dramatic rise to prominence of Sumerian culture at that time, something that puzzles traditional archeologists. An attempt to assuage his guilt, perhaps?

Bottom line? When the Israelites passed down their oral legends that eventually became the OT, they made great play of their *YHVH* who protected them. But over the last 3,000 years, the nature of *YHVH* has changed from being their flesh-and-blood ET ruler into some supernatural being 'out there' somewhere. Meanwhile, we have been robbed of the real Source of All That Is, of which we are each an integral part … and very much 'in here.'

Critics of Sitchin claim he's 'just one voice out in the wilderness,' but that's not so. In 1999, a furor broke out among Hebrew scholars, triggered by Prof. Herzog of Tel Aviv University, who announced: "The Israelites were never in Egypt, did not wander the desert, did not conquer the land, and did not pass it on to the twelve tribes. Moreover, the Jewish God *YHVH* had a female consort—the goddess Asherah."

Herzog further claims that Judaism adopted monotheism (the one god concept) only in the 7th century BCE, rather than centuries earlier when Moses received the Ten Commandments on Mt. Sinai. The name *YHVH*, he states, means "I am who I am," indicating that, for some reason, this being did not want his real name to be spoken.

Other ancient writings clearly confirm that this *YHVH* was only one among many, and that in Judaism, his real name was *El Shaddai*, which means 'the *YHVH* of the mountain,' possibly referring to Mt. Sinai, his temporary home. Herzog adds that the Sumerian name for *El Shaddai* was ISH.KUR, or 'youngest son of En-lil,' and someone renowned for his violent streak and contempt for humans (which is why he too went around smiting everyone), and his open opposition to his father, to the point of consorting with his own mother, Asherah.

Herzog has driven one more nail in the coffin of biblical claims that the Hebrew (and hence Christian) deity is the only God of Creation. In fact, *YHVH* was just one of hundreds of Anu's wayward grandchildren doing battle with each other and with their human subjects.

At this point, you may be asking: So what? Just that you are now free of the 'God Is Watching' mentality. There is no 'God-out-there' watching you, judging you and waiting to punish you. Instead, *you* are the sovereign master of your destiny.

As a synopsis of thousands of tablets containing ancient Sumerian, Chaldean and Akkadian historical accounts, the OT was translated from Hebrew into Latin and Greek about 1000 CE, and later into English. So everything in the OT that you read suffers from a major condensation plus at least three translations, all of which depended on the translator's personal views. Worse, one language may not have a particular concept in its vocabulary, so the original concept must be translated to a similar concept.[9]

To see how translation can create monstrosities, here's a rendition of The Lord's Prayer, translated directly from Aramaic to English, performed by two scholars, Mark Hathaway and Neil Douglas-Klotz. Without all the disciplinary 'sinner' stuff, it's quite beautiful—something I could get behind if it were dedicated to soul:

> *O cosmic, Birther of all radiance and vibration!*
>
> *Soften the ground of our being and carve out a space within us where your Presence can abide.*
>
> *Fill us with your creativity so that we may be empowered to bear the fruit of your mission.*
>
> *Let each of our actions bear fruit in accordance with your desire.*
>
> *Endow us with the wisdom to produce and share what each being needs to grow and flourish.*
>
> *Untie the tangled threads of destiny that bind us, as we release others from the entanglement of past mistakes.*
>
> *Do not let us be seduced by that which would divert us from our true purpose, but illuminate the opportunities of the present moment.*
>
> *For You are the ground and the fruitful vision, the birth-power and fulfillment, as all is gathered and made whole once again.*

If the OT God is a myth, what then *is* the all-powerful force in the Universe? For answers, the best source is ETs themselves, for they've been around the cosmos a lot longer than we have.[10] They see the Source as a 'transcendent matrix of consciousness,' or a supremely intelligent and loving electromagnetic field that pervades the entire universe ... that *is*, the entire universe. Everything, from your body to the stars, is composed of this Source energy. It is deeply personal, infinitely loving, and, being all things, is the energy from which your body, mind and soul spring, moment-by-moment. At the same time, and *without contradiction*, this same energy obeys its own impersonal laws, such as the Law of Resonance

9   For example, the word 'God' has an interesting origin. Apparently the Sanskrit word huta, meaning 'that which is invoked' became the Old Teutonic gheu, or 'invoked by sacrifice.' In Old English, when combined with the Latin deus meaning 'from the skies,' gheu deos came to mean 'invoked from the skies.' Ultimately this was contracted to the word god.

10   If you are still in any doubt about the reality of UFOs and ETs, a Roper Poll published in December 2002 finds that 56 percent of all Americans now believe in their reality, so you're now officially in the minority.

and the Law of Attraction (more later). You are free to work with these laws or against them. However, the more you deviate from Universal Law, the more unhappy you will find yourself.

ETs do not have formalized religion *per se* so, far from worshipping this matrix, they just go about their daily lives, aware of it and working with it. They accept reincarnation as fact, and view the concept of one lifetime followed by judgment on the part of some deity as impossibly simplistic.

Hopefully, ET contact will help quash the childish human notion that we're born and die once only, having lived a single life, and will strengthen the notion that we are souls that incarnate countless times in a variety of roles on a variety of planets. So in some future incarnation, *you* might be the ET who is visiting another planet. Each incarnation is carefully orchestrated to bring learning, wisdom and insight as to the nature of the Supreme Oversoul of which we are each an essential part. (Chapter 14 goes into more detail about ET spirituality.)

Does the 'fact' that our bodies were genetically engineered to serve our ancient ET overlords devalue us in any way? No, because it refers to *just* our bodies, and not to who we really are. The Anunnaki did such a good job, we as souls are able to attach to these bodies, interact through them, and make them serve our needs brilliantly.

I recently read about a Boy Scout who was denied Eagle Scout status because he didn't believe in the narrow Christian God, instead believing in a more amorphous Supreme Source. A scouting movement spokesman talked about the importance to the movement of being 'a good person.' In effect, this equates one's worth as a member of society with blind faith in the Christian God-myth— a scary revelation of how deeply the myth penetrates our lives.

Rather than worshipping the God-myth spawned of Sumerian ETs, this book will introduce you to who you *really* are—a soul that is an integral part of the Source's energy … so you should be worshipping yourself if anyone. However, the entire God industry has sprung up around acting as middlemen between you and its mythological God, when all you need do is close your eyes, clear your mind, talk to yourself as part of the Source … and then listen.

I'm often asked, "Do you believe in God?" That's difficult because I don't believe in the questioner's God, usually the narrow Christian God that people kneel and pray to. Of course, there is a Source because all this stuff around us didn't just happen. Look up in the night sky at the billions of galaxies, each with billions of stars … and that's only in one dimension. The universe also exists up through gazillion dimensions, and there's a lot more stuff packed in at the higher frequencies. So *something* has to be hard at work. Locally, that vast Source being forms your higher self, or soul, so if you pray, that's who listens. It's not the vindictive little 'God-out-there' slave-master but 'Source-in-here' that is the 'active ingredient' in your life. However, an entire industry has sprung up to convince you otherwise, rather like an institutional Santa Claus, created in order to explain something otherwise inexplicable … unless you're an Old Soul who is ready for the truth—or at least as much truth as can be expressed in human languages. However, this is perfectly fine; younger souls need some simplistic explanation of reality and, as we will see in a later chapter on soul ages, the concept of an authoritative God serves their needs well. Not everyone is ready for the truth about reality as a transcendent matrix of consciousness.

Implications

If the Sumerian paradigm is true, then the implications are staggering:

1. Deep within our racial memories lies the fact that we were created as a worker race, completely subordinated to beings so vastly superior in terms of technology and cosmic understanding that our legends portray them as gods. The Old Testament focuses on just one of the Anunnaki 'gods' and the tribe he took under his wing, a god to whom Jews, Christians and Muslims still see themselves as subservient. Blowing this God myth apart is tremendously liberating, allowing us to live as free souls-in-flesh, creators not beholden to some mythical deity.

2. One means of controlling the early humans was to enforce loyalty to their particular ET overlord. This fostered obedience and provided the Elohim with armies to go up against the armies of other Elohim, hence all the 'smiting' in the Old Testament. And so that the humans loyal to one Elohim could not get in cahoots with those of another, each group was taught a different language, as in the Tower of Babel story. Language barriers also fostered lack of trust and animosity between different groups, and wars based on each group's God myth, which we are still fighting millennia later. Blowing apart the myth that human groupings are based on fundamental differences, a myth meant to control us, opens us up to the possibility of planetary unity, peace, and eventual membership of the Federation of Planets.

3. Fear is a way of life for most people. This is because deep in our racial memory, we remember a time when we *needed* to live in fear, when we had no more rights than the animal in the fields, and could be killed for the slightest infraction. Learning the source of our fear-based mentality would allow us to dispel it, and restore ourselves to our soul legacy of sovereign identity.

4. Accepting that the Anunnaki engineered our bodies by combining their DNA with that of *Homo erectus* would allow us to reverse what they built into our DNA—short lifetimes, vulnerability to disease, and aging. Our DNA can and should be far more robust, with more effective self-correcting replication, but the Anunnaki needed nothing more than expendable worker drones to mine gold and keep house for them. The advent of the Indigo Children, with their superhuman gifts, is an encouraging sign that we are moving beyond our ancient, inbuilt, genetic limitations.

It is *essential* to keep in mind, however, that the Sumerian legends record *only* what the Anunnaki told them … and they may have omitted or distorted some of the truth but we have no way of knowing. Another scenario might be that when they came to this planet, the Anunnaki found us to be a profoundly spiritual race, highly telepathic and living in full harmony with nature. Our two races may have coexisted for millennia but, when the Anunnaki mining operations proved too onerous, the newcomers may have forcibly hi-jacked our DNA and 'dumbed down' our genetic make-up by stripping our 12-strand DNA down to two strands. This would have robbed us of our telepathic powers and deep connection to soul. Floundering in psychic blindness, we would have been easy to enslave.

In fact, many channeled sources corroborate this version. For example, the Group (about a dozen angelic beings under Archangel Michael) speaking through channel Steve Rother (see www.lightworker.com) says this is *precisely* what did happen. Back in those days, we were collectively pretty much at the level of today's advanced metaphysicians, and we were literally enslaved and genetically engineered.

Some ET sources claim that in Earth's ancient past, they enhanced our DNA with their own, so they regard us as distant cousins. Then along came the Anunnaki, who enslaved humanity by genetic manipulation, so we would toil in the mines, helping them plunder our planet of its resources.

The skeptic might protest, "What about fossil remains from those pre-invasion days, or old buildings or artifacts?" Well, if we really were that advanced, we would have had the power to dematerialize our bodies when we decided to leave them. As for buildings and artifacts, either we didn't need them because of the material simplicity of our richly spiritual lives, or the Anunnaki did a thorough clean-up job, destroying all evidence of our pre-invasion culture.

If this latter scenario were true, the Anunnaki obviously would not have revealed the whole truth to the Sumerian humans, but would have stopped at the story we have read about—that the Anunnaki 'created' human DNA, and omitted the hi-jack part. Thus they would look like rescuers rather than conquerors. (History is always written by the victors of a conflict.)

If this alternative were true, it does not change the issue with the God myth. Whether we are enhanced primates or dumbed-down avatars, our Sumerian ancestors still regarded the Anunnaki as Lords of Earth. So when the latter finally left the planet, *human* leaders stepped forward and, over hundreds of generations, told us those flesh-and-blood ETs with the high-tech toys were actually a supernatural being called God, and the God they were peddling was the only true one, all the others being fakes.

If we *are* ex-avatars as the ET sources tell us, it's time to reclaim our stolen heritage. Whatever really happened, we as soul *allowed* it to happen as another avenue for learning more about ourselves, but now it's time to move forward into our destiny as Divine co-creators.

The Bible Code

With the worldview in this chapter, especially the assertions that: (1) the Old Testament God was actually an ET grandson of Anu, and (2) the OT is actually the story of the interaction between this being and the Hebrew people, what can we make of the phenomenon known as the Bible Code? The premise is that embedded within the Hebrew text are hidden messages that emerge only when the text is sampled—every 27th letter, say—starting at a particular character. Before the computer, such an analysis took years, but now takes only seconds. One technique is just to sample randomly and see what comes up, but if you specify a search word such as 'KENNEDY,' the software will analyze the text, beginning with equidistant letter sequencing (ELS) of 2, say, then 3, and so on.

This is nothing new; since the 12th century, scholars have explored the OT for 'the handiwork of God.' Sir Isaac Newton was fascinated with the task and learned Hebrew just for that purpose, spending years looking for hidden messages. And just after WWII, a Rabbi Weismandel discovered that by starting with the first Hebrew letter 'T' in the book of Genesis, and counting forward 49 letters gives 'O' as the 50th letter. Letter 100 = R, 150 = A, and 200 = H, spelling out the word TORAH, the name Moses gave to the first five books.

Once personal computers came along, looking for a cryptic pattern, or matrix, became easy, and scholars have found matrices that spell out messages, such as:

- WRIGHT BROTHERS … AIRPLANE
- SARS … EPIDEMIC
- AMERICAN REVOLUTION … 1776
- REVOLUTION … RUSSIA … 1917
- HITLER … NAZI … EVIL MAN … SLAUGHTER
- WORLD WAR … ATOMIC HOLOCAUST … JAPAN … 1945
- PRESIDENT KENNEDY … TO DIE … OSWALD … ASSASSIN

Scholars claim that whoever authored the OT embedded the patterns in the text, and that God himself dictated the first five books. Of course, being omniscient, God was fully familiar with events that would occur millennia into the future.

One of the most startling messages is the so-called End of Days matrix, decoded by a Roy Reinhold in April 2004. Three of the six lines of the matrix are:

- Leviticus 2:5, starting at letter 23: *In 5770, a lion is against Har Megiddo. He laid it waste. You are finished.* Reinhold believes this refers to the lion of Judah, meaning that in the second coming in Gregorian year 2010, the Messiah will return as a warrior, not a gentle preacher, in charge of an army that will vanquish the Antichrist at Megiddo in central Israel.
- Genesis 30:32, letter 55: *He covered the coldness of 5770; command days of HaShem.* The Messiah will, in 2010, begin a special time for Hebrews known as the Days of God (*HaShem* is Hebrew for 'the name of God,' or *YHVH*).
- Numbers 28:3, letter 52: *Who comes from them? He scorned Bel of Sheol, the head of it.* The Messiah will scorn the ancient god of hell who was cast out of heaven.

Two other ominous messages scholars have decoded are:

- EARTHQUAKE … LA … 2010
- METEOR … END OF DAYS … 2012

The book *The Bible Code* by Michael Drosnin brought the phenomenon out of obscurity and into the mainstream, but Drosnin himself does not believe the Torah was penned by the Almighty. "Clearly it was not someone omnipotent, or he would simply prevent the danger, instead of encoding a warning." Another researcher, Dr. James Price ran an exhaustive test on Exodus 19:8–23. The 16 verses yielded 3,773 3-letter words, 2,567 4-letter words, 1.376 5-letter words and 541 6-letter words. You could make up pretty much anything with all those words.

To the skeptics, Drosnin challenged in *Newsweek* magazine: "When my critics find a message about the assassination of a prime minister encrypted in *Moby Dick*, I'll believe them."

That's exactly what Australian mathematician Brendan McKay set out to do. He claims the whole thing is just a statistical anomaly, and any lengthy text yields the same results. For example, when applied to *Moby Dick*, the technique predicts the deaths of Princess Diana (with the names of Dodi and Henri Paul actually crossing her name), plus the assassinations of Indira Gandhi, Abraham Lincoln, Yitzhak Rabin, Leon Trotsky, Martin Luther King and John F. Kennedy (JFK … HE SHALL BE KILLED).

That pretty much wraps it up for me but if you want to research for yourself one rainy day, just Googling on 'bible code' will give you over 100,000 URLs to explore.

Note on the Human Genome Decoding Project

In February 2003, the Public Consortium Team, tasked with decoding the human genome (the genetic code within our cells), revealed their findings. The human code is made up of about 20,000 genes, or discrete pieces of genetic information. (Oddly, the maize plant has about twice that number, and theoretically shouldn't even exist.) Researchers found that we share 99% of our genetic material with other terrestrial species, notably chimpanzees. Apparently, that 1% difference (only 223 genes, which researchers call 'alien' genes) accounts for the proteins and enzymes that govern all our higher functions, such as abstract thinking … and was introduced *recently*, in evolutionary terms, i.e., there are no precursors to them on the planet.

Those 223 genes are found nowhere on the planet except for a few in bacteria, so where did they come from? Although this doesn't confirm Sitchin's Anunnaki translations, it opens a huge question that his work answers very nicely. (Of course, the mainstream genome researchers can't go there or ponder whether those bacteria also have an Anunnaki source.)

As a species, we simply should not exist according to the tenets of evolution. *Homo sapiens* appeared out of nowhere about 200,000 years ago, with no genetic precursors, or missing links to what should be our ancestors. And many genetic anomalies separate us from our nearest possible ancestors:

- We have little body hair, and what we have doesn't grow to a certain length and stop, but keeps on growing, as do our finger and toenails. Without body hair, our skin is sensitive to sunlight, as if we were designed to work indoors or underground.
- Our bones and muscles are much weaker than those of other primates, as if we were designed to work with machinery.
- Our bodies are simply not designed to walk on all fours, which makes us more mobile and flexible as workers.
- Human skulls are of a totally different design, as if to allow for a larger forebrain.
- Our larynx is in a very different place than with primates, which facilitates speech. (This is courtesy of just one gene added between 100,000 and 200,000 years ago.)
- Human female sexual cycles are completely different, so the birth of our young is not tied to the availability of food in the summer.

Starting with the famous Scopes "Monkey Trial" in the 1920s, the creationism/ evolution debate has waged, with both sides presenting limited arguments. Creationism holds that God created the universe in six days about 6,000 years ago, but studies of mitochondrial DNA and human fossils tell us that *Homo sapiens* goes back at least 250,000 years. Evolutionists fare no better. They tell us that life began as an accident as the Earth cooled down within the last 4 billion years, and random mutations led from a single-cell organism to complex bodies such as ours. Now while there is evidence of natural selection *within* a species, there is *no* evidence that one species can mutate into another. Even Darwin himself said his hypothesis would fall if no fossilized evidence of transitional forms were found. Well, they haven't, so it has fallen. Further, as soon as the first modern man appeared, they showed up *everywhere* on the planet, almost instantly.

All this makes one thing clearly obvious—that our genetic lineage was 'recently' totally reworked (about 200,000 years ago), which throws out both Darwin's Theory of Evolution and Creationism, leaving only a couple of alternatives— Intelligent Design and Interventionism.

Two other odd things happened 12,000 years ago after The Great Flood:

1. Dozens of varieties of domesticated animals appeared 'out of nowhere,' all distant relatives of wild creatures, but with no 'missing links.' For

example, the huge aurochs suddenly became tame cattle, and the wolf gave us dozens of breeds of dogs, suited to various tasks such as hunting, guarding and herding.

2. Species of wild grasses with tiny seeds of little nutritional value suddenly became dozens of species of grains and cereals with large, nutritious seeds seemingly designed for easy harvesting. And species of puny wild fruits suddenly became large and succulent.

Studying nuclear DNA, geneticists have concluded that all humans sprang spontaneously from a common father around 270,000 years ago. And from mitochondrial DNA, they have identified a common mother around 250,000 years ago. Both parents of humankind lived in a small sub-Sahara region of Africa. This places the origins of *Homo sapiens* exactly where and when the Sumerian texts say we originated—the ancient goldmines of Africa. Other geneticists claim the initial matriarchal gene pool was small, maybe a dozen or so, while yet another DNA research group claims that most Europeans are descendents of just seven women who lived about 45,000 years ago. Furthermore, the earliest fossil remains of modern Caucasians have been dated back to 100,000 years ago in Java, and 60,000 years ago in Europe, again stemming from a tiny initial group. (It's interesting to speculate on how KKK members feel about having African ancestors.)

Paleontologists estimate that due to random cell mutation, evolution crawls along at 3 percent/million years. On this basis, it is *impossible* for a whole new species to appear overnight. But, on evolution's timeline, these dramatic changes *did* happen overnight, when such genetic mutations should have taken millions of years. Again, the answer can only be the work of a highly advanced civilization.

Studying ancient Sumerian accounts of our history leaves us with some puzzling questions that paleontologists will not even consider:

1. Why is there no evidence of a 'bridge' between *Homo sapiens* who we are today and *Homo erectus*, our nearest living genetic ancestor? (DNA studies prove that Neanderthal man was not our ancestor but a parallel branch.)

2. Why did our 'evolution' occur in a few thousand years, giving us large brains, hairless bodies and speech, when it should have taken tens of millions of years?

3. How did we progress from the Stone Age to the Bronze Age almost overnight? We didn't have time to figure out metal-smelting and alloys, plant-grafting, animal cross-breeding, spoken and written languages, astronomy and mathematics by ourselves, so who taught us?

In earlier chapters, we saw how the physical plane flows down from higher dimensions, where all is carefully planned. Anyone doubting this would do well to study highly complex systems, such as our DNA or endocrine system. Astronomer Fred Hoyle estimated the odds of DNA emerging randomly out of chaos at 1 in $10^{40,000}$ (10 with 40,000 zeroes following). He also likens it to a tornado blowing through a scrap yard and assembling a fully operational Boeing 747 out of whatever junk was lying around.

The more we uncover of the inner world of physics, the more scientists are concluding that the universe is 'telic,' from the Greek *telos*, meaning 'end,' which means the universe is intelligently designed with an end purpose. All that remains is to figure out: (1) whose intelligence and, (2) what purpose.

In his book *The God Gene*, Dean Hamer identifies gene VMAT2 as possibly involved with faith, hope and optimism because it may be linked to levels of dopamine, the 'happy hormone.' People with higher levels of dopamine are more sociable and optimistic, which makes them more attractive to potential mates, and hence more likely than some mean grinch to have children. Thus the 'happy' gene setting is more likely to be passed on to future generations. These people are also more likely to gravitate to religion or spirituality, and such 'people of faith' live up to seven years longer and in better health, due to a happy outlook and tendency to laugh more. Again, this gives them an evolutionary advantage. Of course, this does not automatically translate into belief in God or gods, just to faith in the bigger picture, which may include faith in a deity. This is yet another example of how DNA is hard-wired to best propagate itself.

Implications

Why is the information in this chapter so important? Because the notion of the supernatural God of the Christian Bible is the chief stumbling block to you knowing your soul, and a monstrous affront to your sovereignty. Let's see why.

Towards their human subjects, the Anunnaki stance was, "If you worship me as your Lord, I will protect you from the other Lords. If you rebel against me, I will throw you on their mercy or destroy you myself." Humans were thus engrained with obedience to authority, which human rulers appointed by the Anunnaki perpetuated. Central to worship was the offering of sacrifices, usually a prime farm animal, but after the Anunnaki departure, priests often demanded the life of a slave, captive or child, to persuade the absent Anunnaki to return. The priests' jobs depended on the masses believing the priests were still in contact with the

ET overlords. Since the masses were conditioned to obedience, they acquiesced to the priests' demands.

The demise of Anunnaki power was rooted in the war between the Houses of En-lil and En-ki, which culminated in the nuclear war of c. 2024 BCE that destroyed Sodom and Gomorrah and enlarged the Red Sea. The nuclear fallout cloud drifted east, rendering the Tigris-Euphrates region uninhabitable for centuries. The few Anunnaki returnees resumed the family squabble, leading to a final pullout between 1500 – 1000 BCE.

When the Anunnaki finally left for good, the resulting separation anxiety became the defining theme for western religions that still persists today. Left to their own devices after being obedient worshippers since their very creation, humans were servants with no masters to serve, and woefully ill-equipped to take their rightful place in the natural world.

So, we may ask, why didn't humanity breathe a collective sigh of relief and begin to enjoy its newfound freedom, autonomy and independence? Basically, they didn't know how to. The Anunnaki had managed every aspect of human life so thoroughly, humans had no idea how to self-rule. (When Yugoslavia collapsed, the Balkan states were at each other's throats. And when Britain left India, civil war erupted between Muslims and Hindus, and no one knew how to make the trains run on time.)

In *Gods, Genes and Consciousness*, Paul Von Ward identifies three stages in the evolution of human consciousness at work here:

1. Natural dependence on Anunnaki rule as a fact of life.
2. Departure of the Anunnaki, triggering rituals devised to implore their return because the absence is believed only temporary.
3. After hundreds of generations, *memories* of the Anunnaki evolve into worship of *imagined supernatural gods*, such as the *YHVH* worshipped by the Hebrew cult.

In Stage 1, it's not surprising that ancient humans regarded the Anunnaki as gods. They seemed to live forever, had amazing technology, could fly, and with their medical skills, could apparently raise the dead. And most of all, they created us. So it was not therefore a big jump for our superstitious forebears' impression of them to go from *superhuman* to *supernatural*. However, this put them *outside* the natural world, from where they ruled it. All their worshippers could do was appeal to their mercy and good graces, which varied from ET to ET.

But what do you do in Stage 2, when the object of your worship goes away? First, you try to entice it back with ritual, and instruct future generations about those rituals. But hundreds of generations down through time, empty ritual is all people have, plus descriptions of how magical everything once was when your cult's god-like protector walked the Earth.

During Stage 3, succeeding generations are indoctrinated with those memories and forced to worship them, while negating other cults with different memories. Thus *exclusivity* becomes a hallmark of all cults. Also, the most successful cults are those where the priests allege continued contact with their deity by some form of channeling; such cults can impose the harshest sanctions for nonconformity, as in Judaism.

So the Stage 3 God-focused cult that ultimately evolved into Judaism, Christianity and Islam was based on subservience to the memory of a flesh-and-blood ET overlord, later worshipped as an unseen, supernatural, transcendent being named *YHVH*. This subservience caused major dysfunctional dependence, and stripped humans of all personal responsibility for their lives and destinies. Rather than looking inward for their psychological identity and safety, humans looked to the heavens for a divine scapegoat to blame for any misfortune.

Today, the priests perpetuate the lie that their deity still cares, but from a distance, which continues human dependence by proxy, a disastrous thing for human consciousness and our relationship with our own souls.

The priests' God concept replaces direct experience of our soul with a supernatural higher power, who rewards our good deeds with 'heavenly brownie points,' punishes our misdeeds with the threat of eternal damnation, and requires us to follow 'God's will' while being kept ignorant of what that actually is. So we always have someone else to blame.

On the other hand, realists in the natural world would follow the inner urging of their soul, accepting full personal responsibility for the outcome. They would know their natural place in the order of things, and use inner senses to interact with other natural systems such as the weather, as do aboriginal peoples in the U.S., Australia and S. America. They would also commune with the spirits of animals and deceased ancestors.

These abilities are our birthright, stolen from us by subservience to our ancient Anunnaki overlords, and more recently to our memory of them. Preventing such contamination is the purpose of a policy of nonintervention in more primitive cultures (as in *Star Trek*'s Prime Directive) but because the Anunnaki created *Homo sapiens*, they probably believed it didn't apply to them. Anyway, they seem to have been arrogant enough not to care.

Do Intelligent Design and Interventionism have any credibility? Lots. On April 8, 2001, *The New York Times* ran an article about how ID is rapidly making inroads in states outside the Bible Belt, saying that its proponents claim: "The Designer may be much like the biblical God ... but we are open to other explanations, such as life being seeded by a meteorite, or possibly involving extraterrestrial intelligence." And *The New York Times* editorial of March 17, 2002 was headlined: "Darwinian Struggle in Ohio," and read: Adherents of Intelligent Design carefully shun any mention of God in their proposals. They simply argue that humans, animals and plants are far too diverse and complex to be explained by evolution and natural selection, so there must have been an intelligent designer behind it all. Whether that designer is God, an advanced civilization from another world, or some other creative force, is not specified."

However, the scientific community jump on proponents of Intelligent Design, claiming that it's simply Creationism in disguise. Creationism holds that God set the Universe running and left it alone to play out as it would. ID maintains that some agency (God, ET or whatever) has stepped in periodically to make 'adjustments' by means of genetic engineering. But opponents of ID claim that IDers are closet Christians who want a modified Creationism taught in schools. Meanwhile, a fourth option has emerged—Interventionism, which so far hasn't been the target of Evolutionists. This option looks firmly at the ET community as the agent of intervention in our genetic lineage. But none of this is new.

The notorious 1922 Scopes 'Monkey' Trial rocked the world when John Scopes, a Tennessee high school biology teacher, was found guilty of teaching the theory of evolution and fined $100. Eighty years later, the issue is still very much alive in 40 states across the country. For example, in Georgia, roughly half the students attending teacher training colleges believe in the creation account—that god created the earth 6,000 years ago. When these students graduate as teachers, they will be going into Georgia high schools, with some of them teaching science classes. If that's not a scary thought, I don't know what is.

In 2003, 2,000 parents in Cobb County, Georgia complained to the school board that a biology textbook stated that evolution is a fact. These believers that the Bible should be taken literally insisted a disclaimer be added that stated: "Evolution is a theory, not a fact, regarding the origin of living things. This material should be approached with an open mind, studied carefully, and considered critically."

In Atlanta, six parents objected to the disclaimer, and in 2005, a federal judge ruled the disclaimer should come out, saying, "It misleads students regarding the significance and value of evolution in the scientific community." That's quite a step forward for evolution, because 80 years earlier, teaching it had been a crime.

The southern states took a large leap backwards in March 2005, however. IMAX theaters in many cities in Georgia, Texas and the Carolinas withdrew a movie about underwater volcanoes because it contained a reference to human DNA and evolution, to which fundamentalists objected. So everyone else in those states is denied access to a thrilling movie because a few creationists are offended. Give me a break!

In Dover, Pennsylvania, on May 17, 2005, residents voted on candidates for the school board, and the town was strictly divided on only one issue—should the school curriculum teach Creationism alongside Evolution? The twist was that Creationists were calling their fundamental premise "Intelligent Design." So the Dover Area School Board told its schools to acknowledge ID, along with the other two explanations. Next, eight pairs of parents sued the school board in federal court, demanding that the ID statement be dropped. The board chose Prof. Michael Behe of Lehigh University as their figurehead. He testified that: "evolution cannot fully explain the complexities of life, suggesting the work of an intelligent force." Being Catholic, he added that he believed that force to be God.

"Not fair," shouted the Evolutionists. "That's just window-dressing for the biblical version." The problem, of course, is that whenever someone who believes in the God-myth talks about ID, they assume the designer is God, and not some other agency. Oh, well, at least we now have Interventionism.

The battle between the evolution and creation is mirrored across the population. A Gallup poll taken in November, 2004 showed that 35 percent of respondents believe the evidence proves evolution and 35 percent say it does not, with 30 percent saying they don't know. So here we are, 80 years after the Scopes Monkey trial and we're still floundering around over probably the most important foundation of our world view. The beauty of Intelligent Design is that it proves that Creationists and Evolutionists are both right … and both wrong.

Example: The Great Healthcare Conspiracy

The Anunnaki established a pattern in humanity of bowing down passively to whatever faction presents itself as authority. An excellent example of this today is the egregious seizing of control within the U.S. healthcare industry on the part of the Big Three—the AMA, the 'pharms' and their federal extension, the FDA.

The AMA was formed in 1847 as a trade union for doctors and initially had no more authority over medicine than the Teamsters do over the rules of the road, for example. In the early 1900s, J.D. Rockefeller controlled the oil industry and wanted to control the pharmaceutical industry, since most drugs back then were derived from oil. He shrewdly observed that whoever controlled the doctors controlled the pharms, and proposed to Congress that the AMA be the governing body over medical training. Thus Congress gave to the AMA the power to accredit medical schools and determine their curriculum. (This is akin to putting the Airline Pilots Association in charge of air traffic safety!)

Of course, the first casualties of the AMA's 'approved medical curriculum' were any disciplines that did not involve surgery or drugs, such as Homeopathy and Eastern approaches, despite 5,000 years of tradition. The AMA even went after chiropractors, but lost in the courts in 1987. Anyone practicing outside the AMA's narrow regime—of using drugs for 'symptom suppression' and surgery for symptom removal—by treating the whole human got to enjoy the inside of a jail cell.

In return for prescribing newer, more expensive drugs before they went 'generic,' the pharms paid kickbacks to doctors and lavish campaign contributions to politicians and senior FDA officials, plus golden parachute positions on their boards when the latter retired.

Why would the FDA want to suppress any alternative non-drug treatment that resolves medical problems in minutes rather than years? Because sick people are cash cows to the pharms, which want to keep you just well enough to afford their products but not so well that you don't need them. So-called 'alternative' healing triggers the body's natural immune system for full health, whereas drug therapies compromise the immune system by replacing it. (Rightfully, allopathic medicine should be labeled the 'alternative' to natural, or holistic, healing.)

Among the therapies banned by The Big Three are:

- *Oxygen therapy*, based on hydrogen peroxide (H_2O_2), water with an extra oxygen atom that when released in the body is bad news for any pathogens, which hate oxygen-rich environments. (You can use the standard drugstore 3% solution for topical use on cuts and as a mouthwash, but for internal consumption, use diluted food grade 35% solution.)
- *Ozone therapy*, where again the molecule breaks down to release an oxygen atom that will kill anything that doesn't belong in your body.
- *Bioelectric therapy*, including the famous Rife machine (see Chapter 8) for which Rife was horribly persecuted, plus Bob Beck's Multi-Wave Oscillator (that was so effective at curing 'everything,' it was singled out for 'special' attention), and blood electrification, which involves passing a low voltage current through the blood, where it kills every pathogen it finds, including the AIDS virus, with no side-effects.

- *Alkalizing the body* whereby pathogens and cancers, which need an acidic environment, quickly die out.
- *Diets* that provide nutrition to the body but the 'kiss of death' to pathogens. Can you imagine a doctor saying, "You've got cancer, so take ten grams of flax seed oil and a pint of cottage cheese a day and it will be gone in a month"? Don't hold your breath.

When a single cancer patient can pump $300,000 into the world of The Big Three, why on earth would they let you get away with spending a mere $600 on a box of electronics that would kill the cancer-causing bacterium in just half-an-hour? Sorry, it doesn't make sense, hence the rigid control on 'alternative' therapists, who, they claim, are just after a quick buck at your expense. As a healthcare consumer, however, you get to choose. So choose wisely.

The medical world talks about finding *the* cure for cancer, but what they really mean is a cure that can be *patented*, so that lots of money can be made. There are plenty of extremely effective natural cures on the planet; for example, ask anyone under medical care for cancer if they've heard about the following from a doctor:

- *Artemesinin*. Made from the twigs of the common wormwood tree, it has been used for millennia by the Chinese to cure malaria. However, cancer cells share something in common with malaria—both cells need huge amounts of iron to replicate, and artemesinin uses this weakness to destroy the cells. In clinical tests, it killed 25% of the cells in eight hours, and the rest within 16 hours. At only 20 cents a day, it's very inexpensive.

- *Graviola*, a native medicine from the very common *Annona muricata* tree, has been used for centuries to kill bacteria, viruses and parasites, reduce blood pressure, lower heart rate, relieve depression, stop spasms and convulsions, reduce fever, expel worms, and treat stress, depression and nervous system disorders. The biggie, though, is that it kills cancer cells dead in their tracks by attacking the enzyme processes that occur in cancer cell walls, with *absolutely no side-effects at all*. Normal cells are completely unaffected, so no hair loss, feeling weak, or other violent symptoms resulting from chemo or radiation. Since 1992, the big pharms have tried to find some way to patent this natural substance and have failed, so this pennies-a-day miracle cure has been quietly shelved. Pity, when it's 10,000 times stronger in killing colon cancer than commonly used chemo drugs, and also specializes in hunting down and destroying prostate, lung, breast and pancreatic cancers, while leaving healthy cells alone. Graviola is widely used worldwide, in fact, in every country except the U.S. Oh well …

- *Paw paw.* Another common tree delivers a substance that kills the chemo-resistant cancer cells that are responsible for cancer returning after treatment due to a few cells that escape and become multi-drug resistant. At $1 per day, it's a little more expensive, but highly effective.
- *Essiac tea.* This Native American blend of eight herbs cures just about everything, including arthritis and cancer, and is readily available.
- *Laetrile.* The FDA banned this controversial substance because it was too successful, and was making enormous inroads into the cancer treatment cash cow. A safe and effective form of vitamin B17, it is in wide use in Europe and elsewhere around the world.
- *Shark's cartilage.* Also banned by the FDA, this substance is widely used in Cuba and was the subject of a *60 Minutes* special, in which half of the confirmed cancer patients were still alive and healthy after three years. The National Institutes of Health didn't even bother watching the show.

Of course, there are some quacks out there but, according to an article in *The Journal of the AMA*, July 26, 2000, *doctors*, not disease, are responsible for over 250,000 deaths every year! This includes misdiagnosis, wrong medications, and OR mistakes, making doctors the third leading cause of death in the U.S. after heart disease and cancer. So, having conspired to limit society's healthcare options, they can't even deliver those few options.

To be fair, the March 2005 issue of the *New England Journal of Medicine* published a survey of 12,000 patients who had used alternative cancer treatments. The article reported that 3 percent saw total remission, 8 percent saw substantial shrinkage, and 34 percent saw some shrinkage or at least stabilization, with fewer side-effects than allopathic treatment. However, the test subjects were those who had been written off of as *incurable* by the cut-chemo-radiate brigade. The tests focused on just *one* alternative treatment, so if you combined all *six* of the above and also made diet changes that turned your system alkaline, you'd probably be in pretty good shape. (Don't ask doctors about whether cancer can exist in an alkaline environment. You're better off not knowing what they do and don't know.) Finally, if experiencing cancer is part of your soul's plan for this lifetime, you must also engage the medical profession in treating it because, in most states, treating cancer (yours or someone else's) without a medical license is a crime.

The multi-billion-dollar cancer industry is an excellent example of how the god-myth has tentacles into every aspect of our lives, only here the gods wear white coats. Until we can throw off the yoke of external authority to which we have become beholden, we stand little chance of understanding who we really are—emissaries from the heart of Creation, charged with learning all we can about that Creation.

Needless to say, Americans are by far the most medicated nation on the planet. Every year, 3.5 billion prescriptions are written for 130 million Americans, worth a total $250 billion. This averages out at $850 per person, or what we typically pay at the gas pump for a year. About one third of those prescriptions are for life-savers—keeping hearts going or blood sugar levels under control—but most are for keeping healthy people healthy, thanks to 'incentives' to doctors and high-pressure marketing.

Often drugs are prescribed for vague, poorly defined conditions such as 'depression,' which is really an illness of the psyche. This has resulted in an 11 percent growth per year in business for the pharms, but often the side-effects are worse than the symptom, such as suicidal tendencies. Today, people pop pills for conditions that just come with being human, so in a sense, people are dehumanizing themselves. And when a doctor says, "There's a new drug on the market," it's assumed that it's better, but that's often simply not true—it's just new . . . and more expensive.

On the downside, over 125,000 Americans die each year from drug reactions, making it the fourth leading cause of death, after heart disease, cancer and stroke. If that thought depresses you, there's something new to make you feel better—living with soul.

The Antacid Scam

When the patent on the old, reliable proton inhibitor antacid *Prilosec* expired, maker AstraZeneca stood to lose billions, because suddenly anyone could market a generic knockoff. So what did they do? Change a couple of molecules, patent the new product as *Nexium*, and mount the largest TV ad campaign ever, costing $2.2 million annually. It worked! Doctors now write 25 million prescriptions a year for *Nexium* for an average of $120 each, totaling $3 billion. Now them's good odds! Why take an over-the-counter *Prilosec* costing 90¢ when your insurance company will pay for a $4 *Nexium*, even though they are chemically identical? Because the fancy TV ads talk about 'better,' and insurance doesn't pay for

OTC drugs. Just don't be surprised when your employer stops paying for health-care insurance. Buy AstraZeneca stock instead.

The Great Flu Myth

For another example of how authority is used against us, let's look briefly at flu deaths as an exercise in fear. Every year, the CDC trots out the same old tired press release: "Flu kills 36,000 people a year, so get your flu shot," even though it's totally ineffective, as was the case in the 2004/5 season.

But is that 36,000 number true? No, according to a report by the National Center for Health Statistics in the *Report of Final Mortality Statistics, 1979-2001*, published by the American Lung Association. Over that 12-year period, the average was actually 1,312 deaths annually, ranging from 3,000 in a bad year to 250 in a good year. So,

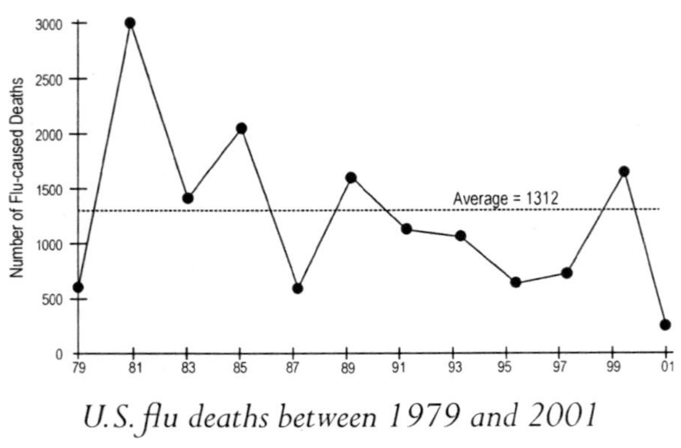

U.S. flu deaths between 1979 and 2001

what's going on here? Why is the CDC instilling fear in the population?

The Highlights page on the CDC website shows that influenza *and pneumonia* killed 62,034 people in 2002, and they simply halved that to come up with 36,000. But if you dig more deeply, you find that total flu deaths for 2002 were actually only 753, with 65,231 deaths due to pneumonia. In 2001, total flu deaths were a mere 257. Lumping these two causes of death together and then attributing half to each cause is simply irresponsible ... unless there's a hidden agenda.

To bolster its case, the CDC site informs us that the Hong Kong Flu pandemic of 1968-69 killed 34,000, which is close to what the CDC now calls 'average.' What's going on? Every year, a joint CDC-AMA National Influenza Vaccination conference is held, attended by the major pharmaceutical companies and state and local health departments. The main topic involves streamlining the manufacture and distribution of flu vaccine, which is a cash cow of close on a billion dollars a year.

For the 2004/2005 season, a British manufacturer had to dump 40 million tainted doses, creating panic in the streets of the U.S. But before the shortage was apparent, in preparation for the 2004 season, the CDC addressed the conference about how to present the flu season to the public in ways to best motivate vaccination numbers, namely how to use fear to sell the cure.

When the CDC gets together with the major flu vaccine manufacturers to figure out how to scare us into being injected with something that's as low as 16% effective, when an average of only 1,300 people a year die, that sounds like conspiracy to defraud. (To put that in perspective, according to the U.S. DOT, between 40,000 and 50,000 Americans die each year in vehicle accidents.) And using fear to sell vaccines is also misusing the authority of the CDC.

Far worse is the effect it has on us, the public. We are being told that the world is a dangerous place, which we should fear, and are encouraged to discount the most powerful aspect of our immune system—a healthy dose of self-love. Sadly, in 2004, tens of thousands of people lined up all day for a week, hoping to receive one of the few hundred or so vaccine doses available, and panicked when the clinics ran out. That fear will kill far more people than the flu virus. A crime wave also sprang up as clinics were broken into and their vaccine supply stolen. And tragically, one elderly lady in line fainted in the heat and cracked her head open on the sidewalk—the first fatality of the season.

If ordinary flu isn't bad enough, in 2004, the World Health Organization publicized its fears of a global mega-pandemic of a strain of avian flu to which humanity has no immunity, such as mutated avian flu (*aka* Hong Kong bird flu). WHO researchers forecast up to 30 percent mortality worldwide, or around 2 billion people. Before you go into fear, later in this book, you will learn that your soul wrote the time and means of your return to the soul plane into your flight plan, so it is already cast in concrete. If the means is flu-related, there is nothing you at the personality level can do about it despite a thousand vaccinations; if it's not flu-related, don't worry.

Following the Hurricane Katrina debacle, the Harriet Miers fiasco and the 'Scooter' Libby indictment, Bubba Bush jumped on the avian flu bandwagon in November, 2005. In a transparent attempt at image recovery, he announced a $7.1 billion package, of which he assigned $2 billion to Swiss giant Roche for 20 million doses of Tamiflu. That's a whopping $100 a shot (you can buy it on the Internet for $40), and there is no evidence it's remotely effective against the N5N1 virus. And even if it were, the virus would need to mutate to be contagious among humans, rendering Tamiflu ineffective. Interestingly, Roche manufactures the drug under license from California-based Gilread, in which Donald Rumsfeld reportedly has a large stake. Ah, it's a small world.

A study by the National Institutes of Health published in February 2005 reported that over the last 30 years, there has been *no correlation whatsoever* between whether seniors had a flu vaccine and mortality rates from flu. In each year of the study, between 20 and 65 percent of seniors had the shot, but that number had absolutely no impact on the number of deaths. The study leader said no matter which way she ran the numbers, the outcome was the same, but that having the vaccine may reduce the severity of symptoms. Predictably the white coats at the CDC dismissed the study as insufficient to cause a review of their policy of vaccinating all seniors.

Another victory for We the People came in late 2004 with the publication of an article in the *American Journal of Clinical Nutrition*, which revealed that the body's way of excreting heavy metal toxins such as mercury and lead depends on the peptide glutathione. Without this substance, the body simply accumulates heavy metals, from the womb forwards. By the time the child is four years old, it may have had up to 50 vaccinations, each one potentially containing the mercury-based preservative and known neurotoxin thimerosal. Experts at the CDC claim the 25 parts per million of mercury in vaccines is not in itself harmful, but if the body cannot excrete mercury, it accumulates and impairs brain development, resulting in autism. Researchers find a genetic vulnerability to autism that in some children renders the body unable to excrete mercury, made worse by the mercury ingested by the pregnant mother in fish, dental fillings and contaminated water. Autism causes enormous financial and emotional strain on parents, and up to 80 percent of marriages fail (compared with the average of 50 percent). Parents' worlds are turned upside down because the disabled child becomes the focal point of their lives, and parents grieve for the loss of 'normal.'

By claiming that these levels of mercury are safe, the CDC has dug itself into a big hole from which it cannot escape because, if the truth were told, millions of parents would bring class action lawsuits for medical and other expenses plus pain-and-suffering that would bankrupt the pharms. Of course, the CDC is a branch of government and cannot be sued. Fortunately, once autism is diagnosed, it can be treated to some extent with folic acid and vitamin B-12.[11]

A secret meeting in 2000 of the CDC, FDA and pharms discussed the clear correlation between autism and thimerosal and the enormity of the liability issue. There were 520,000 autism cases, and 40,000 new cases were being added

---

11 In a stunning revelation, the Environmental Protection Agency (EPA) admitted 'cooking the books' in a March 2005 report. The report quoted the cost to industry of lowering mercury emissions would be $750 million a year, whereas the savings in health care costs would be only $50 million, and concluded that reducing emissions was not economically feasible. However, that report was a rewrite of one that used to include the results of a Harvard University study paid for by the EPA which revealed the annual health care costs of mercury poisoning to be $5 billion. Money is thus being siphoned out of taxpayers' pockets and into the pockets of power company shareholders. And this doesn't even begin to look at the human costs of shattered dreams that parents have over their autistic children's futures.

each year. The cost of special care for each victim is about $50,000 a year, and over 4,000 claims for damages had been filed with the special federal "Vaccine Court." If found liable, damages could run at a staggering $30 trillion a year! To bail out the pharms, Senate Majority Leader Bill Frist embedded legislation deep in the Patriot Bill to hold the pharms harmless from lawsuits by imposing impossible burdens of proof on plaintiffs. In thanks, the pharms contributed millions to Frist's 2002 campaign. Ah, the power of the dollar.

Thimerosal (mercury acetate) in vaccines has two purposes. First, it's a preservative, and second, it's an *adjuvant*, i.e., it irritates the immune system to catalyze it into creating 'search-and-destroy' antibodies to attack the injected dead or inactive viruses or bacteria in the vaccine. Due to its bad press, however, it's being phased out in favor of a new adjuvant that's *much* worse—squalene, derived from shark liver oil. Taken *orally*, it offers many potential health benefits, ranging from skin health, an antioxidant that protects against radiation, pesticides, and toxins, and enhancing oxygen transport. However, if *injected*, it's a biological disaster. Yes, it catalyzes the immune system into attacking squalene's components, but one of those components is so close in nature to the protective myelin sheath around human nerves, the immune system goes after that, too. So your immune system attacks your nervous system! As fast as the body can make more myelin sheath, the immune system makes more antibodies to destroy it, and a huge war begins that can never be stopped, because both processes are simply the body doing what's it's designed to do. The outcome depends on many things, such as an individual's toxin levels, diet, and general health, but the end result is a system-wide syndrome of nonspecific illnesses, leading inevitably to death.

The FDA acknowledges that squalene was used in the anthrax vaccines given to Gulf War troops and that veterans' bodies contain anti-squalene antibodies, even though it was not licensed for adjuvant use in 1991. Off the record, many doctors believe it's the real cause of Gulf War Syndrome, whose symptoms include MS, lupus, fatigue, headaches, depression, insomnia, and memory loss—all nervous system conditions. And experts do not know why ALS, or Lou Gehrig's disease, a rare, incurable disorder of the nervous system, is more common in Gulf War veterans than the rest of us. In fact, squalene programmed their immune systems to destroy the myelin sheath that protects that nervous system. (Of course, don't forget the megatons of depleted uranium[12] (DU) dust and blown-up Iraqi

---

12 According to an Associated Press story run in October 2005, a group of children in Baghdad was found
    playing in a burned-out Iraqi tank, destroyed by a DU shell. The level of radioactivity in the tank was a
    staggering *1,000 times* the acceptable background level. That's quite a legacy we're leaving them.

chemicals that everyone also breathed in.) The Pentagon cannot admit that it used untested vaccine on its troops, hence the cover-up, secrecy and foot-dragging. Small comfort to the 20,000 already dead veterans, and the 45,000 just barely alive, along with their wives, children, and even family pets. And spouses of veterans are routinely told to avoid getting pregnant because of almost certain birth defects. But that's okay because most couples can't even have sex anymore; semen causes blisters on contact with skin and intense genital burning in both partners. So far, it's only affecting the military, but the National Institutes of Health is looking into squalene as the standard vaccine adjuvant, so before you get another shot, ask your doctor if it contains this slow-death time-bomb.

Mandatory Mental Profiling for Children

Another very nasty example of Big Brother surfaced in 2002, courtesy of an Executive Order (which bypasses the U.S. Congress and all that inconvenient public debate) by which President Bush launched the New Freedom (ha!) Commission on Mental Health, which calls for regular, mandatory 'routine and comprehensive' mental health screening of every schoolchild in the U.S., including preschoolers. The resulting mental health profile will become part of the child's official record, along with immunization records, and will follow the child for life. Any child not meeting the highly subjective 'normal' profile will be forced into a regime of psychological counseling and drug therapy.

A pilot study by Columbia University revealed that roughly one-third of American children will test outside of 'normal.' So, given a population of 52 million children aged 0 – 18, 17 million will be labeled 'mentally abnormal,' and placed on highly controversial, expensive and largely ineffective medications, or risk not being allowed to attend school. Dissenting parents could be charged with child endangerment and have their children taken away and put into the state foster care system.

One barrier to blanketing school populations is financial, for many children are not covered by insurance. Simple. Medicaid is being extended to cover them, thus siphoning off billions from taxpayers into the big pharm coffers. For example, in 2002, anti-psychotic drugs were already a $6 billion-a-year business, with over 7 million prescriptions written for Zyprexa alone—that's $2.7 billion, and the NFC program hadn't even started!

So one of the administration's goals of this initiative is clear. The Pennsylvania Inspector-General's office reported that their state's medical leaders responsible for the plan received kickbacks from the drug companies to ensure that their products were on the list of drugs to be prescribed. In Texas, this list includes the following (with monthly prices and side-effects):

Paxil ($74) —suicidal tendencies

Zyprexa ($387) — pancreatitis, diabetes

Adderall ($85) — dizziness, blurred vision, habit-forming

Zoloft ($75) — agitation, insomnia

Seroquel ($104) — spasms, sweating, fever, death

Prozac ($121) — eating disorders, obsessions, depression.

Obviously, these medications turn the child's body into a toxic waste site, but worse, they are largely ineffective. There is no data available about the long term side-effects of children taking psychiatric drugs, but already horror stories abound regarding suicide, violence and psychosis among teens taking them. For example, Eric Harris (one of the Columbine shooters) was on such a drug at the time of his crime and seemed dissociated from what he was doing.

The only clear winners here are the pharms, who stand to make untold billions by providing the mind-numbing drugs to the system. The losers are the insurance companies, which will have to cover the cost, and taxpayers, who will pay for the drugs for non-insured families. But the REAL losers are the children, who will never know who they really are, having been doped up all their lives.

The next piece of the agenda is that mental health screening will also cover the 0 – 5 age group. Imagine what such babes will reveal about their family life: "Do your parents use bad words? How much do they drink? Do they criticize the government? Is there a gun in the house? Do they raise their voices?" (This is reminiscent of the Nazi Youth movement members being told to report their parents to the Gestapo for listening to Radio London during WWII.)

The New Freedom Commission may also be Big Brother's way of ensuring that the New Children grow up drugged out of their minds, so never get to develop and explore their full potential. It may work initially, but eventually their voices will be heard.

The Coming Medicare Crisis

On July 1, 2004, over 36 million Americans were 65 and over, which accounted for 12 percent of the total U.S. population. By the year 2050, this number is projected as 87 million, or 21 percent of the expected population. Baby boomers (those born between 1946 – 1960) will have an unprecedented impact on services in America, no more so than in healthcare. People worry about Social Security and its $3 trillion shortfall, but this is tiny compared with Medicare's expected $75 trillion shortfall. The only way boomers will be able to take care of themselves is by becoming experts in alternative healthcare, such as herbs and supplements.

For an example of this, half of all Americans will develop cataracts in their eyes around age 60. These are deposits of protein in the cornea that turn it cloudy and add ghost shadows around objects, especially at night. Initially these effects can be countered with prescription lenses, but eventually they cannot. Standard practice is then to replace the cornea with an artificial one, at the cost of around $3,000 per eye, along with discomfort and risk of infection, even blindness. In fact, this is the most common operation that Medicare pays for, with 1.5 million operations a year, costing $3.5 billion annually. (In England, under the National Health Service, the wait is so long, most people are blind by the time their name reaches the top of the list.)

An alternative to surgery is to dissolve the protein deposit. For example, the herb Eyebright has been in use for over 3,000 years, and was used by John R. Christopher, the famous naturopath (see www.drchristophers.com), in his eye drops. Cost is about $10 per month. Users report that dissolving the cataract takes about three months, but they notice a difference even after one day.

Another cataract agent is Nu-Eyes, eye drops that contain L-carnosine, a potent anti-oxidant that scours tissues, scavenging for the free radicals that oxidize the protein in the cornea, turning it cloudy. Cost is about $30 month, and most users report that clearing up their cataracts takes 4 – 6 months, depending on how progressed they were.

Not only do these products dissolve cataracts, they also work to reverse glaucoma and macular degeneration, both devastating eye conditions if not treated.

If you are a baby boomer with health insurance, the cost of premiums will soon be crippling, especially when you retire, and if you have no insurance, you're on your own. Either way, your survival may depend on alternative healthcare, but even that is under attack. Americans spend $35 billion a year on prescription drugs and $12 billion on alternatives, and the big pharms want to muscle in on that market, or get it regulated out of existence. Hopefully they will not succeed.

On the bright side, this planet is home to 380,000 species of herbs and plants, and although herbalists know what many of them do, few know how they do it—Nature keeps her secrets well hidden. The herb Echinacea, for example, (used to boost the immune system) contains thousands of compounds, but no one has identified all of them. For this reason, Dr. Christopher[12] insisted on using the *whole*

12   Although he never received a medical qualification, his patients called him Dr. Christopher, which the medical profession hated. As a result, he spent many days in jail on trumped up charges of 'practicing medicine without a license,' when really he was just offering someone a cup of herbal tea.

herb in his products—flowers, leaves, stems and roots—and was able to help thousands whom allopathic medicine had given up on.

Christopher developed 66 blends, combing 120 herbs for everything from acne to weight loss. So why spend over $100 a month on Prozac, when $10 a month spent on Valerian root will do the same thing but without the side-effect of wanting to grab an Uzi and shoot up a MacDonald's?

A Perspective

What would things look like today if the human history presented in this chapter had never happened? We would be living according to our own spiritual nature, forging ever-stronger links between our ego-personality and higher selves. We would be living along the lines of Taoism, where we accept that All That Is—all aspects of all dimensions, including our body, mind and spirit—flow from a common Source. As part of All That Is, we would commune with any other part and, in doing so, the whole learns more about itself. This is the theme of the rest of this book, as we strive to learn more about soul.

Today, we have many ET species telling us that humanity must collectively take responsibility for our spiritual and planetary hygiene, and that they are not here 'to save us.' It's time to purge ourselves of our belief in a Santa Claus-like entity who will absolve us of individual and collective responsibility. This means transcending lines drawn on the ground and then going to war with those on the other side. And we certainly must not war with our neighbor because 'God tells us to.'

The previous section may seem out of place in a book on strengthening your bond with soul, but you also came to this planet with a mission, which probably involves spreading the Light in some way. Therefore, it is vital that you know where the pockets of dark are. As long as we live in a dualistic world, we must acknowledge the dark as well as the Light. Pretending that Lightworkers are not matched by Darkworkers is folly, because what you don't know can harm you. If you blindly trust politicians to conduct fair and equitable elections, and govern you without self-interest, you could be in danger.

Don't expect the media to help out, either. Disney owns the ABC network, and military supply giant General Electric owns NBC, and both parent companies take orders directly from the White House and the Pentagon, which in turn take their orders from shadowy organizations such as the Bilderberg Group and the Council for Foreign Relations. Your best bet for independent news is the Internet, but be careful because that, too, is prowled by wolves masquerading as sheep. For example, a good half of what you read about UFOs and ETs is disinformation placed there by Cabal agents.

Television, incidentally, is the ideal brainwashing tool. The medium causes right-brain activity to swamp left-brain activity, which releases endorphins, the body's opium, and makes you feel good. The subliminal flickering puts you into an Alpha state (much more on this in Volume Two, Chapter 15), which makes you highly suggestive, so you are highly suggestive to the messages of commercials. And it's all perfectly legal. An East Coast department store put TV monitors around the store and peppered 'innocent' commercials with subliminal 'Do not steal' messages. Shoplifting losses dropped 37 percent in the first nine months of operation, more than paying for installation.

Children are especially vulnerable; over 90 percent of them are in Alpha within 30 seconds of starting to watch TV, and they have no 'censor' to question whatever suggestions are beamed at them. By age 16, children have been exposed to between 10,000 and 15,000 hours of Alpha-inducing programming—three times the rate in the 1970s—turning Americans into a nation of zombies. Are we headed for the Orwellian future of 1984, with glassy-eyed robots meekly responding to instructions given via the TV?

Could It Happen Again?

Is it possible that scientists today could replicate the Anunnaki genetic engineering feat? Until 1998, the answer was no, but in that year, everything changed. That's when the role played by human stem cells was discovered. Stem cells are present in the human embryo, and are unique in that they can be programmed to grow into *any* type of cell in the body. If human stem cells are placed into an animal fetus, the result will be a human/animal hybrid whose actual characteristics will depend on timing and quantity of cells. Such a hybrid is called a *chimera* (pronounced ki-MER-ah). For example:

- In California, mice have been born with human brain tissue
- In Nevada, sheep have been born with largely human livers and hearts
- In Minnesota, pigs have been born with human blood.

No one would grant human status to farm animals, but already chimps exist with higher brain functions such as speech and self-awareness, so at some point, we will need to face the ethical question of, "How much human is enough to be treated as human?" This is a key debate, because animals can legally be kept in cages and experimented upon, whereas humans cannot. And at the rate the scientists are moving, that debate will need to happen within a decade.

Rather than impose a knee-jerk ban on chimeras, we need to take a deeper look. Stem cells allow us to grow human organs in compatible animals such as pigs, which have organs with identical genetics to humans. A genetic pig farm could be a plentiful supply of replacement hearts, livers, kidneys, etc., that could be transplanted in humans with no risk of rejection.

Extrapolate to 100 years from now, to when we have mastered interstellar flight. You are the leader of the expedition, and find, orbiting a nearby star, a garden planet that has rich veins of precious metals that are vital to Earth's survival. You colonize the planet, but rather than toil in deep, hot mines, you ask your Chief Medical Officer to inject human stem cells into the fetus of a primate indigenous to that planet. Human DNA happens to be compatible, and the resulting human/primate hybrid is ideal for working in the mines, so you make thousands of them. Although they are smart and can speak, they have no clue about the technology responsible for their creation, so how would they regard you, with all your technology and the ability to fly? Would they form a religion around you? And when your expedition returns to Earth, would they worship your memory as a departed god?

So, to silence those who dismiss the genetic engineering of the Anunnaki as impossible, we *can* duplicate their feat today. And who's to say, maybe in some top-secret lab somewhere, it has already *been* done.

Interesting.

We end this chapter with this. In reference to the S.E. Asia tsunami of December 26, 2004 that killed over 150,000, Rev. Greg Boyd of St. Paul, Minn., author of *Is God to Blame?* was asked why God allowed this natural disaster. His response was, "Because the first humans sinned, the laws of nature have been corrupted and don't all operate now the way God originally intended. That doesn't mean there's a demon behind every tsunami or hurricane, but it means that if it wasn't for the angelic and human rebellion, we wouldn't have tsunamis or hurricanes or AIDS or anything of the sort." So this guy wants us to believe the tsunami was God's way of punishing the people of Sri Lanka and Indonesia because Adam and Eve ate from the Tree of Knowledge. Puh-lease. When will the madness end? That quote jams together a 'slave revolt' on the part of early *Homo sapiens sapiens* against their Anunnaki overlords and a covenant between the Israelites and an ET called *YHVH* who lived on Mt. Sinai and left Earth about 1000 BCE. Nice work, Rev. Tell *that* to the folks with HIV because they received an infected blood transfusion. And while you're at it, pass the Kool-Aid again.

If we moved from religiosity to spirituality, we would seek ways to serve humanity instead of looking for ways to exploit it. We would open to the magnificence of our true nature, and explore the full potential of what that is. Chapter 5 onwards is all about that. However, 2,000 years ago in the Middle East, things were about to get worse. Much worse. On top of the Great *YHVH* Deception, a huge spin-off of the God industry occurred—the Great Jesus Conspiracy—and it was a public relations masterpiece that still has millions enthralled. Let's take a look in the next chapter.

CHAPTER 4

THE GREAT JESUS CONSPIRACY

ROOTED in a real-world covenant whereby the ET *YHVH* traded the Promised Land for Jewish obedience, Judaism began as a 'here-and-now' religion, paying scant regard to the after-life. When *YHVH* left Earth, thus breaking the covenant, the priests had to invent some kind of future resurrection, in which *YHVH* would return to recreate people's bodies from a single bone fragment. (This explains Jewish disdain for cremation and burial at sea.) This promise of messianic return allowed Jews to tolerate inequities in this life, such as Roman occupation, with rewards to be dispensed in the reconstructed second physical plane life. Early Judaism had no concept of an 'after-life,' at least until conquered by the Greeks in 167 BCE. (Of course, the designations BCE and CE were still far in the future. The world ran on Roman time back then.)

Under Roman rule from 40 BCE, the Promised Land became a province of the Roman Empire. Anger grew against increased Roman suppression of Jewish life, resulting in sporadic violence that escalated into a full-scale revolt in 66 CE. Superior Roman forces led by Titus were finally victorious, razing all evidence of Jerusalem and renaming Judea as Palestine.

Around Jewish year 3860 and Roman year 820 (the Julian calendar was still centuries away, but this would turn out to be around 100 CE), amidst the Jewish uproar against occupation, they longed for the return of *YHVH* to lead them to freedom from oppression. Several underground messianic sects formed, each with its own rumors of *YHVH*'s Second Coming. One such sect came up with the brilliant idea that the messiah had already returned, lived and died … only a century earlier. However, they wove together their tale with such compelling detail that people began to believe them. This fledgling Jewish cult attracted followers who saw a glimmer of hope amidst the harsh reality of Roman rule. Over the centuries, the stories would be embellished with elements from various Pagan myths, such as virgin birth, deification, and ritual death—a veritable soap opera of the day. Under Roman direction, the promises of a better life after death were emphasized, so that followers would better put up with occupation. This would create a schism between the new cult and its Judaic roots, leading to the big question of whether or not to admit Gentiles.

The cult's central messiah figure would be based on an Essene teacher whose life would form the basis for a story that would, due to a series of unlikely events, be written and rewritten over several centuries, and form the basis for a new world religion—the Jesus Conspiracy. (The Essenes, following the Greek lines of Gnosticism, believed we are eternal souls taking a series of earthly lives on our way to perfection. This put them way outside, and in conflict with, mainstream Jewish orthodoxy.)

Initially Rome would ignore the cult, then persecute it, and finally embrace it, thus unleashing the cult's improbable work of fiction upon the world as a statement of historical fact. A church would grow up to spread the story, and would also grow into the planet's biggest business and landowner. Strange how things turn out. And so, on with the Greatest Story Ever Sold, still believed 2,000 years later by billions of people hoping for a better deal in the next life, sitting on the right hand of God, to make this life more tolerable.

A Myth Is Born

About 2,000 years ago, Judah and Galilee were home to many competing Hebrew factions such as the Essenes, Saducees, Pharisees and Samaritans, all practicing their own brand of Judaism. Every sect of the day knew they were in transit from the war-torn Age of Aries and brutal Roman Conquest to a hopefully more peaceful Age of Pisces. They also knew that a 400-year-old prophecy foretold that a messiah would be born who would lead the Hebrews out of oppression. Of course, each sect hoped the messiah would be one of their members, because all members of the sect would then benefit from the kudos.

As part of their bid for spiritual leadership, the members of one sect took matters into their own hands and decided to come up with their own messiah story. And they set it 100 years in the past so that no one was alive to contradict it. (Many modern writers raise doubts about the NT Jesus story; I recommend Acharya's *The Christ Conspiracy* and www.truthbeknown.com for further reading. The following weaves together some of her ideas along with my own.)

The Library of Alexandria gave the sect's scholars access to every ancient spiritual manuscript in existence that documented the great mythological characters in human history, plus contemporary thinking. Many of these earlier myths had almost identical elements—virgin birth, precocious boyhood, conflict with elders, beginning a ministry about age 30, martyrdom for the sake of followers, and resurrection after three days. In an intellectual feeding frenzy in the library, the scholars wove together their own story from bits and pieces of all the others. They were determined that *their* messiah cult would push all others aside by having their account accepted as *historical fact*, whereas the source legends admitted to being only mythological.

They loosely based their messiah character on the life of a real Gnostic[1] teacher named Jeshua ben Joseph, who had lived about 100 years earlier and, according to some sources, had evaded persecution by the Sanhedrin (the Hebraic governing body that Rome expected to keep the Jews in order) by fleeing to Gaul (now France) with his wife, Mary Magdalene, and their daughter. However, we will never know because all the evidence is 2,000 years old.

They also credited their fictional messiah with the teachings of Apollonius of Tyana,[2] a well-traveled and knowledgeable scholar and contemporary of Jeshua. To give their messiah supernatural powers, they plagiarized the Persian sun cult of Mithra and the ancient legends of Horus and Osiris, myths that were already centuries or millennia older and based on the characters of the Anunnaki royal family. So, long after the deaths of Jeshua and Apollonius, a great legend emerged telling a remarkable story of miracles, wise teachings and martyrdom.[3] And because their story was set almost a century earlier, it could not be contested by eye witnesses.

---

[1]   Rather than seek to know God externally, Gnostics (from the Greek *gnosis*, meaning 'knowledge') seek to know self, leading to direct knowing of the Source-spark within. Thus one does not need a priest class to act as intermediary, which explains why Jeshua was so hostile towards them.

[2]   Son of a wealthy family, brilliant and exceptionally handsome, this charismatic teacher and miracle worker lived in the first century BCE. Born in Tyana, in the south of modern Turkey, he traveled widely, discussing philosophy with other brilliant minds of the day. Apollonius was a *visionary*, knowing more than ordinary people, a *healer* to whom sick people traveled, and by all accounts, a *magician* and *alchemist*, although any magical talents probably stemmed simply from his arcane knowledge. His prolific writings were housed in the Library of Alexandria and available to the scribes.

[3]   It is unlikely that the real Jeshua, being of the lineage of the revered King David, would have received a common criminal's death such as crucifixion. Exile to a distant country is far more likely.

The messiah story slowly caught on but caused a tremendous ruckus among the Jews in Judea. The common people wanted to believe that a messiah would free them from Roman occupation but the Sanhedrin was unwilling to displease Rome by embracing the new cult.

Mary Magdalene had been pregnant with their daughter Sarah at the time of the supposed Crucifixion, and fled to Alexandria. When Sarah was 12, they went to Gaul (now France), and many say that Jeshua went with them. By the time Christianity started up, of course, they had long since died in Gaul but not before siring a new royal blood line in Europe that, allegedly, would eventually produce King Arthur of England and the legend of the Holy Grail. Old French for 'royal blood' was *Sang Real*, which became corrupted to *San Grail* in Old English, later translated into Middle English as Holy Grail, and woven into the Arthurian legends.

Over the next 50 years, the scribes wrote down the oral stories and wove countless accounts, or 'gospels,' about the life of their messiah. We don't know when the canonical gospels of Matthew, Mark, Luke and John were written (some sources claim between 170 – 180 CE) but none of them were eye-witness accounts and some experts believe the names of the apostles were used just for legitimacy. So anonymous authors penned the gospels to document the life of Jeshua over a century after the alleged facts occurred. The stories were then edited over the next two centuries before being stabilized as what we know today. Based on commonality of content, scholars believe the Gospel According to Mark was the first to be written, probably by 100 CE, which was then copied under the names Matthew and Luke. The writers took the same material in the same sequence but Matthew groups Jeshua's words into lengthy discourses while Luke scatters them about. John, however, seems to have used a different later source that is still unknown.

Again, borrowing from countless ancient salvation cults, the messiah story included the notion that their savior had *already* been crucified to erase mankind's sins. (Note that, wisely, they did not predict a future coming because that would have ticked off the Romans, so they claimed he had already come and gone. Oddly, no accounts of the central character appear in Roman records even though they were meticulous record-keepers.)

Most of the uneducated people of Judea could not fathom the more esoteric teachings attributed to Jeshua, so the proponents of the messiah cult simplified the issue by telling them, "Jeshua died so your sins would be forgiven. All you need to do is accept him as the messiah and *YHVH* will reward you by taking you into heaven." This lack of the need to make personal sacrifices made *their* cult more palatable than all the other competing cults, but a few zealous preachers, desperate for numbers, crossed the line and promised: 'The Wrath of *YHVH* will befall those who do not accept this messiah'—a fire-and-brimstone mentality that is still seen today.

As a marketing ploy, this worked and cult membership grew steadily between 200 – 300 CE. However, they were persecuted by all the Pagan (polytheistic) cults because Christians didn't worship the traditional gods. The many unanswered questions resulted in dozens, if not hundreds, of splinter groups, although an orthodox mainstream Christianity appeared around 300:

- Was the God Jeshua spoke of the same as the God of the Hebrews? Some radical sects claimed there were, in fact, several Gods.
- Should the cult be open to non-Jews? If so, would the Sanhedrin allow into the temples gentiles who were not circumcised or who ate unapproved foods?

The governing body firmly opposed the cult going outside Judaism and admitting gentiles, but when citizens of Rome joined the cult, the rabbis were powerless to prevent them. So it happened anyway, and the many competing Christian cults split off from Judaism.

The savior angle of the conspiracy grew during the next four or five generations over the next 100 years, and turned out to be a master stroke because the then Roman emperor, Constantine, had littered his road to power with the corpses of his murdered wife, son and nephew, and none of the other cults wanted anything to do with him. But here was a cult that would forgive him his sins with one quick-and-easy (but not cheap) absolution if he simply accepted Jeshua as the savior who had died to expunge man's sin. So, following a vision in 312 CE[4], he converted (but still worshipped the old Pagan gods) and promptly placed the Roman Empire behind the cult. The timing was perfect because, after 700 years, the Roman Empire was rotting from within and coming under intense pressure from warlike tribes from northern Europe. Also, Romans worshipped the memories of the ancient Anunnaki overlords, even though Rome had come to prominence after the ETs' power had waned and was never culturally influenced. Constantine hoped that a new faith-based religion anchored on one supernatural god would strengthen the crumbling Republic.

---

[4]   Legend has it that before the battle of Milvian Bridge in 312, Constantine had a vision of the words *in hoc signo vinces*, or 'in this sign, victory' on a Christian cross. He pledged to convert if he won the battle. He did win and did convert, but only many years later on his deathbed.

Under the patronage of Rome, the rash of the new Jesus cult immediately put many of the others out of business as it grew from cult to religion and wrested control from the Sanhedrin. So, due to another fluke of history (Constantine's guilt trip), one messiah cult was instantly elevated above all others, and took off like wildfire. However, Roman patronage meant this exclusively Judaic cult became wide open to all gentiles, so one no longer had to become a Jew in order to convert to Christianity. (Judaism, of course, still awaits its messiah.)

Once Constantine legitimized Christianity, persecution by Pagans ceased, but there were hundreds of radical, little splinter groups. So early Christianity did not come neatly gift-wrapped, and the relationship between Jesus and *YHVH* was bitterly debated. Different splinter groups placed the Jeshua character somewhere on the scale between being 100 percent human on a *mission* from YHVH, and 100 percent divine and, as *YHVH*, therefore able to *manifest* into any shape imaginable, including human. Bitter wrangling among the 150 or so Christian splinter cults threatened to destroy the very movement Constantine was relying on to unite his Empire, and he realized that consensus was essential, so in 325 CE, he convened the Council of Nicea, a group of leaders of the principal Christian cults of the day. Unfortunately, these were not great thinkers like the Greek philosophers, but rabid desert preachers and rabble-rousers, whose twisted reasoning still haunts us today because Constantine ordered this mob to unify the Jeshua stories into one composite teaching. In those days, they already accepted that Jesus (as they started calling him) was a messiah sent by *YHVH*, but they confirmed Jeshua's status by declaring him the Son of *YHVH* and with the same 'divine' nature, which guaranteed the cult's power. They also hijacked the idea of life force energy, called it 'Holy Ghost,' and made up the Holy Trinity.

In *The Curse of Ignorance*, Arthur Findlay writes, "The decision reached at the Council of Nicea, which raised the Christian Church to the position of State Church of the Roman Empire was the greatest and most tragic event in history. Instead of the world being guided by the thoughts of the great philosophers, it fell under the domination of the hierarchy of ignorant priests. Greek and Roman educational systems were replaced by theology, and ignorance displaced the pursuit of knowledge." It's true; if we hadn't spent 1,600 years believing the world was flat, we might be exploring nearby star systems.

Deification of Jesus also strengthened belief in *YHVH*, in whom many were beginning to have doubts. The priests could now claim that *YHVH* had sent Jesus rather than show up himself, which was good for their cult, as the absent ET overlord on whom the myth of *YHVH* was based had long since left the planet, leaving the Hebrews to fend for themselves.

The bishops also declared that upon death, one could *only* join *YHVH* in heaven by having accepted Jesus as one's personal savior, who would wash away the original sin of being the result of one's parents having had sex. However, this gave the bishops a problem. Even though Jesus was the son of God, he still was a mortal man, also subject to original sin. To exempt Jesus from this, the bishops decided to reclassify his mother from *alma* (meaning pure woman) to literal virgin, leaving open the question of who Jesus' father was. (This would be resolved in 431.)

The council was also told to ignore any views that conflicted with the political agenda of Constantine or the new Roman Church. This left out many fine manuscripts, some of which today make up the Apocrypha. Other writings not selected, such as the Gospel of Enoch, were sealed away in the Vatican so people would not know of any information that contradicted the stories that would one day be called *The Bible*, although that would not be finalized until 376 by the Bishop of Alexandria.

Constantine was happy with the way the Council assembled an 'all in one' universal (or *catholic*) doctrine around the Jeshua character. For example, in order to appease Judaism, they gave Jesus the honorary title of *Christos*, meaning 'savior' or 'anointed one,' hence the name Jesus Christ. The church then renamed itself the Roman *Catholic* Church and the religion became known as Roman Catholicism. Rome approved of the 'obey Rome and pay your taxes' mandate and the one-God concept, inherited from the ancient *hibiri YHVH* cult, because it gave them two 'big sticks' for controlling the peoples of the countries occupied by the Roman Empire. (Keeping armies stationed across the huge empire was costing a fortune, so Rome seized on any way to control its unruly subjects.)

During this time, the nature of God was also up for grabs. The Gnostics portrayed it as the Divine Spark within each of us; the followers of Paul (the majority) saw it as an external authority figure that held life-or-death over mortals. Long and bitter were the debates until Rome stepped in and chose the latter. To reinforce the edict, Gnosticism was declared heretical upon pain of fire, to purge such heresy from one's soul: "It's for your own good, citizen."

For the next couple of generations, joining the new Roman Catholic Church was a matter of personal choice until 391, when emperor Theodosius proclaimed that *all* citizens of the far-flung Roman Empire must become Christians, or be guilty of the crimes of *treason* and *heresy*. There was much dissent among Romans about abandoning their old gods (and privately, many didn't), but the threat of becoming lion chow in the arena of the Coliseum guaranteed public acquiescence. Jews and so-called 'witches' were particularly persecuted and died by the thousand.

Further, Theodosius knew the weakness of the Christian cult's dogma—that it had all been patched together from older cults' beliefs—and ordered the destruction of all the bodies of knowledge on which the gospels had been based, plus all references to the Anunnaki. Tragically this included the priceless collection of writings in the Library of Alexandria[5], whose loss set back the evolution of human understanding by millennia. But Christianity could not risk the faithful knowing that their One True God was based on an ET leader's now absentee grandson. Thus the conspiracy was almost complete. (Fortunately, the Romans did not know about the thousands of Sumerian tablets tucked away in ruined temples.)

As the new Christianity drew further away from its Jewish roots, it further distanced itself by rewriting the Gospels to blame the Jews for murdering its central figure, a plague that would haunt Judaism throughout history, and lead to horrors such as the WWII holocaust. It would even resurface in 2004, with the release of Mel Gibson's movie, *The Passion*.

So not only did the early Christian Church fabricate its dogma as a recruiting campaign, it also compounded the atrocity by destroying all evidence that could prove what they did. Gloating over the orgy of destruction, the fifth-century Archbishop Chrystostom said, "Every trace of the old philosophy and literature of the ancient world has vanished from the face of the Earth."

By sacking and burning all non-Christian schools and temples in the name of a mythical god, the Roman Catholic Church made itself the only repository of books and historical records, which it then freely edited. The Church also built over any religious site to do with Pagan[6] worship, thus denying it to worshippers and further obliterating history. Holy days in older religions were also 'covered over' with Christian religious observances, to become holidays (holy days). This resulted in idiocies, such as having lambs around for Jesus' alleged December birth. Christmas was actually timed to coincide with Pagan winter solstice observances, hence the Pagan symbols of Yule logs and indoor trees, and was based on the December 25 birth of the Pagan god Mithra. (This little gem was decided in 527.)

St. Valentine's Day, which the Pope linked to the Purification of the Virgin Mary also covered over the pagan celebration of Lupercalia (named in honor of

---

[5]   The Christian mob pulled Hypatia, the library's head, from the building, stripped her and, while she was still alive, carved the flesh from her bones using abalone shells. Then they burned her body and went on to destroy the world's greatest repository of learning and knowledge.

[6]   The word *pagan* simply means 'country dweller,' people who were the last to submit to the new religious cult issuing from Rome. Pagans saw the divine in everything, but Christians vilified them as godless, soulless heathens, who should be put to the sword with impunity. However, Socrates, Plato and Archimedes, arguably the world's greatest thinkers of all time, were Pagans.

the wolf that legend says suckled Romulus and Remus, founders of Rome). This Roman purification and fertility rite evolved into a rite of passage in which young men and women play-acted mock betrothals. Cupid is actually a greatly watered down symbol of erotic love. And Easter covers up celebration of the Spring Equinox; those Easter bunnies and eggs are actually pagan fertility symbols.

The year 431 saw the Council of Ephesus, which decided that the Holy Ghost had impregnated Mary, so Jesus was fathered by *YHVH* and thus free of the 'original sin' stain. In 550, Emperor Justinian went even further by declaring the death penalty for anyone who questioned Roman Catholic doctrine.

Just three years later, he convened the Second Synod to remove a major block to the wider acceptance of the cult. The prevailing Greek view was that we are eternal souls who incarnate into flesh, live, die and return to the soul plane, from where we will reincarnate once more. The cult's view (based on the Hebrew model) was that we are born, grow a soul and, depending on how many good works we did while alive and whether we adopt Jesus as our personal savior, go to Heaven. If not, we're hell-bound. Justinian favored the cult's view to appease his new wife, an ex-prostitute, who was worried about future lives in which she would have to atone for her sins, whereas everything was hunky-dory with Jesus. To expunge the many references to reincarnation littered throughout the Bible, 14 books were dropped because they discussed three topics—pre-birth existence of the soul, reincarnation and karma. These references also weakened the hold of the Church and threatened its revenue, for believers in reincarnation did not need the sin-confession-sin cycle or Christ as their savior. Instead, they strived to improve themselves, and thereby get off the karmic wheel of future reincarnations.

The Church, therefore, willingly dropped reincarnation from its doctrine because it was proving bad for business. The bishops reasoned that because the people knew they had plenty of lifetimes to 'get it right,' if they were told their soul came into being at birth and had only one shot to impress *YHVH* enough to get into heaven and enjoy everlasting salvation, they'd really pay attention … and also pay tithes. The faithful would be desperate to erase their sins by paying money to the Church, and the business of selling indulgences would go through the roof. Thus, to even mention the pre-existence of the soul before birth was declared *anathema*, a state that usually required death by fire to purify one's soul and rectify one's erroneous thinking.

Wherever it could, the Roman Catholic Church responded to resistance by fire and the sword, or even worse atrocities, often involving deviant sexual torture of women who were perceived as temptresses of men and the cause of all ungodly behavior. In this way, the celibate priests could indulge their perverted sexual fantasies with any poor woman unfortunate enough to be accused of witchcraft. Evidence-gathering involved shaving the suspected witch's pubic area, and close examination for evidence of consorting with demons.

Interestingly, Jeshua never had a problem with carnal pleasures and allegedly enjoyed a fruitful relationship with Mary Magdalene that produced a daughter. The cult that sprang up around his name initially allowed its priests to marry, but insisted on celibacy for unmarried priests because of numerous scandals involving priests and married female followers that threatened to bring the cult down.

In his painting *The Last Supper*, Leonardo Da Vinci portrayed John sitting to the right of Jesus, wearing complementary colors and forming a V-shape—an ancient esoteric symbol fully understood by the painter. Oddly, Leonardo portrayed John as very effeminate, maybe just to keep us guessing. (Also, notice that there is *no* Grail Cup on the table in front of Jesus.)

Da Vinci's Last Supper, with detail showing the table contents and the mystical V-shape formed by Jesus and John / Mary

In his book, *The Da Vinci Code*, Dan Brown's premise is that, for 2,000 years, the Catholic Church has oppressed the female principle, as exemplified by Mary, casting this priestess and wife of Jeshua as a whore. (Some Jewish sects did not practice the subjugation of women and many women served as priestesses in their churches.) Brown suggests that the figure of John in the painting is actually that of Mary; but we will never know what was in Leonardo's mind. However, Brown misses the mark by asserting that the Holy Grail was Mary herself, as the mother of Jesus' child, the bearer of the royal bloodline of the House of David. In fact, the Grail is about the female principle in *all* of us, something the early Church tried to deny when it stamped out the goddess-oriented Pagan religions. However, to most early Christian sects, women were useful only for bearing Christian sons. So, guys reading this, we have our work cut out—restoring our inner female as counterpart to our inner beast. (With worldwide sales of over 30 million, Brown has stirred up magnificent debate, much to the Vatican's horror, which has issued many edicts condemning his book as heretical. What's that I smell burning?)

In the first few centuries, therefore, many books and epistles were removed and many verses would be added later to bolster the decisions made about the Jesus character. For example, in the KJV of the NT, Acts 8:37 records Philip saying, "I believe that Jesus Christ is the Son of God." This verse is pure forgery, because it does not appear in the 4th century *Codex Vaticanus*. The first time it appears is in the 1582 Rheims version—the Catholic standard. So some scholar injected the verse between the 5th and 16th centuries, easy to do when the scriptures were copied by hand.

Brown was on solid ground with his mention of the Priory of Sion. Its existence is historical fact, as its mission of safeguarding the proof that Jesus didn't die on the cross, but feigned crucifixion and emigrated to France (then Gaul), and started the Merovingian bloodline. Proof that this proof exists turned up in 1891 when the curator of the church at Rennes-le-Château in the French Pyrenees was restoring the old building. The curator, a Mr. Saunière, found four carefully hidden scrolls—two New Testament texts in Latin with an embedded message in code, and two lengthy genealogies. Deciphering the coded message plus a few clues on a gravestone led

Priory of Sion at Rennes

him to a cave full of treasure, believed to have been that of the Knights Templar who found the fortune of King Solomon when they built the Temple of Solomon in Jerusalem. The treasure was safeguarded by a group known as the Cathars (whom we will meet again in Chapter 13), who were brutally persecuted by the Roman Catholic Church and finally wiped out in 1244 because of two heretical beliefs: (1) that the Crucifixion is actually cruci-fiction, and (2) reincarnation is real. Enough of the Cathars escaped, taking with them the proof of their beliefs and the treasure, which somehow ended up hidden in Rennes-le-Château, to be found five centuries later. Somehow, the shadowy, secret organization called the Priory of Sion spirited away the genealogies that purportedly show the lineage of Jeshua, and are rumored today to be in a safety deposit box in a London bank.

Beginning in 1096, a series of popes launched waves of Inquisitions and Crusades, which killed millions in Europe and the Middle East, and later the Americas, just because they didn't buy Rome's God and Jesus myths in their totality. But does this mean that Jesus never existed? It's not a simple yes/no answer. On the physical plane, the character was largely fictitious, being a composite of Jeshua and Apollonius, both of whom *did* exist, plus countless mythological characters. However, on the astral plane, the answer is 'sort of,' and the astral and physical planes were almost interwoven back then. According to the Seth entity, as channeled by Jane Roberts, the Ascended Master hierarchy decided the fictional Jesus character was a good vehicle for spreading compassion and wisdom, so they threw their weight behind it. Led by one of their number (Sananda), they induced mass dreams about Jesus in the population, which resulted in dreams and reality being interwoven. (Dreams were far more influential in those days and colored waking life, so the mass dream, spanning scores of generations, drove the myth of Jesus into the realms of historical fact and strengthened the religion's power base.)

Does this conspiracy erode the validity of Jesus' words? Not in the least. Great truths are always great truths, whether spoken by a flesh-and-blood teacher such as Jeshua, the Buddha, Lao-Tzu, or even a Shakespearean character. The words ascribed to Jesus still stand as unparalleled wisdom to live by ... if only Christians would. As with the God concept, the Jesus myth was created for the benefit of younger souls who need support over and above advanced knowledge about soul. The concept of a savior to forgive their sins serves their needs well.

Today, those on the soul plane report meeting Jesus, actually a projection by Sananda, and an incredibly wise and loving ascended master, but no one over there expects Jesus to 'save them' because over there, no one believes they need saving.

Over two millennia (roughly 100 generations) of political wrangling, much of the real message of teachers such as Jeshua and Apollonius—the Source is within you, and love your neighbor as yourself—was lost. Deifying the messenger as the 'Son of *YHVH*' and 'Savior of Mankind' further obscured the message, but enough remains for us to get the point. At one point, Mary told the disciples that Jeshua had told her his teachings were about seeking union with God through inner knowing, adding, "He is calling upon us to become fully human," i.e., to find the God within. However, Paul believed in a patriarchal, external God and completely ignored her, going on to establish Christianity as the authoritative, male-dominated institution we see today.

Supporters of the Jesus story look to the Bible for their proof, but that is self-serving and circular because the New Testament was compiled for marketing and promotion, so we must look to contemporary accounts for validation. And since the Romans were prolific record-keepers, we should find plenty. However, not a single reference to the Jesus story exists outside the four canonical gospels of the New Testament. This includes the works of Philo (30 BCE – 54 CE) and Justus of Taberias (30 CE – 100 CE), two inveterate commentators of all things Jewish. A brief passage appears in the works of Jewish historian Josephus (37 CE – 105 CE), but this is a clear and flagrant forgery, added centuries later.

If the dogma of Christianity is fiction written to elevate the status of one Hebrew sect, and then rewritten to control the unruly citizens of Judea, and if the lead character of Jesus has no more historical credibility than a TV soap opera star, where does that leave us? It leaves us FREE! Free of two millennia of rigid church dogma. Free of 'God's rules' about the way you should think, be and act. Free to follow your own spirituality, guided by your heart and inner teachers. And free of a submit-or-perish-in-eternal-damnation God based on ancient ET slave-masters.

Does this mean throwing out the New Testament? Of course not, because its creators called on many of the world's great traditions and wove a rich tapestry of wisdom to live by. As for worshipping the character of Jesus, that is a valid step in a soul's growth in its cycle of lifetimes when it needs a simplistic set of rules to follow daily. However, one is less likely to find older souls in church on Sunday morning.

Just a few hundred years ago, not attending church was enough to get you burned. In 1231, Pope Gregory launched the Inquisition, targeting witches, imagined or real. This spread fear and suspicion throughout Europe, as neighbor accused neighbor, usually over some petty disagreement. The only proof needed of being 'in league with the devil' was, say, a mole on the skin. You were then immersed in water, and if you drowned, you were not a witch. But if you didn't drown, you *were* deemed a witch and tortured until you confessed. The torturers were very skilled, thorough and had no time limit to do their work, so confession was inevitable, followed by public burning.

In 1648, the madness came to the American colonies and incited Quaker men, who had hostility towards women due to guilt over finding them attractive. In 1692, this culminated in Salem, Mass, with accusations against over 200 men and women, including a four-year-old girl, who quickly confessed so as to be with her mother, also in jail for witchcraft. The witch-hunt turned into hysteria as the girls who started the whole thing couldn't back down and admit having made it all up. Instead, their claims got progressively more outrageous, as even the clergy were accused and hanged. After 20 executions, suspicions finally arose when the girls accused the wife of the state governor, the very man who was heading the trials.

The story started in winter 1691 at the house of Salem's minister, when some grain used for making bread got damp and a mildly psychotropic fungus called ergot contaminated it. The household also had a black but free housekeeper, who regaled the minister's daughter and her friends with tales of voodoo. She was quickly accused, tried and sold into slavery, but the girls had gotten to like the limelight, so they got their thrills by accusing women villagers for something as simple as not attending church or owning a cat. The girls loved being the center of attention, and their parents encouraged the accusations as a great way of getting rid of anyone they didn't like. The local constable also loved it because he got to confiscate the witch's property.

Ain't religion grand?

The tourist guides at the Grand Canyon have an interesting dilemma. When someone in the group they are leading asks about the age of the canyon, the guides say the rocks are about two billion years old and the gorge itself dates back about five million years. "Nonsense," fundamentalist Christians say. "It can't be more than 6,000 years old, because that's when God created everything." On October 26, 2004, *The New York Times* ran a story by Cornelia Dean titled, "Creationism and Science Clash at Grand Canyon Bookstores." The article talks about the controversy caused by the park bookstore carrying a book expounding the creationist view. Scientists complain that by doing this, the Park Service endorses the idea.

So where *did* the idea come from? Around 1650, King James took it upon himself to rewrite *The Bible*, and asked one Bishop Usher to determine the time and date of the first day of Genesis. The good bishop came up with 9:00 a.m. on October 8, 4004 BCE. Considering that many years have been added to and subtracted from the calendar countless times over the centuries, exactly how the bishop pulled off this feat is a mystery.

Those who insist the Bible is 'God's living word' have many interesting dilemmas. For example, Genesis 29:17-28 stipulates that marriage shall consist of a union between one man and one or *more* women. Furthermore, II Samuel 5:13 states that marriage shall not impede a man's right to take concubines in addition to his wife or wives. In biblical times, a woman's lot was not a happy one. Deuteronomy 22:13-21 tells us that a marriage shall be considered valid only if the wife is a virgin. If she is not a virgin, she shall be executed. On the bright side, Genesis 38:6-10 states if a married man dies without children, his brother shall marry the widow. If he refuses to marry his brother's widow or deliberately does not give her children, he shall pay a fine of one shoe and be otherwise punished in a manner to be determined by law. However, God's living word makes no allowance for the widow declining the offer other than in Gen. 19:31-36, which says that, in lieu of marriage, if there are no acceptable men in your town, you and your sisters must get your father drunk and have sex with him. Guess the Bible was written by men.

Leviticus is also a goldmine of rules to live by. Lev. 25:44 allows you to own slaves as long as they are foreigners; Lev. 15: 19-24 prohibits contact with a woman during her moon time; Lev. 11:10 declares eating shellfish an abomination up there with homosexuality; Lev. 19:27 prohibits getting your hair cut; Lev. 11:6-8 declares you unclean if you touch the skin of a dead pig. Darn! There goes football!

A breaking news story in January 2004 gives a fascinating inside glimpse of a 'fundy' religion. The town of Colorado City, Arizona is owned by the Fundamentalist Church of Jesus Christ of Latter-Day Saints, a breakaway cult of the Mormon Church. Its leader, the so-called Prophet, claims to speak with 'the Voice of God,' and routinely marries off teenage girls to older men and 'reassigns' wives to other husbands at 'God's Will.' If they refuse, he excommunicates them, evicts them from their church-owned house, and makes sure they never work again in the church-owned town. The Prophet basically controls every detail of the lives of the 6,000 residents, including their sex lives, and they willingly comply because they believe his word is God's word. (Remember this story when we talk about Baby Souls in the next chapter.) To eliminate any competition for the women, the male elders evict young men as they graduate high school, casting them out into a world for which they are unprepared.

Meanwhile, in Brunswick, Georgia, several teenaged girls testified in the trial of the 58-year-old leader of another religious cult. Apparently, he made the older girls groom the younger girls in the art of pleasing him sexually. Girls who did please him were rewarded, otherwise they were punished. Will someone please pass the Kool-Aid? I'm outta here.

After having given us a 'potted' God-concept, how have organized religions fared in helping us develop a relationship with it? In assisting us to strengthen that relationship, religions have been abject and miserable failures. Rather than bolster our bonds with our spiritual nature, they have systematically driven huge wedges between our human and spiritual aspects—hierarchies of priests, bishops, cardinals and popes. As for them being role models, many of the so-called celibates have more sex than most of the faithful, and often with the very girls and boys they are charged with protecting.

In February 2004, a John Jay College of Criminal Justice study of self-reported cases of sexual abuse by Catholic priests between 1950 and 2000 revealed that 4,329 clergy (that's 4% of the total of 109,694 priests who served in the U.S. during that time) were responsible for 10,667 claims of abuse, costing the Church $533 million in settlements. But these figures are from less than half the dioceses (84 of 195), so the final numbers will probably be more than double. And because these are only *self*-reported (many offenders are no longer alive to report), some sources claim the real numbers could be ten times higher. According to the survey, 78% of those abused were aged 11 – 17, 16% were 8 – 10, and nearly 6% were 7 or younger. The survey also said several factors contributed to the problem, including failure to grasp its gravity, overemphasis on avoiding scandal, misguided willingness to forgive and insufficient accountability, with bishops simply reassigning abusers to other churches. It seems that these 'men of God' are not quite so godly after all. Some interesting life reviews coming up on the Other Side, I'd say.

The purpose of organized religion is to bind us to the one true creator Source—there can be only one—but they end up dividing us over how to worship that entity, and exclude all those who disagree on the specific protocol for worship … as if the Source cares how you worship it, or even if you even *do* worship it. I'm sure the Source would prefer us to stop blowing each other up in order to please It. How can religions give their followers license to kill those with a different God-myth, all in the name of their supposedly loving God? And the sad thing is that no religion comes even close to defining the Truth.

An evolved spirit-based 'religion' would put you in ever-closer contact with your own higher self and help you to create openings for more of its energy to percolate down into your daily life. You would live in full attunement with your soul and need no 'middle man' to intercede on your behalf. This would add immeasurably to the love and wisdom in your dealings with others and yourself. You would take every opportunity to remind yourself and others of your glorious true identities and encourage all to assimilate more.

The truly brilliant coup that religion, especially Christianity, pulls off is to convince millions of Baby Souls that they are automatically damned by virtue of being descended from Adam and Eve. As abject sinners, they are told that their only hope is to turn to a savior for salvation, which Christianity just 'happens' to have. But you must join their church to be saved; otherwise it's fiery pit time. However, this is okay in the big picture because all souls need to live at least one life of blind adherence to authority figures just to know what that is like. All just the Source learning more about itself.

However, the Catholics can't take all the credit for sexually abusing our children. The Jehovah's Witnesses seem to have their own claim to fame. According to the website set up to disclose the Church's track record (www.silentlambs.org), the Church gives complete anonymity to sex offenders when they are discovered and threatens parents of molested children with 'disfellowshipment' if they try to warn other members whose children may be in danger.

The primary purpose of organized Western religions is to perpetuate themselves for the ongoing job security of their officials. They therefore have no interest in 'saving souls,' for each saved soul who no longer needs the religion reduces its income. Imagine officials going before the faithful and saying, "We have misled you. The God you seek is within you. In fact, you *are* the God you seek. You no longer need us."

Or the Pope admitting, "We made up the Jesus character as a composite of many ancient myths from history. So there really is no one to worship. And you don't need anyone to forgive your sins because you have not sinned; you have just acted with less than full knowledge of the truth."

Don't hold your breath. Those two scenarios are pretty unlikely, but as an Old Soul, at least *you* should know the truth. Old Soul? What's that? The next chapter goes into it in some detail.

Core Beliefs and Religion

The major problem with our core beliefs is that, because we focus on our physical body, we operate from the body's agenda, not the soul's agenda. Thus we focus on physical survival and pleasure. The soul's agenda is to explore the nature of reality—i.e., the *insides* of the Source—to realize the oneness of creation and to bask in its unconditional love. To the soul, there is no such thing as death, but only the cycles of experience.

Remember, you are not your body; you are soul, eternal and infinite. This calls for a fundamental revision of who we really are. We are soul, and the body grows within its field, or aura. Soul is a focal point of Universal Life Energy (*chi,* or *qi*). So every soul is really only a focal point in the One Soul, which is one manifestation of the Source. There is literally no separation and no difference between these focal points. So, whatever you do to harm or benefit another, you do to the whole, hence to yourself.

However, organized religion teaches the exact opposite—that we are separate from each other and from God, that God wants us to behave in a certain way, and that we must redeem ourselves by admitting our sinful, flawed state, and then begging for forgiveness and salvation.

We need a New Spirituality to give people the gift of knowing who they *really* are—an integral part of the Source, here to learn about itself. So it is impossible to not ultimately do the Source's will, to offend the Source, or to lose Its love. In the final analysis, we *are* that love.

The core belief within organized religion is that we are separate from God and must work our way back to His good graces by trying to figure out what He wants, and then giving it to Him. This is flat-out wrong. We were never *not* part of All That Is; in fact, it's just not possible to be separate. By definition, nothing can exist that is not part of All That Is so, of course, you're Source-stuff.

Religions *should* be training us to wield our god-like powers wisely, not separate us from them; and to postpone short-term gratification for the long-term evolution of humanity. In every moment, we get to choose between immediate satisfaction and evolution of the species.

For example, religion should be helping us with decisions such as cloning ethics and *in utero* treatment of diseases. We may ascribe illness and disease to 'the Will of God,' but *we* actually choose these things, not God. And science gives us the power to reverse many of them through techniques such as stem cell therapy.

Religion clouds ethical decisions about genetic engineering by proclaiming it as 'God's territory' and leaving us to suffer 'God's will.' But, as long as we see ourselves as separate from God and God's will, we cannot fully harness technology.

Humanity will always survive because soul cannot be destroyed, but our survival in physical form is questionable. This *should* concern us because most of us know no other form. However, many of our decisions to pollute the planet show that we don't really take seriously our physical demise. And so we continue to work against the collective good by taking a 'me first' attitude, rather than thinking as a unified One Soul.

In summary, then, yes, there is a Source of All That Is, but it is far from the limited God-myth of the Bible. And yes, there is a Jesus on the soul plane but Sananda is far from the Jesus-myth of the Bible. So why is getting out from under these myths so important? Because they represent authority in your life and reinforce every other authority figure—parents, bosses, government, etc. It's vital to live with only *one* authority in your life—your Higher Self, your soul, your Divine Spark of the Source of All That Is.

We see the true crime against humanity that organized religions have perpetrated when we look at the nature of the deity they propagate. In Walsch's *Conversations with God*, we read that God wants us to behave in a certain way and if we do not behave in that way, He (note male gender) will be angry with us and judge us unworthy of spending everlasting eternity with Him. So, we spend much of our lives, figuratively and literally, begging this God to forgive us pathetic, whimpering sinners (although we're not sure exactly what our sin is), and trying to figure out what will make Him happy. What arrogance to think that anything we could do or not do would remotely concern the Source of All That Is, who gave us that free will in the first place. Or that toeing the line or not, will determine whether God is a happy camper.

Next, we're told that because we *are* sinners, God has distanced Himself from us, beginning with the eviction of Adam and Eve from the Garden of Eden. But even though we are distanced from Him, we must *still* figure out what He wants, and He will *still* destroy us if we can't, even though He created us. Religions don't actually tell us why God would go to all the trouble of creating us only to destroy us if we can't figure out in one short lifetime what He wants us to do ... *and* deliver it.

This is a brilliant, no-win, Catch-22 situation devised by the priesthood and guaranteed to keep us going back to them so they can continue to tell us what the God they created wants from us. Again, brilliant PR on their part! 'Create a need and fill it.'

Even if you are not a practicing Christian, Americans live in a Christian-based country—one nation *under God*, with the words: "In God We Trust" on our dollar bill. If you went to Sunday School as a kid, you were brainwashed, especially if it was Catholic. Subtle or gross, organized religions erode our self-esteem and personal power. Fortunately, their gods are purely fictitious, made up to control the Baby soul masses (see next chapter for an explanation of Soul Ages). The real Source is very different ... as we've seen.

And It Still Goes On

The Anunnaki long ago put in place measures to control us by creating differences and amplifying them, so that we become afraid of those who are different and begin to fight them. ("Divide and conquer" is an old Machiavellian trick that works very well.) Fighting each other weakens us and keeps the warmongers strong by selling weapons to both sides.

What are the differences that are exploited? First, we divide ourselves up into nations and proudly wave our country's flag. But from space, you can't see national borders unless they follow a large river. So, down in Arizona and New Mexico, there's no difference between the U.S. and Mexico, yet we draw a line in the sand that arbitrarily divides two peoples—one that consumes 75% of the world's resources and the other, practically nothing. Therefore, we have competition, with the poorer group often dying as they try to sneak in among the richer group.

Because of the disparate distribution of resources and raw materials, we fight wars over them, such as oil, mineral and water rights. On a civilized planet, all would be apportioned equally, but by carving us up into territorial groups, the Anunnaki worked hard to keep us separate.

Twice now, the world has divided itself up into two evenly armed camps and thrown billions of dollars of munitions at each other—armies and civilians alike—supplied, of course, by the agents of the Anunnaki. And every few decades, nations destroy each other's cities and spend billions (borrowed) on rebuilding.

Different languages further enforce our separation: "People who speak other languages are 'foreigners' and cannot be trusted." Even in Canada, the presence of the French-speaking Quebeçois is a source of separation. But things can get even more tricky for, in Rwanda, the Tutsi and Hutu speak the same language and share the same culture, but are bitter enemies, killing each other in huge numbers.

The first example of this is the Genesis story of the Tower of Babel, in which humans decided to build a new city, complete with a tower that would 'reach the heavens.' The *Yahwehs* didn't approve of such a move of power, so they 'confounded the human tongues,' i.e., made them speak different languages. Of course, their collaborative building project quickly fell apart.

Another enormous wedge between us is division by religion, each with its own god icon. When the Hebrews emerged as a distinct group about 4,000 years ago, they made themselves different by their eating habits and male circumcision. Then, 2,000 years ago, a small messiah cult grew out of that and declared itself separate by accepting Gentiles. When the cult of Islam emerged, things got *really* interesting, and we had the Crusades, with Christians, Jews and Muslims having a three-way hate-fest in which millions died. And the fighting still goes on today.

In Northern Ireland, Christian kills Christian, divided over transubstantiation, i.e., whether sacramental wine actually *becomes* the blood of Jesus or only *symbolizes* it. As if *he* cares! In August 2003, the Episcopalian Church in the U.S. was in an uproar over the consecration of an openly gay bishop (Rev. Gene Robinson of New Hampshire), with all manner of groups threatening to walk out on each other. So much for brotherly love. And the issue derailed delicate talks between Anglicans and Catholics because only days earlier, the Pope had sharply criticized homosexuality as 'morally disordered.' Tell that to all the young men molested by Catholic priests over the years.

Wedges are not limited to Christianity. In Iraq, free of the tight control of Saddam Hussein's Baath party, Sunni and Shi'ite Muslims went at each others' throats in a centuries-long dispute over whether the Imam speaks with the infallible voice of Allah (Shi'ite view) or whether he's just a spiritual leader (Sunni view). This is akin to Catholic killing Catholic over whether the Pope is the voice of God or just head of the Church. March 2004 saw the deaths of hundreds of Shiites during the most holy time of the year for them, courtesy of Sunni suicide bombers. And in India, during April 2003, Muslim terrorists exploded two car bombs that killed Muslim and Hindu alike.

Also in August 2003, the people of Alabama were split over a two-ton block of stone sitting in the state's Supreme Courthouse because it displayed the Ten Commandments. Now, if the content of Chapter 3 is on the mark, these words of wisdom were given to Moses by one of the Anunnaki nobility named *YHVH*. However, 'Roy's Rock' raised interesting constitutional issues.

The Founding Fathers ensured that the Constitution prohibited the establishment of an official religion for the United States and the individual states. They also wanted to keep the government's meddling hands off the religions being practiced. But today, being such words of wisdom, the Commandments form the basis of the American legal system. So Alabama's Chief Justice, Roy Moore, believed it was in order to display those words in the state's Supreme Court building, claiming that "God's Law (i.e., Anunnaki law) is above Man's Law."

At issue is the question: Does placing a monument to the Ten Commandments in a state facility constitute establishing a state religion? Is this a state-mandated endorsement of Christianity? Or is this a Christian imposing his personal views on other people 'because he can' … or at least thought he could until he was fired. And those commandments are not even Christian, for Christianity stole them from the Jews; they were first given to Moses, after all.

In response to the firing of the good judge, a group of extremists known broadly as Dominionists started pushing the *Constitution Restoration Act of 2004* through Congress. This bill would 'acknowledge God as the sovereign source of law, liberty and government in the United States.' Furthermore, it would forbid all legal challenges to government officials who use the power of the state to enforce their own view of 'God's sovereign authority.' Any judge who dared even hear such a challenge could be removed from office.

If enacted, this will effectively transform the American Republic into a theocracy, where the arbitrary interpretation of the word of God by a judge, policeman, bureaucrat or president can override the rule of law.

The Dominionists' openly expressed aim is to subject every aspect of society to 'biblical rule,' placing 'the state, the schools, the arts and sciences, law, economics, and every other sphere of public domain under Christ the King.'

According to Dominionist literature, the phrase 'biblical rule' means execution by stoning of homosexuals and other deviants and enslavement of debtors. Legal challenges to 'God's order' will *not* be allowed. And because this order is divinely ordained, the 'elect' can use any means necessary to establish and sustain it, including deception, subversion, and violence.

"Yeah, right," many will say. But the Dominionists are bankrolled by some very deep-pockets in the Republican Party, and are in alignment with such names as Supreme Court Justice Antonin Scalia, who wrote in the theological journal *First Things* that: "The state derives its moral authority from God, not the consent of the governed. Government is the 'minister of God' with powers to 'revenge,' to 'execute wrath' including even wrath by the sword."

Of course, this has nothing to do with restoring the Constitution, but drives a Mack truck through it. Fortunately, enough good people revere that document as the prime law of the land, but if you want to read something scary, do a Google search on 'dominionists.'

On the other hand, we also have political correctness insanity. In November 2004, a Christian fifth-grade teacher in California sued his school principal for discrimination because he'd been censured for using the G-word while discussing the Pledge of Allegiance. Schoolteachers simply cannot teach current affairs or world history if they cannot mention God, because many wars have been, and still are being, fought over which side's God-myth should prevail.

Then we have skin color. We all know that, "People with _____ colored skin are _________." However you fill in the blanks, a fight is guaranteed. In fact, the peoples with different skin pigmentation were seeded over many millennia by different groups of ET colonists who either left or ended up interbreeding with their human subjects. So only the genetic creations of the Anunnaki can be said to be true Earthlings; the rest are 'imports.'

Finally, let's not forget gender, where one-half of a population enslaves the other half out of fear and ignorance. Gender stereotyping and mutual distrust have been a favorite tool for millennia because it's so easy. Fathers teach sons and mothers teach daughters, so we're self-policing.

Until we can rise to the level of unconditional love, compassion and tolerance, the above differences will continue to drive wedges between us, and continue to keep humanity at less than full strength.

Armageddon: Fact or Fiction?

We have always worried that life as we know it could end, and all cultures have their 'Armageddon beliefs.' Islam believes that Allah has already set the schedule for the end of humankind, and the Old Testament book of Daniel claims that God has too. In 1978, Jim Jones sought paradise for 900 disciples and, in 1993, David Koresh and 90 followers went after them. March 1997 saw 37 Heaven's Gate members going to meet God in a UFO. And still the madness continues.

Christianity obsesses on this subject, as witnessed by the very popular *Left Behind* series, which predicts ecstasy for believers and horrible suffering for everyone else. Pandemics, asteroids, crime, warfare and terrorism are all heralded by Christians as signs of the Second Coming of Christ. The Book of Revelation purportedly foretells that the Second Coming will be accompanied by untold and terrifying horrors. But it's all a huge misunderstanding.

Back in 81 CE, Roman Emperor Domition demanded that Romans worship him as a god. A preacher called John refused to do this, so the emperor exiled him to Patmos, an island in the Aegean Sea. In a cave there, he claimed an angel revealed to him a vision concerning the fall of Rome. However, he had to disguise his predictions for Rome's demise in 'apocalyptic form,' which simply means 'veiled,' a codeword which told readers that the revelation was symbolic of Roman oppression and doom. For example, the seven-headed monster actually referred to the Seven Hills of Rome. Revelation was really a harsh condemnation of all things Roman but today, Christians misinterpret it as *real*. So TV evangelists preach the imminent Second Coming by totally misunderstanding a book written 2,000 years ago for pretty much the same reasons that Thomas Paine wrote *Common Sense*. This has engendered two millennia of fear, especially concerning the seven seals (war, pestilence, plagues, earthquakes, antichrist, etc.).

Christians wrestle daily with Revelation, and wonder when the world will end. Also, they totally miss the message of Jeshua, who never said he would return. In fact, he constantly dodged the issue of his being a messiah. Nevertheless, since its inception in the fourth century, the Christian Church has been predicting the date—first 365, then 1,000, then 1033, all of which fueled 'End of Times' art as seen in the work of Hieronymous Bosch.

When Christianity spread to America, it developed its own Armageddon myths. Cotton Mather predicted 1691, and when that didn't happen, he came up with the whole list of dates. The most dramatic predictor was William Miller. In the 1813, he predicted that Jesus would appear in 1843, which gave rise to a sect called Millerites. A huge crowd assembled but Jesus was a no-show, so Miller then came up with October 22, 1844. Thousands sold their belongings in readiness for the big event, and another no-show led to the formation of the Seventh Day Adventists.

About 250 million people in 180 countries have heard his message: "God loves you and gave his son to die for you; repent and take Jesus Christ as your savior." Ordained a Baptist minister in 1939, Billy Graham was there when the post-WWII world needed him. And his mentor, William Randolph Hearst, made sure the world heard him. Just 25 years after the divisive Scopes Monkey Trial had polarized American Christians, people needed a unifying voice.

In 1949 at age 30, Graham held a 6,000-seat tent crusade in L.A. that was to last for three weeks but was extended to twelve. Taking full advantage of the newly emerging mass media, he quickly became a household name, and remained so for over half a century. Opening his new HQ in Charlotte, NC, he said, "We are living in a world of great spiritual hunger and this place will be a center for proclaiming the gospel to the world."

From humble beginnings in the tent, he ended up filling football stadiums and touching one in 25 people on the planet. But what were his followers looking for? Simply something larger than themselves and a sense of higher meaning in their lives. As we will see in this book, because of childhood indoctrination, younger souls in the U.S. interpret this 'something larger' as the Judeo-Christian God. The messages of this book are that: (1) You would be better off praying to Santa Claus than the ET-based God myth, and (2) True meaning can be found only in your own soul and its role as a node in the matrix of consciousness through which the Source seeks to know itself.

Today Graham's son and daughter are following in their father's footsteps, but with less expansiveness. In fact, son Franklin says, "The god of Islam is not our God. It's a different God and I believe it is a very evil and wicked religion." Obviously we Old Souls still have work to do.

The Rapture

In the 19th century, a Brit called Derby came up with the idea of 'The Rapture,' which heralds the Second Coming, an idea that has caught on among millions of fundamentalist Christians worldwide. It is a glorious prospect wherein, at the sound of a trumpet, Jesus will appear in the clouds to take believers up to meet him, thus escaping the horrible calamities foretold in the *Book of Revelation*. Those who aren't lifted up will be left behind to suffer the consequences of the 'Great Tribulation,' a seven-year period, the last half of which will see enormous suffering and devastation. Non-believers, including members of other religions, will be left behind to suffer and perish. At the last moment, those accepting Jesus as their savior will be saved; the rest will perish.

Rev. Tim LaHaye, co-founder of the Moral Majority in 1979, and his co-author Jerry Jenkins are largely responsible for taking the Rapture mainstream, via their *Left Behind* series of apocalyptic novels. Sales of nearly 60 million copies of their 12-volume series ensure frequent appearances on the bestseller lists. LaHaye says, "I see many signs of the Lord's return. This could be the generation that's going to hear Jesus shout from the heaven and we'll respond to be with him. And you don't want your loved ones to be left behind."

According to Barbara R. Rossing in her book *The Rapture Exposed*, "The rapture is a racket, a fraud of monumental proportions, as well as a disturbing way to instill fear in people. The *Left Behind* books instill terrible fear in children that people are going to be left behind. It is not biblical. There is no Rapture in the Bible. In the early

Roman Empire, when it looked like violence was getting out of hand—much like things today—the *Book of Revelation* was a message to people that the empire would not last much longer and that the emperor was not the one in charge of the world."

Some liken the series to ethnic cleansing. One columnist wrote: "If a Muslim were to write an Islamic version and publish it in Saudi Arabia, jubilantly describing the massacre of billions of non-Muslims by Allah, the world would have a fit. It's disconcerting to find ethnic cleansing celebrated as the height of piety."

All of this is very sad and results in stories such as the following.

On September 23, 2003, a Las Vegas mother sent her 8-year-old son and 4-year-old daughter 'to be with Jesus' by caving in their skulls with a baseball bat. Then she jumped in front of a fast-moving big rig. She recovered but faces two murder charges, with a possible death sentence. And what of the poor husband, who came home to find his children lying in pools of their own blood? He's lost both his wife and children. Apparently, a rabid fundie minister took advantage of her simple intellect and convinced her that the world was a sinful place and that her kids would be 'better off with Jesus.'

As we'll see in this book, you are not a sinner, and no one is coming to save you, because you don't need saving. YOU alone are responsible for your own salvation by realizing you were never separated from the Divine; you were only *told* that you were separate by those who sought to control you. And, as an innocent child, you believed those limited opinions handed to you by parents, schools, and churches. (By the way, the word 'salvation' comes from the Latin *salvus,* which simply means safe or comfortable.)

The God and Jesus myths were, and still are, brilliant ploys to take all your power and project it 'out there.' Then, the hierarchies of priesthood step in to serve as middlemen between us 'sniveling little sinners' and the all-powerful God-out-there, completely denying the all-powerful God-in-here. So why did we allow this to happen? Because these limitations were exactly what the Earth Game needed—one more layer to obscure the truth and make things interesting.

To close the subject of the Rapture, you may wish to visit the Rapture Ready web site (www.raptureready.com), which features a 'rapture index,' a compilation of 45 key indicators that signal conditions are ripe for the return of Jesus to save the faithful. Factors such as the inflation rate, the price of oil, crime rate, and level of global turmoil are ranked on a scale of 0 – 5. At its worst, the 45-factor index would top out at 225, but the indexer says anything over 145 means that the Rapture is imminent. In October 2005, we were at 156. Hold on, kiddies!

Final Word

A couple of centuries ago, a new game came into town with its own twist—science. As a discipline, science sets itself up to tell us what is real, but also got into the Great Identity Theft by telling us we climbed out of the primordial ooze, little better than pond scum with legs, and into some enormous machine that randomly generates events to which we must respond ... assuming the events don't kill us first.

Add to that, western organized religion's take about God watching us closely, ready to pounce on any false step in our response and judge us 'unworthy' of spending eternity in His Kingdom. Again, brilliant PR for the churches, who become indispensable middlemen to pray for our troubled souls, and the scientists who become the new priesthood.

To Sir Isaac Newton (1642 – 1727), the founder of modern science, the universe was a huge machine, a giant clockworks, which we could understand by studying its parts. Quantum physics, however, has trounced that worldview. The *atom* (Greek for 'indivisible') is known to be made of far smaller particles that are not particles at all, but energy packets coming from somewhere other than the physical plane. They cross a quantum barrier into 3-D from a higher dimension and appear to cooperate in order to make up atoms, and they seem to know exactly what they are doing.

In ways we haven't got a clue about, subatomic particles get together and create the *appearance* of atoms, which our instruments can detect. Thus the world around us is actually energy flowing across the quantum barrier and somehow organizing itself on the fly.

Working through the brain, our Subconscious Mind creates the world we see by 'approximating' trillions of energy packets into familiar objects. The mind/brain has evolved to be selective, and to 'notice' only those patterns important to our survival. As we drive down the road, our visual cortex 'sees' every leaf on every tree, every bird in the sky, and the cat sitting in someone's window, but we notice only the red light up ahead.

Researchers estimate we perceive less than one-tenth of one percent of what our visual cortex sees, our mind discarding the other 99.9%. Thus our *conditioning* governs what we perceive about the world around us. Of the estimated 40 million bits of information we receive every second, we notice only 16 bits.

In the miracle of Creation, every moment, massive amounts of energy pour across the quantum veil that separates the physical plane from the higher dimensions, and then behave as subatomic particles, which collaborate to form the seemingly solid matter of daily reality. Science and religion ignore our ability to influence that energy as it makes up reality, an ability we'll look at in Vol. II, Chapter 9, and one that boggles the mind once you know you can do it.

So, if anything in the last two chapters is true, having slaughtered all our sacred cows, what's left? Something infinitely better that leaves you as an all-powerful spiritual being who existed long before the life you're currently living, and who will exist long after you have returned to the soul plane. So go to the cosmic 'Lost and Found' and reclaim your true identity that was stolen from you.

Remember, it's just like the movie *Groundhog Day* where you get to do it over and over until you arrive at unconditional love. The movie is a brilliant parody of reincarnation, with each day in the evolving of Bill Murray, analogous to a lifetime. For the first few hundred days, he's barbaric and cynical, but he changes into a talented and loving person. Once he was able to say "I love you," and mean it, everything changed. Once *you* can look life in the eye and say, "I love you," you're free to move on to bigger and better things ... only right now you can't even imagine what those things could be.

If we drop the concept of a god who listens patiently to our pathetic whining, and instead focus on the soul that we really are, how do we deal with *that*? Possibly the most useful stance is found in *Taoism*. Taoism is neither a religion nor a philosophy but a way of life, often associated with the force that flows through the entire universe (variously called orgone, chi, qi, or prana).

Founded by Lao-Tzu, Taoism began in China about 500 BCE and today has roughly 50 million believers. The *Tao-te-Ching*, or *Book of Reason and Virtue*, is a slim volume because the Tao, or the Way of undivided unity and ultimate reality, is left for the seeker to discover within. Taoists believe in the oneness of all creation, in the spirituality of the material realms and in the brotherhood of all men.

Not having been exposed to Anunnaki conditioning, *Eastern religions* in general teach there is one true and absolute Supreme Unified Divine Principle, of which we are a part, and which dwells within us. This Principle is love and all souls are a facet of it, but a veil keeps us from realizing our personal relationship with it. We receive its grace through our experience according to our soul's understanding, temperament and maturity, developed over the course of countless lifetimes. Salvation comes through the descent of its grace through spiritual enlightenment. Moral living is essential to spiritual progress, for unrighteous thoughts, words and deeds keep us from spiritual liberation.

The soul is immortal and will ultimately be liberated from the cycle of reincarnation when it feels it has no more to learn by Earth incarnations. The universe exists in endless cycles of creation, preservation and destruction. There is no absolute end to the world.

The foundation of Eastern religions is personal, inner and often mystical, experience of the Divine Principle. We can, and ultimately must, come to direct knowledge of the Divine Principle during earthly life. Each soul is guided as it experiences karmic interactions into dharma, or alignment with universal laws.

Hell is not a physical place, but is the lower astral plane. Karmic suffering is a state of mind during life or between lives. There is no intrinsic evil because all things are within the Divine Principle.

Taoism is commonly represented by the yin-yang symbol, which stands for the balance of opposites in the universe. *Yang* is the radiant, masculine principle; *yin* is the receptive, female principle that absorbs the yang. When they are equally present, balance prevails. When one principle outweighs the other, there is confusion and disarray, from the cells in your  body all the way up to our galaxy. Only in balance can happiness be found.

The Tao (pronounced 'dow') is the first-cause of the universe, a force that flows through All That Is, and becoming one with it is the path to enlightenment. The Taoist has no concept of a personified deity or of the creation of the universe, since it is recreated in each now moment. They do not pray as religions do, because there is no God to hear the prayers or to act upon them.

The basis of Taoism is focus on the world around you to keep the forces of yin and yang in harmony by meditation and contemplation. At its core is the art of *wu wei*, or action through inaction. The practice of minimal action is much like standing in the river and letting it flow past you because it's easier than struggling against it by going upstream. However, Taoists also live life intensely and intently, enjoying health, vitality and longevity.

This does not mean being a pacifist. Taoists hope to avoid violence or the need for military action by means of looking ahead to prevent it, but when violence is inevitable, the Taoist will fight, albeit with a heavy heart.

The essence of the Tao (way or path) is unknowable but its manifestations can be observed in nature, a practice that is the basis of a spiritual approach to living. Taoists hold that the order and harmony of nature are more stable and enduring than the institutions of man, and that we flourish better when we flow with nature in a simple approach to life. Thus life has less to do with externals, such as monetary reward or fame, and more to do with internals, such as creativity, joy, and sense of purpose. To the Taoist, the chief task is developing virtue, or the Three Jewels of compassion, moderation and humility. Taoists believe in the innate compassion of human beings, and that left to their own devices, people will show this compassion without expecting a reward.

Apart from the yin-yang symbol, the Tao cannot be symbolized in any other way. In fact, at its heart is the saying, "The Tao that can be spoken is not the Tao," which suggests that this ineffable, eternal, creative force is best known through mystical experience. Such personal transformation is the opposite of religion's morality and community orientation. And the ultimate transformation within the Tao is our return to the soul plane, to begin the cycle again … or not.

On the website of The Campaign for Philosophical Freedom, www.cfpf.org.uk, its founder, Michael Roll, sums up this chapter well, so it closes with his words:

"To mislead people when the motive is pure is forgivable and excusable. To deliberately mislead people, after gaining knowledge, is unforgivable and inexcusable. There is no greater crime in the cosmos than to deliberately indoctrinate young trusting minds with false teachings for selfish ends. From this one heinous crime stems all crime. The perpetrators of this evil deed will pay a terrible price in mental remorse when they pass from this world.

"We only have to look at Northern Ireland, the Middle East and New York to see what happens when babies are got at from birth by priests, mullahs, rabbis, 'holy' men and ministers of religion. Those guilty of mental child abuse will wish they had never been born when they enter into the etheric wavelengths. The tragedy is that this is not brainwashing, it's mindwashing, because we leave our brains behind when our physical bodies pack in. The victims of priestcraft carry on hating in the so-called next world."

Anthony Borgia and Monsignor Benson

Between 1951 and 1957, psychic medium Anthony Borgia channeled a compelling series of afterlife accounts from Catholic priest Monsignor Robert Hugh Benson about life on the other side. He did this because he had been a prolific Catholic writer and, when he crossed over, he realized everything he'd written was a lie. He was so mortified at having misled mankind, he asked 'the powers that be' for permission to set the record straight should a suitable medium be found. One was, and Borgia compiled the session notes into six books: *Life in the World Unseen*, *Facts*, *More Light*, *Heaven and Earth*, *More about Life in the World Unseen* and *Here and Hereafter*.

Msgr. Benson (1871 – 1914) was a son of Edward White Benson, Archbishop of Canterbury from 1883 until his death in 1896, and has much to say to correct the teachings of his life as an influential Christian. His words are frank and honest. For example, "These spirit realms are full of people who, when they were on earth, denied that such things as psychic faculties existed. They know better now. They know that such faculties are part of the natural make-up of man."

Monsignor Benson

When it comes to orthodox religions, in retrospect, the good priest has this to say: "The Church says 'the dead' cannot come back, or would not come back if they could. They say, 'It is only devils that come back, who impersonate our own kindred, deceive us, and thus try to ruin us spiritually, so that we jeopardize our immortal souls.' What arrant nonsense! The Church professes to have the spiritual care of man in its hands—and knows next to nothing about the matter at all. The Church has become stupefied by its own fantastic doctrines and beliefs. It has become inflated by its own self-importance. It has become hypnotized by its own apparent security. It has become absorbed in the details of dogma and doctrine, and the outward displays of showy ritual. It has poured money into bricks and mortar because it really believes the House of God warrants a lavish expenditure in art and architecture. This may be justified only when all else is fully provided for—the poor people, for instance, for the needy always come first. Because we see things in a clear light in the spirit world, we regard the Church on earth not as a help to man in his spiritual progression, but as a downright and deliberate hindrance. The Church is blocking the way to the diffusion of spiritual truth and knowledge throughout the earth world.

"The Church can provide no answers to vital questions, questions that are in the minds of so many people. Can the Church answer these questions, for instance, as applied to yourself: What becomes of me when I die? What has become of all my relatives and friends? Why is there this seemingly profound silence between them and me?

"To the last question, I would answer that there is no need, no need whatever, for that profound silence, for it can be and is broken, just as I have broken it, even as I am now breaking it to you, my good friend, and even as I shall continue to break it for just so long as I can serve a good and wholesome purpose.

Hard-hitting words from a man who dedicated himself and his life to Roman Catholicism. On the topic of Adam and Eve and 'original sin,' he rails: "The complexity of Church doctrines and creeds that have their origin or basis in the fable of our first parents is a totally inadequate attempt to explain what the early churchmen were completely unable to explain. It was the sin of these supposed first parents that led the Father of the universe to invent the 'death' of the physical body. He cast them out of Paradise, condemned them to 'death,' and that 'death' became communicable, like some pestilent disease, to all future generations of mankind. The whole fabrication of the history of the creation of man and his subsequent disaster is a gross insult to the Infinite Mind."

For a highly respected 'man of the cloth' to say that Church teachings are an insult to Creation and the Source is a major heads up. The good Msgr. Benson goes on to say: "Indeed, it may be said that orthodox religions base the only hope of the soul's 'salvation' upon the merits of another. It is in this respect that orthodoxy has taken the spirit world and made of it a Christian world, or, at least the religious teachers would say that the Christian element more than predominates.

"As an inhabitant of the spirit world, I soon discovered that the spirit world is so much greater than what the earth world denominates 'the Christian religion.' Indeed, it is away beyond all earthly religions of whatever denomination. It is made up of peoples from every quarter of the earth world, representing every school of earthly religious thought. In the realms wherein I dwell, we have cast aside *forever* the allegiance to the Church of our earthly lives. We have no orthodox religion here. We are all of one mind, and that mind is regulated by the strict truth.

"The spirit world, in short, is undenominational. Orthodoxy may make as many claims as it wishes in respect of its self-arrogated right to be the guardian of man's 'immortal soul.' Admittance to the spirit world is not through any one Church or collection of Churches; nor is it obtained through the merits of any one person or body of persons."

Despite the author's 19th century verbosity, hopefully the above excerpts will prompt you to look in depth at Borgia's 'must read' books. New and used copies of three of them (*Life in the World Unseen, More about Life in the World Unseen* and *Here and Hereafter*) are available on Amazon.com, and for the others, you can read or download (which I strongly suggest so that you have permanent hardcopy) them from the Angelfire website. To download *Facts*, go to www.angelfire.com/ne/newviews/facts.html and progress through the series.

Downloading from Angelfire will take time, but I guarantee that those who do will be richly rewarded. For example, in *World Unseen*, Msgr. Benson is given a tour of Halls of Learning, and in the Hall of Fine Art are displayed paintings as the artists originally *intended* them to be and not how they ended up on canvas. On the soul plane, artists can use colors not available on the Earth plane and show true, living 3-D. The Libraries contain books where the deceased authors have filled in the *truth* rather than the potted versions in history, so we can learn the *real* reasons why history took the turns it did. And the Halls of Music put on symphony concerts where, in addition to incredible acoustics from instruments that do not exist on the Earth plane, concertgoers also get to see the architecture of the symphony in wonderful, living, colorful geometrics. He also visits the Hall of Science, where every scientific discovery is tried and tested before being dropped into the mind of an Earth plane scientist for development. Benson's description of how everyone is actively living and growing on the soul plane makes a mockery of the phrase 'Rest in peace.'

In his 90 (Earth) years of residence in the soul plane, Benson has run into Sananda (the Ascended Master behind the Jesus story), who is 'embarrassed at the 'only begotten son of God' myth woven around the character in the 4th century. We can see why; it's hard to listen to his wise words while groveling at his feet and proclaiming what a miserable sinner you are.

Benson talks at length about communication between the soul plane and Earth plane, whereby those on the soul plane know fully what's going on with us, and attempt to guide us. Their two main avenues are: (1) spirit guides, who are largely ignored by most people, and (2) inventors, scientists, musicians, etc., over there who drop inspirational thoughts and prompts into our dreams and meditations, and urge us to take certain actions, in the hope of improving Earth plane life … again with varying success. This information should be well known, he says, claiming that the beatitude: *"Blessed are they that mourn, for they shall be comforted"* is an example of how the New Testament has been hopelessly mangled. That sentence fails to reveal exactly *how* mourners will be comforted, so Benson went to the Akashic record (the blow-by-blow, living history of the planet and every human ever on it). There, he discovered it was the title of an entire sermon in which Jeshua taught people how to talk to deceased loved ones across the veil, and/or enlist the services of a psychic medium. Of course, that's the last thing the 4th century clerics wanted people to hear, so they deleted the actual sermon itself. In fact, organized religion strongly discourages such things as 'communing with evil forces.' Read Borgia's books for yourself and decide whether the good monsignor is evil or not. Oh, well.

Chico Xavier and the Physician

Msgr. Benson seems to have ended up on Level 4 of the soul plane (in the Chapter 2 model). Another famous account concerns a community of about a million souls dedicated to healing on Level 3. Unlike Level 4, souls still consume food and use transportation to get around, and the city is associated with the geographical location of Brazil, which gives the realm an 'informed Catholic' vibration.

In the 1930s, a prominent Brazilian physician died and, due to some serious arrogance problems, spent many years wandering the Lower Zones, as he called them (in this book, we term that Level 2, with Level 1 the home of unspeakably monstrous low entities, the truly unrepentant and genuinely evil). Eventually, from the wastelands of Level 2, he cried out to God to rescue him and almost immediately a high being showed up and led him to what he calls the Astral City on Level 3. There, he underwent months of healing and eventually dedicated himself to helping those who had recently crossed over in confusion, just as he had done. After working in the soul plane for about 60 years, he contacted Chico Xavier, Brazil's leading psychic medium, and dictated his story, resulting in the book *The Astral City* (available for download at the website: *www.geae.inf.br/en/books/ac/index.html#TC.*

The life of Xavier itself is worth a brief detour. By the age of four, he was hearing voices and having visions. His family thought he was possessed by the devil, and he was ordered by the local priest to say a thousand Ave-Marias. But the voices continued and, as a teenager, Xavier began to study the teachings of Allan Kardec, the Frenchman who was the father of the spiritualist movement in Europe, which became the spiritist movement in Brazil.

Xavier went on to become Brazil's most respected medium, a position of great moral authority in a country where an estimated 20 million people believe in spiritism, a hybrid of Catholicism and communication with those who have crossed over. In a career spanning 75 years, Xavier became its most important figure.

Even though barely educated, he published more than 400 books dictated to him telepathically by the spirits of dead people. All told, he sold an estimated 25 million copies, the profits of which were all channeled into charity work, while he himself lived close to poverty.

In the late 1990s, Xavier's health began to deteriorate, and he died in 2002 aged 92, of heart problems. Xavier had prophesied he would die on a 'day of celebration,' so the immense grief would be lessened by national happiness. On the day of his death, the Brazilian football team won its fifth World Cup. (We see a parallel here, with Mother Teresa choosing to cross over just a week after

Princess Diana. True to form, the saintly lady did not want a fuss made over her departure.)

The crux of this piece is the need for 'right living' while here on Earth, to prevent serious 'hard time' on the other side. As a physician in Rio de Janeiro, he had enjoyed prestige and a lavish lifestyle, but had neglected the spiritual side of life, and found himself 'on the bottom rung' of the soul plane. He muses in *The Astral City:*

"If my earthly experiences might be classified as a 'wreck,' it was all my own doing. Now that I had the opportunity to observe the vibrations of intense and constructive work at the Astral City, I could not help wondering how I, when on Earth, could have wasted so much time on trifles.

"True, I had loved my wife dearly, and had tenderly cherished our children, yet on examining my conduct as a husband and father, I realized that I had failed to build up anything solid and useful within the spirit of my family. I realized it only now, now that it was too late. Whoever advances along a road and neglects to sow the seed for a future harvest along the way, and fails to protect the fountain that quenches his thirst, cannot turn back expecting to find all he needs. These thoughts kept recurring in my mind with an irritating insistence."

In one highlight in the book, the physician recounts a lecture he attended by a high being in the Astral City, given to a few hundred new arrivals to answer some of their questions:

"I am here to talk to you about certain thought processes. Among us tonight are a few hundred listeners who are still surprised about the similarity of forms on the physical plane and in our spirit sphere. They have learned that thought is the universal language, and have been told that mental creation is the most important factor in spirit life. Numerous brothers are asking themselves questions, such as why they find earthly dwellings, utensils, and even the same forms of speech here. Yet this fact should not be a motive of surprise to anyone. We must not forget that, up to now, while in the physical body, we have lived in circles of antagonistic vibrations. Thought is the basis of all spiritual relations, but we must keep in mind that we are millions of souls in the Universe still far from perfect obedience to universal laws. We cannot, as yet, be compared with our older and wiser brothers nearer to the Divine Spheres [Level 4]. We are millions of entities living in the undisciplined 'inferior worlds' of our Ego. The great instructors of physical mankind teach divine principles and expound eternal truths, but in our earthly life we generally learn these laws without obeying them; we acknowledge these truths without consecrating our lives to them.

"Now then, do you imagine that by just admitting the power of thought, man can be purged of his inferior condition? Certainly not; it would be impossible. A hundred years on the planet represent much too short a period of training for us to become divine cooperators. During our earthly apprenticeship, we learn the principles of mental force, but forget that, for thousands of years, we have used our thought energies to form destructive mental creations, or at best creations harmful to ourselves.

"We follow courses of spiritualization in the various religious schools of the world, yet, with most of us, it is frequently a question of mere verbal adherence, of lip service and nothing else. No one, however, can attend to his duty through words alone.

"We all know that thought is an essential force, but we overlook the fact that we have misused that force over centuries. We all know that it is man's duty to provide for his own children; likewise each spirit is compelled to maintain and nourish his own creations. A criminal idea will produce mental creations of the same nature; a lofty principle will observe the same laws. Let me illustrate the fact with a more objective example. After rising to great heights, water is purified and carries vigorous vital fluids, returning as the vivifying dew and generous rains. Keep it on Earth, mixed with the impurities on the soil, and it will become a foul mire, a habitat for destructive micro-organisms.

"Therefore, the Astral City as a transitory spirit colony is a great blessing granted us as an 'additional mercy' in order that a few may prepare themselves to rise to higher spheres, and the majority may return to Earth on redeeming missions. I beg you, my friends, let us all realize the importance of the processes of the mind and live up to them from now on.

"Who is willing to try?"

[Note that residents of Level 3 still talk of returning to Earth lives to redeem some undesirable traits and/or teach other Universal Principles to others.]

As a soul that existed long before the moment of conception from which grew the body you now occupy, you were instrumental in planning the life you're now living. Your body, personality, and life circumstances did not 'just happen.' In fact, the planning process is the most fascinating story ever told. Let's join you-the-soul, about to take the most monumental journey a soul can undertake in this part of the universe …

CHAPTER 5 ══—

EARTH LIFE PREPARATION

Let's Get a Life

Suppose, as a soul busy with your soul plane research on emotional states, you've taken theory to its limit and need to test something out. You-the-soul have realized you need an Earth life.

With the help of your spirit guides and soul plane colleagues, you identify your goals, such as to study the balance between arrogance and humility, or how to create a concert symphony. Then the two big things you will need are:

- The *situation* that will best support you in achieving your goals, which includes choosing the most appropriate physical body. Remember, that body will be conceived and born, regardless of which soul chooses it. The soul for whom that body will best serve gets to 'appropriate' it. (If you hadn't chosen your current body, some other soul would now be living there instead of you.)

- The *personality structures* that will allow you-the-soul to operate in that situation and hopefully achieve your goals. (Accepting that you created your personality allows you to change it. You created it so you can recreate a new one at any time.)

What's all this talk about goals? Are we not just born and left to figure out what life is about? Absolutely not. Your reasons for incarnating are carefully planned, although ego-personality is kept in the dark until it returns to the soul plane for debriefing … unless you can figure it out while still here. And *that* puts you in the driver's seat.

When a soul decides to incarnate, it begins a planning process that involves countless spirit guides and counselors, and the souls of everyone who will be involved in the Earth life, such as parents, siblings, mates, children and significant co-workers. You also use a time-travel 'technology' that cannot be described in our language to preview how the life you're planning will turn out.

Each time a soul incarnates, it transmits a characteristic vibration, a fragment of its energy, plus the template for the personality it has designed, across the veil—the boundary between the soul and physical planes—and 'attaches' to the fetus that will be its focal point for that incarnation. As we will see, when the incarnation is over, that soul vibration or fragment, along with the levels of mind and the etheric body (your higher frequency double that looks to other souls just like your physical body), all return to the soul plane to continue development, growth and learning. After a few thousand years, possibly several hundred of these fragments (all part of the same soul) exist, work and play on the soul plane and are aware of each other as 'soul siblings' in the same soul family.

When the soul plans a new incarnation, these soul siblings all have their say in the goals and challenges the incarnation will take on, because they know the gaps in their soul's collective experience and understanding that must be closed. For example, suppose the soul siblings have shown a tendency towards arrogance while incarnate. The soul may plan a few lifetimes that explore humility, which would move the aggregate soul energy more into balance. If on its return to the soul plane, the soul fragment successfully led a lifetime of humility, that helps the other siblings, who can tap into that energy and moderate their arrogant streak. Therefore, each returning soul fragment helps and supports all the other fragments, past and future, in its soul family by pooling what it has learned and achieved.

This also means that while you are incarnate here on Earth, the knowledge and achievements of all the other fragments of your soul are available to you, but you must ask. Even as a soul fragment yourself, you are a sovereign entity and no other part of your soul can force anything on you, not even wisdom and understanding. However, what a resource once you know about it!

All the people who will be in your new life are 'supporting actors' drawn from your soul's soul group, a band of maybe a thousand or so other souls who hang together for eternity. After 40 or 50 lifetimes, you all know each other very well and count on them to incarnate with you and put on a good performance. Of course, you have your smaller group favorites, or family, and turn to them for the intense interactions, such as becoming your mate or even murdering you if your soul needs that experience.

First, however, you define your intent for the upcoming lifetime. What facet of the Source's experience do you wish to explore in your own way? Creativity, humility, courage, humor, nurturing, being nurtured? Or a talent such as music, art or mathematics.

Once you've pinned that down, you-the-soul choose the circumstances that will best help you, such as gender, location, socio-economic class, and timeframe in history. (Because the entire timeline is available to the soul plane, you could drop into any period you wished, so the 'next' lifetime could actually be lived in ancient Greece if that culture best supports your goals.) You also need to find other souls who want to explore that era with you and agree to co-incarnate with you. To study courage, for example, you may choose to incarnate into a country planning a war in 20 years, when you will be a young man. To study culture, you may choose to incarnate in Italy during the Renaissance, as did Michelangelo. Or Leonardo da Vinci, who studied everything.

Pinning all this down could take the equivalent of many Earth years and involve consultation with a council of wise elders, and countless meetings with the other souls whose lives will be intertwined with yours. You also use the holographic 'time machine' to preview possible lifetime scenarios. (This may sound complex but it's as much fun to souls as planning a vacation is to us, as we decide what countries and landmarks we want to visit and where we will stay.)

What if two souls are interested in attaching to the same yet-to-be-born fetus because, say, it will be born to wealthy parents or even royalty? The higher selves of the souls involved sort it out because, at that level, we are infinitely wise and can see the larger ramifications of the choice.

Knowing that most soul growth comes from overcoming the most challenge, souls deliberately build some adversity into the life plan … and how the incarnation deals with it is what the Earth plane is all about. From the common perspective down here, someone leading a charmed life of opulence, luxury, and an easy, painless death may seem fortunate. But from the soul perspective, however, that is a wasted life, for nothing is learned and no growth occurs. Of course, it may be a 'vacation life' after a particular grueling lifetime of torture, rape, extreme pain and a grisly death that caused such disturbance in the soul's energy that an easy lifetime is needed to compensate. Therefore, no one can or should judge any incarnation's circumstances because no one has all the information. The down-and-out wino lying drunk in the gutter may be a soul studying advanced sociology on the soul plane, looking at compassion during this lifetime.

Who Shall I Be? The Michael Teachings

The next major group of decisions concerns the personality for the upcoming incarnation. Personality does not 'just happen' but is carefully crafted beforehand. Two facets that soul cannot change are its basic nature and the overall Earth experience it has mustered from previous incarnations. These constitute 'soul-level personality.'

Discussing how a soul crafts a personality needs a model of personality, and a soul entity that goes by the name Michael has given us one. The Michael entity is a soul group of 1,040 souls that speak with one voice. Through a number of mediums, the group has given us what are called The Michael Teachings (see Resources), which present a model for learning and understanding. However, the entity stresses that this is a model only, presented as a rudimentary teaching tool, and the truth is far more complex. (The following has been synthesized from many sources, including live channeling of the Michael entity and some of the sources in the Resources section.)

According to the Michael Teachings, souls close to the Earth plane tend to fall into seven types of energy, or Roles, and souls operate consistently within Role across the entire Earth cycle of incarnations. The Roles are listed below (percentages are for the USA); the examples are taken from the database in Emily Baumbach's book (www.itstime.com/famous.htm) and reproduced with kind permission):

- *Priest* (3-5%), whose incarnations are spent working for the best interest of others in a spiritual sense by inspiring them through their compassion. This helps them to grow and take on challenges. Priests are driven by a vision of what they see to be the higher good and will urge others on to it. Famous Priests include Joan of Arc, Julius Caesar, Princess Diana, Adolph Hitler, Napoleon, Malcolm X, Jesse Jackson and Oprah Winfrey.
- *Artisan* (30%), who incarnates to creatively manifest something new and original. They tend to express their nature through creating things, ideas and the moods of groups. Although usually warm and friendly, they tend to be uncomfortable on the physical plane, being so far ahead of other roles, they can feel 'odd' and misunderstood. Famous Artisans include Elvis Presley, Vincent Van Gogh, Michael Jackson, Shirley MacLaine, Marilyn Monroe, Cher, Elizabeth Taylor and Michelangelo.
- *Sage* (15%), who communicates wisdom to large groups from center stage, using language in new and creative ways. Their incarnations are gifted and

highly creative, but because they take life less seriously than any other role, they want to inform while entertaining and having fun, rather than inspiring spiritual growth, as do Priests. Famous Sages include Bill Clinton, Ronald Reagan, Mikhail Gorbachev, Bill Cosby, Dr. Ruth and Robert Kennedy.

- *Warrior* (30%), who tends towards doing and getting things done through others by persuasion. They are physical and goal-oriented, highly focused, clear-thinking strategists, inveterate planners, organizers and executors, and make good business people. Warriors can be in the military, where they excel, but are not limited to that sphere. They can be single-minded, even ruthless, with those not similarly motivated or in agreement with their plans. Famous Warriors include John Wayne, Sylvester Stallone, Hannibal the Great, Hilary Clinton, Dwight D. Eisenhower, Gen. Norman Schwarzkopf, Ayatollah Khomeini, and Ulysses S. Grant.

- *King* (1-2%), whose incarnations naturally fall into governing the outcome of events by personal direction and mastery. Their exaltedness gives them an expansive, broad vision that leads to easy learning and natural, charismatic 'presence.' Monarchs are not automatically King Souls; in fact, Queen Victoria was a Server Soul. Famous Kings include Charlemagne, Queen Elizabeth I, Madonna, Katherine Hepburn, John F. Kennedy, Jacqueline Kennedy Onassis, Aristotle Onassis, Martha Stewart and Donald Trump.

- *Server* (10%), who incarnates to work for the best interests of others in a physical sense. They are often modest and self-effacing, and exude reliability, practicality and productivity. They truly like to help, support and nurture others and will do practically anything for them without seeking reward or praise. They make things happen quietly in the background. Famous Servers include Mother Teresa, Martin Luther King Jr., President Jimmy Carter, and Queens Victoria and Elizabeth II.

- *Scholar* (15-20%), whose incarnations study, assimilate and organize knowledge into integrated structures for the benefit of all. They feel and act neutrally in situations that would rouse other roles. Their panoramic vision and few personal opinions make them excellent mediators and recorders of events. Their incarnations are more solid than fluid, well grounded and physically oriented. Famous Scholars include Beethoven, George H.W. Bush, Bach, Henry VIII, and Britain's Margaret Thatcher.

To help you determine your role if it isn't obvious from the above, the Michael Education Foundation offers a quiz on their website at www.mef.to/seven_roles/the_roles.html. For those who are Internet-challenged, it also appears at Appendix B (with the kind permission of MEF).

Table 1 summarizes the Roles, which Michael breaks down into the Inspiration, Expression, Action and Assimilation Axes, and categorizes into Local or Ordinal, and Global or Cardinal. By 'local' is meant someone's 'small story' of personal growth; 'cardinal' means the 'big story' of global influence, such as the life and death of JFK, Jacquie and Onassis, three famous Kings. The positive and negative attributes or qualities depend on whether the person is operating out of love or fear.

AXIS	LOCAL/ORDINAL		GLOBAL/CARDINAL	
Inspiration	**Server (30%, US 10%)**		**Priest (7%, US 3-5%)**	
	+ve Service	−ve Bondage	+ve Compassion	−ve Zeal
Expression	**Artisan (20%, US 30%)**		**Sage (11%, US 15%)**	
	+ve Creation	−ve Self-deception	+ve Dissemination	−ve Verbosity
Action	**Warrior (20%, US 30%)**		**King (3%, US 1-2%)**	
	+ve Persuasion	−ve Coercion	+ve Mastery	−ve Tyranny
Assimilation	**Scholar (13%, US 15-20%)**			
	+ve Knowledge	−ve Theory		

Table 1: The Seven Roles of the Michael System

Soul Age

The other attribute of the soul is *Soul Age*, which is a function of the understanding and wisdom gleaned from the soul's various incarnations. Michael breaks this down into seven Ages:

- *Infant Soul* (5%), who is born into primitive situations and easily frightened by everything, especially animals. They react to stimulus without thought, showing fear in the eyes. Their humor can be cruel and sadistic. They perceive a clear distinction between 'me/not-me,' seeing 'not-me' as hostile. Intimacy is alien; personal relationships are based on want and lust without conscience. Many sadistic serial killers are Infant Souls. In fact, famous Infant Souls include David Carpenter, Richard Ramirez, Larry Singleton, all criminals.
- Baby Soul (20%), whose incarnations perceive the world as 'me/other-me's' and may develop early unshakeable views from those around them,

plus a rigid perception. They are normally agreeable until an opposing view is encountered which they can't handle and may react with hostility and possibly violence. Guilelessness shows in the eyes as a blank wall. They may be uneasy about their own sexuality, possibly feeling it to be shameful, which may prevent enjoying sensual pleasure. They are immaculate and antiseptically clean. Baby Souls make good small town police chiefs. Famous Baby Souls include Queen Elizabeth II, Adolph Hitler, Stephen King, Jimmy Swaggart, Rush Limbaugh, Benito Mussolini, and Col. Kadafy of Libya.

- *Young Soul* (30%) incarnations have developed more discrimination and awareness, and their eyes show more unrest and activity. They are doers and architects of the physical plane. They see 'me/you' but see 'you' as different from 'me' and a target to be won over to their point of view. They are transformers, converters, idealists but, being still of limited perception, may not question their own motivations. They see other soul ages as not as motivated as they are, and lacking in initiative. They can manifest love but often see it as erotic. For appearances' sake, they are socially polished, poised, externally tidy, and seek high-status jobs and homes, seeing the purpose of Earth plane life as a game of 'he who dies with the most toys wins.' Famous Young Souls include Saddam Hussein, George W. Bush, VP Dick Cheney, Billy Graham, Bonaparte Napoleon, Dan Quale, British Prime Minister Margaret Thatcher, Lucille Ball, Cher, Johnny Carson, Eddie Murphy, John F. Kennedy, Jacqueline Kennedy Onassis, Mike Wallace, Saint Joan of Arc, O.J. Simpson and Donald Trump.

- *Mature Soul* (35%), whose incarnations are the most difficult and demanding because the Mature Soul begins to see and experience other people from *their* point of view, so social interaction occurs at a deeper level of perception and usually involves mixed emotions. They seek understanding and begin to look inward for the answers. Towards the end of the cycle, they begin to see the truth but, being still surrounded by the illusion of Earth plane, their behavior may be artificial and stylized as they strive for external validation. Mature Soul incarnations know they are searching but not always for what. This causes great stress and often requires therapy, occasionally from a bottle or other substances. Famous Mature Souls include President Bill Clinton, Hilary Clinton, VP Al Gore, Tipper Gore, Shirley MacLaine, Martin Luther King, Jr., Elizabeth Taylor, Vincent Van Gogh, Ernest Hemingway, Michael Jackson, Princess Diana, Willie Nelson, Mozart, Marilyn Monroe, Bette Midler, Jack Nicholson, and Oprah.

- *Old Soul* (10%) incarnations epitomize "Live and let live." They see others and self as part of a whole, and realize that Earth plane problems stem from the ego in self-defense. After so many lives, they are able to avoid ego traps by being fully aware of the outcome of choices. Their broad integration, wisdom and understanding show in their direct, penetrating gaze. Their quest becomes more ardent and more creative. They tend to be competent in anything they attempt and could master any field but tend to focus on spiritual evolution. They are usually drawn to situations that offer freedom and lack of interference, realizing the futility and transience of material gain. They can easily switch between spirituality and personality, making them powerful. The barrier that personality presents to the soul is weak and memory of co-incarnations bleeds through, giving them access to knowledge and wisdom far beyond the current life's experience. Old soul incarnations are not automatically 'laid back' however; some seek difficult challenge for dramatic growth. Their spirituality tends to be expansive and unorthodox, free of dogma. They may be casual about sex because of its lack of use in the quest, but are intensely sensual and enjoy physical contact. Old Souls confuse Young Souls because they can do anything but prefer not to. They sense the emptiness on the physical plane, and yearn for Home. Famous Old Souls include George Washington, Thomas Jefferson, George Burns, George Carlin, Leonardo da Vinci, Carl Jung, Abraham Lincoln, Michelangelo, John Lennon, Yoko Ono and Mother Teresa.
- *Transcendental Souls* (< 0.01%) incarnate as teachers and inspirers. They keep away from all organized religions and are not fooled by the Earth plane illusion. They naturally express their soul's wisdom, without force, for us to hear and act accordingly. Mahatma Gandhi and St. Francis of Assisi are good examples.
- *Infinite Souls*, while few in number, lead lives of enormous impact. According to Michael, the Earth plane has known only four: Lao-Tzu, Sri Krishna, Buddha and Jesus.

Soul Age and Life Passages

As people go through life from birth to midlife, they go through the Soul Ages, topping out at their native soul age. Each 'age' is categorized as fulfilling certain needs, as identified by the famous psychologist, Abraham Maslow. He postulated five layers of need: survival, safety and security, love and belonging, esteem, and self-actualization:

1. *Survival needs.* To survive, we need air, water, food, sleep and sex.
2. *Safety and security needs.* Once survival needs are handled, we work at finding safety, stability, and protection, which might also involve a need for structure, order, and some limits.
3. *Love and belonging needs.* Once survival and safety needs are assured, we move on to satisfy our need for friends, a life companion, children, pets, affectionate relationships and a sense of community, which manifests as membership of a church, a fraternity, a gang or a social or sporting club.

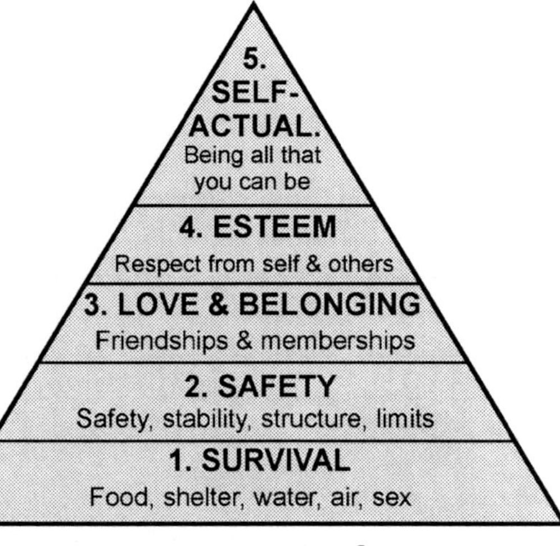

Maslow's Hierarchy of Needs

4. *Esteem needs.* Once we feel safe and part of the world, we look for esteem from two sources:
   - *Respect from others*, in the form of status, fame, recognition, good reputation, appreciation, and dignity.
   - *Self-respect*, in the form of confidence, sense of competence, achievement, mastery, independence, and freedom.
5. *Self-actualization needs.* Finally, we address our need to fulfill our potential, to 'be all that we can be.' This involves becoming the most complete and full expression of who we are. Sadly, Maslow suggested that only about two percent of the population ever gets to this level. His list of those who did includes Abraham Lincoln, Thomas Jefferson, Mahatma Gandhi, Albert Einstein and Eleanor Roosevelt.

If at any time, a lower need stops being met, we drop down to that level to take care of things. For example, if you're an artist busy painting a masterpiece (level 5) and the tornado warning siren goes off, you drop down to level 2 and scramble for the storm cellar just like everyone else.

Maslow also taught that one must go through the five levels systematically, starting with Survival. You cannot 'skip' a level in hopes of achieving Self-Actualization by cheating.

Maslow's Needs and the Michael Teachings

Maslow's five levels of need dovetail with Michael's soul ages and our life path between birth and mid-life:

Maslow's Needs	Soul Age	Age Preoccupation	Actual Age
1. Survival	Infant	Survival	0 – 5
2. Safety	Baby	Rules for living	5 – 10
3. Social	Young	Competition	10 – 20s
4. Esteem	Mature	Relationships	30s & 40s
5. Self-Actualization	Old	Wisdom/expression	40s onwards

The Infant Soul's preoccupation is survival. They cannot manage their life or see the larger picture. Even the Old Soul goes through this age for the first few years, maybe to age five.

Once we're through infancy, we begin to look out for our own *safety*, and come to see ourselves as part of a larger whole, and start to make friends. In order to structure our dealings with others, we seek a sense of order in our lives. This is comparable to the *Baby Soul's* preoccupation with rules and guidelines for living, between the ages of around five to ten. Actual Baby Souls will freeze development at this stage and live out a Baby Soul life.

As our *social needs* become our focus, we seek to belong to groups, and desire their acceptance, which leads to competition, be on the football field or in the back seat of a Chevy. This social focus equates to the *Young Soul* age, and may last through one's twenties. Actual Young Souls will freeze development at this stage and live out a Young Soul life.

Maslow's *esteem needs* focus on the search for self-respect and the respect of others in our groups. This equates to the focus of the *Mature Soul,* where we strive for trust and cooperation in our relationships, and may occupy our 30s and 40s. Actual Mature Souls will freeze development at this stage and live out a Mature Soul life.

Our *self-actualization needs* manifest as the need for ongoing self-improvement and striving to become all that we can be, including teaching what we know. This equates to the *Old Soul's* focus, where we define success not as having the most toys or being lauded, but as feeling good about ourselves and being in touch with our soul. This focus occupies us for the rest of our lives.

The two facets of Soul Age and Role color all a soul's incarnations and are analogous to a soul's own 'personality.' The combination goes a long way to explain the wide variations between people. For example, a younger soul age cannot under-stand an older age, so dynamic Young Souls cannot fathom the Old Soul's *laissez faire* approach to life. With Roles, too, a King cannot understand why everyone else doesn't want to govern. And a Sage's incessant talking may annoy those of other Roles.

Countries tend to have aggregate soul ages. The United States, for example, is a Mature Soul country, which explains our emphasis on social programs. However, many of our politicians are incarnations of Young Souls, who have the energy and drive to win elections, but then turn around and rob the cookie jar simply because they can. Iraq has a Baby Soul population that had a Young Soul leader. Iraq's Baby Souls develop early, unshakeable views and rigid perception, and react with hostility and violence to opposing views; while Hussein wanted to be seen as a 'mover and shaker' in the Arab world and used his people's blind loyalty and adherence to Islam to further that ambition. His regime was also part personality cult. (Vol. II, Chapter 9 continues this topic.)

Suppose you're driving on the freeway and some jerk cuts in on you. If you're a Baby Soul, you might begin a tirade about, "They shouldn't allow people like that on the road!" A Young Soul will respond with, "Okay, you S-O-B, I'm gonna get you!" A Mature Soul will look nervously at his watch, wondering if he'll be on time for the appointment with his shrink, and the Old Soul will mutter, "Chill out, dude. What's the hurry?"

Because the entire planetary timeline is available to souls, if an Old Soul wished, it could choose an incarnation set in a much earlier era of history, such as Ancient Greece, so we cannot assume a linear sequence of lifetimes through history.

Levels within Soul Age

Within each Soul Age are 7 sub-levels, each moving the soul through completion of an Age. Each level requires about 200 years, or about 3 lifetimes, but there are no firm rules for what should be accomplished in each life because of the complexity of the chosen personality traits and the Challenges a soul packs into each incarnation:

- *Level 1* lifetimes are bridges that exhibit about 30% of the new soul age and 70% of the previous age.
- *Level 2* reflects the beginning of the new Age's intensity (70% new vs. 30% old), often coupled with emotional centering or the goal of growth. The soul is pushing onward whereas personality may want to hold back.
- *Level 3* is often marked by introspective lifetimes, where one is able, knowledgeable and accomplished.

- *Level 4* builds lifetimes of consolidation and application, and is often the level where karma is generated through identifying too strongly with problems encountered. Mature Souls may suffer mental disorders because of such over-identification. Extroverted people are often drawn to a power mode.
- *Level 5* is the level of exploration and pushing to the limits of that soul age, often appearing eccentric. If intellectually centered, the person may have chosen extreme intelligence. Level 5s are drawn to spirituality and may appear 'not of this planet.'
- *Level 6* can be demanding and inherently difficult because of the need to deal with all obligations of the Age, particularly for an Old Soul. Goal of Growth is often chosen with a hard-working, driven life, possibly as a teacher.
- *Level 7* marks the enjoyable end to one Age and preparation for the next, usually lived without problems. This level brings together all the lessons learned in all levels of the Age, making someone a good teacher for lower levels of the same Age. Old Souls prepare for cycling off the reincarnation wheel altogether.

Soul Age and God

If an incarnation is imprinted with a belief in a deity, how that concept colors one's life depends partly on Soul Age:

- *Baby Souls* carry with them for life whatever God-concept they are first imprinted with, rarely stopping to question it. They may be religiously fundamental with a strongly personified concept of a god, and believe in evil as a reality. Those with a Role of Priest may end up as evangelists, such as Jim Bakker and Oral Roberts, who see things as fairly black and white. As a Baby Scholar, Jimmy Swaggart has a slightly different pitch.
- *Young Souls* tend to put a 'socially acceptable' face on their relationship with their deity, worshipping for show, such as dressing in their Sunday best for church and having the largest, shiniest SUV in the parking lot. God is still very much 'out there' to them, and a force to be bargained with. Their relationship with it can be superficial and discounted when the chips are down. They may use their god-concept as a battering ram to convert others, or play holier-than-thou games such as 'my God's better than your God,' or, 'my worship is purer than yours.' A Young Warrior such as George W. Bush may use his God to win Baby Soul votes, and to

justify his actions. An exalted Young Soul such as Billy Graham (King) may launch his own Crusades that influence millions, but still with no concept of soul as our primary identity.

- *Mature Souls* tend to have a deeper relationship with their Almighty and see it as something far larger than themselves, yet as something of which they are a part, leading to a possible glimmer of soul recognition, but with God still firmly in charge. As they go through the inevitable Mature Soul 'dark nights of the soul,' they may question the nature of God and revise their early imprinting. And they might weave religion in with social issues, as with Rev. Jesse Jackson (Priest) and Rev. Martin Luther King, Jr. (Server).

- *Old Souls* who believe in God see it more as All That Is, both 'in here' and 'out there' at the same time. Any involvement with social issues may be exalted, as with early Old Soul Mother Teresa. Late Old Souls are usually on the way to soul recognition and accepting their place in their soul's cycle of reincarnation, having thrown off the denial by organized religion. In fact, Old Souls are rarely found in churches, except for Unity or Spiritualist.

Michael Teachings: The Optional Qualities

In addition to the two unchangeable qualities of Role and Soul Age, Michael identifies three variable personality components that *can* be chosen for each incarnation: Goal, Mode and Attitude.

Goal

Goal is the primary motivation in an incarnation, and soul sets up situations to facilitate goal achievement. Failure leaves you feeling blocked and frustrated; things flow smoothly when you're on track as helpers appear and events unfold with a sense of inevitability. Again, the table is organized along the four axes and the local/global distinction. (See Table 2.)

The Goals are:

- *Growth* (40%), the most common goal, results in a very active lifetime of seeking new experiences for their growth potential rather than for fun or enjoyment. In fact, this goal may actually involve suffering. For example, John Lennon and Yoko Ono are two Old souls in Growth. In entertainment, Kevin Costner, Tom Hanks and Shirley MacLaine are also doing Growth.

AXIS	LOCAL/ORDINAL		GLOBAL/CARDINAL	
INSPIRATION	**Reevaluation (1%)**		**Growth (40%)**	
	+ve Simplicity	−ve Withdrawal	+ve Evolution	−ve Confusion
EXPRESSION	**Discrimination (2%)**		**Acceptance (30%)**	
	+ve Sophistication	−ve Rejection	+ve Agape	−ve Ingratiation
ACTION	**Submission (10%)**		**Dominance (10%)**	
	+ve Devotion	−ve Exploitation	+ve Leadership	−ve Dictatorship
ASSIMILATION	**Flow (7%)**			
			+ve Free-flowing	−ve Stagnation

Table 2: Goals in the Michael System

- *Acceptance* (30%), the next most popular goal, involves a strong desire to explore accepting life's situations and being accepted by others. This may cause discomfort, but to assert oneself would risk rejection and cause even worse discomfort. Positive incarnations may be warm, friendly, altruistic, and understanding, and negatives may be insincere, with a false desire to please in order to avoid rejection. Mel Brooks and Pierce Brosnan are two Mature Sages with a Goal of Acceptance. Bill Clinton, too, although Hillary is in Dominance.

- *Submission* (10%) explores submission to the belief system of a guru, party or religious body. Depending on other qualities, it may result in either someone who is caring, helpful, sensitive, selfless, dedicated, and loyal, or someone who appears helpless, dependent, and a victim. Princess Diana explored Submission in her dealings with Britain's royal family and 'the Palace.' Mature Server, Martin Luther King, Jr. and Old Server Florence Nightingale dealt with it by committing their lives to larger causes.

- *Dominance* (10%) is the goal of taking charge in family, career, and social situations. So incarnations may be authoritative, determined, capable, and outgoing, or demanding, pushy, dominating, selfish, and insensitive. Actor George C. Scott (Mature Sage) was in Dominance, as was his most famous part, Mature Warrior Gen. George Patton.

- *Flow* (7%), a less common goal, is usually chosen for a rest life, for just going with the flow and enjoying a comfortable life-style with little drama, say, when born into a wealthy family, such as Britain's Prince Harry. So-called sex guru Baghwan Rajneesh is also a good example of someone in Flow.

- *Reevaluation* (1%) is a rare goal that involves introspection and consolidation, either before or after a 'busy' lifetime. Soul may arrange for a physical disability, such as Stephen Hawking and Helen Keller, mental incapacity such as Howard Hughes, or a temporary condition such as drug addiction.
- *Discrimination* (2%) is another rare and challenging goal usually associated with creating and resolving karma or exploring heavy judgment of one's own and others' life experiences. Incarnations may display prejudice and snobbishness, and be prickly and difficult in dealings with other people. Vincent Van Gogh, for example, was harshly critical of the Paris bourgeoisie, who did not appreciate his work. Also, Bette Davis criticized everything other people did and was generally difficult to work with.

Mode

Michael identifies the next quality of personality the soul chooses as *Mode*, or the primary form of expression and the approach taken to achieve the Goal. It is 'how you do things' behind 'what you do,' and how other people see you. (See Table 3.)

The seven Modes are:

- *Observation* (50%) is the preferred Mode of incarnations in the West, and involves watching as a way of learning and achieving goals. Its positive aspects are clarity, awareness, and alertness; its negative aspects are spying, obtaining information as a means of power and control, and jealousy. They make excellent commentators, such as Jim Lehrer, Jay Leno and Bill Moyers.
- *Power* mode (10%) exudes an outward sense of confidence, authority, flair and style. (For example, a Young King with a goal of Dominance and a

AXIS	LOCAL/ORDINAL		GLOBAL/CARDINAL	
INSPIRATION	**Repression (2%)**		**Passion (10%)**	
	+ve Restraint	−ve Inhibition	+ve Actualization	−ve Identification
EXPRESSION	**Caution (20%)**		**Power (10%)**	
	+ve Deliberation	−ve Phobia	+ve Authority	−ve Oppression
ACTION	**Perseverance (4%)**		**Aggression (4%)**	
	+ve Persistence	−ve Immutability	+ve Dynamism	−ve Belligerence
ASSIMILATION	**Observation (50%)**			
		+ve Clarity	−ve Surveillance	

Table 3: Modes in the Michael System

mode of Power would be a formidable force to reckon with, as was Alexander the Great.) Its positive aspects are a commanding presence (as with Madonna, a King), a natural assumption of responsibility, and stepping in to take over when others hold back, such as Henry Ford and H. Ross Perot. On the negative side, an incarnation may threaten, bully, and push others around, as did Ivan the Terrible.

- Passion mode (10%) involves intense emotions and movement based on what the incarnation feels. Mature souls often choose Passion so they can identify with others, but their responses can cause energetic chaos, as did Lucille Ball. Positive qualities are self-awareness, intensity, and aliveness, as with actors Richard Burton and Martin Sheen. If negative, watch for over-involvement with dramatic situations, such as friends' problems.

- Perseverance (4%) says, "Do it until it's right," which differs from stubbornness by not being rooted in a fear of loss of integrity. This mode focuses on the problem and drives relentlessly at minute detail, as with Gandhi, who toiled endlessly to free India from British rule, and Nelson Mandela of South Africa. It may manifest as self-discipline, endurance and ruggedness, or an inability to focus on the big picture.

- Aggression (4%) says, "My way or no way," and can show up as dynamism, risk-taking, fast action, and adventure-seeking. Or if blocked, it can be belligerent, destructive, and being on the offensive, as with Khrushchev and his famous shoe-banging incident at the United Nations, and Mussolini's famous strutting stance. Teddy Roosevelt and Arnold Schwarzenegger are both Young Warriors in Aggression.

- Caution (2%) shows up as either careful risk-avoidance or a fear of doing something wrong, always worried about the consequences, and terror of responsibility. Almost by definition, those in this mode do not become famous. Author Stephen King is a notable exception.

- *Repression* or *Reserve* (2%) involves holding the self in and uncertainty of one's own feelings. On the positive side, it's self-contained, self-disciplined, and refined; on the negative, it's being emotionally blocked, withdrawn, reserved, and unable to express oneself. Actor Hugh Grant is a good example.

Attitude

Attitude is the third quality, and the primary perspective with which we look at the world, which determines what things we take into account and how we interpret them when deciding what to do and what position to take on issues. Attitude determines how we see the world and through this, we then use our Mode to go about achieving our Goal. (See Table 4.)

The seven attitudes are:

- *Realist* (30%), which sees situations, experiences and relationships with clarity and simplicity. The Realist sees all sides and helps others out of confusion. Those with positive traits live in the moment and see what's going on. They flow with things rather than trying to change them. Scholars often choose an attitude of Realist, as has the author. Realists tend to show up more in older soul ages, having begun to dissolve the ego's insistence that things be other than they are.

- *Idealist* (30%) is enthusiastic about making progress, but are full of 'ought's' and 'should's,' and may put others on a pedestal, only to be disappointed if they fall short. Idealists can suffer from low self-esteem when failing to meet their own very high standards, but they can also be a model of how to meet the fullest personal potential as their eternal dissatisfaction stimulates much growth and progress. Priests often choose this attitude, as did Ralph Nader, the tireless campaigner.

- *Pragmatist* (20%) tends to see things in terms of simplicity and efficiency, although not always in the most pleasurable way. Notions of productivity may cause them to avoid the 'scenic route' and stopping to smell the flowers. They can become workaholics, ignoring emotions, beauty, relationships, etc., as we see with Donald Trump. On the positive side, they are efficient, simple, sensible, and functional. On the negative, they are opinionated, narrow-minded, rigid and ruled by the rules, as with Richard Nixon and Pat Robertson.

AXIS	LOCAL/ORDINAL		GLOBAL/CARDINAL	
INSPIRATION	**Stoic (5%)**		**Spiritualist (5%)**	
	+ve Tranquility	−ve Resignation	+ve Verification	−ve Faith
EXPRESSION	**Skeptic (5%)**		**Idealist (30%)**	
	+ve Investigation	−ve Suspicion	+ve Coalescense	−ve Naivete
ACTION	**Cynic (5%)**		**Realist (30%)**	
	+ve Contradiction	−ve Denigration	+ve Objectivity	−ve Subjectivity
ASSIMILATION	**Pragmatist (20%)**			
		+ve Practicability	−ve Dogmatism	

Table 4: Attitudes in the Michael System

- *Stoic* (5%) takes the attitude that whatever happens is to be borne and that is okay because it's all part of the fabric of life. This attitude leads to dampening of feelings and putting up with adverse circumstances without speaking up. (This attitude suits Warriors and Servers, exemplified by Queen Elizabeth II who completely surrendered her personal life to her public persona.)

- *Spiritualist* (5%) sees the big picture with a broad perspective, how things *could* be, and what others could achieve if only they tried. Although often drawn to religion, as with Tammy Bakker, the vision could be applied to any arena. Taking things on faith may make them naïve and gullible.

- *Skeptic* (5%) is the natural doubter and disbeliever. Their highly intellectual and conceptual approach takes a "Too good to be true" attitude, and the better it is, the greater the doubt, as with actor Woody Allen.

- *Cynic* (5%) takes Skeptic to the next level of "It will never work," which is often a self-fulfilling prophecy. Cynics can be natural humorists, seeing the other side of the world of idealists, as do comedians Whoopie Goldberg and George Carlin.

Why do we need seven different perspectives on life rather than one absolute viewpoint? According to Michael, we each live in our chosen Attitude as our native natural viewpoint. This colors our entire view of the world, ourselves and other people, but we can visit other attitudes and often do. We can cultivate the habit of being aware of our Attitude at any point in time, and being able to envision how a situation would look from another attitude.

Also, reality is multidimensional and no one human being can handle all aspects of any situation, so we must specialize in only one or two aspects during one lifetime. The combined understanding of *all* lifetimes occurs at the soul level. Also, during one lifetime, we associate with people of differing perspectives and must therefore stretch to recognize other views. Recognizing the validity of one's own and others' views is a maturing process. On the Earth plane level, there are no truths, no right views and no wrong views, and we must overcome the danger of invalidating ourselves in order to be accepted and to conform to the majority. Further, understanding that the seven basic attitudes inevitably mean that individuals must see things differently, allows us to accept why people differ.

Challenges

Finally, souls take on one or more *Challenges* as a stumbling block designed to neutralize our attempts to achieve the Goal. But why do we need such a handicap?

Without obstacles, life would be a breeze, we would meet no opposition and achieve little growth--so we build in Challenges to push us to a higher level. Coming to know your Challenge explains much about your reactions and allows you to overcome the 'first strike' mode. You become more understanding and therefore tolerant of the behavior of self and others.

Challenge varies greatly in intensity and degree, and is usually selected by adulthood but may change many times. Old Souls may not manifest any challenges at all. Some Challenges can be self-karmic, holding you back, leading to self-blocking, self-destruction, self-deprecation and martyrdom. Others may lead you to be outgoing and self-serving in terms of greed, arrogance and impatience.

The Challenges that Michael identifies are (see Table 5):

- *Arrogance* (15%), stemming from a fear of *being judged wanting*. Low esteem is covered by a veneer of appearing to feel okay or superior, often deceiving even the self. You attract a great deal of attention to yourself, so much so that you can react by appearing shy. Fearing that others will pass judgment and find you wanting, you may pass heavy judgment on yourself and project any shortcomings on to others. It looks like a shield held up for protection or a 'cardboard cutout' of the sort of person you would like to be. Any penetration of such a shield mortifies you. You can erase this Challenge by building your self-esteem and realizing your self-worth. Saddam Hussein, Osama bin Laden and Mohammed Ali are typical.

AXIS	LOCAL/ORDINAL		GLOBAL/CARDINAL	
INSPIRATION	**Self-deprecation (10%)**		**Arrogance (15%)**	
	+ve Humility	−ve Abasement	+ve Pride	−ve Vanity
EXPRESSION	**Self-destruction (10%)**		**Greed (15%)**	
	+ve Sacrifice	−ve Suicidal	+ve Appetite	−ve Voracity
ACTION	**Martyrdom(15%)**		**Impatience (15%)**	
	+ve Selflessness	−ve Victimization	+ve Audacity	−ve Intolerance
ASSIMILATION	**Stubbornness (20%)**			
		+ve Obstinacy	−ve Determination	

Table 5: Challenges in the Michael System

- *Self-destruction* (10%) is based on the fear that *life is not worth having*, and can lead to self-sabotage through drugs, alcohol, and masochism, as with Martin Downey, Jr., Jimmy Hendrix, Jim Morrison and Janis Joplin.
- *Greed* (15%) shows the fear of *not having enough*. It may also show up as a need for ever more experiences or relationships, which may ironically drive others away. Jimmy and Tammy Fae Bakker are good examples of Young Souls in Greed.
- *Martyrdom* (15%) is based on the fear of *being a victim of circumstance*. Martyrs constantly complain about how they suffer for others, and how they are victims of others' pleasure and freedom. Silent martyrs hold that their suffering is too great to talk about, or that no one wants to hear. They can never acknowledge pleasure for fear of damaging the image. James Dean typified this while alive.
- *Impatience* (15%) arises from the fear of *missing out on something* that others might enjoy or use up, to your detriment. May easily slide over to Martyrdom if one feels helping others is responsible for missing out.
- *Stubbornness* (20%) fears *loss of integrity* or one's position, so it takes a stand in the face of real or imagined opposition, as with crusader Billy Graham.
- *Self-deprecation* (10%) stems from a fear of *inadequacy*, in which you assume your self-worth to be low and apologize in advance. Despite protestations on the part of others, you eventually annoy others, resulting in a self-fulfilling prophecy. We saw this clearly with Beatles George Harrison and Ringo Starr.

Baby and Mature souls select Martyrdom and Impatience to facilitate these Ages' lessons in interacting with others and experiencing feeling out of control. Infant souls select Greed for amassing material for survival and Young souls use Greed to prove they are winners. Old souls tend towards Self-deprecation and Arrogance to examine questions of self-worth that come from knowing too much in some ways yet not enough in others.

Personality Density

Personality density is also important. Imagine that each of the five main personality components is a sheet of plastic colored by the chosen trait to some extent, where the denser the coloration, the more the personality trait is evident. Then put the five sheets together and shine a light through them, analogous to the light of the soul. A 'strong' personality will block the soul's light and deny the soul much influence in that incarnation's life. Lighter hues, however, will allow more soul light through, which will have more say in that lifetime. The softer ego will better hear and listen to the soul's bidding. With a great teacher such as Yogananda, personality can be fully transparent.

Centering

Centering determines how we will react in the moment to a sudden stimulus, and the soul also chooses which centering will predominate. Centers are the communication channels between spirit (soul fragment) and personality, and determine how you will act most naturally when faced with an unexpected situation—whether you think, act or feel first. Your centering may create difficulty in understanding those with different centers. For example, the intellectual center cannot easily appreciate the emotional center and may see it as hysterical. On the other hand, the emotional center may see the other as cold. We all have all three centers, and understanding that each center is prejudiced in its own favor increases self-knowledge and allows you to understand how other people, operating from different centers, interpret and respond to the world.

In more detail:

- *Intellectual Center* is linked to the fifth chakra and holds concepts and reasoning. The units of storage are words and vocabulary, hence retrieval is slower than for the other centers. The center stores the 'intention' behind the operation of the other centers, so a strong intellect will ensure consistency of effort until a job is done rather than until the personality is tired or bored. This center also operates in linear time, relating cause and effect, and past, present and future. In a positive intellectual center, original ideas appear spontaneously out of nowhere; a negative center logically relates a series of ideas, slowly and tediously.

- *Emotional Center*, linked to the Heart chakra, holds perceptions and feelings. Emotional responses are fast and dramatic, backed by the body's physiological responses to internal and external stimuli. Over-development of the Emotional center results in hysterical behavior, but when balanced with the Intellectual center, the result is open and responsive emotion. A positive center is direct and perceptive in its assessment of situations. A negative center gets caught in excessive and irrelevant feelings, blocked from true feeling by nostalgia, for example.

- *Moving Center* is connected to the Solar Plexus chakra (3rd), and holds all that pertains to physical activity, e.g., walking, sports. Moving centered people are whirrs of activity and excel at physical doing. A positive centering works on enduring projects, buildings, etc., and a negative centering dissipates energy by being restless, fidgety and hyper.

Body Type

Michael also identifies body type as a soul choice. Of the seven main body types, most soul fragments combine two, three or four. The body itself has a personality based on its type make-up, and we all have our preferences as to body type in a mated relationship. Body types are:

- *Solar*, petite, even child-like, such as the models of the 1960s.
- *Lunar*, pale, slender, often moon-faced.
- *Venusian*, voluptuous sex symbol-type build.
- *Mercurial*, volatile, swift, and lithe.
- *Saturnian*, tall, athletic and thin, possibly with sullen or pouting features.
- *Martian*, slim, active, always on the go, working out or jogging.
- *Jovian*, typified by the jolly fat person who tends to be passive and enjoys good food and drink.

Bodies themselves have a natural temperament that the soul must work with ... or work around. This can be a source of harmony or conflict for the entire incarnation.

The Nine Needs

Whereas the personality overleaves determine how we respond to the outside world, our needs focus our efforts and drive us through life, giving us a wonderful sense of inner peace when they are satisfied. Michael identifies Nine Needs as: Security, Adventure, Freedom, Expansion, Power, Expression, Acceptance, Communion, and Exchange. Most people select three primary needs when very young, and tend to keep them for the rest of their life.

Read over the descriptions of all the nine needs, and rank them from 1 to 9 in terms of importance to you or another. Or, group them into three tiers: most important, medium, and least. Then, for each need in the top tier, reflect on how you structure your life to meet it. Also, if any need in your top tier is not being satisfied for you, brainstorm changes you can make so that it is.

Repeat the exercise for the people closest to you, talking about your results with them to ensure accuracy. This will reveal to both of you that people act from their own highest needs, not just from a desire to be a pain.

The Nine Needs identified by Michael are:

1. *Security*. Happy with the status quo, these folks don't like to rock the boat because this could mean change. All their decisions are based on ensuring that everything will be all right. Wary of change, they're obsessively cautious, avoid taking risks, and are paralyzed by fear of the new. People with this need who are love-based feel safe, balanced, grounded and connected. Those who live from fear are paralyzed, indecisive, unable to function due to insecurity, and retaliate against those who want to implement change.

2. *Adventure*. The need for Adventure drives people to seek exciting new experiences such as sky-diving or hang-gliding for the adrenaline rush. They love to take risks, meet challenges, plan new trips, start up a new company, create new markets, change jobs, cars and houses every year, and solve new problems. People living from love have higher self-confidence, optimism, and enthusiasm for living. Those living from fear can be reckless, irresponsible, or create crises for their own sake.

3. *Freedom*. Those with this need lead lives with room for independence and spontaneity. They seek mobility, and the opportunity to make their own choices. You won't find them working 9-5, in the standard business 'uniform,' and subject to deadlines imposed by other people. If love-based, these people are self-confident, responsible, and with high self-esteem. Fear-based, they avoid responsibility, relationships, and therefore true intimacy.

4. *Exchange*. These folks are driven to trade information and knowledge with others, through conversation, communication, energy, friendship, services and shared experiences. People with a need for exchange are concerned about the flow of energy in all types of relationships. They like to see things "moving" in some way that expresses balanced equality, integrity and an equal exchange. If love-based, they form solid but dynamic relationships, and promote equality in all interactions. If fear-based, they keep secrets, withhold communications, and gossip, lie and criticize.

5. *Power*. The need for power puts people in charge as an 'authority' in their area of specialty. They tend to be self-disciplined, and good organizers and leaders. If love-based, they wield their power for the greater good; if fear-based, the need to control is obsessive, often to the point of tyranny.

6. *Expansion*. This is the need to build, create, or expand something that no one has done before, whether it is a building, financial empire, or country.

If love-based, these folks show growth and expansion; and know the value of art, science, nature, and physical and spiritual laws. If fear-based, it's growth for its own sake, possibly causing confusion and spiritual separation.

7. *Expression.* People with this need are driven to express their creativity through words, speech, art, music, or dance. If love-based, their creativity benefits self and others; if fear-based, they can be self-centered and intrusive.

8. *Acceptance.* The need for acceptance has people wanting to belong. They are usually easy-going and pleasant to fit in with a group, whether family, work team, church, or club. Acceptance also means being tolerant of self and others. Being love-based leads to understanding, bonding, forgiveness of self and others, and altruistic gestures. Fear-based people experience rejection, jealousy, prejudice, guilt and shame.

9. *Community.* This need drives people toward family orientation and social settings for their own sake. Unlike Acceptance, these people just don't like being alone, and look for any excuse to bring people together, where they are great hosts. If love-based, they're happiest when in a group or when friends drop by. If fear-based, there can be a sense of desperation and an indiscriminate seeking of the company of anyone just to avoid being alone.

The Nine Needs and Relationships

Fulfilling your needs is strictly your responsibility, and not that of your mate, spouse, friends, children or shrink. For this task, relationships are vital. Because we attract people like us, chances are they will share similar needs in a similar ranking. Relationships between people who have no needs in common have little connection or content, and often lead to domestic strife and karma. If a husband wants to learn sky-diving but his wife prefers shopping at the mall, the relationship may well founder. So before making a long-term commitment to a relationship, determine the needs ranking for your proposed partner.

The Michael Teaching is an awesome body of information that makes it okay to be who we are. If someone else is different from you, it's not that they're wrong and you're right, or vice versa; their overleaves make them who they are at the personality level and yours make you who you are. And you're both okay. We at the soul level carefully chose our overleaves for specific purposes, so apart from the need to migrate from any negative poles to their positive equivalent, you're perfect just the way you are. So, if you're emotionally centered and your mate is intellectual, neither of you is going to change the other, so learn to live with them as they are... or without them.

Comprehensive though the Teaching is, its main value lies in revealing we are more than just a bunch of overleaves; we are also the being that put them together before incarnating here. And through *that* being, we are an intimate part of the creator Source.

The whole intent of spiritual work is to render ego-personality more transparent and let the light of soul shine through more brightly. However, that does not mean eradicate ego-personality, but just drop some density—the worries and preoccupations that block the love, joy, peace and harmony of Spirit. As we open to these, everything becomes more immediate and vibrant, and we can study the intricate dance of the universe with childlike wonder.

How do we do this? Most self-help books are 'one size fits all'—everyone is urged to do the same thing—meditate this way, deal with anger that way. But the Michael Teaching offers *over half a million combinations!* (7 Ages, 7 Roles, 7 Goals, 7 Modes, 7 Attitudes, and 7 Challenges, each with two poles—and this is just the simple stuff; we haven't even talked about the Michael Math.)

The Teachings offer guidance on how to work with each of those combinations, and how to transmute fear-based negative poles into their love-based opposites. This is essential groundwork in order to live more with soul. Michael's model is an outstanding tool for examining another tool—our ego-personality—and for putting us in touch with the tool-maker and tool-user, our soul. Once we can regard our ego as a tool for executing soul's agenda, all manner of problems fall away, such as addictions of any kind, and relationship problems. For a tool to take itself so seriously and put itself ahead of soul's agenda becomes laughable. The overleaves are a great way to transmute fear-based False Personality into love-based True Personality ... and then you're living with soul.

In summary, the benefits of studying the Michael Teaching are:

1. Greater self-awareness of who you really are—a soul wearing a 'suit' of personality overlays for a lifetime. This allows you to transcend personality and go 'transpersonal.'

2. The realization that our main freedom is one of *choice*—the power to *choose* how to respond to situations, free of autopilot's knee-jerk reactions to things and people. As a sovereign soul, you have complete autonomy in your life, because you set it up. Once you have mastered the basics of

Michael's system, you can begin to choose how you move around in it, for example, sliding from a negative pole to its opposite positive pole, i.e., moving from a fear-based reaction into a love-based response. (This huge subject is well-covered in the mountains of Michael Teaching books available and on the voluminous site: www.michaelteachings.com.)

3. Realizing that personality is a tool that soul creates in order to better understand the Earth plane on behalf of the Source, leads to realizing that the main flow of information should not be from soul to ego, but from ego to soul. An Earth plane life is not about illuminating and informing the ego about soul, but about soul learning all it can from ego. If ego feels bruised by this, tough. Earth plane lives should be soul-centric, not ego-centric, with soul's agenda running the show, not ego's agenda. Of course, soul would prefer ego to live in joy, but childhood imprinting can batter ego, so that it self-sabotages itself into a life of misery and pain. Hence the importance of choice … once you realize you even *have* choice.

4. Acceptance of other people as souls doing the same thing as you, only with different 'suits,' which makes it okay for everyone to be perfect exactly as they are. You don't need to change others, and they have no right to try to change you.

5. Greater insights into what motivates others and makes them tick, so you can dump the blinders and deal with people as they are and not as you would like them to be.

(The body of Michael Material grows every day as channels bring more in, so stay up-to-date by visiting the websites of the Michael authors listed in the Resources section.)

The Enneagram View

Another fascinating model of ego-personality lies in the Enneagram, brought into modern times by one of Gurdjieff's students, Chilean Oscar Ichazo, in the mid-20th century (some say, given to him by the Michael Entity). The Enneagram consists of nine 'types,' or ways of coping with the outside world and other people, arranged around a circle (so that no one type is 'better' than the others). It is an outstanding diagnostic tool for looking at yourself, your motivations, fears, ideals and aspirations … and those of others, too.

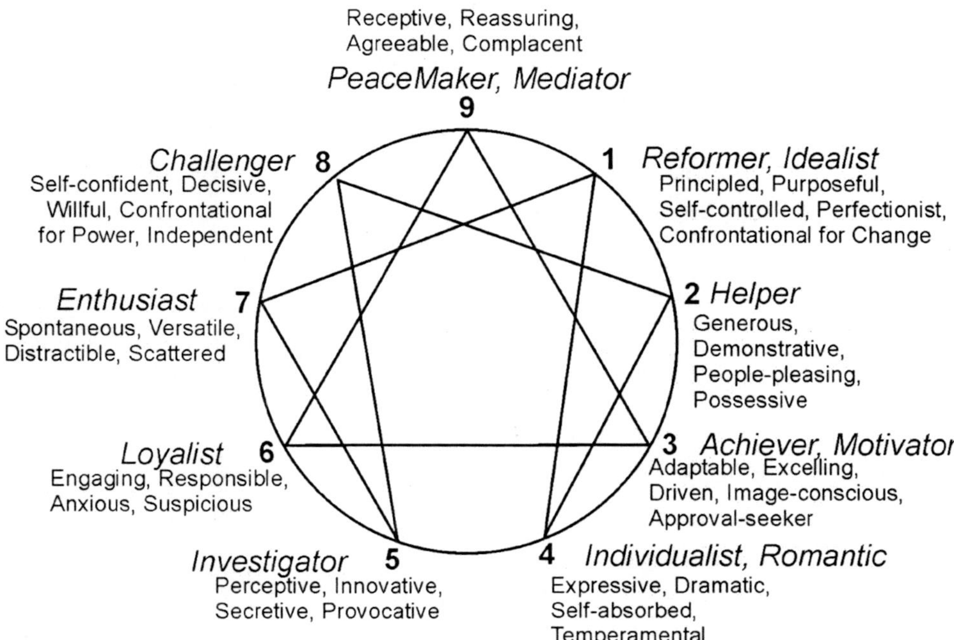

Basic Enneagram Model

The nine Enneagram types are:

- *Type One: The Reformer*—the Ralph Nader type, driven by what they believe to be right but, at the low end of the scale, they can aggressively get in other people's faces. Other famous Ones are Hilary Clinton, Ms. Manners, and Martha Stewart.

- *Type Two: The Helper*—driven by the need to give and receive love, either at the humanitarian level, as with Mother Teresa and Princess Diana, or at the interpersonal level. (Prince Charles thwarted Diana's interpersonal Twoness.) The Two's 'help' ranges from pure altruism to manipulation to achieve their agenda.

- *Type Three: The Achiever, The Motivator*—relentlessly driven by career and life goals, and by the need for admiration from the rest of us. Because the U.S. is a Three society, they may be showered with rewards, but the self-esteem they project may be covering up deep insecurity. Famous Threes include Arnold Schwarzenegger, Tony Robbins, and Britney Spears.

- *Type Four: The Individualist, The Romantic*—driven by an attachment to understand their own emotional processes, they can be self-indulgent drama queens, who leave a string of maudlin relationships behind them. Unable to deal with today's complex world, they can spiral down into addictions of various kinds. Michael Jackson, Wynona Ryder and John Lennon are famous Fours.

- *Type Five: The Thinker*—known for their sharp intellect, they are driven to understand the world and predict what it will do next, often as an attempt to control it. The Five can range from a towering intellect to antisocial weirdness. Famous Fives include Nikola Tesla, Stephen Hawking, Charles Darwin and Isaac Newton.

- *Type Six: The Loyalist*—driven by the need for safety, security and trust, Sixes place high value on loyalty, so betray them at your peril. They work best in groups ('safety in numbers'), to which they will prove totally loyal, while holding back a little 'just in case.' Mel Gibson, Adolph Hitler and George H. Bush are famous Sixes.

- *Type Seven: The Enthusiast*—driven by the need for action, experiences, and fulfilling their dreams, they are talented, exuberant, and full of curiosity. Their youthful outlook and love of beauty makes them fun to be around, except when there's a boring, routine task to attend to, in which case they vanish. Famous Sevens include John F. Kennedy, Madonna, Jesse Ventura and Howard Stern.

- *Type Eight: The Challenger, The Confronter*—driven by the need for power and autonomy, Eights are natural 'winners' (just about every player on a football field is an Eight, as is the team itself). Energized by conflict, they hurl themselves into situations that would scare the rest of us. Joseph Stalin, George W. Bush, Vladamir Putin, Rosie O'Donnell and Bruce Lee are famous Eights.

- *Type Nine: The PeaceMaker, The Mediator*—not driven at all, but just happy to go quietly with the flow. Accepting and supportive of others, they make excellent listeners, even to the point of not looking out for their own best interests. However, once riled up, they can be relentless and unstoppable. Famous Nines include Nelson Mandela, Tiger Woods, Prince Charles and the Dalai Lama.

How do you learn which type you are? The best way is to read descriptions about all nine types and figure which one best fits you. Or you can to the website of The Enneagram Institute, founded in 1995 by Don Riso and Russ Hudson and take their short online test for free (the full test costs $10 to take) at: www.enneagraminstitute.com/dis_sample_36.asp.

Levels of Development

Although not originally part of the Enneagram body of knowledge, the notion of Levels of Development was added by Riso and Hudson to give depth to the otherwise two-dimensional enneagram. The nine levels fall into three groups, which also correspond to the concept of the three sub-types of social, relational and self-preservational:

- *Average levels (4 – 6),* where people are in conflict and seek to manipulate each other to get their psychological needs met. They identify fully with ego, having no concept of spirit or soul. As level 5 devolves to 6, he can overcompensate and become more aggressive in his manipulation. As anxiety and stress increase, he pursues his agenda without regard for others.
- *Unhealthy levels (7 – 9),* where personality becomes increasingly defensive and destructive. These unconscious, autopilot modes are ultimately self-defeating, as one ends up in jail … or dead.
- *Healthy levels (1 – 3),* where we become progressively less defensive of the ego-personality, and more in tune with society, the environment and spirit. Ultimately, we transcend the personality and identify fully with spirit.

	Level	Level Quality
HEALTHY	1	Liberation, identifies fully with spirit
LEVELS	2	Broad psychological capacity
(Social)	3	Social value, balances self with society
AVERAGE	4	Imbalance, with self before society
LEVELS	5	Interpersonal control over others
(Relational)	6	Overcompensation and aggression
UNHEALTHY	7	Violation
LEVELS	8	Obsession and compulsion
(Self-pres.)	9	Pathological destruction Courtesy Riso/Hudson

Levels of Development appear to align with Michael's concept of Soul Age, with Infant Souls matching the pathological destruction of Level 9 (serial killers such as Son of Sam, Ted Bundy and the various 'stranglers' throughout history). These levels correspond to the self-preservational subtype, where the person seeks to control or gain approval of the self, with little or no regard for others. Baby Souls can be quite obsessive and compulsive, to the point of violating the peaceful rights of others to 'just be.' Young Souls clearly exhibit Level 4 and 5 behavior, and correspond to seeking to control or gain approval from others in one-on-one relationships. Mature Souls show Level 3, and Old Souls, Levels 1 and 2. Healthy levels are more comfortable in social interaction with groups. Of course, in the

Michael system, you can't change your Soul Age, but you can try acting older. In the Riso/Hudson levels, you can strive for a more healthy level by study and emulation … which leads to traversing the enneagram.

Traversing the Enneagram

The Enneagram is far from a cop-out, as in, "I'm a Four, so you'll just have to love me as I am," or, "So, I'm in your face. What do you expect? I'm an Eight! Deal with it!"

The internal lines reveal how one can move fluidly to other types. *Integration* occurs as stress levels fall and you feel more confident and at ease in the world. Being a Five normally, I would flow to an Eight as I felt more sure, possibly moving to a more healthy Level of Development at the same time, which would bring out the magnanimous generosity of a Healthy Eight. Then I would slide to a Two, where I would empower others through unconditional love and an outpouring of spirit into the world. Well, at least that's the plan.

However, if I was stressed out and in fear, I would *disintegrate* by sliding to a Seven and maybe dropping a level, and suffer the mood swings of an Unhealthy Seven. I might start to react impulsively, or just get drunk to quell the fear. If things got worse, I'd go to One and look for someone to blame, because "I'm obviously the target of some evil conspiracy!"

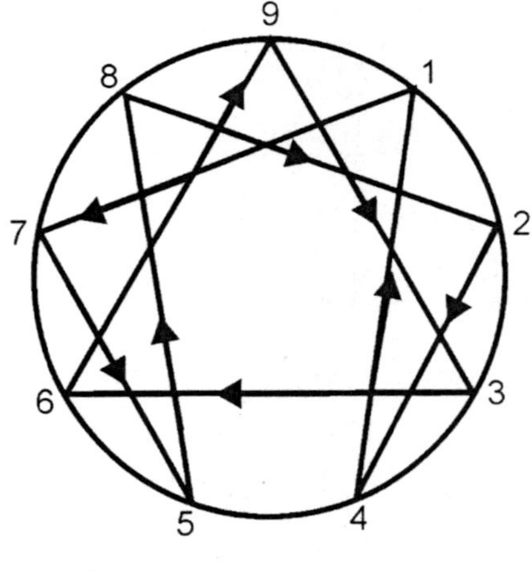

INTEGRATION

1-7-5-8-2-4-1
9-3-6-9

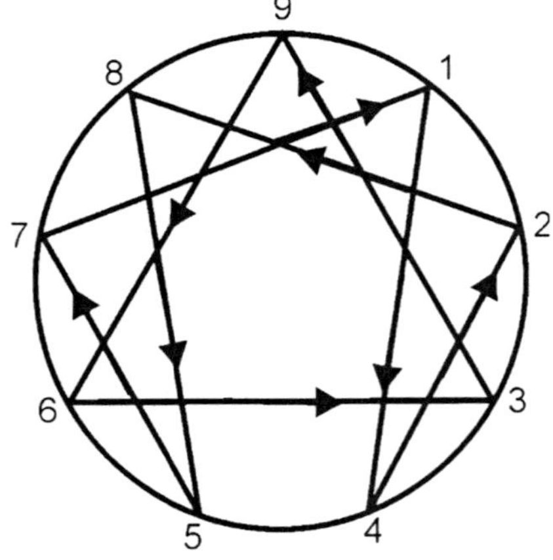

DISINTEGRATION

1-4-2-8-5-7-1
9-6-3-9

The Value of the Enneagram

Used correctly, the Enneagram is another valuable tool for personal growth and spiritual development through analyzing the ego-personality tool:

- It's a tool that reveals how we view and cope with the world. Critics claim 'it puts us in a box,' but really it reveals that we're *already* in a box—our trancelike ego-personality. Once we see that, we can begin to dissolve the walls of the box and embrace soul with greater exuberance.

- Just as the Michael Teaching helps us accept that it's okay to be as we are (our Role, Goal, Mode, Attitude, etc., are perfect just the way soul designed them), the Enneagram makes it okay for you and everyone else to be the very personality types you all are. So people do not need to go around trying to change others to be more like them. However, knowing about the other types allows you to flow around the circle, 'borrowing' any desired personality traits.

- The Enneagram opens your eyes to your interaction with others and leads to an immediacy of, "Why did I just say/do that?" It also helps avoid the trap of trying to be spiritual without first having completed the psychological work of clearing the baggage you've gathered during your life so far. Otherwise, your spiritual house will be built on sand, with no foundation.

- As with the Michael Teaching, the growth from working with the Enneagram may bring up pain that needs to be soothed away. It will also help you define better personal boundaries. This all leads to healthy self-acceptance, and ultimately to profound self-love.

Of course, this brief account doesn't even scratch the surface, and the Resources section lists some excellent online sources of primer material available on the Internet.

Astrology

Another model of personality commonly used is that offered by astrology. Astrology is about the interaction between the planets (including the Sun and Moon), the 12 Signs of the zodiac into which the heavens are divided, and the 12 Houses into which the various aspects of life fall. When you were born, the planets were each in a Sign, and all made certain angles with the Earth (called aspects), so their unique 4th-dimensional energy influenced your new body.

The planets each represent an energetic influence and, at the moment of your birth, appeared in a particular Sign, meaning they each influence an aspect of your life. The important thing to remember is that your life is not the way it is because of what the planets were doing, but you-the-soul chose your moment of birth in order to get those influences. You were the cause; the astrology was the result, and not the other way round. So astrology explains the influences and challenges that you-the-soul brought into your life, which gives you clues about how you can use your 'starting point' strengths to grow and evolve, and the areas you need to work on.

Just as the Michael model describes our *internal* personality make-up, astrology relates to the *exterior* world that soul chooses to best support (or challenge) personality.

The three most influential contributors to that life are: 1) the sign the Sun was in when you were born; 2) the sign of your Ascendant (i.e., the Sign just rising on the horizon); 3) the sign the Moon was in. The Sun Sign reflects who you are at the ego-personality level; the Ascendant reflects how you appear to others, and the Moon tells you much about the inner forces at work in your personality. The 12 Sun Signs (i.e., the Sun falls in that sign) are:

- *Aries* are leaders and organizers. As the first Sign of the Zodiac, they are first in line to get things going. King Souls often choose this Sun sign.
- *Taurus* loves the physical pleasures and material goods of life. They enjoy tender, sensual touch, comfort and being surrounded by pleasing, soothing things. Warrior Souls feel comfortable in Taurus.
- *Geminis* love to talk, being driven by their minds. Intellectually inclined, they are forever probing people and places in search of information. Scholar Souls thrive under this sign.
- *Cancer* takes great pleasure in the comforts of home and family. Maternal and domestic, they love to nurture others. Server Souls are at home in Cancer.
- *Leo* loves being center stage, and their personal magnetism puts them there. Ambitious and purposeful, they accomplish a great deal in life. King, Sage and Warrior Souls make good Leos.
- *Virgo* rightfully earns the reputation of being picky and critical, or attentive to detail, as they put it. Serving others by taking care of the little things brings them great joy. Server Souls love being Virgos.
- *Libra* focuses on balancing the needs of the individual with the needs of the world. Sage Souls find this useful, especially in a political arena.

- *Scorpio* focuses on the essential questions, the secrets behind the scenes, beginnings and endings, and life and death, which helps Artisan Souls.
- *Sagittarians* are truth-seekers, so they talk to anyone who may have some answers. Knowledge is key to these folks, which aligns this sign with Scholar Souls.
- *Capricorn* is all about hard work, and their ambition and determination ensure success by taking a businesslike approach to life. Warriors find this Sign useful.
- *Aquarius* has the social conscience needed to carry us into the new millennium. Humanitarian and philanthropic, they strive to make the world a better place. This fits well with the King Soul's agenda.
- *Pisces* are selfless, spiritual and very focused on their inner journey. Being a water sign, they also place great weight on their feelings. Server and Priest Souls are found opting for this sign.

Add to your Sun Sign the sign that was just on the horizon at the moment of your birth, for that influences how others see you. For example, I am a Gemini Sun, Gemini Ascendant and a Capricorn Moon. This means I love to communicate, people see me as a communicator, and I am driven to work hard on what I am communicating. As an Old Scholar here to teach, that was a perfect astrological choice on my soul's part.

Your astrological profile is no accident of birth, therefore. Your soul worked hard—and may have put your mother through a long labor—in order to get the exact set of planetary influences it needed for the moment of birth, i.e., your natal chart. So your personality is not the result of your astrology; your astrology is the result of careful soul choices.

Life Path Number

Here's another fascinating game for soul to play, and is based on one's date of birth. To derive your Life Path Number, write out your birth date as, for example:

January 2, 1980 = 1 + 2 + 1 + 9 + 8 + 0 = 21 / 3.

Some numerologists claim that your Life Path Number is simply 3, but others claim you will live as a 2 until about age 30, and then as a 1 until age 45, by which time, you manifest as a 3. From the following descriptions, you be the judge.

One caveat: if your Number ends up as 11, 22 or 33, these are master numbers, so do not distill down to 2, 4, or 6 (except on 'bad hair days,' when you will not feel like a master number). For example, I was born on June 6, 1947, which gives me:

$$6 + 6 + 1 + 9 + 4 + 7 = 33.$$

Does this mean that everyone born on the same day as I was is destined to be a world teacher (not my claim, but just the agreed upon designation for 33s)? Yes ... or manifest as an exalted 6. If the numerologists are right, then your soul may well plan your birth for a specific Life Path Number. (Of course, there's much more to numerology than this, just as there's more to astrology than your Sun Sign.)

Here are the interpretations:

1. *Individualism, Independence* —1's stand on their own two feet and do not depend on others. Includes many military, political and corporate leaders. Such people are creative and have the drive and enthusiasm to accomplish a great deal. This stems from an enormous depth of strength, determination and the ability to lead. This is coupled with strong personal needs and desire to follow one's own convictions, often to the point of aggressive self-promotion.

2. *Sensitivity and Balance* —2's see the full spectrum of viewpoints in any argument or situation, which makes them good mediators. They can settle disputes with the most unbiased outcomes, showing sincere concern for others and wanting the best for them. They are totally open and honest, and excel where expertise is needed in handling people and achieving compromise.

3. *Creativity, Self-expression and Sociability* — 3's appear as bright, effervescent, sparkling people with exceptional creative skills, whether verbal, written, speaking, artistic or acting. They are passionate about harmony and beauty. 3's are warm, friendly, and good conversationalists.

4. *Down-to-earth, Trustworthy, and Practical* — 4's demand much from themselves. They are excellent organizers and planners, based on strong common sense. Once they make up their mind, they persevere through to the conclusion, for better or worse. They are obsessively set in their ways and determined to do things their way. They are also loyal, devoted, and dependable.

5. *Adventurous, Progressive and Versatile* — 5's are always striving to answer life's questions. Passionate about freedom and independence, they avoid routine and boring work, and dread deadlines. Good communicators, they

easily motivate other people to explore and blaze new trails. They live a serendipitous life, and do not worry much about tomorrow.

6. *Shouldering Responsibility and Being Needed* — 6's are known for their advice, support and service. They lead by example and always take responsibility. Strong yet compassionate, their wisdom, balance, and understanding are the cornerstones of this Life Path. Their extraordinary wisdom and the ability to understand others' problems allows them to bear more than their fair share of life's burdens.

7. *Reserved, Thoughtful and Analytical* — 7's mine every situation for what they can learn. Studious and intellectual, they dissect issues and come to their own independent conclusion. Their spiritual wisdom also calls for alone and quiet time, and avoidance of confusion, crowds and noise. It also means that their gut feelings can be very accurate.

8. *Material Wealth and Success* — 8's tend to be forceful and competitive, as their ambitions and ability strive to 'have it all.' Competitive to the max, they manage themselves and their world well. In the extreme, obsession with material success can eclipse the values of family and home.

9. *Generosity and Compassion* — 9's are unprejudiced, trustworthy and honorable, which makes them ideal for high offices such as judges, spiritual leaders, educators and healers. Material success is less important than the opportunity to help others, especially the underprivileged. Unfortunately, others often take advantage of their generosity.

11. *Intuitive and Visionary* — 11's are patient, honest and spiritual. They can be great leaders, but also have a mystic side, which makes them attractive to others. And being intuitive makes them good teachers, often from their own life experiences. (On 'bad hair days,' they are 2's.)

22. *Loyalty and Optimism* — 22's are practical idealists who can also carry out their plans to achieve their goals. As master builders, they bring order to the world. Hard-working, consistent, and well-organized, they work well with groups, leaving them better than when they joined. (On bad hair days, they revert to being 4's.)

33. *Planet-wide Unconditional Love* — 33's are here to raise the consciousness of humanity. They are charismatic, magnetic master teachers, who guide through their books, talks, and other media. They demand much of themselves. (On bad hair days, they live as 6's.)

So What Does It All Mean?

Assuming the actual protocol for putting together a personality is *something* like the above overlays of qualities, the soul knows its efforts will be supplemented by the early environment of its incarnation, which it also chooses. So, personality development is far from hit-and-miss.

With a nice, warm, cozy fetus to get to know, the soul puts forth a thread or fragment of its particular vibration to form Superconscious Mind, like a TV transmitter sending out a signal to just one TV set. (The whole soul rarely attaches, for its immense power could fry both baby and mother to a crisp.) The 'flight plan' for the incarnation is also held in the Superconscious and drives major events during the lifetime. This stores all major agreements and contracts between your incarnation and the incarnations of other souls (agreements can be broken by mutual consent; contracts cannot and must be followed through).

Soul also stores past life memories in the newly forming Subconscious Mind, along with skills and talents borrowed from its other incarnations. These will remain locked in the Subconscious Mind until needed, at which point the Superconscious Mind will unlock them. (Stored past life memories explain why young children can often remember other lifetimes lived by their soul. A notable case, researched and documented by Dr. Ian Stevenson, is that of Shanti Devi, a girl in India who recalled every detail of the life of a woman who lived and died in a village about 75 miles away. Their families had had no contact, yet the little girl knew everyone in the other village by name, and even the woman's secret hiding places for her valuables.

Critics of Stevenson's work allege he is selective in presenting his evidence, and ignores inconvenient cases. Some of the most convincing cases of people living apparent past lives under hypnotic regression could possibly be cases of cryptoamnesia, where the subject might have read historical accounts of those lifetimes rather than having actually experienced them. As usual, we cannot say "Definitely!" but only "Maybe?"

However, I personally know a boy who, when aged 7 and on a fishing trip said, "I've been here before but I was older then." Oddly, the boy's mother had a deceased cousin who used to spend many hours at that same fishing hole.

Soul also stores personality in the area between Conscious and Subconscious Minds, which will drive the formation of Ego during the first decade of life. The experiences of and responses to any trauma that ego suppresses will be stored in the Subconscious Mind, waiting to be tapped during hypnosis if necessary. Under extreme trauma, ego will create a sub-personality to deal with it, and then cocoon the energy in the Subconscious Mind, which also has a 'photographic memory' and will record every minute aspect of daily life—also available under hypnosis.

What Else Shall I Take?

Given that you have already had maybe several hundred lifetimes, you will have been hurt emotionally in most of those, so buried in your soul's energy are several thousand emotional wounds that you-the-soul need to heal to become fully whole. Some will be trivial, such as the time you felt insulted in public, and others will be major, as when your mate left you and ran off with your best friend. Yet others will be horrendous, as when invading Vikings plundered your village and ran a sword through your two children. As your throat was cut, the last thing you saw was your children impaled and thrown into a fire. Your dying vow was to never have children again.

Many of these wounds lie beneath your awareness in your Subconscious Mind, and soul seeks to have them brought to the surface for healing. But they will stay there until triggered by some stimulus you plan for this new lifetime. Suppose you hear tribal drumming or old English dance music from Elizabethan times, and you suddenly feel a wave of nausea or extremely angry or sad. You may even feel a physical pain, as if a hot poker has been thrust into your body. You know an old past-life wound has just been triggered, and has come up to be healed with love and forgiveness. (We'll see how later.)

To make matters even more interesting, we often incarnate in pairs or groups of incarnations of the same souls who originally gave us our wounds. If your mate in this lifetime had killed you in another, your wounds get triggered every day, so you may feel as if you're not even safe in your own home. The barrage of criticism can be endless, with everything always your fault. This can go on for years because your mate is oh so nice in public, and your friends have no idea you're living in hell. But can you leave the relationship? Usually not, because you two are karmically bound to each other. After a particularly bad argument that may have resulted in violence, you gather some things together, planning to leave, but your mate pleads with you to stay, claiming it was stress-induced and promising it will never happen again. So you stay ... until the next time. And there will be a next time, probably worse than the first. The outcome? Either your mate kills you, or you kill your mate, so one goes to heaven, the other goes to jail. But it doesn't have to end that way. However, you must realize you can't solve a problem such as this without going to the lifetime where it began. And this means past-life recall, either informally on your own or formally with a regression therapist, where a couple of sessions will do more than years of traditional therapy.

The problem with the latter is that blame must be assigned in this lifetime, when there really isn't any. The blame may go back hundreds of years, to different people in different bodies and different lifetimes, *but it's still in your subconscious!*

Preparing for Departure

From the soul plane, the soul monitors its parents-to-be and may be present during conception of its new home (that's a scary thought). The soul itself or a genetic specialist (in spirit) may influence the actual genetic cocktail as sperm and egg fuse, in order to obtain just the right physical characteristics the soul requires for meeting its life goals. This presence is what many women sense when they know conception has occurred.

If the parents' circumstances point to a possible abortion, none of this may happen, of course, and the fetus may remain just 'tissue growth' in the mother's body, with no soul stepping forward to 'claim' it. Or a soul fragment may come forward as soon as conception happens, and come and go at will from physical to soul plane, until the abortion occurs. Occasionally, a spirit associated with a first-trimester abortion shows up in psychic readings, but generally an abortion in the first trimester would not be considered 'murder.'

Once into the second trimester, however, and if the fetus is 'viable,' the intended fragment of soul begins to make more frequent forays to its prospective home to acclimate itself. There is much to learn, as it familiarizes itself with brain chemistry and the neural network with which mind will work. Fortunately, much is already built-in, thanks to the miracles of the autonomic nervous system and DNA, which guides how stem cells split and specialize as parts of specific organs, bones, blood, tissue, etc.

In such an incredibly complex process as growing a human body, things can go awry and the soul may realize the body will not be a viable home, so it leaves, resulting in miscarriage. The spirit (soul signal) and personality had already formed, so they return to the soul plane and may undergo the same development track as in cases of infant death. (This explains why mediums notice unborn children and count them with other siblings who have crossed over. The parent/child agreement still counts even though birth did not occur.) Or the soul fragment may wait for a new pregnancy.

Why does the soul plane need babies growing up over there? Because crossing over as an unborn or infant, and growing up solely on the soul plane (sorry about the pun), surrounded by loving relatives is a completely different experience than crossing over as an adult. The young incarnation grows up in wonderment and awe, knowing only of love and freedom, and nothing of fear or limitation. The soul needs that variety among its hundreds of fragments.

If everything goes according to plan, sometime in the third trimester, the soul becomes increasingly involved with its new biological home and the mother's energy. As the time for birth approaches, the soul fragment may still pull back, resulting in stillbirth. While a tragedy in Earth terms, the soul has gained valuable experience and the mother gets to explore intense grief on behalf of the main soul entity—not much consolation, but she can take comfort from knowing her soul thought she was strong enough to bear the pain. This may sound callous, but in its quest to know itself, All That Is strives to probe every nuance of every emotion, which includes a mother's grief over the loss of her baby—arguably the most intense feeling possible on the Earth plane. True callousness is the remark, "Oh, don't worry. You're young and can have others." That denies the spiritual bond that had already formed between mother and baby. Of course, chances are that the same soul will show up again in a subsequent pregnancy—it happens all the time. (In a famous case in England, twin daughters died in an accident, and the mother later had a second pair of daughters. As they grew up, they could remember every tiny detail of the first twins' lives, even down to the pet names for their favorite dolls, which the parents had kept—an obvious case of reincarnation.

As an example, hypnotherapist Marge Rieder describes in *Millboro and More* how she regressed her daughter Evie back to the moment of conception, and asked her to talk about her experience. Her spirit (that part of her soul focusing on this incarnation) reported fascination over which egg would leave the ovary and attach to the womb wall, knowing the person the incarnation would become, depended on that to some extent. Conception was 'planned chaos' as if a horde of attackers was trying to break into a walled city, but when one eventually succeeded and its head punctured the egg wall, everything calmed down.

Over the next five weeks, cells replicate at breakneck speeds, with a background noise of humming (the sound of the mother's blood flow), but this growth is driven by DNA and not the spirit. As cell division calms down, a sense of individuation begins to dawn. However, these weeks are 'iffy' because the tiny fetus could easily be dislodged from the womb.

At two months, spirit begins to associate with the fetus and individuated consciousness starts recording everything that goes on. Most of the spirit, however, is still at one with the soul plane. At three months, specific organs are under construction, starting with the brain and eyes. At five months, things begin to feel cramped for Evie, and she begins to get tangled up in the umbilical cord.

By five months, the spirit is becoming increasingly committed to this remaining a viable pregnancy; until now, it was noncommittal and wouldn't have cared either way. Fetal consciousness is increasingly aware of its surroundings, and getting really irate at near-strangulation by the umbilicus. Four months later, Evie was ready but badly positioned and completely wrapped in the cord, so delivery took an amazing four hours. Once out, Evie is shocked by the cold and all the rough physical handling that passes for SOP in delivery rooms.

This fascinating account shows how spirit and emerging body consciousness work together to establish a focal point of awareness, one that is recording the world outside itself after only a few days.

It is vital for parents to know that, as the soul spends increasingly long sojourns in its new body, it is storing impressions of the world around it in its Subconscious Mind, the most obvious source of these being the mother's energy. The soul is eager to begin its learning process about the world, and starts while still in the womb. Children rarely have conscious memory until the second year, but the Subconscious Mind begins forming deep feelings of being either wanted and safe, or unwanted and unsafe, even while still in the womb.

Knowing this, enlightened parents play beautiful music at this time, or even spend time in a dolphin tank, for souls are familiar with their languages. Dolphin-assisted births are the ultimate in serenity, as the female dolphin 'midwives' use their high frequency sonar to minimize labor pain, even though we humans do not know how.[1] Next best is water birth, for a gentle transition from the *in utero* environment to the outside world. The *worst possible* start in life is being held upside down under bright lights, being smacked, and taken away from the mother. This lays a foundation in the Subconscious Mind of punishment, danger and abandonment, which emotionally scars the person for life. And because these are deep foundational percep-

---

[1] According to Ms. Newland, the founder of the Cetacean Commonwealth and pioneer of dolphin-assisted underwater childbirth, "The Cetacea have had a complex language for millions of years, have the largest brains of any creature on the planet and have a history of friendship, cooperation, even partnership with humans. ... They are conscious beings to the point where they deserve full protection under human laws." New research has shown that our DNA is sensitive to vibrations and electromagnetic fields, more so than to drugs. Somehow the acoustic and electromagnetic fields emitted by dolphins seems to turn pieces of our DNA 'on' and 'off' and induce electrochemical changes in our blood. This explains the many reports by swimmers of spontaneous healing after coming into contact with dolphin pods. The remarkable implication of this is that somehow dolphins are able to read our DNA, looking for defects, and then make just the right signals, both acoustical and electromagnetic, to correct those defects. Of course, how they are able to do this is a complete mystery.

tions of the world, they are hard to get to except by hypnosis. However, this negative imprinting is *exactly* why we come to the Earth plane, with things beginning badly and just going downhill from there.

What should *not* happen in the last few months of term are energies of conflict or hardship. For example, being born soon after WW2 in England, I picked up on the deprivation and scarcity of post-war rationing, and lived for a long time with the deep subconscious core belief that "life is hard.' Also, we all lived with my father's mother, who did not get along with my mother, adding additional tension and conflict. Of course, at the soul level, I had anticipated that and had deliberately sought out that imprinting as a challenge. As a result, I have probably been more diligent and hard-working than if everything had been smooth sailing.

In one study conducted by psychologist Dr. David Chamberlain and documented in his book, *Children Remember Birth*, he studied ten mother/child pairs. He regressed the children back to the birth process and had them describe it. Then he compared their accounts with those of their mothers, and found the pairs agreed on an average of 14 points, with no discrepancies. One pair had an amazing 24 points of agreement, again with no discrepancies. This study proves conclusively that our birth process is recorded in our subconscious minds, down to each minute detail.

Parents, therefore, would do well to remember that their unborn child is a sponge, studiously recording everything about the energy it senses while in the womb. Particularly harmful energies flow if the child is unwanted or deemed 'a mistake,' for that inflicts incalculable harm on its emerging self-concept, harm that may never be expunged during its lifetime, and cause irreparable emotional scarring. But again, souls choose these Challenges for their own reasons.

Planning Illness and Disease

The soul plans all aspects of life, including major health issues in order to challenge the ego-personality to look within and reevaluate attitudes or beliefs, to develop compassion, to turn to Spirit as a Resource and, of course, as a means of leaving the Earth Plane.

Some illnesses are not planned but are self-inflicted due to stuffed, unresolved anger or resentment. Holding grudges is probably the worst thing you can do to your health, so forgiveness of those who harm you in any way is essential to avoid creating cancers, immune system deficiency, and high blood pressure. However, the soul allows this illness to proceed as a teaching tool.

Some or all the benefit of this reevaluation may accrue to the next incarnation as, say, a deeper level of compassion, but that's no consolation if you're the incarnation suffering the disease or illness, and life will seem unjust. Only when you see your life as just one pearl on the necklace does *anything* make sense. Until then, nothing does.

When faced with an illness such as cancer or AIDS, how should you respond? First, seek why you-the-soul arranged this. What spiritual purpose does it serve? Use meditation, a medical intuitive, a psychic counselor, or just ask your guides.

Next, your mental and emotional states are crucial during serious illness. Anger, self-hatred, blame and fear will work against restoring health and may well be the root cause anyway. Instead, practice courage, hope and self-love because these change your body's chemistry and put you in alignment with Spirit. And without self-love, *no* healing can take place.

At the very worst, the odds of recovery are 50/50, and whatever positive steps you can take will tip the balance in your favor. Begin by smiling (a lot), reading uplifting, inspirational books and listening to tapes. Instead of assuming things will only get worse, assume they'll only get better. This stimulates your body chemistry to release natural healing hormones in the endocrine system.

Pull in *all* your Resources—guides, healing angels, your own higher self and any Earth plane healers you know. Even pester the Source itself, affirming that you are part of it and deserve good health. Finally, check the Internet for dietary changes that can send cancer into remission.

Above all, remember that this is a growth opportunity, so look for the growth, even if it must be carried through to another of your soul's incarnation's lifetime.

Past Life Trauma

Many souls carry past-life trauma into a new incarnation to be healed, especially when the trauma involved death and couldn't therefore be healed in that life. This usually shows up as an irrational phobia, say of heights, water or fire. One of my friends, for example, is terrified while driving on bridges that span water, which points to how she died in a previous life. The fact that she suffers from chronic asthma tends to confirm death by drowning in that lifetime. Asthma may also indicate a prior death by asphyxiation or hanging—anything that makes breathing difficult.

Working with a regression therapist is a quick and easy way to release the trauma energy in order to diffuse the phobia. In these cases, healing the past life is the only way the problem in this lifetime can be dealt with, and lack of awareness or acceptance of reincarnation means: 'you're just going to have to live with it.'

Planning Your Exit Strategy

Equally as important as entry strategy is the soul's exit strategy or strategies, the means of returning Home. This, too, is carefully chosen for maximum growth for the incarnation and those around it.

If the incarnation's goals are limited, such as 'just testing the physical plane waters,' an early return may be planned via SIDS, which will allow parents and siblings the opportunity to explore grief, for the death of a child is always seen as tragic. Unless those around the baby or child brought about its demise, there should be no guilt, for the exit was well-planned in advance, and the returning soul fragment is always met by relatives who have already crossed, and even by the soul itself. (The latter is the radiant, all-loving being of light sometimes seen during an NDE.) Parents should never worry about their child being alone on the soul plane. It never happens! Children are always met!

If someone *did* have a hand in the child's crossing, however, incredible karma has been generated, which will need to be rebalanced in this or another lifetime, so the perpetrator can experience both sides of the equation.

Karma is poorly understood, and this is the source of much misery. Karma simply means 'balance' and is never punishment. Universal law requires that whenever one soul's deliberate actions impact another, the first soul must experience that impact itself, so that it gets to experience the full energy dynamic, and not just one side of it. Therefore, if a soul in any way *intentionally* infringes upon or limits the free will of another, the first soul itself demands to know what that infringement felt like to the second soul, so it must set up the appropriate circumstances for the experience.

As part of planning a lifetime, the soul decides how much karma it will create, and how much it will balance, and make arrangements with the other souls involved. The incarnation then spends the early part of its life attending to karmic issues, and when done, that person may return to the soul plane or switch to what the East calls dharma. This may differ widely and might involve volunteering to work with sick or dying adults, children or animals—anything that involves giving of the self for the benefit of others, and for aligning self with Self. When complete, the soul fragment crosses over via one of its planned exits.

Souls can define a number of exit points and, as each one's time comes up, will decide whether or not to take it. Some exits are for soul growth, such as the slow, thoughtful process offered by AIDS. Other exits make a public statement, such as Nicholas Green, a young boy on vacation with his family in Italy. He crossed over when thieves 'randomly' opened fire on their car. When his parents offered his organs for transplant, the resulting publicity revitalized Italy's languishing organ donation movement, saving thousands of lives.

The only death not carefully planned is suicide, although the soul knows if it stacks up too many Challenges, the ego-personality may feel overwhelmed and believe it lacks the necessary Resources to meet them. It may then seek to leave the situation, in the mistaken belief that something is being solved or avoided. Surprise!

The combination of difficult Challenges and a weak ego-personality is always a risk and requires extra care in life-planning, such as having a few supportive relatives in the family. Because suicide is really a soul-level planning snafu, those crossing over in this way are given extra healing to help the soul fragment examine its actions. Suicides are NEVER punished. Again, *suicides are NEVER, EVER punished*. Suicide is treated simply as an action taken with less than full understanding of the consequences and is, therefore. just another learning experience. And surviving relatives should never feel guilty about 'missing the signs' because this is purely an issue for the soul to deal with.

Some folks believe a suicide is immediately bounced back to the Earth plane to repeat the experience. In fact, successful suicides spend a long time in counseling and reflection as to why the suicide happened. Yes, a similar circumstance will be set up at some point, but the same soul fragment does not return. The new fragment will have much of the previous one's energy, but hopefully, the balance between Challenges and Resources will have been tweaked to lessen the chance of a repeat outcome.

Compounding the suicide's sense of failure is often the guilt that comes from causing grief and instilling guilt in those remaining on the Earth plane—which is often massive in intensity. Those who cross due to so-called 'natural causes' suffer along with those left to grieve (although they do see the larger context, which helps). But those who deliberately *cause* that grief suffer incredible remorse. And the remorse goes off the scale with murder-suicides because they also have to deal with the taking of one or more other lives, which is never condoned on the other side under any circumstances. When murderers come to on the other side, the horror they feel at what they have done is indescribable (except in cases of no remorse, in which case, they arrive on the other side to circumstances that are appropriately unpleasant as we'll see later).

Of course, none of this applies to suicides in cases of terminal illness, where great pain is involved. Once the soul fragment has experienced some of the pain, the learning is over and nothing is gained from further suffering, so self-induced exit is acceptable.

Anyone contemplating suicide should remember that it is a permanent solution to a temporary problem, and no problem is insurmountable, given the right Resources. So if you or anyone you know is contemplating suicide, reach out and gather up those Resources. Far more people than you think are willing to admit having considered suicide at some point, and will not be shocked or think any less of you if you ask for help. Remember, your soul may have factored in precisely those additional Resources when it set up the Challenges for your lifetime, so it behooves you to take advantage of them, and not just give in to the Challenge. Because it's all just the Source learning more about itself, let's try to make it fun. Asking for help and gathering Resources will not prevent death, but may prevent suicide as the vehicle.

Who or What Actually Incarnates?

Usually, when a new incarnation begins, a fragment of soul splits off, forms a personality, inhabits a body, develops an ego, lives a life and returns to the soul plane. Then it does something extremely clever—it merges back into its soul, while retaining the same focal point of consciousness that it had on the Earth plane. So, if you visit a medium, your great-grandmother who crossed over 50 years ago can still come through even though she long ago merged with her main soul entity. (Those on the other side say this feat cannot be explained in words.)

When the soul decides to form a new incarnation, it 'borrows' skills, understanding, wisdom and memories gleaned during the lifetimes of whichever of its incarnated fragments are needed. (This pool of wisdom determines soul age rather than the actual number of lives lived.) This 'borrowing' gives it a jump-start on personality-building. But the new soul fragment is still a sovereign first-timer, never before having incarnated. However, the soul may include significant portions of fragments that have already incarnated, especially if there is 'unfinished business,' as in the case of suicides. But those fragments that have returned to the soul plane do not, themselves, incarnate again, instead continuing their development on the soul plane.

The degree of 'borrowed' memories that a new fragment takes on could result in an "I've been here before" sensation, even though that fragment per se has not been there before. It only has the borrowed memory of having been there. The original fragment that had been there is still alive and kicking on the other side, waiting for its loved ones to join it. For example, during WWII, General Patton experienced this while on campaign in Italy, when he 'remembered' ancient battles he'd fought as a Roman soldier.

Departure and the Dreaded Amnesia

As the time for actual birth approaches, the fragment of soul vibration that is to incarnate as the new human being attaches permanently to the body, with the mind interfacing with the brain in ways that are yet to be understood. However, to see why amnesia happens, we must revisit the topic of 'mind.'

As we've seen, the human mind is a complex psychic structure with several levels:

- *Subconscious Mind* contains soul memories, including details of its other incarnations (past, present, and future, because they are all happening simultaneously from the soul's perspective). All this is accessible under hypnosis, and holds details such as the license plates of cars that passed you on the street when you were playing as a child.

- *Conscious Mind*, the surface part that is the rational, decision-making level, where we consciously evaluate and interpret the data coming in from the five senses ... and a few others if you're psychic, which many children are. Children often have bleed-through from other incarnations, but this usually ceases by age seven, when the child accepts society's consensus reality model, which does not allow for this phenomenon. (Aware parents would do well to ensure this does not happen, especially with an Indigo Child (see Vol. II, Chapter 14.)

- *Between the Conscious and Subconscious Minds* lies a border region that becomes home to the personality that soul wove together. Because it lies beneath your Conscious Mind, this interface to the world governs your automatic responses to events around you. If you overlay this personality pattern with one that says, "I will be nice to others so they will accept and validate me," internal conflicts will arise on days when you don't feel like being nice ... and you may get a nasty headache. This area is also home to sub-personalities and other fragments of consciousness created in response to mental and emotional trauma, especially experienced as a child.

- *Superconscious Mind* houses the soul vibration that connects you to your identity on the soul plane. Often termed 'the higher self,' it is usually eclipsed by the intensity of sensory input and chatter of the lower minds, but makes itself known during so-called peak experiences such as Tantra and meditation. You can consciously communicate with this level of your being using the Superconscious Technique (described in a later chapter).

Having all the neat stuff locked up in either the attic or basement and normally inaccessible may seem a huge waste, because we then need to figure out our reaction to everything, or rely on knee-jerk responses of personality or sub-personalities. However, things have been carefully arranged to be this way to further the soul's primary purpose—that of placing ego-personality in various situations and seeing how it responds. If the ego-personality knew everything about everything, including the reason for incarnating, that would skew the results, for ego would want to deliver the 'right' response ('right' from the soul's perspective) and move on to the next Challenge, which defeats the purpose, of course.

In his books, remote viewer Bruce Moen describes how he visited the soul plane Exit Portal through which pass spirits departing for an Earth life. It was shown to him as an energy funnel into which souls enter for 'compression,' a process that squeezes their huge soul energy down into the form that will incarnate. My take on this is that it's where past life memories are compressed into the Subconscious Mind, and details of one's karmic mission, or flight plan, are compressed into the Superconscious Mind, effectively leaving the Conscious Mind a blank slate to record memories as the fetus begins forming them.

Moen also noted that spirits often grouped together, with slender cords connecting them. He was told that those spirits were unified or connected in their missions, such as those going down to become the parents of the others in that group, or spirits that had a soul agreement to work on the same Earth plane mission, such as a research project or establishing a hospital together.

So why *do* we wipe the slate clean and forget our flight plan? Imagine knowing your life plan in great detail. You wake up in the morning knowing exactly what was going to happen that day as in *Groundhog Day*. "Great! It's July Fourth and I'm going to a barbeque, where I'll meet my next soul mate—a red-haired beauty with blue eyes and sparkly laugh called Jennifer." Or perhaps, "Oh no, this is the day of the routine dentist appointment, where I have a bad reaction to the anesthetic and die in the ambulance on the way to the hospital. At least it will be painless. Better get up." I think I'd just pull the covers over my head and hide. Wouldn't *you*?

Also, as Moen points out, we stumble on our way to unconditional love by gauging the emotional impact our behavior has on other people. And we learn who we are by the impact that others have on us. None of this would be necessary if we had soul's perspective on exactly who we were and what was going to happen at each turn.

At this point, you might be feeling used or set up. If being dropped into situations to test your mettle makes your ego feel like a lab rat, ask who is running the lab. You are … at your soul level. Remember that ego is not who you really are. Your primary identity is soul, not ego. You created your ego as an interface or buffer to the world around you, and built in some responses called personality traits to save yourself the trouble of having to think from scratch about what to do in the hundreds of situations you encounter every day … thousands if you have kids.

The next question may be, "How can my response to situations possibly be of interest to the universe? Doesn't it have something better to do than watch me?" The answer is no, because the physical plane was created precisely for this reason. The original Source set this all up within its huge mind so that its parts (i.e., us) could explore reality and see how they respond in all manner of situations. In this way, the Source learns more about itself, which is really quadzillions of us parts running around, having experiences and reporting back.

The combination of your unique ego-personality in the unique circumstances you call your life has never occurred before and will never occur again, ever! So how you respond to your life is unique and vital information the Source needs in order to more fully know itself. Quite a responsibility, eh?

There's something else. Who you are and how you respond to the world changes as you live and grow, and that, too, is a source of delight and fascination to the universe … and again unique to you. But the real biggie comes when you, having been mind-wiped of the fact that your true nature is pure, unconditional love, can return to that state consciously. Of course, in your Subconscious and Superconscious Minds, you know that to be true, but the clamor of the world keeps it hidden, so most of us do not regain that truth until we cross back over to Home. But the entire soul plane rejoices when human incarnations break through the petty ego stuff and become the unconditional love they already are. This is termed 'self-realization' because you yourself realize who that self truly is—and no two people do it quite the same way. (Enlightenment is a huge subject and the real reason why everything exists at all, so we'll revisit this topic later.)

The amnesia, i.e., forgetting the soul plane, past lives, unconditional love, etc., comes automatically, as sensory input from the world around us begins to drown out higher and lower minds, leaving ego-personality aware only of the contents of its Conscious Mind. (This is analogous to the dawning sunlight of a new day drowning out the stars.) This means you forget all about your flight plan and its contents, your soul and its past lives, etc., which leaves you with a blank slate to begin your new Earth plane experience, with your ego-personality and the imprinting you get from early caregivers, plus whatever spirit influence can get through.

For the same reason, we dumb down our telepathic powers, which are in full flow on the soul plane. We do this for peace and quiet. Imagine walking down the street and everyone has a boom-box blaring out their favorite music or talk show. Rap music, Reggae, rock-and-roll, Rush Limbaugh and Howard Stern all mingle in a deafening cacophony. Or worse, how about being on a long plane flight during which you get to experience the fear-of-flying of half the passengers? No thanks! (This happened to my friend, Lauren Zimmerman and it almost drove her crazy until she learned to control her receptivity.)

The Human Chakra System

One of the trickiest things the incoming soul manages, apart from working with the three levels of mind, is to master the body's chakra system. The chakras are a series of energy centers that transform and distribute soul energy and life force energy within the physical body. There are seven located within the body and seven outside. Knowledge of the function and maintenance of at least the seven in-body chakras is essential for health and well-being. They are:

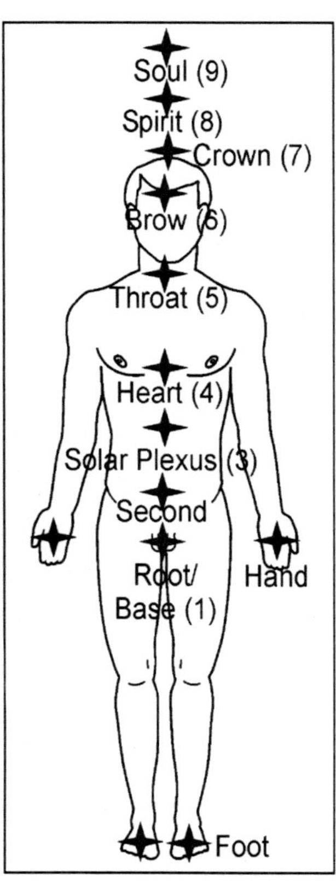

Human Chakra System

1. *Root Chakra*, located at the base of the spine; its 'color' is seen as red by clairvoyants. It grounds us to the Earth plane and holds the basic needs of stability, security, and survival. In our body, the root chakra influences the hips, legs, rectum, kidneys, bones, colon, and lower back.

2. *Second Chakra*, located in the abdomen, is orange, and deals with our sexuality, self-esteem, creativity, and the lower emotional

body including our unhealed inner child. Physically, it involves the ovaries, vagina, genitals, uterus, lumbar spine, kidneys, bladder, and large intestine.

3. *Solar Plexus Chakra*, located at the base of the sternum, is yellow. It is home to our self-confidence, personal power, intuition, material learning ability, self-empowerment and will. It rules the stomach, bladder, pancreas, small intestine, liver, and gall bladder.

4. *Heart Chakra*, located in the chest, between the nipples, is either green or pink depending on our purpose. Pink represents earthly, personal love; green is universal, healing and unconditional love for self and for humanity. It houses our ability to give and receive love, to love ourselves and others. It rules the heart, circulatory system, lungs, shoulders and upper back.

5. *Throat Chakra* is located in the throat, and is light blue. It rules expression, hearing (physical and psychic), communication, and higher creativity. It holds the potential for change, transformation and healing, including healing one's future through karmic release of the past. It influences the throat, neck, jaw, teeth, ears, hearing, and thyroid gland.

6. *Brow Chakra*, located in the forehead, is indigo. It holds our ability to see beyond physical realities into the psychic realm, for understanding non-physical truth. It rules the eyes, face, and brain.

7. *Crown Chakra* is located on top of the head, and is violet. It is the point where soul enters the body at birth, and remains our soul portal throughout life. It rules the spine and nervous systems.

The eighth chakra, visualized a few inches from the Crown Chakra, is the seat of higher communication with your spirit guides and loved ones; the ninth connects to the soul. The remaining chakras connect to progressively higher levels of cosmic experience. There are also minor chakras in the palms of the hands and soles of the feet.

So, there we have it. The fragment of soul has attached to the fetus and caused its tiny body to release hormones that will trigger the mother's labor. Then it waits for just the right moment, often based on astrology, particularly the ascendant sign. (As we've seen, the Ascendant is the sign just coming up on the eastern horizon. This changes every two hours, which is why astrologers need the time of birth and longitude in addition to birth date.) Then you begin the scariest ride of your life that all souls hate—being squeezed through the birth canal and out into the waiting world. But there is an alternative to being born in; we can walk in …

Walk-Ins Welcome

The 'walk-ins welcome' sign in the windows of many hair salons reminds us of the other way to incarnate that avoids the messy infant years. Here, one soul 'walks out' of the body and a new 'one walks in.' It's a lot more complicated than it sounds and is *always* done with the total agreement of both souls and a bunch of higher souls who supervise things.

First, why would a soul want to walk out? Many reasons:

1. Its life objectives are complete. After 10, 20, 30 or so years, it feels done and would normally leave via death, as in an accident, war or illness.
2. Maybe the soul only wanted to experience life's early years and didn't need the growing old and death experiences. So before incarnating, it arranged for another soul to take its place and live out the remaining years.
3. The soul miscalculated the Challenges and took on too much … and wants out. But rather than commit suicide, the soul finds a soul that wants in and they arrange a swap.
4. The first soul is doing a favor for the second soul by preparing the body and then stepping aside at the appointed time.

Why would a soul want to walk in?

1. Walk-ins have planetary missions and don't need the messy early years, so they skip those and arrive ready to begin work. They are seasoned Old Souls, so have done the messy years often enough. And the personal history of the walk-out serves as good cover.
2. Their mission usually doesn't involve tangled karmic relationships with parents and siblings, so they usually walk into a family setting of non-soul group members.

The walk-out/walk-in process itself is lengthy and complicated, as the walking out spirit (soul fragment) actually goes through a death-like experience of disengaging from the chakras and leaving via the crown chakra, severing the silver cord and heading off to the soul plane. Then the new soul enters and engages with the chakra system. This is usually done during physical body trauma, such as when unconscious after an accident or during a severe illness. In my case, my soul walked into a body aged 7 during a high fever associated with a childhood illness that the walk-out spirit arranged.

The switch is usually preceded by a period where the incoming spirit 'shadows' the body, to get used to it, often during sleep so as not to alarm the ego-personality. Because the memories and ego-personality's traits initially remain, the switch may not be apparent, even to the ego, but the incoming spirit soon begins to assert itself. Tastes in food, clothing, music and even friends begin to change, and a new belief system and personality emerge. In my case, the previous occupant's ego was chronically shy and I spent years overcoming that—vital because public speaking is a large part of my mission on Earth. My mother remembers being surprised at how quickly I 'grew up' around age seven, suddenly more scholarly and studious, always with my head in a book.

So, if you have ever been unconscious, in a fever, or undergone a period of intense personal angst, and then people begin to tell you, "You're not quite the same person after your accident (or illness),' maybe this is what happened. After about seven years, the walk-in process is complete.

Spirit Guides

A major resource known by few people is the team of spirit guides that works with us. These are trusted members of our soul group who choose not to incarnate while we do, so they can help us. They specialize in various facets of our life, such as life direction, health, career, and spiritual growth. And we take turns. When we are not in a body, we serve as spirit guides to those of our soul group who are.

Whenever you need help with some aspect of life, call upon them, silently or out loud if you wish, and state the problem. Specifically ask for their help, for they cannot intrude until asked. Request their input to your decision-making, for synchronicities to reveal new options, or for actual direct intervention. Make this as much a habit as talking to your physical friends, and know they are rooting for you.

Never worry that you're bothering them, for helping you is actually their job and they like to feel useful. Also, helping you provides growth and learning for them, something for which they are eager. Turn the tables and see how you would feel if you volunteered to be a spirit guide to someone who ignored you all their life. Of course, you deliver the guidance you contracted for with the person's soul, but the soul's incarnation doesn't even know you exist. Then imagine how you would feel if the person learns about you, begins a dialog with you and starts asking for all kinds of guidance. Suddenly you're pretty busy ... and happy.

This chapter has focused on the preparations that go on in the soul plane. The next chapter looks at how the soul actually makes the leap and takes up the challenge of an Earth life.

Chapter 6 ═──

Earth School and Back Home Again

Starting with being held upside down and having your little butt smacked as your first Earth School impressions, you have just embarked on the toughest, most challenging experience available to souls that exists anywhere in this galaxy. Scary thought, but you did choose it, confident you could handle it. In fact, you-the-soul spent years planning and preparing for it. Why? Because it's the single most powerful way to accelerate your growth. You-the-soul will learn more in the next few years on Earth than you could in a million years (literally) on the soul plane.

Imagine a friend recounting at great length how thrilling a roller coaster ride was for him. But his account is limp and pallid and, never having been on such a ride yourself, you just don't get it. Then, one day, you take the ride yourself and are blown away by the sensory overload of the experience. That's the difference in the intensity between the Earth and Soul planes. Now this intensity only applies to negativity, because what we call 'love' here on Earth is limp and pallid compared with the intensity of love on the Soul plane.

On the Earth plane, we forget who we really are and say, "Let's pretend we're limited mortals" for a few decades, with you-the-soul (the creator of you-the-ego) watching and wondering, "Will he get it?" Or, "When will she realize who she really is?"

The Earth School is the only plane where your soul can experience surprise, pain and death, and only then through your ego-personality. Every day sees hundreds of ways your life can take unexpected (by ego) turns, and how you-the-ego respond is a source of great fascination and delight to you-the-soul.

The Early Years

During the first year of your new life, how your primary caregivers treat you has a major impact on you for life. If your material needs (being fed, changed, etc.) are met promptly, if you're picked up when you cry, and you're made to feel loved, safe and wanted, you record in your Subconscious Mind that, "The world is a safe, loving place that nurtures me. I am wanted, I belong, and I am lovable."

But if your needs are not met, you record, "The world is a cold, hostile place and I must fight for what I need. I am not wanted, do not belong, and am not lovable."

Throughout the rest of your life, whenever you encounter a situation that requires a response, you turn to your Subconscious Mind for your 'world view.' If you had recorded the first imprinting, you will respond with warmth, love and confidence, and exude the energy of, "Of course my needs will be met." And magically, they will.

With the second imprinting, however, you respond with fear and low self-esteem, and transmit to the world, "My needs will not be met, so I will have to struggle to get what I need." And, of course, this response will elicit a totally different reaction from the world outside.

Parents do not set out to deliberately undermine their children's self-esteem, but children's needs are so enormous, it's inevitable that some will not be met. The child innocently interprets this as rejection, abandonment, etc., and goes further to reason, "My parents are perfect and infallible, so if I am not getting the love I need, it's because I am unlovable."

To prevent future disappointment and pain, children lower their expectations with, "I am unworthy and undeserving of love, so I won't expect any. Then I can't be hurt." Unfortunately, the millions of such children who grow up to be adults help shrinks put their kids through college, because by closing off to the pain as children, they also closed themselves off to love. (More on love blocks later.)

Decades later, as an adult, say you need a ride to pick your car up from the repair shop but your spouse or mate says, "I'm sorry but I'm too busy." The minor pain of that rejection resonates with the major pain of childhood, faithfully stored in your Subconscious. But this old pain surfaces as 'now pain' because your Subconscious has no sense of time. All the times when your parents were too busy for you as a child, crash into your adult life and you explode, saying things you don't mean and that are just not true, such as, "You're never there for me when I need something." If one of your volcanic eruptions triggers your mate's childhood pain, you've suddenly got a huge fight on your hands. However, it's not you two fighting as adults but two four-year-olds who wanted to go to the zoo or the beach but your parents were too busy. Of course, it feels like 'now pain' because emotions do not obey time.

The Big Secret

Knowing how crucial is that first year's imprinting, why would a soul knowingly choose caregivers who would imprint the child with the second, negative type of experience? Because the greater the challenge, the greater the potential for growth when it's overcome ... which leads to The Big Secret: *You Create Your Own Reality*.

Of course, I can't claim those words as my own; they were made famous by the Seth entity channeling through Jane Roberts but, from personal experience, I *can* claim that they work. (By the way, the Seth books should be required reading for any serious metaphysician—all 20 or so of them, I'm afraid.)

The two different imprints we've just talked about result in different life realities for our two hypothetical babies, which brings us to the single greatest secret ever hidden in plain sight, and something that is well known and taken for granted on all other occupied planets. In fact, the ETs observing our planet are amazed that we don't know The Big Secret, and wonder how we stumble around and just make it through the day. So, what is it?

On the Soul plane, everything is created by thought. If you want to live in a huge castle, just conceive of the architecture in your mind and bingo ... there it is. You want the turrets taller? Then think them taller and watch them grow. The great secret is that the Earth plane is like that too, but with a dampening field applied so that a stray thought doesn't wreak havoc or create monstrosities we can't handle.

Specialized souls on the Soul plane are busy thinking the thoughts that sustain the Earth plane for us, but your thoughts influence what those souls create for you. To be effective, you must hold a thought with clarity and consistency, and exclusively for about 20 seconds. Most of us do that anyway, of course, only they are not positive, life-enhancing thoughts, but negative, fearful thoughts. That's The Big Secret, and if you don't know this, you can create a life you really don't like. *Your thoughts create your reality whether you know it or not.*

For example, a man with low self-esteem from childhood carries the thought 24/7 that he is unworthy of happiness, abundance, loving relationships, a rewarding job, a fulfilling sex life, etc. Thoughts are electromagnetic waveforms that he transmits from a special area in the brain, and they ripple outward into what we will learn later is called the *morphogenetic field*, or M-field. When his low self-esteem thought signal encounters a complementary thoughtform put out by someone looking for a victim to victimize further (say a mugger), the two thoughts mesh together and amplify each other. This changes the probabilities around the victim, and shifts reality slightly, opening him to an encounter that a man with high self-esteem just would not attract.

On the other hand, a woman with high self-esteem applies for a job. She signals high self-worth to the interviewer, who is subliminally influenced by the thoughts she projects and thinks more highly of her than the other candidates. Her answers and experience may be the same or even less stellar than the others but the interviewer thinks subconsciously that there's something different about her. Somehow she seems to exude more competence ... and gets the job.

Our successful candidate has actually programmed the M-field, which, of course, also includes the interviewer. So, even though she may not have the strongest resume, her self-esteem makes her the 'best' candidate.

The best example of this is in relationships, where the self-image you transmit determines *precisely* the kind of people you attract into your life. Someone with low self-esteem will attract only users, losers and abusers, because those with high self-worth wouldn't put up with such behavior in a partner. A woman with low expectations of men will attract only losers, because men with high self-esteem just wouldn't be attracted to a woman with that belief.

This brings us to the second part of The Big Secret: *your life is a reflection of your beliefs*. If your life sucks, don't complain about life; examine your beliefs because that's where the root of the problem lies. This is classic 'chicken and egg.' Does your life suck because your beliefs suck, or do your beliefs suck because your life sucks? Contrary to popular belief, it's the former. Thoughts come first and reality follows. Of course, it looks the other way round ... which is why it's still The Big Secret.

So, to change your reality, first change your thoughts *about* reality, and your reality will then change, albeit slowly. What you believe and how you think are habits that took years to form. The good news is that you formed them unconsciously; now that you're conscious, change will come more quickly.

Why is this big secret still The Big Secret? Why isn't Reality Creation 101 taught in first grade? Who's keeping the secret from us ... and why? For the oldest reasons in the world—power and greed. Since the beginning, powerful groups of people have been brainwashing us into believing that the real power lies outside ourselves in some God somewhere who wants us to behave in a certain way and punishes us if we don't. Of course, with their help (and for a fee), the Church will petition this God-out-there to maybe ease your suffering a little. Or if you must suffer, they will petition that you grow strong enough to bear the pain.

The truth? The real power lies in you and the thoughts you hold in the miraculous electromagnetic complex called 'your mind.' The real miracle is that, although your mind contains your beliefs, it also contains the tools to examine those beliefs and change whatever isn't working for you. But you must first realize that your beliefs *about* reality have little to do with reality itself. Worse, your beliefs aren't even yours … you inherited the opinions of other people as a child and never got around to reviewing your inheritance. If, as a child, you were inculcated with a belief in a 'hellfire-and-brimstone' God, and didn't bother to reevaluate that belief as you grew older, then, to you, God is still hellfire-and-brimstone.

Again, your beliefs about reality are just arbitrary opinions and may have little or nothing to do with reality itself. In a way, what you believe is relatively less important than why you believe it. So, why *do* you believe whatever you believe? Because when your young 'sponge mind' was trying to figure out the world, you grasped at whatever you were told by people you thought had it already figured out—parents, teachers, priests, etc. If they're grown up, you reasoned, then surely they know, right? Wrong! *The truth is, they haven't figured out a thing and are faking it!* They were just regurgitating what *they* heard as kids. And so it goes on, down the generations. But, knowing this, YOU ARE FREE to believe in whatever you wish. Of course, it will help if those new beliefs actually work better than the old ones … and bear some resemblance to reality.

There is a downside to learning of the amazing power to change your beliefs, however. Suddenly, you become responsible for your life. No excuses. No side-stepping. You're it—the creator of your reality. No one to blame except the person in the bathroom mirror. And once you learn this, you can't 'unlearn' it; you're stuck with it and if you don't use this new ability, you'll begin to feel even worse than before you did know this.

Changing those pesky little critters called your beliefs is easy on the one hand … but also hard on the other because, for a while, you will be flying in the face of what *seems* to be true. Your less than rosy life won't necessarily become magic overnight (although there's always room for a miracle). New thoughtforms may take a while to ripple out and make changes, but all the while, reality is staring you in the face, challenging you to persist. Many times, you may say, "The hell with it. It's too hard. I'm going back to sleep." And it *is* hard, which is why it's still The Big Secret.

But once the eagle has hatched, it can't crawl back inside its eggshell. So, immerse yourself in reality creation books, tapes, and seminars so that you're in the company of other eagles also on the path. Whatever you do, run away from people who still see themselves as victims of the world they are unknowingly creating. It's simple: eagle or chicken? The clear blue sky or KFC via the *back* door?

Challenge and Change

We have seen how the Earth School is a constant tension between Challenges and Resources. Up pops a Challenge—you lose your job, say—and need to call up Resources to deal with it. If you engaged just your ego-personality, you might feel overwhelmed and helpless. But, summon up a Resource instead. For example, you might meditate and say, "Okay, guides, I need some help down here. You know what the problem is, so get off your etheric butts and do something. I'm open to suggestions." Then, *listen*. Suddenly, the memory of an old high school buddy jumps into your mind, so you call him, only to learn that the company he owns needs a new marketing director—exactly your specialty—and the job will be advertised beginning the following day.

"Yeah, right," you may say. "That stuff never happens in real life." Oh, yes it does, but not to everyone, because most people just don't know how to go about marshalling their Resources. Your soul doesn't build in Challenges so that you will fail. *Challenges are opportunities that you-the-soul give you-the-ego to succeed.* That's why they exist--so, fearless eagle, jump on them, and become a *creator* rather than a *reactor*.

Remember, for every Challenge, there is an equal or more powerful Resource, and matching up the two is what the Earth plane is all about. It's the tension that enlivens the game, but if you don't know that, who you really are, what your Resources are, and what the game is really about, you may be missing out on many, or even most, of your Resources. But one thing is for sure ... new Challenges will still come along.

Given that it is a *fact* that we create our reality, you can:
1. Step up, accept this fact, and consciously manifest reality as a creator, or
2. Remain ignorant or deny this fact, in which case, the reality creation mechanism still operates, but your creations then control you, so you are a victim who must react to your creations, however monstrous.

Most of the population falls into category #2, and just dismisses their own power, so when challenges or problems arise, these chickens fall victim to their own creations and end up in KFC.

Moving from human to spiritual, therefore, involves taking responsibility, not just on a personal level but globally. Responsibility and authority go hand-in-hand. Ironically, we knew this 15,000 years ago when we were 'one with nature,' but we grew more sophisticated, separated from our unity, and began to see our creations as 'not us.' We began to see ourselves as *victims* of reality, and not its creators. But the reality creation mechanism didn't cease, and still operates full-force today … only we have forgotten about it. Worse, the delay between cause and effect is getting shorter every day.

Over 15,000 years, we have placed all authority outside ourselves, ably abetted by organized religion—authority over what is real, what is 'right,' and what our options are. We defer every aspect of life to the 'experts'—health, finance, law, even the plumbing in your house. Our technology has gotten so complex, we *need* experts to get through the day. So the very technology that's meant to empower us actually enslaves and leaves us powerless.

American hospitals kill almost 100,000 people a year (i.e., their actual cause of death is not the reason they went there) as people relinquish responsibility for their health, and fall victim to their own bodies. By placing reality creation outside ourselves, we develop left-brain technology to *change* reality, completely overlooking the fact that our right brain *creates* it.

Advertising is a classic example. We look to the media for our self-image, and for the means to achieve it by buying certain products. Ad agencies are the 21st century priesthood, giving us new role models and icons to worship. Each image is a cynical manipulation of a Subconscious Mind archetype of how we *think* we should be, in order to win the approval of others—richer, sexier, thinner, more hair, less hair, etc.

Our culture demands that we trade in our personal authority (about what's real, true, okay, etc.) for societal acceptance. But we can only be bullied into this trade-in if we lack a strong sense of who we are and are open to an identity being imposed from outside. Ask Madison Avenue, "Who should I be?" and you will be swamped with input.

Part of the 15,000-year trade-in has included the rip-off of our spiritual nature, stripped from 'in here' and repackaged as 'out there' … and accessible only in church on Sunday mornings, on your knees to show due respect and awe. Now, when you pray, you don't realize you're praying to YOU at the soul level, but it's true—there's only *you* on the other end of the phone, an aspect of the Source of All That Is.

So, forget the latest guru, the 'sacred sites trip to Peru,' and all the other New Age fads. Find a comfortable rock, sit down, and get to know the creator-in-here. And if you don't feel worthy, declare yourself worthy—you're the only one who can.

Interestingly, the break-up of Jennifer Lopez and Ben Affleck, begun in September 2003, prompted the experts to go public with a curious malaise called 'Celebrity Worship Syndrome,' a condition where people develop pathological association with celebrities, and suffer as their heroes suffer. Our entertainment-saturated society bombards us with information about our icons and the vacuum of most people's lives lets it in. Worship based on fantasy relationships with celebrities displaces relationships with real people. In the old days, we'd just say, "Get a life, already!" (As I edit the manuscript in January 2004, the trials of Michael Jackson and Martha Stewart dominate the news, even as dozens die every day in Iraq.)

Let us continue with the story of a newborn arrival to the Earth plane. (To avoid the pronoun problem, let's make him a boy called Joseph, or Joe for short.) During Joe's first three years, he receives a neutral upbringing: basic needs met but no great experience of love either. He hasn't got the 'me–not me' distinction figured out, so he sees the world as an extension of himself. A couple of his spirit guides hang out with him and the three chatter endlessly while in private. One day, his mother overhears the conversation and demands that he stop, with, "You're just imagining them. They're not real. Go out and play with the other kids. At least they're real." Our young hero is crushed, for he's just lost two good friends, and wise ones at that.

By age seven, Joe's ego-personality is well-anchored and his motor skills well-honed. He is a Little League star and no longer even remembers his guides, but they never leave his side. They distract him when he was about to go out on ice that was too thin; they thwart a pedophile who has just been released from jail; they arrange for a fever on the day of a big game so he isn't in the minivan that overturns, killing all the other kids. In other words, along with his guardian angels, they all just do their jobs.

When puberty sets in, raging hormones bring a bad case of acne and our hero spends more time looking in the bathroom mirror than out on dates. Deep depression sets in and his first major Challenge pops up. He doesn't yet know of all his Resources, and thoughts of suicide become more frequent, putting his guides on 'scramble.' Time for Plan B.

One day, after school, the bus 'just happens' to be full except for a seat next to the class nerd who the other kids avoid because he's 'too weird.' It doesn't seem to bother him, however. Joe learns that the boy's father is an inventor. "He's invented this skin cream made of energized colloidal silver. Hey, you should try some. It works killer on acne. Why not come home with me and we'll ask my dad?"

The pair go to the boy's home and meet the father, who is frustrated because he can't afford the FDA approval process for his invention. He gives Joe a month's supply and four weeks later, the acne is history. Odd how things turn out, isn't it? Score one for the guides.

Joe studies journalism at college but drops out when both his parents die in a plane crash. He begins to squander his inheritance by experimenting with drugs, particularly a lethal mixture of Ecstasy and speed. One day, even his young heart can't handle the potent drug cocktail, and he collapses at an all-night rock concert.

Joe is puzzled. Finding himself in pitch blackness, he asks, "Where am I? Am I dead? But if I am dead, who's asking the questions?" Suddenly, he senses black shapes gathering behind him and, terrified of the dark, he begins to move towards a white glow in the distance and possible safety.

Once inside the white cloud, Joe relaxes. A tall robed figure emerges from the cloud's center, arms folded in reproach, looking sternly at Joe. A mixture of love and disappointment pour from this authority figure.

"Are you God?" a nervous Joe asks.

"No, I am your soul," the figure replies.

"What am I doing here? And where *is* here, anyway?"

"Here is not the problem. What are you doing back there is the problem."

Suddenly, Joe's parents emerge from the cloud and he is mortified to see his mother crying. She reaches for him, with desperate pleading in her eyes. Joe blinks back his own tears and everything goes black again. Then he hears a woman say, "Tell the doctor he's coming round."

Just as Joe opens his eyes, he hears, "You're very lucky to be alive, young man. You were gone for almost an hour."

Joe doesn't care. The look in his mother's eyes still haunts him, with their look of feeling betrayed and let down.

Joe underwent a type of Near-Death Experience (NDE) called 'less than positive,' or LTP. Unlike the 75 – 80 percent of NDEs that celebrate the spiritual, the LTP is more of a disciplinary hearing and usually triggers life changes for the better. One LTP experiencer describes himself as a most unpleasant person, who disdained anything good and loving. While awaiting emergency surgery, he left his body and was 'kidnapped' by several demon-like beings who clawed at his body, causing him intense pain. In panic and desperation, he called on God to save him, and was suddenly enveloped by a warm, loving Light. For the first time ever, he knew he was loved, but argued that he was unworthy of such love. Several beings in the Light told him, "We don't make mistakes," and that he had to return to his body. After more argument, he finally returned, had the operation, and now lives a totally different life full of love. Now *that's* a wake-up call!

Some psychologists say of LTP NDEs that they result from fear of death. Because they occur in a mental realm, if you go in with fearful thoughts, these will be magnified and produce monstrosities, but it is more likely (to me) that soul orchestrates the experience for the wake-up.

The Near-Death Experience (NDE): Window on Eternity

Thanks to improvements in medicine, more and more of those who die during operations or from accidents are being resuscitated and are returning with fascinating stories of what happened while they were clinically dead. Each experience is different, but seem to contain one or more of the same core components:

- Leaving the body, often looking down on it as medical staff rush to resuscitate you, as in the cases of the Red Shoe and the White Sneaker[1].
- High-speed travel towards a light, usually through a tunnel, possibly accompanied by a buzzing sound.
- Being met by a 'greeter,' who may be a deceased loved one or favorite pet, a notable religious figure, or even the Presence of God (as experienced by my friend Lauren Zimmerman, whom we will meet in a later chapter).
- Intense light with no apparent source, which answers all your questions, even though you may not remember the answers later. Despite its intensity, it doesn't harm vision.

---

[1] Two often quoted anecdotal cases reported to hospital staff involve NDErs who leave their bodies and see things not easily visible. One woman reported to Prof. Kimberly Clark that she had traveled out through the wall and noticed a white sneaker on a high outside ledge. The staff member recovered the sneaker by leaning out of the window of a locked room, and attested there was no way the patient could have seen it from the ground. In the other case, the experiencer went up through the ceiling and once above the hospital noticed a red shoe on the roof, which the janitor subsequently retrieved. Of course, an out-of-body experience proves nothing about NDEs but it does dismiss doctors' skepticism about the phenomenon. Such incidences are known as 'vericidal,' in that they verify the phenomenon by allowing the experiencer to garner knowledge not otherwise knowable by that person.

- Overwhelming feelings of love, acceptance, forgiveness and homecoming in the Light, which may involve a profound encounter with an all-loving Being of Light.
- Panoramic life review that examines significant life events and reveals what is *truly* important about life on the physical plane. It also includes the emotional impact you and your actions had on other people.
- Colors, sounds and scents that dwarf everything on the physical plane.
- Overwhelming desire to stay but being told or just knowing it's not your time. This is not surprising considering you're being loved by all of Creation, and a pain-wracked body may well await you on your return.
- Suddenly being slammed back into your physical body.
- Trepidation about sharing the experience with others for fear of being thought weird.

A recent Gallup Poll of NDErs identified the prevalence of the major NDE components:

- Feelings of peace, painlessness   32%
- Being in another world   32%
- Panoramic life review   32%
- Out-of-body experience   26%
- Encountering other beings   23%
- Accurate visual perception   23%
- Audible sounds or voices   17%
- Light phenomena   14%
- Traveling through a tunnel   9%
- Precognition of events   6%

About a third report feeling totally different than when in a body: "As the awareness of gross matter and gravity slips away, you feel light as a feather. Being without a body is about lightness, freedom, comfort, relaxation. At first, of course, you are afraid because you have lost some of your senses, but you soon gain an entire fresh set of senses, and they open a whole new world of beauty and experience such as you never thought possible."

We can see that NDEs give us a wonderful glimpse of the soul plane, as they are reminded of the flight plan they filed and the goals they established for this lifetime. One man was taken back to a pre-life planning session about challenges group members would take on. The counselor told them that, for growth, they could meet challenges at a slow but on-going pace, or cram them full with severe illness. The man recalled volunteering for cystic fibrosis so as to study response to constant pain. His NDE gave him the first break from lifetime pain, and recalling his choice removed any 'why me?' element.

A woman NDEr relived the life-planning process, meeting the soul who would one day become her son, and a counselor telling her how much her difficult life challenges she had chosen were advancing her soul age. Another woman relived meeting all her siblings-to-be, where they had decided the birth order and debated which of three couples they wanted as parents. A male NDEr was taken back to a meeting with the spirits who would later be his children, and was surprised to find them full-grown long before their birth.

When Betty Eadie visited the soul plane during her NDE, she was relieved to learn that Earth is not our natural home, but is just a place for brief (from soul's perspective) learning sojourns.

In about 6% of cases, NDEs can also reveal future events. Upon dying following a hernia operation, a man was greeted by his long-deceased daughter who told him, "It's not your turn yet." She then listed three other family members who would precede him: his son, then his mother, then his wife. He then returned to his body just as a priest was administering Last Rites, and made a miraculous recovery. Just weeks later, his four-year-old son fell very ill and told his father that the sister he had never met had come for him, adding, "She says that when you were in the hospital, she told you this was going to happen." Three hours later, the boy slipped away with his older sister. Within two months, his mother died after being told by her doctor that she would 'outlive us all.' Six years later, his wife crossed over, presumably to a grand family reunion.

During her NDE, one young woman met a spirit who pleaded with her to return to her body because he had chosen her as his mother and, without her, his important mission on Earth could not be accomplished. Another young woman saw a tall man walking with two small children who got excited when they saw her. She just 'knew' they were her family-to-be, and that she had to return to Earth to wait for them to show up. They did.

Another NDEr was approached by the spirit of a man who had been murdered, who asked him to relay to family still on Earth that he was fine and busily at work on the soul plane. In another case, a woman who had died and whose relatives were grieving excessively, returned just long enough to tell them she would be fine on the soul plane if only they would not grieve as much, as it was interfering with her work there.

During an NDE, a woman was introduced to two little girls in spirit and exclaimed at how beautiful they were. A counselor asked, "Do you want to be their mother?" When she said yes, the being replied, "Good. This is why you were brought here. Now you must return." As she recovered, she told her husband they were to have two more children. The girls were born one year and three years later, and looked *exactly* as they did during the mother's NDE.

Such NDEs reassure us that, despite appearances to the contrary, our lives *are* carefully planned *by us* long before we as soul approach the Earth plane, and that planning includes our finest achievements as well as our more dire failures. So we are *never* victims of life or other people; everything that happens to us happens because we planned it that way.

Countless NDErs have been told that the *only* things you can take with you when you cross over are *knowledge* and *love;* the rest stays here. Melvin Morse summarizes this as: (1) love your neighbor, (2) cherish life, (3) clean up your own messes, (4) be the best you can be, and (5) be of service.

The knowledge and love you take with you are important to your continued studies on the other side. You might ask, as I once did, "What's the point of my seeking knowledge on this side, when once I cross over, I get total access to Universal Knowledge?" Well, it's the quest itself that's important—how you go about your discovery, your mental machinations as you strive to figure things out. For example, when I first read Zecharia Sitchin's books, I was amazed at how much sense the information made and how it answered many of my questions. Then doubts set in: "If the information *is* true, why doesn't everyone know and accept it? Maybe Sitchin and I are the only people in the world who believe it." Only later did I realize that whether or not it's true is less important than my brain-wracking in weighing the evidence.

Another reason for searching for the quest is that once you know, you spread your wisdom and insights to those on the Earth plane ... if people are ready to hear you. This is no more important than when it involves a potential suicide that your words can help avert. Everyone has a life mission, and suicide robs the world of the fruits of that mission, so it's the duty of each of us to dissuade a would-be suicide from applying a permanent solution to a temporary problem.

At the moment of death, people can be confused because they find themselves in a duplicate body that looks and feels every bit as real as the one they just left that's lying in bed or mangled in a car wreck. They can pull their hair and pinch their skin, and it feels totally real. They can even see their fingerprints, although their hands are glowing. The only clues as to a change are that any pain has ceased, and those still living cannot see or hear them, but those who have crossed over can. Still, realization can take a while because we are so accustomed to our physical body being our focal point. If realization does not come, one can end up caught in limbo, or what Dannion Brinkley calls, in *The Secrets of the Light*, 'the blue-gray place.' There, he saw spirits wandering aimlessly around, endlessly repeating the same day, often since as long ago as the Civil War. Armed with fore-knowledge, you can zip past that place on your way to the soul plane.

Another clue is that when we cross over, our spiritual bodies are perfect, younger, taller, and more radiant, as are the bodies of those we meet who have already crossed over, yet we still know who they are. Also, we suddenly possess many more senses and abilities, such as being any place or beside anyone we think of.

Apart from LTP NDEs, thousands of returnees describe the soul plane as the most exquisitely beautiful environment, beyond anything they could ever have imagined. The scenery, flora and fauna are breathtaking and defy description, as do the colors, sounds and smells.

A few 'lucky' NDErs get to visit a city, where the very buildings emanate light and are separated by lawns and gardens that are beyond perfection. Some buildings have soaring marble or crystal walls and columns, topped by domes of finely worked gold, and are pervaded by reverence for their purpose, whether it is learning, research, teaching or study.

If family ties are important to NDErs, they may briefly visit with family members. One woman found crossed-over relatives busily preparing for the arrival of an aged aunt who was expected, but was told that she, the woman, had to return to Earth. When she came out of her NDE, she learned the aunt had just died.

NDErs routinely hear that life on the soul plane revolves around ongoing learning, teaching and service to those on both the soul and Earth planes. Learning over there is easy for two reasons: (1) we are no longer limited by linear brains, and (2) we have instant access to unlimited knowledge. We learn at our own pace and can study whatever subjects interest us. The corollary of learning is teaching, in vast, university-type settings dedicated to every conceivable body of knowledge.

We also serve as spirit guides and guardian angels to those still on the Earth plane, and many NDErs are reassured to meet their guides on the other side. Such meetings are characterized by profoundly intense love and assurance of ongoing 24/7 support. (Countless anecdotal accounts describe how a stranger just 'shows up' to warn of impending danger, which helps one avert it, and is then nowhere to be found—all evidence of the other side busy at work.)

The truly great gift of NDEs is that they put the particular life we're living, into the larger context of soul growth. We come to Earth to experience certain things, so it's impossible for anyone to be a 'failure' because we learn from each experience. We may not fully understand a lesson until we return to the soul plane, but that doesn't matter, for down here, we are *fact-gathering* for later study.

Of course, fact-gathering can be painful or joyful, the difference depending on how much love you allow to flow through you to others. Also, seeing the larger context ensures that your actions and how you treat others follows the Golden Rule. And knowing about the life review process means you will always test the love quotient in your actions and examine the long-term consequences.

Context is revealed in the pre-life planning that goes into an incarnation and the meetings between all those spirits involved. NDEs also reveal the life's mission and goals, plus the help available from the other side.

The duration of Earth lives is predetermined, and if they suffer a life-threatening situation before the appointed time, NDErs are told to return to their bodies to continue their mission. A life review and advice from counselors and deceased relatives are also often part of the package. And occasionally, the actual soul shows up to reveal additional background as to particular challenges. The paramount benefit is the realization that whatever your life circumstances, *you chose it!*

NDEs also show us that we carry on pretty much on the soul plane as we did on the Earth plane, automatically adjusting our level there according to the love energy in our aura. And on the soul plane, there is *no* hiding because our memories are intact and open for all to see.

In summary, NDEs reveal that we lead *very* active lives on the soul plane, and put them on hold for a few decades to plan, execute and conclude an Earth sojourn. Then we return to the soul plane, review how we did, and resume our soul plane activities, each phase smoothly dovetailing with the next in a well-orchestrated symphony of love, learning and service. Knowing this helps us immeasurably to lead more productive Earth lives and better prepare for what lies beyond. As we will see below, NDEs are *always* life-changing. It is *vital* we know that whatever preparations we make here will greatly help us over there, and that worldly achievements here count for nothing in the big picture over there.

The NDE phenomenon is crucial because it proves there is a part of us that can and does operate independently from the physical body, and has far better senses than just our normal five. However, the phenomenon also raises more questions than it answers, such as what actually lifts out of the physical body, how can it see, what exactly *is* the Light, and *where* is it? First, the etheric, emotional, mental and spiritual bodies together lift out of the physical body. In an NDE, the bodies are still connected by the famous silver cord, which is actually severed when we cross over for good. The etheric body has etheric eyes, which many NDErs report as having 360° vision. These eyes can see both etherically and physically, which is why people talk about floating above their body while medical staff try to resuscitate it.

The tunnel (shown here in a painting by Hieronymus Bosch titled *Ascent into the Empyrean*, in the Doge's Palace, Venice) is actually through dimensions rather than space, and usually takes one to the Light, which is often described as a bright, luminous fog. In this fog, one feels unconditional love and a sense of all-knowing. As to its location, it's in a part of the spiritual plane reserved for temporary visitors and new arrivals for beginning the necessary orientation and energy cleansing. Most NDErs do not go further, and may just

Ascent into the Empyrean

have a conversation with a being in the light, but some, notably Dannion Brinkley and Betty Eadie, are taken further in to see cities and landscapes. Dannion actually met 13 beings who showed him 117 visions for Earth's future, all of which have come about (except for those that are *still* in our future, and are discussed in his third book, *The Secrets of the Light*).

Noted neurologist Wilder Penfield discovered, by stimulating parts of the brain, that different areas are associated with different functions. He found that the right temporal lobe (see diagram) just above the right ear is the seat of the NDE. This does not mean it's just a brain function, but that the part of the spiritual body, mind, or spirit involved with the NDE anchors to the brain in that area, which undergoes a change when impacted by the Light that is at the core of the experi-

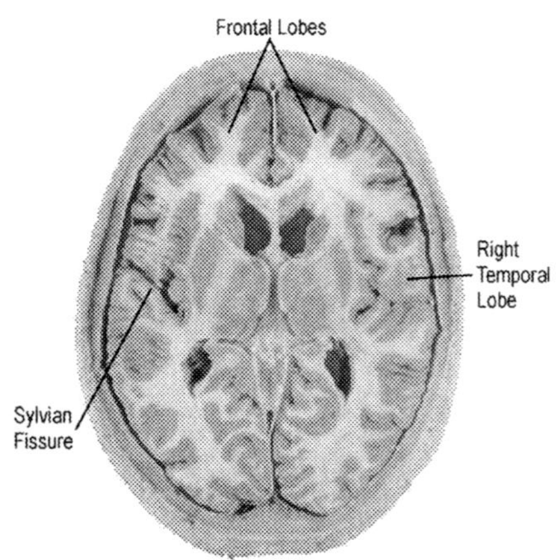

Cross-section of the Human Brain

ence. Those who encounter the Light come back with enhanced psychic abilities, which shows up as increased temporal lobe activity on MRI and CAT scans. There is no enhancement with NDErs who do not encounter the Light.

Interestingly, another area of the brain associated with anchoring psychic abilities is the Sylvian Fissure, just over the left ear. It is also the seat of higher intellect (as opposed to the frontal lobe's normal intellect). Einstein's brain displayed a highly unusual Sylvian Fissure, which may account for his remarkable ability to 'think outside the box.' This, too, is a major anchor for mind to connect with the brain, along with the pineal and hippocampus glands.

As a quick aside, previewing relationships, an MRI done on male subjects while being read a fiction story shows activity in the left hemisphere only, while women show activity in both. This suggests that in conversations between a couple, the man listens analytically, missing the emotional cues that his mate gives, while the woman 'hears it all.' So heads up, guys, and listen with *both* ears.

Life-changing Nature of NDEs

The important lesson of NDEs is not that they happen, but what they mean. How do they change the NDEr and the rest of us in the areas of self-view in terms of how we perceive and hence treat other people? How do they change our larger worldview, and our relationship with soul?

The key component to a life-changing experience seems to be the Light, seeing it, being enveloped by it, and better yet, meeting a Being in it. NDErs who do not encounter the Light report having a pleasant out-of-body experience, but those touched by the Light undergo radical life changes.

All of us search for personal meaning, often in our jobs and relationships, but many fail to find it. We are really searching for our unique place within the matrix of All That Is, and NDErs usually come back with the certainty that they *do* have meaning within the larger scheme of things.

NDErs routinely return with higher self-esteem and self-confidence, and a passion for their perceived mission, reporting *significant increases* in:

- Appreciation of life, treasuring small, ordinary things and events, and an increased love for, and reverence of, nature. When one woman woke up after her NDE, the first thing she saw was a vase of flowers; she broke into tears at their beauty.
- Sense of partnership with All That Is, in which they have a responsibility to the Source, but are also infinitely supported by it. They are filled with awe for the majesty of Creation, from the tiniest bug up to entire galaxies, and

everything, including themselves, is held sacred. A common phrase used by Native Americans is, "For all my relations," and they mean *all*.

- Concern for others, in the areas of helping others, increased compassion, patience, tolerance, love, greater insight and understanding, and more acceptance of who and how other people are. As Albert Einstein said, "Human beings are part of the whole, yet we experience ourselves as something separate from the rest—a kind of optical delusion of consciousness. This forms a kind of prison for us, restricting us to our personal desires and to affection for the few persons nearest to us. Our task must be to free ourselves from this prison by widening our circle of compassion to embrace all living creatures and the whole of nature in its beauty."

- Enhanced quest for meaning, involving higher consciousness, meaning of life, purpose, and self-understanding. (As one NDEr said, "I am here to learn the laws of Creation and to love unconditionally. Since my experience, I am no longer content to live for myself. My sense of fulfillment comes from developing my potential for service to others.") Loving, compassionate service comes more naturally to NDErs, as exemplified by Dannion Brinkley, who has spent thousands of hours in hospices at the bedsides of the dying.

- Profound gratitude both for having a unique place in the Universe *and* knowing about it. Even those who come back to impaired health or compromised bodies still display wonderment and awe at being part of All That Is.

NDErs also show a *significant decrease* in:
- Concern for impressing others, including becoming well-known and worrying about what others think. (This stems from higher self-esteem but without self-inflation. Superficial social games become irrelevant as NDErs present their secure authentic selves to the world.)

- Pursuit of pleasure for its own sake. They find that happiness and pleasure flow from throwing yourself wholeheartedly into life. Dr. Victor Frankl said, "Happiness cannot be pursued; it must ensure as the unintended side-effect of one's personal dedication to a course greater than onself.

- Concern with materialism. A car is just a means of getting from A to B, and doesn't have to be the latest foreign import to do that.

NDE researcher Dr. Ring concludes that the NDE catalyzes a marked shift from materialism to spirituality, and puts NDErs on the spiritual path. This does not mean 'religious' but a 'universality,' which he defines in terms of seven qualities:

1. Spiritual but not religious (This doesn't always mean pulling away from the church. In fact, 40 percent found deeper ties, but they were less into empty church ritual than before and more into private prayer.)
2. Feeling close to the Supreme Being (seen as much larger than the Christian God)
3. Absolute conviction in the reality of life after death
4. Openness to the concept of reincarnation
5. Realization of the underlying unity of all religions, based on appreciation for the Supreme Source, leading to an interest in the beliefs of others
6. Desire for one unifying religion.

NDErs also undergo remarkable physical changes, too, according to Ring. They are likely to be more sensitive to light, sound and humidity. They also experience decreases in metabolic rate, temperature and blood pressure. They sense that their brains actually function differently and can process more input more efficiently. Also, electronic equipment tends to burn out in their presence, and they can even scramble data in computers. Light bulbs often glow when NDErs just hold them. It seems that whatever part of us 'goes to the Light' (etheric double and that part of soul that projects into the body as a conscious focal point) returns with a more powerful electromagnetic field. (Other researchers theorize that this electromagnetic power may also be a result of a spontaneous *kundalini* experience.[2])

Other physical symptoms include heat and tingling sensations, especially in the hands and feet, energy flows around the body and unaccountable vibrations or shaking, which are also symptoms of kundalini rising.

Another issue tackled by Ring is that, of those who are resuscitated after clinical death, only one in three reports having an NDE. Why? What's different about them, he asked. His survey reveals that, compared with a control group, NDErs were 2.5 times more likely to have been prone to alternate realities as children. They were also 2.2 times more prone to having psychic abilities, compared with the control group. This includes playing with invisible friends and seeing into astral realms. This ability to disassociate from everyday reality may be why some people report having NDEs and others do not.

---

[2] *Kundalini* is a Sanskrit word for a bioenergetic 'pool' that sits at the base of the spine. Certain spiritual processes can cause it to rise up the spine. It can also rise spontaneously, causing pain, confusion and fear if one does not know what's happening.

For most NDErs, spirituality becomes the bedrock of their lives, on which all else rests. Those of us who have not had an NDE would do well to ponder that, which brings us to the big question: Can what is true for the NDEr be true for the rest of us? Of course it can. Try reading NDE accounts and note how the experiencer feels. Then pretend the experience happened to you, too. How do you feel?

It's possible to tap into the experience of others without needing to drown, or fall off a cliff and get smushed on the rocks below. Make believe *you* have basked in the unconditional love and acceptance of the being of Light, that *you* were told you have an important mission and must return to Earth, that *you* met your deceased loved ones waiting for you, etc.

Nothing marked NDErs as 'special' before their NDE ... or after it. We're all just bozos on the bus of Life, but they got to talk with the driver, and we can eavesdrop. Here are a few ways you will benefit:

1. You will fear death less or not at all, for you will be sure you exist independently of your physical body, and in a state of divine ecstasy.
2. You will know that everything happens as it should and for a reason, even if you can't always see what it is.
3. You will enjoy feelings of well-being, self-acceptance and a greater zest for life.
4. You will know that spirit guides are all around you, and you will become more open to their guidance, such as noticing, appreciating and acting upon synchronicities, whereas before you had dismissed them as coincidences.
5. While you may not 'meet God,' you will know of the Divine Order behind life and sense that a Supreme Source is ultimately responsible ... and know that you are an integral part of that Source.

Obviously this 'borrowing' technique falls short, because NDErs undergo actual changes, such as the acquisition of the gifts of clairvoyance and healing. But probably the most important thing to 'borrow' from NDErs is their absolute certainty in life-after-death, the continuance of consciousness, and the exalted nature of life on the Other Side. Even hardened skeptics return with such certainty. We also realize that religious bias has no effect on the experience; soul alone determines what the individual experiences.

At this point, debunkers may protest that NDErs are already interested in spiritual matters and make their NDE account to bolster their beliefs. However, researchers find that only about 1 in 50 or so had any prior interest in esoterica before their NDE. Also, many spiritual people 'die' and are resuscitated without having an NDE.

The information imparted in NDEs can come in three 'flavors,' although an NDE can contain all three:

1. Advice and insights specific to the NDErs themselves about life goals and directions. A being of light is often encountered, possibly a spiritual icon or maybe one's own higher self, but always exuding such unconditional love that it's often hard to bear. Once back to health, the NDEr's life, beliefs and behavior usually undergo dramatic changes as a result.

2. Insights important to humanity as a whole, such as being shown the outcome of not halting pollution or nuclear arms proliferation. The insights can be shocking in order to get our attention, and the NDEr is charged with coming back and telling the rest of us.

3. Vast spiritual truths, such as the reality of life-after-death, the unity of Divinity, or the perfection of the Divine Plan. Not a single NDEr has ever returned who is not certain that some ultimate, transcendent reality exists, of which we are all a part. And during the encounter with the Divine Light Being, they briefly know what it knows about the purpose of Creation, although this often doesn't come back with them. They also see the profound connection between all things in Creation, and experience deep gratitude for being part of it. As one put it: "The serenity and peace were nearly overwhelming … an intense feeling of love and joy."

Dannion Brinkley's NDE, documented in his book *Saved by the Light*, triggered by a lightning strike in September, 1975, contains all three aspects:

1. During his grueling panoramic life review, he got to experience being on the receiving end of his roustabout youth and his military service exploits.

2. He was then shown a series of 117 visions, of which 95 had come to pass by 1993 when he wrote *Saved by the Light*. These included the dismantling of the Soviet Union, Chernobyl and Desert Storm in 1991. He was told that the remaining dire predictions were not inevitable and that humanity could deflect the worst outcomes.

3. He also got to meet a number of Beings of Light in a beautiful crystal city, feel their overwhelming unconditional love, and see the perfection of their Plan. They also charged him with setting up a number of healing centers.

To sum up this section, the NDE phenomenon is incredibly important because people have crossed over the soul plane and returned to tell us about it, with incontrovertible plausibility. And their testimony changes our worldview of the universe around us in many ways:

1. There *is* a soul plane, and meaningful things *do* happen there

2. Consciousness *does* survive physical death without so much as a blink

3. Our lives are meaningful sojourns within a much larger tapestry of meaning that itself is part of an infinite and eternal venture on the part of Spirit.

Implications of the NDE Phenomenon

Strictly speaking, the two elements—(1) having an out-of-body experience in which you see things from a different vantage point, and (2) having a spiritual encounter with Beings of Light—do not actually answer the life-after-death question. Yes, your consciousness does operate independently of your body during an NDE, sometimes for up to an hour of clinical death, but the body is still capable of being resuscitated. Can we make the leap that says the resuscitation issue doesn't matter? That clinical death for 45 minutes is the same as for 45 years? NDErs all say yes.

For those who are about to cross over, the phenomenon tells them:

- Actually crossing over is not painful, and is often ecstatic.
- Your experience is real, and not the result of an oxygen-starved brain.
- You cross over, not to oblivion, but to a beautiful, light-filled environment, to be met by your loved ones who are already there and quite fine. Thus there is nothing to fear.
- Any deathbed visions you may have are real, and the people and places you see are real.

For the friends and family of someone about to cross over:

- Those who have deathbed visions are not "going senile" or hallucinating. What and who they see are real; you just don't have the psychic senses that would allow you to see them too. As people approach the threshold, new senses come online that allow them to see and hear what you cannot. Their final look of serenity is justified.
- With effort, those on the soul plane can contact those on the Earth plane, and even materialize for a while. This is real. Be open to contact with, and visions of, those who have crossed over.

For medical staff attending those who are crossing over:

- You are not in control of their process; they are. So do what you can but do not fight the process. Relax whatever rules get in the way, such as visiting restrictions.
- Accept the reality of deathbed visions, and that your dying patients have senses you do not.
- Do not impose your beliefs about the process on them and on surviving family members because you are probably wrong. Never invalidate what your patients and their loved ones claim to experience.
- Treat those in a coma as being fully present but just not active, for their senses are often fully functioning.

Before leaving this topic, let's just revisit the big question: Does the NDE phenomenon 'prove' the survival of consciousness after death? Many NDErs report some kind of barrier or 'line in the sand' that, if crossed, means their *near*-death becomes *actual* death. It is inconceivable that if they crossed that line, they would suddenly vanish into oblivion with a 'poof,' especially as the deceased loved ones who came to greet them often approach from behind the *line*. However, far more compelling evidence comes from other phenomena such as cross-correspondences (later in this chapter) and reports from the deceased through reputable mediums with concrete evidentiary information that is not known to the medium or sitter but is later verified.

Although the near-death experience does not prove survival of death, it does provide three strong indicators:

1. *Improved mental processes* such as reasoning at a time when we would expect mental functioning to have ceased or at least greatly diminished due to loss of the body's vital signs. This strongly suggests that consciousness operates independently from the physical body and could continue after physical death.

2. The *out-of-body experience* demonstrates senses that operate over and above the five physical senses and are non-local to the body. This allows the NDEr to gather sensory information from the immediate environment and beyond which is not available to the body, usually due to lack of consciousness and/or mobility. This strongly suggests that the psychic senses are independent of the physical body and therefore could continue after physical death.

3. *Paranormal experiences*, such as visiting the light in a nonphysical realm where things are learned that transcend physical means of learning them,

such as learning of the death of others in the same accident by having met them in a nonphysical realm. This suggests that consciousness really does operate in a different dimension independent of the physical body, and could therefore continue following the death of the physical body.

Again, while not *proving* survival of death, NDE components are *strongly suggestive* of it. Add to this the categorical insistence of survival on the part of those returning from NDEs and we have a pretty strong case for survival. One of the most remarkable NDE accounts follows:

In 1982, Mellen-Thomas Benedict died from terminal cancer, having been in hospice care for about eighteen months. He awoke about 4:30 am and knew he was going to die. Suddenly, he found himself fully aware and standing up, looking down at his body in the bed. He noticed a strong Light, magnificent, tangible and alluring. As he moved towards it, he knew if he went into the Light, he would be dead, so he decided to have a conversation with the Light first. As the Light changed into different figures—Jesus, Buddha, Krishna, archetypal images and signs—he wondered what was going on.

The Light transmitted the information that our beliefs mirror back the kind of feedback we receive. Then he became aware of a Higher Self matrix, an oversoul part of our being that connects all as one being, making all humans literally the same being. He also experienced love beyond imaginable, the kind of love that spontaneously cures, heals and regenerates.

Then the Light turned into the most beautiful thing he'd ever seen—a mandala of all human souls on the planet—which changed in an instant how he saw humanity and reality in general. He was particularly astonished to find there is no evil in any soul. Although people do terrible things out of ignorance, no soul is evil. The Light told him, "What all people seek, what sustains them, is love. What distorts people is a lack of love."

"Does this mean that humankind will be saved?" he asked. The Light replied, "You save, redeem and heal yourself. You always have and always will. You were created with the power to do so from before the beginning of the world." In that instant, he realized *we have already been saved!*

Next, he entered into another realm more profound than the last, and was aware of an enormous stream of Light, vast and deep. He asked what it was, and the Light answered, "This is the *river of life*. Drink of this water to your heart's content."

Suddenly he rocketed away from the planet and the solar system, flew through the center of the galaxy, and learned that the entire universe is teeming with myriad varieties of life. As the universe shrank into a speck, he passed into a second Light and could perceive forever, beyond Infinity. He was in the pre-Creation Void, at one with Absolute Consciousness, and realized Creation is the Creator exploring its own Self through every way imaginable. Every hair on your head, every leaf on every tree, every atom, is the Creator exploring its Self. *That's what it is all about.* The truth became obvious to him that there is no death, that nothing is born and nothing dies, and that we are immortal beings within a natural, living system that endlessly recycles itself.

As he began his return to the life cycle, he asked never to forget the revelations he had learned on the other side. He expected to reincarnate into a baby somewhere, so was surprised to be back in his old body, with a hospice nurse crying her eyes out. Initially, he had no memory of the experience, yet within three days, he was feeling normal again, clearer, but different than before, and the memories kept coming back.

Three months later, a doctor at the clinic said, "I can find no sign of cancer."

"A miracle?" Benedict asked.

"No," the doctor answered dourly. "Just spontaneous remission."

However, Benedict knew it was a miracle. So, how did his NDE change him? In this own words:

"I now know that our heart, not our intellect, is the wiser part of ourselves. I experience the Light spontaneously, and have learned how to get to that space almost any time in my meditation. You can also do this. You do not have to die first. You are wired for it already.

"The body is the most magnificent Light being there is. It is a universe of incredible Light. Spirit is not pushing us to dissolve this body. We don't need to commune with the Source; the Source is communing with us in every moment. When I asked it, "What is the best religion on the planet? Which one is right?" it said with great love, "I don't care." So it doesn't matter what religion we are. Religions come and go. Buddhism and Catholicism have not been here forever, but they are all about to become more enlightened. Many will resist, believing that only they are right. But the Source doesn't care if you are Protestant, Buddhist, or Jew. Each is a reflection, a facet of the whole. Each has a different view … and it all adds up to the big picture."

Two Brains in One

Before leaving the fascinating topic of the brain, let's see how our brain actually works to support our mind. The two hemispheres of the brain support two very different modes of the mind's processing:

1. *Left hemisphere* supports linear, rational, deductive reasoning, where everything that is known has come in via the five senses or has been logically deduced.

2. *Right hemisphere* supports intuitive, insightful processing that includes peak and mystical experiences, and exercise of psychic talents, e.g., clairvoyance and the ability to see patterns, such as when you stare at those images made up of visual clutter and a 3-D image suddenly pops out at you.

Ideally the two hemispheres work together via the *corpus collosum*, but if this is impaired, a person can actually be two entirely different people who know nothing about each other. For example, one woman had her right eye covered and was shown an erotic image, causing her to blush. When asked why she was blushing, her left-brain response was that she had no idea, because her left brain hadn't seen the image; her right brain had responded to it.

The idea of two minds first emerged to explain hypnotism. We have:

- An *objective mind* that deals with practical issues in the outside world, using reason and the five senses

- A *subjective mind* that deals with the inner world through intuition and insight.

During hypnosis, the subjective mind is engaged and the person can speak in languages not learned in this lifetime, and know things beyond the physical senses, such as the text of stories in an unopened newspaper or book. To many people, this mind is a mysterious stranger whose promptings are drowned out by the objective mind. Its worst enemy is skepticism, which shuts it down completely.

Genius results from balanced, free flow between the two minds, but those with a dominant right brain may not be able to communicate their insights or put them into a real-world context, as with idiot savants. If the left brain dominates, its adult, rational approach can dampen or even stop the childlike wonderment and awe of the right, leading to depression, neurosis and even suicide.

Another dampener is that we tend to live life on autopilot, where our jaded responses cause us to miss life's exquisite moments. We become bored, wooden and closed off to input from soul via spirit, which comes via the right-brain mind. We then live in a 3-D trance, consumed by the illusion, like the figures in Plato's cave, fascinated by shadows, yet unaware of the vaster reality creating them. With our senses dulled, we sleep-walk through life, missing its magic, as if a blanket had been stuffed into a piano to dull all the strings.

Indigos and psychics do not have such a blanket to dull right brain operation. But what can the rest of us do to reawaken the right brain to its full potential? Begin by forming a new habit—really *noticing* things. Study the petals on a rose or the pattern of seeds in a sunflower. Really *listen* to the intricacies of birdsong. Stop seeing things as symbols, and see them for what they *really* are. (Symbols are autopilot's way of dealing with complexity—by reducing everything to simpler patterns.)

It would be wrong, however, to cast the left-brain mind as a soulless jailer of our creative side, for both sides have evolved to work together. Early man could have all the mystical visions he wanted, but he still had to fashion weapons and go hunting, and design and erect somewhere to live. Left-brain mind gives us our sense of 'I-me' and also anchors us in time-space, whereas right-brain mind would be having out-of-body experiences and flitting along the time-line into past and future.

An example of this is the widely reported phenomenon of 'time-slips,' where people suddenly find themselves transported to a totally different time. Two women of impeccable credentials were touring the Palace of Versailles but rather than being surrounded by other tourists with cameras, they were in the midst of people of the 1750s era. Two other women were in an old Civil War era building and suddenly found themselves in the middle of a field hospital, where they saw limbs were being sawn off without anesthetic, and other horrors of war. In both cases, both women saw the same thing, so it wasn't imagination. Somehow, their right-brain mind had done a 'fast-reverse' and stopped at a point of strong energetic imprint on the timeline. How and why is not known, but it makes us glad of the left brain anchoring in the 'here and now.'

In the English Civil War Battle of Edgehill in 1642, 30,000 soldiers clashed in three hours of hand-to-hand combat. Both sides were so badly mauled that a 'draw' was declared, but the fighting was so violent, the episode stamped itself on the fabric of time-space, and for three centuries, historians would visit the site and watch the battle 'replay' itself. King Charles I even sent an envoy to report back to him on the phenomenon.

The challenge is to blend left-brain mind's 'planning and control' of *outer* life, with right-brain mysticism and connection to *inner* life, so that structured discipline co-exists with spontaneous creativity. How do we do that? Meet in the middle during meditation. Or buy a hemi-sync machine. (If you can't afford a new one, buy a used one on eBay.) Or play with books of optical illusions that exercise both hemispheres.

The left-brain mind can be likened to roaring down the freeway at night with your headlights illuminating just the road ahead. You see none of the scenery passing by, but just what's in the field of your headlights. The right-brain mind kicks in when you sit beside a lake at night and open your senses to everything that's going on—lapping of small waves, the wind sighing in the trees, the plop as a fish breaks the surface to catch an insect, the whoosh as a night heron swoops in to take the fish, and the rustle of undergrowth as a fox comes down to the water's edge to drink. In this open state, we are clairvoyant, clairsentient, and can talk to dead people. The whole point is to break left-brain mind's obsession with life's daily trivia, so that right mind's wonderment and awe can surface. Then all doubt, depression and suicidal thoughts would evaporate, and we would know of our innate 'rightness' in the physical world and the realm of spirit, *and* of life's *meaningfulness*.

Back in our story, Joe describes his experience to the staff but is brushed off with the usual 'neural activity of a dying brain starved of oxygen' explanation. Not satisfied with this, Joe begins a lifelong spiritual quest to discover what happened, and also resumes his college classes. Odd how things turn out, isn't it?

Joe joins the college spiritualist group, where members communicate with those who have crossed over, and meets Sally, an incarnation of an old soul buddy whom his soul has chosen as his life mate. They become inseparable.

Nearing graduation, on his way home from a job interview, by 'coincidence,' Joe goes down an unfamiliar street and just 'happens' to see a group gathered around a tree. On stopping, he learns that a cat is stuck, so with the invincibility of youth, he climbs the tree and rescues the animal, but not before receiving a bad scratch on his arm. The cat's grateful owner takes him into the house to treat the scratch. When her husband comes home, she regales him with stories of Joe's bravery. The husband owns the local newspaper and is about to advertise for a junior staff reporter. Joe gets the job. Funny how things turn out, isn't it?

Ten years later, Joe is a reporter for the local TV station, and receives an unusual assignment from the crabby news director. "This weirdo is in town who claims to talk to dead people. Try to figure out what his scam is, okay? Someone else was supposed to cover the story but he's got car trouble."

Joe's heart leaps at the chance to interview the famous medium, whose show is syndicated nationwide. On meeting, the medium looks at Joe, smiles and asks, "Do your parents follow you everywhere?" Things are off to good start and Joe shoots a very sympathetic piece, which enrages the news director, whose wife just 'happens' to stop by the studio on her way to … the medium's evening seminar. She threatens divorce if her husband doesn't air the interview. It airs as the human interest segment on the six o'clock news that night and changes countless people's views on survival of death. Odd how things turn out, isn't it?

Years later, Joe retires and spends his days writing a book about his passion—survival of death, naturally. One day, he meets his last Challenge. A sharp pain stabs in his chest and he slumps forward. Sally, his wife and an ex-nurse, calls paramedics and keeps him alive with CPR. In the ICU, Joe watches from the ceiling as the doctors open his chest and massage his heart. Bored, he notices a tunnel and moves into it, unafraid. Knowing where the tunnel leads, his only regrets are not finishing his book and leaving his beloved Sally, who he knows will join him anyway in what will seem a blink on the soul plane.

At the end of the tunnel, a magnificent Being of Light envelops him and he is bathed in ecstatic love for the Being. He asks/thinks, "Who are you?"

"I am your soul," booms in his mind. "Yes, we really are this magnificent. Now you see why only part of our energy can incarnate on Earth. Like this, we would burn up the physical body in an instant. It is not yet your time. You will go back and complete the book. Use this experience to tell everyone they are infinitely more than they believe themselves to be. Your recovery will be swift."

Joe is suddenly back in his body, bright-eyed and alert, showing no signs of being under anesthesia. Three days later, to the amazement of the hospital staff, he's ready to go home. He resumes work on the book, which is published four months later to great acclaim.

Return Home

Three years later, Joe and Sally are returning from a book signing in the next town when a runaway big rig slams into their car. They leave their bodies before impact and, standing together surveying the tangled mess of steel and flesh, they look at each other and smile. "Guess we won't need those anymore. Ready for an adventure?" Joe asks.

Sally grins impishly and takes his hand. "Which way to the tunnel?"

When the two emerge, they are greeted by a huge crowd of friends, relatives, the son they lost to SIDS and now a tall, handsome 30-year-old, various dogs and cats they have loved, and even the horse from Sally's childhood. Suddenly a hush falls over the party as a tall, robed figure approaches. His long hair, beard and loving eyes leave no doubt as to his identity. Instinctively, Joe and Sally drop to their knees before the figure, but hear the gentle words in their minds, "Stand. It is I who should kneel before you in gratitude for your service. Welcome Home."

The figure's eyes bathe the pair with infinite love and he slowly dissolves, leaving them shaken to their very core. The rest of the group looks on in awe at the special honor just bestowed.

The party resumes until Joe's spirit guide tells them it's time to go to the Hall of Healing to have all vestiges of Earth energy transformed into the higher frequencies of the soul plane.

Joe looks at his wife of 50 years and gasps at the radiantly beautiful 30-year-old woman standing beside him. Picking up his thought, Sally smiles at the tall, muscular young man Joe has become. "Plenty of time for that later," she jokes. "We're here for a long, long time."

Is It Real?

Fact or fiction? It depends on who you ask. To career skeptics (really professional debunkers), all the accounts of those hypnotically regressed can be dismissed as suggestions implanted by therapists as fodder for their next book. Or the delusional ramblings of hopeful but deranged people who are so afraid of death, they will stop at nothing to assuage their fears.

On the other hand, you can go to any public library or metaphysical bookstore and read thousands upon thousands of accounts that are all very similar to each other and to the hypothetical story of Joe, created from a collage of true stories. If it *is* all bunk, then it's the largest mass conspiracy of all time, going back thousands of years to ancient Greece, and philosophers Plato and Socrates.

Despite overwhelming evidence, the debunkers keep up their monotonous denials in the name of protecting you, the gullible public, from the charlatans who claim to unite us with deceased loved ones, while separating us from our wallets. Fortunately, most of us do not need such patronizing protection.

Here are a few of the debunkers' favorite weapons and, in *italics*, how Dr. Schwartz of the University of Arizona ensured they could not apply to his clinical trials involving John Edward and George Anderson:

- Outright fraud using researchers or private detectives *(sitters were randomly chosen)*
- Cold reading by studying facial expressions, voice stress and other cues *(mediums could not see sitters, who communicated with researchers using only nods and shakes of head)*
- Sitter remembers only the 'hits' and forgets the 'misses' *(scoring of accuracy was based on typed transcripts of sessions)*
- Information vague and general *(seven levels of 'hit' were used to score sessions)*
- Lucky guesses and not replicable *(each sitter was read by five mediums, with 'chance' correlations estimated at over one in a trillion)*
- Protocol bias or errors *(stringent checks and balances, with 'near hits' scored down a level)*
- Mediums motivated by greed and with an ego need to be right *(results guaranteed to be made public, which would discourage fake mediums from endangering their careers)*
- Mediums are just 'mind-reading the sitters' and can't read the dead because, well … they're dead *(readings revealed details that couldn't be confirmed until later, or that the sitter was mistaken about and corrected later)*
- Medium reading from 'universal memory' *(contactees retained unique personality and often argued with the medium)*
- Medium is contacting merely the 'after glow' of the deceased who really is dead and gone *(interplay between medium and contactee is dynamic, fluid and driven by personality of the contactee and often involves events that occurred in the sitter's life after the contactee crossed over)*

What drives the debunkers, apart from royalties from their book sales and fees for TV show appearances? Some are driven by fear that it is all actually true and of having to be responsible for what that means. It's easy to say that death is the end so we don't have to be accountable for our life beyond death. It is a different matter to say, "I am responsible for, and will be held accountable for, every action and interaction in my life, so I will strive for the highest and most noble expression of my divinity."

When all else fails, the debunkers also resort to dirty tricks by, say, publishing scurrilous articles in attempts to discredit the spiritual arena. One debunker was so determined to bring John Edward down, he wrote an article claiming that on *Crossing Over with John Edward*, production assistants interviewed audience members to get family tree information, and that a network of hidden microphones under the seats secretly recorded conversations between audience members. Let's look at three reasons why this is nonsense:

1. John Edward's level of integrity is so high, he will refuse to do a session if he knows anything about the sitter beforehand. Also, going in, audience members are specifically told not to discuss any personal information with staff members.

2. Out of the hundreds of audience members per show, many would raise a great stink if they suspected they'd been duped into giving information that John then turned back at them. And often, those being read cannot validate information until they contact family members after the show, so how could they have even given that information in the first place?

3. A network of hidden microphones would need to be installed and maintained by the sound crew, any of whom could blow the whistle if fraud were taking place. Would the show's producers risk career suicide by instructing sound engineers to install the microphones? And how would the production team have time to listen to all the hundreds of conversations, sort out some juicy nuggets, and coach John as to which information belonged to which audience member?

The principle of Occam's Razor applies here, i.e., the most plausible explanation of any phenomenon is probably the simplest and most economical. In this case, that explanation is that John really does what he says he does, and that *after-death communication is valid*. Far more complex and expensive is a vast, high-tech conspiracy throughout the entire TV production team, fueled by a desire to get rich at the expense of gullible Americans—less likely, and more a product of debunkers' fear-driven attempts to wriggle off the hook of personal accountability.

My favorite John Edward story aired on September 18, 2003 (in the Las Vegas area), when John brought through the deceased husband of a woman in the audience. John said, "He's talking about … I'll say it as I get it … a piss-stained carpet. What's that all about?" (Of course, the p-word was bleeped out for national television.)

The woman revealed that just as she was leaving for the studio that morning, one of her dogs peed on the carpet but she didn't have time to clean it up. This story is significant for several reasons:

- Proof that John was indeed talking to *someone* on the other side because the woman had been 'alone' and hadn't mentioned the embarrassing incident to anyone.

- Our deceased loved ones really do hang out with us and notice what happens in our lives.
- It's the trivial little things that provide the best personal evidence of survival.
- John is not fabricating or cold-reading because he could never have made that story up by just looking at the woman.

In 1855, philosopher William James said in order to disprove the assertion that all crows are black, it's necessary to find only one white crow. So to debunk the debunkers, John Edward is such a white crow—the real deal. In his third book, *After Life*, John describes how a corporate executive made debunking him her passion. She spent weeks poring over tapes of his shows and attended four live seminars to uncover his 'scam.' However, she was thwarted at every turn and ended up convinced that he really does what he says he does, and was furious with the professional debunkers for trying to rob people of the beautiful experiences John brings them.

William James is also credited with 'James' Law,' based on his observation that paranormal phenomena provide just enough evidence to convince those who are willing to be convinced, but never enough to win over the skeptics. If you look at a photograph in a newspaper using a high-powered magnifying glass, all you see is lots of dots. One dot in of itself is meaningless, but together with thousands of other dots of varying size, they make up a meaningful image. Similarly, one paranormal instance alone may not be compelling but, viewed against the backdrop of hundreds or thousands of instances, they all add up.

Much also depends on one's predisposition to the paranormal in that, if you don't believe in fairies, say, you will probably never see one, but being open to such phenomena makes one more likely to witness them. It's widely known that when the Spanish conquistadors arrived in the Caribbean, the natives saw the rowboats coming ashore but just couldn't see the huge galleons at anchor in the bay because such large ships simply did not register in their minds. And where does such predisposition come from? Your own soul and your spirit guides are busy working with your belief system to gently pry it open to let in a larger perspective than younger souls are okay with because 'they just can't see the ships moored out in the bay.' But let's see them try to dismiss the following cast-iron evidence of survival of death.

Many say that information received through a medium from those who have crossed over may be entertaining but would never stand up in court. Well, it did, back in 1979. A Filipino nurse named Teresita was brutally murdered in her Illinois apartment during a robbery, and the police were baffled as to who was responsible. Two weeks later, Teresita showed up in full body to a co-worker, Remy, who was terrified. Soon after, Remy was in a hypnagogic state, and her husband heard the words coming out of her mouth in her native Tagalog, "I am Teresita. I want you to tell the police that my killer is called Allan."

The couple decided to do nothing, but a few days later, it happened again. "My killer is called Allan Showery. He stole my jewelry and gave it to his girlfriend." She even gave the phone number of someone who could identify the jewelry as hers. This time, they told the police, who interviewed Allan Showery, who also worked at the same hospital, and his girlfriend, who said that Allan had recently given her rings and some other pieces. The phone number turned out to belong to two of Teresita's cousins, who identified the jewelry as hers.

In the trial, the judge overruled the defense objection that information received psychically was untrustworthy, but the trial ended with a hung jury. At the retrial, when the new jury seemed more sympathetic to the source of the evidence, the accused entered into a plea bargain to avoid a life sentence and admitted his guilt. He was sentenced to 14 years.

Skeptics could argue that Remy had picked up the information telepathically from Showery's mind, except for one thing … the cousins' phone number, which he couldn't have known.

Case closed.

Cross Correspondences

For the still unconvinced, for irrefutable confirmation of the survival of the spirit, we can go back one hundred years to 1901, when, in a series of demonstrations, someone from the other side would send messages to two psychic mediums, say A and B, telling them both to convey the messages to adjudicator C. Neither message made sense in of itself, but when C put them together, they dovetailed perfectly. This eliminated debunkers' claims of mental telepathy where A and B are reading each other's mind, because neither knows about the message to the other, or even who the other is. This leaves only spirit communication as the explanation.

It all started with a Frederick Myers, one of the founders in 1882 of the Society for Psychical Research (SPR), based in Cambridge, England. Myers, author of the classic *Human Personality and Its Survival of Bodily Death*, researched many spiritual mediums at that time, and became very good at validating the real ones and debunking the frauds. He died in January 1901, but a few years earlier, he had entrusted an envelope to Sir Oliver Lodge, already a prominent member of the SPR. Myers told him to keep the envelope and open it only when a medium claimed to be in communication with Myers.

After Myers' death, the daughter of one of his friends tried to use automatic writing to contact him, and through her, he wrote: "Myers' sealed envelope left with Lodge … it has within it the words from the *Symposium* about love bridging the chasm." The medium knew nothing about the envelope or about Plato's *Symposium* (a philosophical debate about love set within a Greek drama), but immediately sent word to Lodge.

When Lodge opened the envelope, he was puzzled. It read: "If I can revisit any earthly scene, I should choose the Valley in the grounds of Hallsteads, Cumberland." Just how brilliant this was soon became apparent. Someone remembered that, years earlier, Myers had privately published a book containing the words of Plato's *Symposium* as a memorial to Annie, a woman he had once loved and who had lived at Hallsteads, and was buried there in the Valley. So the reference to the Valley was actually a reference to Annie, and via her, to the words of *Symposium*.

Myers' brilliant strategy involved several people, each holding a piece of the puzzle, but not one of them knowing about the other piece-holders. It was only when the whole thing came together that the pieces fit, and proved unequivocally the truth of spirit continuance after death.

After this start, many such researchers followed suit, most notably Houdini, who left an envelope with his wife. The message was delivered after his death through psychic medium, Arthur Ford. Controversy still rages over Houdini's message, but no one has ever proven that Ford did not receive the message from Houdini himself because no other way was feasible.

Arthur Ford was the principal spirit who communicated through writer Ruth Montgomery, *(1913 – 2001)*, once president of the prestigious National Press Club. Beginning as a Washington DC reporter, she wrote a book about the world-renowned psychic Jeanne Dixon, who warned JFK not to go to Dallas on that fateful day. The book's success prompted Ruth to look further into the world of the paranormal, and she discovered her gift of automatic writing. Despite all the ridicule and criticism heaped on her, she and Arthur brought in over a dozen books from the other side answering questions such as: What happens after death? Where do we go? What is it like over there?

Modern research into the spirit's survival of death actually goes back to the Fox sisters, Margaretta (14) and Kate (12), who in March 1848 were disturbed by rapping sounds in their bedroom in upstate New York. Rather than be afraid, the girls began rapping back, and soon had a 'conversation' going with the source. Their worried mother said, "If you are a spirit, knock twice." The house shook as two thunderous explosions boomed out. Through a code they devised, the spirit revealed he had been a 31-year-old peddler named Charles Rosma who said he had called at the house five years earlier. The then tenant, a Mr. Bell, had murdered Charles for the $500 he carried on him, and buried the body in the basement. Armed with shovels, the girls' father and some neighbors found a false wall behind which were a skeleton and the peddler's things.

Word of the Fox sisters spread rapidly, and their talents grew to include table-tipping, objects flying around the room and automatic writing, all by the spirits of those who had crossed over. Suddenly, all manner of people were holding séances and Spiritualism exploded in America, quickly spreading to England and then sweeping Europe. Of course, some were charlatans, but the genuine mediums were excellent, no more so than Daniel Douglas Home (pronounced 'Hume'). Born a sickly child in 1833 Edinburgh, Scotland, at age nine, his family moved to the U.S., where he contracted TB, which would haunt him his whole life. Powerfully psychic since childhood, at age 17 he was thrown out of his home by his mother, who accused him of 'the devil's work.' He caused an enormous stir wherever he went, being the darling celebrity of séances in the parlors of the aristocracy on both sides of the Atlantic. For 25 years (less one year when the other side remained silent to punish him for arrogance), he brought the Earth and soul planes together, not once missing a beat. Of course, Victorian England was in the thick of the Industrial Revolution, and many reductionist scientists wanted him debunked, so they were delighted when the formidable Sir William Crookes began to investigate Home. To their absolute horror, Crookes wrote a book concluding that Home really could talk to dead people, move grand pianos by thought, float out of a room by one window and reenter by another, and apport *anything* out of thin air. Home died of TB peacefully in 1886 at age 53, leaving behind absolute proof positive that there's a lot more to our world than our five senses tell us.

The world of Spiritualism had a resurgence following WWI and the ensuing flu epidemic that put 20 million folks on the other side in just a few years, but sputtered out again during WWII and never did regain widespread popularity; but the message is clear: None of today's interest in communicating with the other side is new; and it's been thoroughly validated for at least 150 years. Professor

James Hyslop, the tough-minded, skeptical researcher for the SPR, wrote in *Life After Death*: "I regard the existence of discarnate spirits as scientifically proved, and I no longer refer to the skeptic as having any right to speak on the subject. Any man who does not accept the existence of discarnate spirits and the proof of it is either ignorant or a moral coward. I give him short shrift, and do not propose to argue with him on the supposition that he knows nothing about the subject."

Evidence from Houdini, Ford and Pike

Harry Houdini, the renowned escapologist, was also an arch-skeptic of the spiritualist movement. Just before his death in 1926, he and his wife arranged a coded message that he would try to get to her from the other side … if it was real. After he crossed over, his wife did the rounds of mediums until, in 1929, the famous medium Arthur Ford successfully received the message from Houdini. Ten words were a code that spelled the one key word 'Believe.' The wife confirmed the code and newspapers blazoned the headline: "Houdini Communicates with Widow." She later retracted, leading to the next headline: "Houdini Message a Fraud"—another example of James' Law.

In 1958, Ruth Montgomery met Arthur Ford, a renowned psychic of the time, when he was giving a lecture. She interviewed him as a skeptic, but their meeting changed her entire life. He taught her automatic writing, and urged her to begin writing books about life after death.

Ford later became famous for a televised séance in 1966 involving the Episcopalian bishop James Pike that resulted in a huge scandal in its day. This fascinating story began when Bishop Pike's son Jim overdosed on drugs in London in 1966. After crossing over, Jim left his father plenty of evidentiary clues that he was still around, so Pike arranged a sitting with Mrs. Ena Twigg, a famous British medium of the time. In great distress, she told Bp. Pike that his son was pleading for forgiveness. Back in the U.S., the bishop sat with Arthur Ford, who relayed amazing details from Jim in the scandalous TV show. Pike told his story in the book *The Other Side*, published in 1968. As a result, he was charged by the Church with heresy, which he countered with another book *If This Be Heresy*, published in 1969. Pike died in 1969 in the Israeli desert during a trip to the Holy Land. He had been reported as missing, but on September 4, he came to Mrs. Twigg and told her he'd been dead for 24 hours. Further, through her, he told authorities of the remote location of his body, where it was soon found. Mrs. Twigg was consulted by many of the royal families of Europe and the Middle East, and had her own BBC television program—the John Edward of her day.

As the result of a bad car accident, Ford developed morphine addiction and then alcoholism, and died in 1971 aged 74. However, he soon began working with Ruth Montgomery to continue his work from the soul plane, and became a major guide in her dealings with 'the other side,' publicized in her many books. For example, in *Herald of the New Age*, written in 1986, Ford told Ruth, "The purpose of the book is to clear out the minds of those who still cling to mistaken ideas about the beyond. We are the co-creators with God of what we find for ourselves here. Ruth, we want you to wake the people up to the importance of this towering truth. They, with their thoughts, are not only creating the pattern of their future lives, but their own heaven or hell."

Ford mentioned God so frequently, Ruth finally asked him to define the term. He replied [apologies for the Ford/Ruth gestalt making the Source male], "God is the core of the universe from which all else flows forth. He is truth and energy. He is matter and spirit, and all things of heaven and earth. He is also the essence of our being, without which nothing would exist. ... Because we are imperfect in our reactions and behavioral pattern, we must strive ever onward through many earth cycles until we achieve sufficient perfection to rejoin God as cocreators. Thus our ceaseless attempts to return to the physical state in order to erase our rough edges and be able to fit into the Godhead as perfect segments of the whole."

So it's time for the debunkers to cease their endless prattle, and let people enjoy communicating with those on the other side. After reading thousands of 'survival of death' accounts over the decades, I see them as jigsaw puzzle pieces that fit together to reveal the larger picture. Each of us is free to accept or reject that picture, but if you reject it, ask yourself why. Make sure it isn't fear of the responsibility implicit in accepting the truth of the survival of death.

Life on the Soul Plane

Meanwhile, back on the soul plane, Joe and Sally are having a blast. On the way to their Life Reviews, Joe remarks, "You know, the colors here are so incredibly vibrant that being on Earth was like having a near-life experience. Life there was only a fraction as 'full' as it is here."

At the Hall of Records, their respective guides sit with them as every detail of their lives is replayed in a three-dimensional holographic reconstruction, much like the holodeck on *Star Trek's USS Enterprise*. But, in addition to just watching, they also 'become' the other people they interacted with, feeling their emotions and thinking their thoughts. Joe, for example, gets to feel the fear of the cat he'd rescued from the tree many years earlier.

Of course, the only 'judge and jury' during your panoramic life review is yourself, but now you are pure soul, free from the lower ego's traits of fear, greed and jealousy, and its need to defend and justify. This makes you your own 'worst judge,' and you feel waves of remorse over hurtful things done and loving things left undone. Your guide is present to ensure balance by pointing out the loving things you *did* do. Joe learns that once he got his act together after his first NDE, his life was one of such exemplary service, the few blemishes along the way were trivial.

Joe's guide then takes him to a special chamber in the Hall where sit three members of the Council, whose wisdom, love and high vibration make Joe reel. Initially incandescent balls of pure light, they manifest as elders, with long white hair, the two 'males' having long white beards. (They ceased incarnating eons ago, so gender is irrelevant to them, but appearances still matter to new arrivals.)

The Council members show Joe in his mind the goals that his soul had for the lifetime he's just lived and ask, "Well, how do you think you did?"

Joe is amazed at the careful and precise planning that went into his life path. Even as a spiritual man, he'd figured that much of his life had 'just happened.' He saw all the missed cues and wasted opportunities, but noted the important things were always backed up with contingency plans so he couldn't really stray far off-track. After some thought about his performance, Joe says, "C-minus, I reckon."

"Joe," the three voices say soothingly in his mind, "an Earth life is the greatest challenge any soul can face. You're too hard on yourself. We give you an A-plus."

The wave of love that then hits Joe knocks him backwards into his guide, who, knowing from experience what's about to happen, is ready to catch him. After bathing for what seems an eternity in an ocean of blissful love that transmutes any remaining Earth plane energy, Joe hears the question, "So what will you do now?"

Pulling his scattered thoughts together, Joe answers, "As a journalist and author, I've developed a passion for writing, so I would like to be a spirit guide to authors on Earth who write spiritual and inspirational books, especially those to do with survival of the soul after death."

The Council members consult with Joe's main soul entity, which agrees and Joe feels an overwhelming sense of approval, along with the message that his own guide will teach him 'the way of the guide' if he wishes. Then, with great humility, the Council members rise and bow deeply to honor Joe, for they still remember just how tough Earth lives are. And then … they're gone.

Joe sighs deeply and follows his guide out into the perfect 75 degree, blue-sky day. His guide says, "You two need somewhere to live. You both want a log cabin beside a stream and waterfall, so I've got a team of landscapers, architects and builders waiting. Sally's already there. Fix on my thought and it will take us there."

Instantly, Joe is beside a stream and sees Sally working with the landscapers, who are 'thinking' various rock faces into being to form the waterfall. She greets Joe and points to a 20-foot cascade. "That's my favorite," she says. "What do you think? We can always change it later if we get bored with it."

Joe is blown away by the sparkling water droplets that seem to actually enjoy flying through the air, shimmering with colors that Joe has never seen before. The water appears to *love* being water. "It's the most beautiful thing I've ever seen," he gasps. "Perfect."

"Glad you like it. Now let's design the cabin."

Sally, Joe and the architects form a telepathic link and visualize various designs. As they do, lines of light appear in thin air, moving around as the four play with designs. Meanwhile, the builders pet a pride of lions that wander up, curious about what's going on. A small family of deer join them and the lions use their rough tongues to groom the newcomers' coats.

The idyllic moment is broken when the architects telepath to the builders that the design is complete. A seemingly complex web of light-lines fills the air, and the two builders sit on a rock and focus on them. One-by-one, logs materialize in exactly the right place and of exactly the right size. Once the builders get into their pace, the house comes together in literally 'no time.'

As Joe and Sally watch in awe, Joe asks his guide, "So how do thoughts differ here from on Earth?"

"Well, down there, the average person has about 60,000 thoughts a day, most of which are fleeting, such as 'Gee, I really need a haircut.' Those thoughts quickly evaporate, but some are permanent, such as when Nicola Tesla conceived the entire design for his AC generator in his head. He set it running in his mind and frequently inspected it for wear and tear, never needing to commit his plans to paper. His mental plans had thousandth-inch tolerances, from which he built the real thing."

"So the generator existed in the higher dimensions before it did on Earth?" Joe asks.

"Oh yes, but because most people can't see into those dimensions, they assume that thoughts are too ethereal to be real. Just as well, considering how chaotic most people's thinking is. Here we know different. In fact, those builders are using their training to harness universal energy and form it into building materials that are every bit as durable here as actual bricks and mortar on Earth."

"Okay, seeing is believing. But what happens when one person thinks about another?"

"On Earth, that thought ends up in the second person's aura and its effect depends on how robust his energy field is. Even if it's strong, even a negative thought has no impact, but if it's weak, every thought will have an effect, for better or worse. But if someone thinks about a loved one who has crossed over, the latter is *far* more sensitive to the thought. If it's a grief-ridden thought, it drags the recipient down, and they have to work hard to heal themselves, maybe even needing specialized help in the beginning. But if it's a sincere prayer asking, say, that Divine Love be poured upon their loved one, it feels like a warm energy shower, and boosts the recipient's energy in ways you can't even imagine. So, positive prayer is the best way to help."

"I guess the moral of that is, 'Be careful what you think,'" Joe sighs.

"Yep, so far we've communicated with simulated voices, so let's try the way we *really* communicate up here. See if you get this."

Almost immediately, Joe sees a brief flash jump from his guide and hears the guide's voice clearly in his head saying, "Smell this." Suddenly, Joe sees a beautiful rose in front of him and inhales its overpowering aroma.

"This is so cool," Joe thinks to his guide, who nods in appreciation of Joe's newfound skill.

Right on cue, the builders drop the thought into Joe's mind, "Okay, we're done. Go take a look round."

Hand-in-hand, Joe and Sally explore their dream home, delighted at the exquisite workmanship and attention to detail. Then Joe's guide says, "It's customary to thank these folks with a meal, not that we need to eat, of course. But it's a way of saying thank you."

Sally laughs. "Well, I've always been a creative cook. Let's see how creative I *can* get." As she manifests tables of food, Joe's guide advises, "Now, you know you will continue to have this individual 'Joe focal point' indefinitely but, at some point soon, you will need to experience merger with your full soul for an exchange of energy and information. Your main soul will copy into itself everything you have become and learned as Joe so that it's available to all your co-incarnations, past and future. And everything they all know will be copied into your awareness, to accelerate your growth."

"Sounds intense," Joe quips.

"Extremely. I'll lead you in a meditation to prepare you, but even then, it can get wild as you absorb the wisdom of a couple of hundred other lifetimes and identities."

Just then, they receive the thought from Sally that food is ready, and Joe is left to savor full-blown soul merge and meeting all his brothers and sisters-in-soul from across time and space. During the meal, Joe's guide explains that Joe and Sally will need to attend 'thinking school' to get the most out of their new lives. Joe says, "I know this is a weird question, but I want to learn how to play the didgeridoo. How does that work, since we don't have to breathe air?"

"That requires using thought to focus life-force energy and direct it into the instrument. To learn how to do that, you will need thought to transport yourself to aboriginal teachers, and to learn the special 'circular breathing' you need."

"So it's all a matter of thought. And the clearer the better."

"Absolutely. The more people who know this before they arrive, the better for them."

The reality that Joe and Sally experienced when they first arrived was a function of their enlightened beliefs about what to expect. Basically, the soul plane is a mental dimension, created from thought, so you *initially* get what you believe you will; Jews experience their familiar synagogues and Muslims, their mosques. Once the new arrivals have settled in, however, guides show up to reorient them away from their 'small limited gods' and towards their true, glorious identity as souls that are creators within the 12th-dimensional Source.

Crossing Over: What Can You Expect?

Piecing together the thousands of eyewitness accounts by those who've already crossed over, here are some of the highlights:

- It will happen regardless of your beliefs
- Your mind, emotions and etheric body leave your physical body. Initially you will be in the same location, but you very soon find yourself in surroundings that feel every bit as tangible as the Earth plane used to feel to you.
- The nature of those surroundings depends on your beliefs about the afterlife. If you believe in oblivion, you will sleep for a while. If you harbor the beliefs found in this book, you will find yourself in an idyllic setting, surrounded by loving beings who have already crossed over, with whom you

communicate telepathically. It is, therefore, essential to learn as much as possible about what to expect.

- There are many levels to the soul plane and you are automatically pulled to the level that resonates with your own vibration, so it behooves us to clean up our act. You will be able to see down into lower levels but not into higher realms. Even though it may take eons, those in the lower realms will eventually graduate to the highest.
- Any physical disabilities disappear and you find yourself in the prime of life.
- Your mind controls every facet of your experience and you can travel anywhere instantaneously simply by thinking about that location.
- After a period of adjustment, you will conduct your own panoramic life review. This carries no judgment and is conducted purely for the learning involved. Because you review your *entire* lifetime, deathbed repentance does you no good. The only issue is the amount of love in your energy and how you served your fellow man while on Earth. A wise counselor will be on hand to stop you from beating yourself up.
- You meet with one or more counselors to decide on a curriculum of soul plane activities that are consistent with your overarching soul intent, so that you balance learning and growing with loving and playing.

Life Review

How does knowing that this life review *will* happen to you make you feel? That you *will* be on the receiving end of every harsh word you have ever uttered, and of every mean-spirited act you have ever committed.

If someone once asked you for a favor and you declined to help when you could have, you *will* get to feel the other's hurt and disappointment. If you shot a 'holier than thou' look at a panhandler in the street or at a homeless person huddled in a doorway, you *will* experience how it made that person feel—the hopelessness, desperation or panic—because you could have done something but didn't.

The Golden Rule isn't just a platitude. It's a Universal Law and a constant reminder that whatever you do (or don't do) for others, you do (or don't do) for yourself ... and you *will* get to experience that. Fortunately, this also goes for the loving words and deeds, which hopefully outweigh the other kind.

The purpose of reliving your life is not, however, punishment or even the opportunity to forgive yourself, and there are no judges from whom to beg for leniency. The purpose is to *understand* and work towards unconditional love. For once you finally cross over fully into the soul plane, you will need this understanding.

Again, it must be stressed that the review is *not* judgment but an opportunity to see that unconditional love is the *only* true currency—all else is counterfeit, worthless scrip on the soul plane.

All through the review, the tone is loving and compassionate, and the sense that life is a learning experience, with the review as a natural part of the process. There is no blame, just as you wouldn't blame a child learning to ride a bicycle for falling off. It's just part of growth, and a chance to look at your life in a loving environment and examine the things that were 'too close up' on the Earth plane.

The being who guides you through your review is infinitely compassionate, for he or she (gender is just for your comfort) knows how difficult Earth lives can be. This allows you to relive shameful, humiliating episodes without feeling shame, blame, or guilt. After all, few of those episodes were malicious, and more likely done out of ignorance.

(Characters such as Hitler, Stalin, Pol Pot, or someone who preyed on innocence, such as a serial child molester, are special cases who resonate with low frequency energy on the soul plane, and have much work to do before they are even ready for their review. Apparently, Hitler is still strutting around those lower levels complaining that history has misjudged him. Such arrogance needs a *lot* of work, which is why we have eternity.)

The lesson we can learn from the life review process is that of self-forgiveness. Don't beat yourself up for transgressions committed in ignorance. The caveat, however, is, now that you know the yardstick is unconditional love, any non-loving act earns a double penalty, for in your review, *you will know you knew better.* Ouch!

The life review goes way beyond watching a movie. There's one screen for each participant in a drama, but it's more than just audio and visual; in addition to every thought and emotion *you* had, you also get the thoughts and feelings of *all involved.* What does this mean?

Take someone who one day snaps and 'goes postal.' Firing an automatic weapon, he storms into his place of work, and kills a dozen people and then himself. He gets to relive that incident through maybe fifty simultaneous tracks. He feels everyone's fear, panic and pain as they die. From their vantage point, 'he' sees himself firing his gun and, in slow motion, 'he' sees the stream of bullets coming and feels them slam into 'his' body, destroying 'his' internal organs.

He thinks the other people's thoughts and feels their feelings as they die, knowing they won't see their families again. He is each of his victims—the ones who die and the others cowering under their desks—all at the same time. He also experiences the grief of his victims' loved ones who will never see their mother, father, son or daughter alive again. Then, when he puts the gun to his own head, the fraction of a second it took his brain to explode can be stretched out for hours so that in his review, he really 'gets' how dumb a thing it was to do.

On top of this, he also has the psychological insights as to why this happened. He relives his childhood molestation, which destroyed his boundaries and trust, and made him feel unable to cope. Of course, when his molester crossed over, he got to relive the *full* outcome of his actions, which includes his own heinous crimes as well as those committed by all those he molested. Now, that's justice.

The ease with which we slide and experience our own actions from the point of view of everyone we impacted, teaches us that we are all one, part of a super-soul being. The review process also calls us to cease, right now, any thought, word or deed that we might regret, *knowing* we will have to squirm through a replay in exhaustive detail.

As for what's already happened in your life, you can replay events in your mind and rework them, apologizing to everyone you've hurt, but it's much easier to not create any new karma for which you will later need to apologize. Of course, you will still hurt people by accident—forgetting a birthday or an anniversary, say—but these things count for nothing in the review. What really matters is *intentionally and maliciously* causing pain, for replays of this are 'squirm times.' And it's no excuse to claim, "They hurt me first!" Turn the other cheek, remember.

Those who commit suicide can have an uncomfortable review, whether or not the attempt is successful (if not, they have an NDE; if yes, they can report back using a medium). They get to experience firsthand the pain and suffering their action causes those left behind—most unpleasant. One NDEr reported that her review was like an endless loop, with the events leading up to the suicide and the act itself replayed repeatedly, presumably to drive home the point that suicide is never an option. On returning to her body, she vowed, "Never again!"

Anticipating the Review

You can benefit from knowing about the review process without the trauma of having an NDE or dying, by conducting your own review. Pick an interaction you're not proud of, one in which someone else was hurt, and replay it in your mind … but put yourself in the other person's position. Do you feel slighted, put down, made fun of? Is your self-esteem eroded, or your personal power diminished? How does that feel?

After doing this a few times, you will instill the habit of empathy in your future interactions and ask, "If I say or do this, how will it make the other person feel?" Or, if a careless remark does slip out, you will immediately catch it and apologize on the spot. Either way, you'll be a nicer person to be around. You will also find that you feel better about yourself.

In fact, this is the main message of the life review. No matter how much squirming we do, we feel loved regardless, by the being of Light who is with us. If that being accepts us as we are, why shouldn't we? If the Light loves us unconditionally, is it not presumptuous on our part if we don't love ourselves as much? Who are we to second-guess the Light as to our lovability? If the Source loves us, who are we to argue? Do we think we know better? Do we think we know ourselves better than our soul does, and can therefore judge ourselves more harshly and love ourselves less? I don't think so!

People returning from a life review during an NDE, report feeling overwhelming unconditional love and enjoying a higher level of self-love. However, these folks are no different from the rest of us. So we can tap into their experience, too, without all the fuss and muss of nearly dying. *You* can feel loved because NDErs feel loved. *You* can feel self-love because NDErs feel self-love.

The life review process also tells us the only yardstick is the love quotient in our words and deeds, not whether they are politically correct or make you popular. So, rather than speak or act to elicit the approval of others, just ask, "How is this going to show up in my life review?" and let *that* guide you.

More Proof of Survival

In 1937, a 10-man committee of the Church of England sat for *two years* to examine the available evidence on mediums and survival of death. In 1939, the committee concluded, against enormous internal pressure, that spirit communication with the deceased is true. However, the Church was so scandalized by these findings, the report was locked away and forgotten for 40 years before being leaked to the media in 1979.

Sir Winston Churchill routinely used the services of a medium during WWII, who actually predicted the Japanese attack on Pearl Harbor six months before it came. Unfortunately, it wasn't enough to help medium Helen Duncan who was imprisoned during the war, when she was contacted in 1941 by a deceased sailor who revealed that his ship had been sunk. For morale reasons, the Admiralty had not publicly revealed this, so it was a major embarrassment. By January 1944, preparations for D-Day were underway and the landing site was top secret. To prevent Mrs. Duncan from revealing it, the government charged her under the obscure 1735 Witchcraft Act. The Crown assembled a jury of 12 people who did not believe in mediumship and *concluded before the trial* that Mrs. Duncan had to be a fraud. Despite the sworn testimony of 41 of her clients, she was found guilty of fraud and thrown in jail for the rest of the war. A furious Winston Churchill visited her and promised to repeal the Witchcraft Act as soon as he could. By its concern, the British government tacitly acknowledged that Helen Duncan's gifts were genuine

In 1956, police again raided a Helen Duncan séance and brutally manhandled her while she was in deep trance. The shock to her system was so great, she died five weeks later.

Mrs. Leonore Piper

One of the most notable mediums who ever lived was Boston's Leonore Piper. She used a 'control'—a being from the other side called Dr. Phinuit—who brought through a tremendous amount of information and messages from those who had crossed over. In one case, a couple called Sutton (strangers to Mrs. Piper) wanted to contact their deceased daughter who had just crossed over. Through Mrs. Piper, the little girl chattered on about her brother and sister and named her favorite dolls. This left the Suttons with absolutely no doubt that they were talking to their daughter.

Britain's Society for Psychical Research sent their top investigator, a Richard Hodgson, to expose Mrs. Piper as a fraud. He had her followed and used every dirty trick in the book, but in the end, he had to admit, "I can't prove anything at all. I can't prove fraud, I can't prove cheating, I can't prove trickery."

When a friend of Hodgson, a George Pellew, died, the friend took over the role of control, and Hodgson asked his friend literally thousands of questions, every one of which he answered correctly. The initially skeptic Hodgson was so impressed, he reported to the Society, "I cannot profess to have any doubt but that the chief communicators to whom I have referred are veritably the personalities that they claim to be, that they have survived the change we call death, and that they have directly communicated with us whom we call living, through Mrs. Piper's entranced organism."

Even more amazing was the fact that upon the death of Hodgson, he took over from George Pellew as the control, and relayed much information about the afterlife. Professor William James, also a member of the Society, said, "Yes, maybe it is Hodgson transmitting this information, but I'm not so sure," at which Hodgson exclaimed, "If I'm not Richard Hodgson, then Richard Hodgson never lived."

Evaluation

Every element of the story of Joe and Sally has been reported by those undergoing hypnotic regression to past lives and the period between lives, i.e., the interlife. Here are the main points again:

1. You-the-soul plan every detail of circumstance and personality needed to accomplish your specific and well-planned goals for an incarnation. However, the original and true essence of you is soul, which focuses a vibration of itself, often called 'spirit,' into the body it has chosen. Each human body therefore contains and is enlivened by this spirit, an aspect of soul. The spirit vibration also contains the three levels of mind: *Superconscious*, the actual soul vibration; *Conscious Mind*, which accumulates wisdom and surface memories as the life unfolds; *Subconscious*, which contains deep memory and past life identities. Ego-personality lies on the boundary between Conscious and Subconscious layers of mind.

2. You-the-soul choose the other players in your incarnation's drama from your soul group of maybe a thousand other souls, who also choose you to play 'bit parts' in theirs. Those you choose to cause you the greatest harm are your closest and most trusted soul buddies, for they love you enough to create karma by their actions. Just as a school child goes through the series of semesters with the same group of students and forms deep friendships, you meet up with incarnations of the same group of souls in each life time. You have close friends, and others you hardly know.

3. Your main spirit guide works closely with you, along with up to a dozen specialist guides for specific guidance. They too are drawn from your soul group, and when they are incarnate and you are not, you may serve as spirit guides to them. Their love for you is unfathomably deep, but they can and will intervene in your life only on your request or if you are in a danger that is not in your life plan, at which point guardian angels may also intervene.

4. If you stray seriously from your life plan, you-the-soul may intervene by orchestrating a near-death experience. This may be less than pleasant in order to shock ego-personality into changing. The only life event not built

into the flight plan is suicide, and guides work extra hard if they see this as a possibility; but they must always respect your free will. After a period of healing and reflection, you-the-soul will be eager to repeat the circumstances in another incarnation.

5. When you incarnate, you are 'one of a kind' and not some prior soul fragment recycling as you. Your unique combination of soul vibration and ego-personality has never before occurred, and never will again.

6. When you first cross over back to the soul plane, what happens depends on the means of death. A sudden, traumatic passing may leave you disoriented, confused, regretful, even angry, whereas crossing after a long illness may find you relieved to be free of your body and any pain. Next, your immediate surroundings reflect your beliefs, but soon teachers show up to orient you to life on the soul plane.

7. If you have a clear understanding of crossing over and have lived a positive, loving life, you will move quickly through the Astral Plane to the Soul Plane to be greeted by loved ones and beloved pets who have gone on before you. If you firmly believed that death is the absolute end, you will find yourself in a limbo state akin to deep sleep. You will eventually notice the distant glimmer of Light and may become curious about it, or you may respond to one of the many healing angels that 'work' this level, waiting for you to 'wake up.' Once you decide to check out the Light, you're Home.

8. If you lived a negative life, you may be afraid of the Light for, to you, it represents the dreaded Judgment. Or, if you were addicted to some aspect of Earth life, leaving this dark place would mean you could no longer return to your old haunts. Better yet, why not take up residence in an addict's home, so you can tap into his 'high'? Congratulations ... you're now a ghost. You can hang out there, possessing your host until some human or angelic 'ghost-buster' serves you an eviction notice.

9. Most ghosts know they are deceased and just hang out with us for kicks, for something to do, or worse, to generate fear in us and feed off it. Ghosts who don't know they're deceased still appear as they did at the moment of death, such as in a tattered Civil War uniform, covered with blood, etc. When ghost-busting, be gentle in explaining the situation to this latter category, but with the others, chew them out and send them to the Light. Always remember, *we* are more powerful than they are ... after all, the Earth plane is *our* home, not theirs, and they are trespassing!

10. Once on the soul plane, you do not go into limbo to await reincarnation, but continue to learn and grow as your own sovereign focal point of consciousness. The energy and wisdom gained from that lifetime will merge back into soul. But meanwhile, you will be very busy, learning, studying and researching your pet projects, and occasionally meeting and greeting newly arrived friends and relatives.

11. In the long (really long) term, the spirit will no longer retain an individual identity separate from soul. Eventually, once merged with soul, incarnations will be no longer separate or identifiable as separate incarnations. The wisdom and experiences gained in all incarnations will then be part of the entirety of Soul. Until that inconceivably distant point in 'time,' however, each 'spirit' retains its identity and what it learned during its incarnation, which explains why mediums see, hear, and experience a spirit that still looks and feels like the person who has crossed over to the soul plane. Even when full soul merge does occur, soul retains the *memory* of that spirit's original form, experience and wisdom, and can present itself as the energy of the 'original spirit.'

12. Over inconceivable eons, the soul entity will work up through countless planes, merging with its ever-higher creator aspects, until it merges back into the Supreme Source.

13. You-the-soul plan one or more 'exit points,' and when a point comes along, you choose whether to take it, depending on whether you-the-soul feel 'done.' You may walk away from a horrific car wreck … or not. You may miraculously recover from a fatal disease or terminal illness … or not. But *you-the-soul* choose, based on your progress toward your goals; the will of God or the whim of fate has *nothing* to do with it. With only one exit point, the time of death is etched in stone, as is the time of birth, but there may be many choices as to the way in which this occurs.

14. Your goals inevitably involve Challenges because that's why the Earth plane exists. Nothing can exist on the soul plane outside of unconditional love, so to experience fear, hate, jealousy, greed, etc., you must come to Earth. And if you *do* come to Earth, you know exactly what to expect. You wouldn't join the Marine Corps if you didn't want to experience The Crucible.

15. Your sojourn here will involve those you love going Home before you do. Of course, they will be waiting for you, but their crossing gives you the gift/challenge of grief, so use it well. Explore the emotional intensity

while on Earth, because you can't do so on the soul plane, where death is known to be a purely physical plane illusion.

16. The most tragic 'loss' is that of a child, but know that no one is ever 'lost,' and your child is still closer to you than your own thoughts. The child will wait on the soul plane for you, cared for by relatives and kept very busy, often working with animals or helping other children who cross over. Their only regret is that, "Mommy cries all the time," or, "Daddy blames himself and drinks too much." Of course, grief is natural and healthy, but eventually it begins to wear on the child so, instead of mourning what you have lost, celebrate what you had together … and still have. And know that you'll be together in a few short years. Finally, know also that your child's death was carefully planned, so *you are not to blame*. If you turn your back for a moment, and your child drowns or runs into traffic, you were *meant* to be distracted. Obviously, this in no way condones deliberate neglect or malicious harm—you will have to suffer the consequences of that, over there for sure, and possibly over here first. And taking advantage of a child's innocence and inability to protect itself has *major, major* karmic consequences. As the child's soul chooses, the child's spirit may age-progress or remain a child.

17. If you are gifted with a 'challenged' child or one who dies young, it is *never* a punishment for something you, the parent, did. To think that, denies the sovereignty of that soul, who chose the impediment or early return Home for its own growth … and yours.

18. When you do finally go Home yourself, be prepared for the greatest party of your life. As a new graduate of 'Hell Week' on planet Earth, your return is celebrated by friends, relatives, dogs, cats, plus whoever and whatever else shows up. Then, after healing and your life review, you're ready to begin *LIVING!*

19. Our Earth plane is a holographic dream within a dream within … oh well, it goes on forever, all the way up to the Supreme Source, the 'Big Dreamer' itself. And even that entity exists inside the dream of another even vaster entity (my mind has long given up wondering what *that's* like). But, you, as a fragment of your soul, have a vital role to play because of your unique expression within All That Is, and your unique way of experiencing that. Without your experience, the universe just wouldn't be complete. So experience it all with gusto.

20. Finally, no one on the Soul plane looks back and says, "Gee, I wish I'd put

in more hours at the office or the plant," or, "I wish I'd grieved more for my lost loved ones." No, souls are unanimous in saying, "I wish I'd played more, loved more, laughed more, lived more, and prepared better for what's over here when I arrived." As the late Mr. Rogers used to say, "The only thing that matters is whether you mattered to your neighbor," so don't wait until then to change. Begin right now.

Chapter 7 ═══

Life as a Spiritual Being

If you espouse the worldview of the previous chapter, how would this change your life? Completely and in every department of your identity: relationship with self, with how you perceive deity, and with others (romantic, platonic, family, co-workers, children, pets and deceased loved ones). Is that enough?

The spiritual path is not a 'doing' thing, for that leads to spiritual ego and spiritual ambition. It also separates the seeker from that which is sought, which is True Self. The real spiritual path involves getting little self out of the way and dissolving the blocks to love. Then, you can allow True Self to embrace you, and self to merge with Self.

Also, 'searching' implies that the path and Self are 'out there' somewhere, when, in fact, they are very much 'in here.' Worse, you create the illusory 'out there,' so you would actually be chasing your own illusions, much like a dog chasing its tail—not a productive exercise and you get dizzy. Of course, you must interact with 'out there,' but do not confuse it with anything Real; the only Reality is within you, and it is the unconditional love of your True Self, your soul.

Relationship with Self

Again, love is not a 'doing' but a 'being' state, and all you need do is remove the fears that block love's flow and the indwelling presence of your True Self. And that Self 'fits over' your physical body, which you borrow temporarily from

Mother Nature. Anyone who has had an out-of-body or near-death experience will confirm that you are fully functioning and aware, even though detached from physical form.

When you look in the mirror, you are seeing only a tiny fraction of who you are—a physical body. But you now know that's not all you are. That body is just a temporary focal point for your soul and a system of muscles and levers for getting things done to sustain that soul's exploration.

I am an avid nudist and love being around other nudists because most of us are Old Souls who fully accept our bodies as is, since we know there's a whole lot more. When you over-identify with your body, you worry that being nude in public reveals too much of who you are. But if you know your body is only a tiny part of your magnificent soul identity, who cares? To be ashamed of your body would be akin to being so ashamed of your car, you drive around with a car cover on, with just two little eyeholes cut out. The primary keynote of the nudist lifestyle is healthy body acceptance, so if you are a person who says, "Oh, I could never go to a nudist place!" I suggest you look at your reasons for saying that.

If you are not your body, then who are you? Ego-personality? No, that's just an interface that you-the-soul created to deal with the outside world, a characteristic set of behavioral reflexes that avoids the need to evaluate every situation for how to behave. Also, knowing how you will likely respond makes others feel more secure in dealing with you.

So who are you in your life? What do your 'life tags' say? Suppose you break your life identity down as: 50 percent company employee; 25 percent spouse; 20 percent parent; 5 percent church member. That could be dangerous; if you lose your job, there goes half your identity. If your spouse and child are killed in a car accident on the same day you lose your job, that's almost everything else gone. And, you may be so mad at God, you drop out of church. Then there's nothing left of you!

But suppose your life-tags said: 80 percent soul/spirit; 5 percent company employee; 5 percent spouse; 5 percent parent; 5 percent church member. Much healthier. Of course, you would look the same from the outside and still do the same things. But you would *feel* different. When you drive your son to the soccer game on a Saturday morning, you're not thinking about office work; you're thanking soul for having a healthy child with all his limbs, the coordination to operate them, and the desire to join a team and get some exercise. That's a lot to be grateful for.

In a 'worst case scenario,' suppose your spouse and child *do* die in an accident. You have lost 10 percent of your identity, so what do you do? Rather than play victim, you marshal your Resources to meet this Challenge. "Okay, spirit guides, guardian angels and anyone else who's listening, I need some help in coping with this new emptiness in my life. I know my spouse and child are around me and that they're okay on the soul plane, but my grief prevents me from sensing them. I also know we all planned for this to happen but I can't remember why. It's the loneliness I have trouble with. I want to be a survivor here and not the accident's third victim."

Of course, the hole in your life is painfully real. You had heart cords from your chest area to theirs (heart chakra); you had a sexual cord to your spouse's abdominal area (second chakra); plus many other cords, all of which were suddenly severed when they left their bodies. You had a genetic resonance with your child, akin to two identical tuning forks humming happily away together, and one of them suddenly stops. And if you're the mother, you also had a tissue resonance with your child.

Emotionally, you're a basket case, too, because having your spouse and child in your life were almost 'habits,' or pieces of the present that you projected into the future, and suddenly that future has been torn away. But, know that your life plan does not end here. The show can, will and must go on. And so will you.

That's a lot to lose all at once, and probably the greatest Challenge you could write in your life plan. Add to that, normal ego guilt over surviving when they didn't. Given this (or any other) Challenge, it is your right and duty to call for the Resources to meet it. Otherwise, you may put your life on hold indefinitely, function at only a fraction of your performance, or take your own life, none of which your soul wants or intends.

Beyond a healthy grieving period, setting up the rest of your life as a shrine to a loved one who went Home a little earlier than you is self-indulgent. Death is a vital part of life. Once the soul has fulfilled its purpose for an incarnation, hanging around just to please others would be a waste of the soul's energy. Accept that people come into your life so you can all share experiences. Love them while they are here, and celebrate them when they go Home. Do not cling so tightly that the pain of separation overwhelms you. This also applies to our beloved pets.

If your best friend got married and moved far away, of course you would miss him or her but you would not put your life on hold. You would miss your friend deeply and may even be angry about the separation but you honor the free will behind it. It's the same with mates, children, parents and other loved ones who cross over … only they can see things clearly, while you can't.

Meditation is a major Resource, for it puts you in touch with the 80 percent of you that is spirit, and allows your guides to coach you: "Yes, you planned all this, and yes, it was your intent to be alone for a while. But, in your grief, grieve for yourself and not for them. They left their bodies just before impact and felt nothing. They are happily busy on the soul plane now, but are also around you constantly, giving you strength and loving support. As you begin to heal, you will feel them."

Also, know the angelic realm is busily working on you, healing the gaping holes in your aura where the cords were ripped away; but this takes time and cannot be rushed.

Finally, remember that you built grief into your life plan in order to study it, so study with gusto, but do not get so absorbed in your 'pity party' that you let other aspects of your life go, or ignore any other surviving family members. And whatever else you lose, you've always got that 80 percent of your identity.

Of course, such a devastating event will test your faith that you-the-soul pre-ordained it for your growth, growth you simply cannot get on the soul plane; hence the trip to the Earth plane.

For couples who do lose a child, remember that only one couple in five is still together after five years; to stay in that group, keep reaffirming your 80 percent soul identity.

The Quadrant View

Another way to look at yourself is to imagine you're divided into four quadrants: physical, emotional, mental and spiritual.

In case (A), Spirit has little or no influence on the personality, being swayed almost entirely by the needs of the physical body, the emotions and the intellect. Being a property of the Spiritual Quadrant, love is squeezed out, its closest approximation probably being just trading attention with other people.

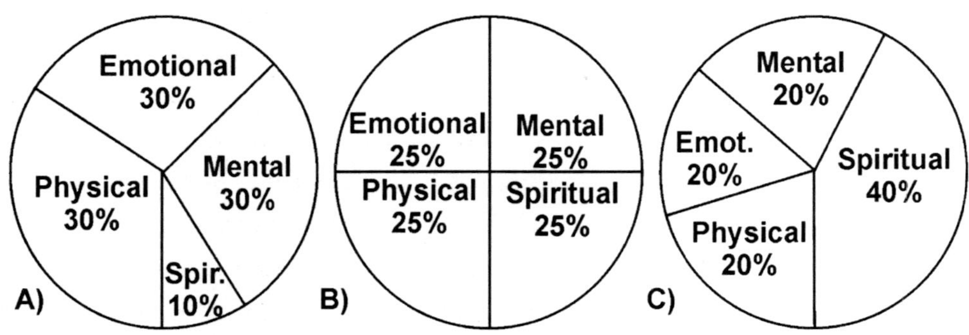

The Quadrant View of Human Personality

Case (B) shows a more perfect balance, with some love squeaking in and being flowed out to others. This is probably where most people on the spiritual path are. Case (C) is definitely on the way to self-realization, with Spirit playing the major role in life. Where are you?

Self-identity and Deity

(The word 'God' is avoided here because of the hooks that Western religions have sunk into most of our minds, such as, "God demands that you behave in a certain way and will punish/destroy you if you don't." More neutral terms such as, Source and All That Is are preferable for those seeking true understanding, free of preconceived, packaged, fear-based mind control. We heard some of the following in Chapter 1, but it bears repeating.)

In its efforts to know itself, an inconceivably vast consciousness decided to play a game. Out of its thoughts, it created points of consciousness within a lower dimension of its vast matrix and interacted with them. These would go on to become universes, in turn would create slightly more limited points of consciousness in their own matrix and in turn interact with them as galaxies. This continued for eons but all the creations (i.e., probes to create and explore progressively lower frequency dimensions) behaved just as they believed the Source wanted them to. They had no other option because, being part of the Source, they behaved and made choices exactly as the Source would. This is analogous to a daytime TV drama where all the cast members look alike, think alike and react alike … and all like the scriptwriter who created them. In other words, BORING!

Then the Source had a brilliant idea. FREE WILL. "I will let my creations go off and create whatever they want, however they want. Now that will be interesting because I cannot predict what they will do. Then, I will learn more about myself and all the potentials within my being."

So the game was on. To cut a long (trillions of years long) story short and breeze over countless progressively lower dimensions, the Source is a vast matrix of a gadzillion sovereign soul entities, each made of Source-stuff. So, the sum of all of us *is* the Source, in the same way the sum of all IBM employees *is* IBM.

Each dimension away from the Source is a little more limited, but nowhere do the inhabitants not know they are Source-stuff and creator-gods in their own right. However, knowing this tends to limit their free will, because no part of the Source wants to cause harm to another part. And since we all exist in pure unconditional love, you couldn't possibly harm them. This lack of *true* free will really stunts your growth, because you can't study the nature of love from the inside; you must somehow get *outside* it … and that requires forgetting that you *are* love.

To fully round out the game and complete the experiment, therefore, one more dimension was needed into which hardy souls would venture and forget they were Source-stuff, so they *could* exercise complete free will. Amidst the complete unpredictability of amnesia and free will lies great opportunities for learning and growth, for creation and destruction. (That this wild and crazy experiment has lasted as long as it has is a miracle in its own right.)

Bear in mind that our Earth plane is still only a miniscule pinpoint in all the width, breadth and height of the dimensions, so where do you fit in? You-the-soul exist for one purpose only—to explore and research the nature of All That Is. You do this in your own way, but you do it thoroughly, which is why we invented reincarnation. There's no way a soul could explore it all in one lifetime. Just to explore both genders requires two lifetimes. Then you've got to try out each race, then rich and poor, gay and straight, etc., etc. So you're looking at hundreds of lifetimes in order to pack it all in. And there are *no* rules; any rules come from a culture, religion, etc., that wants to control you.

When it comes to exploring whether you have a dark side, you can't do that on the higher dimensions because you are bathed in unconditional love. For that, you must come down to the Earth plane (or any other planet inhabitable by whatever species you want to incarnate as … and there are many). You set up a life scenario, attach a fragment of your energy to a fleshy little body, and play out that scenario for a few years to see how that fragment of you handles things. You also bring a three-tiered mind and ego-personality with you, but the ego-personality can access only the middle tier—Conscious Mind. That is brilliant because your true identity is stored in the top tier (Superconscious Mind) and is not accessible to ego-personality, so it knows nothing of you as a creator-god. And all the other lifetimes of your soul are stored in the lower tier, also inaccessible.

So that's where you fit in—a creator probe coming to the physical plane to play out your soul mission of exploration. But what about your relationship to the Ultimate Source? Apart from being made of the same stuff, that relationship exists through your soul. If your mind were to contact the full Source directly, its consciousness is so vast and intense, direct contact would fry your circuits. So you, the soul fragment, do have an intimate relationship with the rest of your soul and its creator—your oversoul. When you pray, that's who you're talking to. Your higher self intercepts the call and is quite powerful enough to have a god-like impact on your life … if appropriate.

However, do not let this make you feel lonely. All these dimensions co-exist with the physical plane (and just vibrate at a higher frequency), but most of us can't see at those frequencies. Now that's strictly one-way, and everything here is accessible to any being in a higher dimension. This allows for intervention from 'on high,' something that happens all the time but we usually miss it. It's called *synchronicity*, and we'll look at it more in a moment.

For now, what does this mean in terms of your day-to-day life?

Your Relationship with Self ... Again

First, who are you? To summarize, the gestalt that is you consists of:

1. *Soul fragment*, in intimate contact with your main soul entity and, as needed, with the other incarnations of that entity (let's just call it 'soul' from now on). This fragment of soul is a vibration transmitted from the soul plane into the aura and, analogous to a complex TV signal, conveys personality, soul vibration, and memories of all other incarnations.

2. *Physical body*, to which your soul attached sometime between conception and birth.

3. *Mind*, an awesome non-physical electromagnetic structure for thought processing. This attaches to the brain at several points, including the limbic area at the junction of the two hemispheres and the brain stem.

4. *Emotions*, which soul uses to guide your mind in its decision-making by moving various energies around your body via the meridians, chakras, and the endocrine system. This Emotional Guidance System (EGS) and the mind are probably the most underrated and ignored marvels in all of Creation, which is why so many species of ET are here studying us. Your EGS is an invaluable but greatly underestimated resource that needs honing.

Mind has three main components:

- *Subconscious Mind* records every minute detail of your life, along with how you interpret events and their outcomes to guide you the next time the event occurs.

- *Conscious Mind*, which makes your decisions, but only if you are fully engaged with your life and are self-aware; otherwise, programs and sub-personalities (created at times of great stress or trauma, such as during sexual abuse as a child, when your mind is overwhelmed) shut the world out, and create a compartment in the Subconscious to deal with it. Stored in the Subconscious, they run your life for you in what is often termed 'being on autopilot.'

- *Superconscious*, or the mental component of soul. Through interaction with Conscious Mind, soul guides decision-making when you consciously live your life and are open to its urgings and your EGS. Otherwise, sub-personalities make your decisions for you.

Residing at the boundary of Conscious and Subconscious Minds is ego-personality, the complex collection of personal qualities, approaches, styles and habits that other people experience as 'you.' As a creation of soul, it is the interface between the real, inner you and the false outer you that you show to the outside world (in fact, *persona* is Greek for 'mask').

Because many people do not know about the inner self, and cannot therefore tap into its wisdom and strength, the ego-personality is given way more authority and power than was ever intended. It cannot make important decisions but, if no one else is at the controls, it will run the show, possibly reaching down into Subconscious Mind for a sub-personality to handle things. How does this work?

Suppose, when you were five, your mother was terrified that you would be kidnapped, so she instilled great fear in you, which at that tender age, you took in without question. You lived your early years in constant terror of a 'bogey man coming to get you.' You made your father check the closet and under the bed every night. Slowly, over the years, you let the fear go from your Conscious Mind and forgot all about it … or did you? No, it's still in your Subconscious Mind, being cared for by a sub-personality.

At age thirty, suppose you've had a hard day, and are at home, trying to unwind with a drink and the TV nightly news. A news item about an abducted child features an interview with the distraught mother. This resonates with the sub-personality created when you were young and your mother obsessed about your safety, with you taking on her fears. As an adult, you get hit with all that fear again. Your concern for mother and child bring up all your old fear energy, which surfaces and feels fresh and new because the Subconscious operates outside time. Because it's 'now fear' and not 'old fear,' suddenly, you're five again … and terrified. If your Conscious Mind were in control, you would ask your fear, "Where did you come from? I'm sitting here watching TV and am in no danger." But you're cruising on autopilot and just assimilate the fear energy into how you're feeling. After a series of other bad news stories, you're convinced the sky is falling … and you pour yourself another drink, a large one.

But, as a fully conscious, spiritually aware being, how do you respond *creatively*, as opposed to *reactively*, which is what happens when you're on autopilot?

First, although spiritual people have bad days, there are many ways to make them not quite so stressful. One is the path of non-attachment. Attachment occurs when ego sees situations as 'win-lose.' It gloats when it wins and plunges into despair when it loses. In other words, it takes everything personally and engages the win/lose battle by stealing other people's energy before they can steal yours. *Detachment*, on the other hand doesn't care, because the enlightened ego knows that all energy comes from Spirit. (*The Celestine Prophecy* offers one of the best explanations of this.) However, detachment can get you branded as cold, 'not committed' or not a team player.

The middle road of 'non-attachment' is fully engaged in the game but sees the outcome as not really about you. It's actually about soul finding out more about itself, not about winning or losing; it's about the quality of the play and how you grow in the process.

Second, accepting that you pick up other people's stray energy in your aura (most people are incredibly sloppy with their energy), which can cause you stress, you can spin your aura to centrifuge out any stuff that's not yours. Looking down on the top of your head, spin counter-clockwise to get rid of junk, letting your aura go far out. Then spin clockwise, bringing your aura in to about three inches from your body. That is a respectful distance, so you're not swamping other people with your energy. (The exception, of course, is during intimate moments, when the whole point is for the two of you to envelope each other in your energy and merge your fields … by mutual consent, of course.)

Hopefully, then you won't go home from your day quite so frazzled. But once home, you can meditate, soak in the tub or do a deep-breathing exercise, or all three. Of course, there's nothing wrong with a drink or two, although it won't take the stress away but just anesthetize you to it, leaving it still locked away in your cells, causing cellular breakdown, illness and premature aging.

As for the TV news, forget it. Are you going to let New York news directors dictate your pictures of reality for you? Remember their motto: "If it bleeds, it leads." They are driven not by your being well-informed, but by advertising revenue, which depends on ratings, so they're going for maximum 'shock and awe' to keep you watching. The more blood, gore, serial killers, child abductions, bombings, plane crashes, train wrecks, rapes, murders, wars and other mayhem they can cram into your living room, the better. Is that what you want? With a newspaper, at least you get to choose which stories you read and how long you spend on each one.

But it's more insidious than that. Psychologists know that when you're in fear, you stabilize yourself and seek security by consuming material things; so the more scared you are, the more you'll pay attention to TV advertising, which is why they scare the bejeezus out of you with their 'bleeds and leads' headlines. So while those TV anchors seem so concerned for your well-being, they're only looking out for the bottom line—ratings. At least now you know how and why you're being manipulated. Have a nice day, citizen.

When you know you are a soul having an Earth plane sojourn, your stress level drops dramatically, for when a Challenge pops up, you know you put the Challenge there specifically to learn and grow from it. So you ask, "Hmm, this is interesting. Why did I plan this? What is it going to teach me about my Resources, and how can I grow from this situation?"

So, your relationship with yourself is with your whole self: physical body, the three levels of mind, ego-personality, emotions, and soul, all operating harmoniously and aligned to the goals in your life plan.

Well, now you know who you are, so the next question is: Why am I here? What is my purpose? Or more accurately: What was my soul's purpose in incarnating as me?

If you've taken the Michael Education Foundation's quiz in the Appendix, you know your soul's Role, so that's a beginning. Next, read up on Michael's goals in Chapter 5, and try to figure out which applies. None of the Roles implies a profession or line of work, so the field in which you pursue your goal is up to you. Is your goal to learn via growth, acceptance, submission, dominance, re-evaluation or discrimination? Also, if you find yourself in the negative pole of a quality, then slide to the opposite positive pole within the same axis. For example, if you're in Confusion, the negative pole of Growth, slide to Simplicity, the positive pole of Reevaluation on the Inspiration Axis. Normally, you would be in the positive pole of Growth, or Evolution, which involves clarity and understanding, but if you're caught in a dilemma, you can stagnate in Confusion. By sliding over to Simplicity, you can sit a while in awe of the wonder of reality, and let the dilemma resolve itself.

Archetypes

Your soul also embodies the energy of one or more vast archetypes, such as truth, love, beauty, passion, abundance, devotion, faith, grace, spirituality, forgiveness and so on. Your job is to explore your archetypes thoroughly and express them in the world for the rest of us to enjoy. Suppose truth is one of yours. What does that mean? You would thrive on discovering new concepts, exploring them with clarity, teaching truth, and maybe even fighting for the right to express it, as did Galileo when he discovered the truth that the Earth revolves around the sun but the Church wanted to suppress it.

How do you discover your archetype(s)? Simply ask. In meditation, or just a quiet space, ask your soul or guides to reveal them to you in thoughts, words, or feelings. Suppose you ask and the first thing that comes to mind is the image of Joseph Campbell, Princess Diana, or Mother Teresa. What quality does that person symbolize for you? Truth? Love? Service? If you hear or see nothing, ask to be shown via synchronicity. For example, you may turn on the radio just as the Beatles are singing *All You Need Is Love* and may suddenly feel your heart swell with loving energy. Big hint.

Next, what is your purpose within the archetype? You may already know this because it's whatever brings you joy. For example, I derive great joy from taking truths from a number of sources and synthesizing them into something larger (as with this book). But if nothing strikes you, ask again. Or talk to your friends because they are your mirrors. They may tell you, "You always see the practical solution. You're so grounded, you make me feel safe.' And stay open to more synchronicity, such as words on billboards that jump out at you, or even overheard conversations in the checkout line at the store. You never know how your guides will bring you the information.

Emotional Wounds

We saw in Chapter 5 that we come into this lifetime carrying wounds from previous lives that our soul has lived. These wounds stem from past-life traumas that were not resolved or healed in those lifetimes (by definition, a traumatic death can only be healed on the soul plane or another Earth life), and in *this* lifetime they manifest as our fears. Being buried alive in medieval times may be the cause of today's claustrophobia, or being once burned at the stake may make us fearful of fire today. Unfortunately, most of us are born fearful and our job is to heal those wounds.

What are *you* afraid of in this lifetime? Fire, falling, loud noises, sharp objects, water, the dark, spiders, bridges, dogs, a particular place? Whatever it is, if you can't recall a childhood cause, its roots lie in a past life, and can only be dealt with by going back to that life. But once you heal it, you remove its charge from your *soul's* energy, and hence *all* your co-incarnations.

According to the Michael entity, our deepest fear is of 'not being good enough.' That no matter how proficient we actually are at the life game, we fear we will be exposed as a fraud, and hence unworthy of love, acceptance, abundance, whatever. This imprinting may have happened in utero if the pregnancy was unwanted or it may be a past-life wound. Either way, regression will uncover it for healing.

Past-life shame and guilt over atrocities we have committed are major emotional wounds that may make us cringe under criticism or compensate with arrogance. Either way, they block love and must be healed, beginning with acceptance. After all, as Old Souls with hundreds of lifetimes behind us, we've all done things we're not proud of. Then come self-forgiveness and self-love. (I myself had to come to terms with having been a genetic engineer in Atlantis who created many monstrosities during my experiments.)

Of course, professional regression is optimum, but many people have great success self-regressing, using what I call Soul's Life Gallery, where you allow your guides and soul to lead you through the healing.

Soul's Life Gallery

First decide what issue you want resolved during regression. Then settle in as if you're about to meditate, breathe deeply for a few minutes, and then ask to be shown an art gallery-type building. It may be anything, from a grand Washington landmark to a south-western pueblo style building in Taos, NM. Enter the building and sense the energy, the lighting, the smell, the sounds. Then ask to be shown your soul's life gallery. There, you will see, hanging on the walls, portraits of every incarnation your soul has ever taken. Walk through the gallery, looking at the figures. What do you see? A Civil War soldier? A Roman senator, or a slave rowing in a huge galley? An intern in a Nazi concentration camp, or a guard there? A combatant in a WWII battle for a Pacific island? A nameless scullery maid in a medieval castle, or the baron? A primitive cave-dweller?

Ask your soul or guides to light up whichever portrait has the answer to your issue. Move to it and watch as the figure comes to life and the still-life becomes a movie screen. Observe as events unfold that yield the key information you need. You may even find yourself in the scene, reliving the life of the character. Be careful not to get too analytical just yet, but go with the flow as it's presented to you.

When the movie stops or the character crosses over, determine whether you were warm and loving in that lifetime, or cruel and mean. Was the world a better place for having you in it ... or worse? What did you learn, and what lessons went unlearned? Were people enabled and empowered through knowing you … or disempowered? Ask if there are any unresolved emotional wounds you can heal in your current lifetime. Or any physical ailments that stem from that lifetime.

If you find this technique easy, you can go back any time and rerun any other life portrait that your guides or soul think appropriate, but be careful not to get lost in there. Your current life is your point of power, and those other lifetimes just contain clues and pointers to this lifetime.

Self-loving or Self-loathing

Crucial to your relationship with self is how you rate *yourself* in your worldview. If minus 10 is feeling despondent about yourself, thinking you're a waste of skin, and plus 10 is feeling transcendentally good about yourself, where do you fit in?

Are you positive and upbeat about who you are? Do you enjoy being you? Are you happy to be alone with yourself? Are you your own best friend? Do you wake up saying, "Fantastic! A whole day of being me!" Yes, there really are people with such high self-love.

Now, some people will dismiss this as self-indulgent narcissism, but it is not. When you know you are primarily soul and have an inkling of what that means, high self-love is *inevitable*, because soul is pure love. You don't fabricate the love; it just flows. But it goes much deeper than that.

As we will see, you cannot love yourself or anyone else for that matter. Loving is not something you *do* but something you can only *allow*. The universe and everything in it, including you, is made of energy vibrating in a particular frequency band, and we call that band 'love,' so you have two options: you can allow it to flow through you from your soul out into the world, or you can block it from flowing.

The first option—allowing—is easy; you just get out of the way and let it happen. You need do absolutely nothing. Self-love is our natural state (just look at newborns … well, some) if only we would get out of our own way and bask in the love of the Source, All That Is and our own soul.

The second option—blocking—takes much hard work but we do it anyway. We must erect and maintain barriers that keep the love out, and this takes years of effort. While you were still in your mother's womb, you were being bombarded with energy and the worldviews of your caregivers, who inherited them from their caregivers, and so on. Therefore, unless someone in your family has broken the chain, your beliefs have been handed down for generations.

How We Block Love

We block love in dozens of ways, all of them laid down during childhood by how we interpreted our perceptions of how our parents treated us. Here are just a few:

- *Unwillingness to deal with feelings*—if we felt hurt, we suppressed our emotions, which means *all* of them, pleasant and unpleasant.
- *Not feeling deserving of love*—one way to deal with lack of love as a child was to convince yourself that you were unworthy of it, so you didn't expect it, and were not hurt when it didn't come.
- *I don't need love*—another coping mechanism was to reinvent yourself as a rugged individualist who didn't need anyone else, especially if you're male, because the culture encouraged this.
- *I've had my shot at love and won't get a second*—in other words, I screwed up the first time and must now receive my punishment.
- *If I open to love, I will get hurt*—that's always a chance in anything we try.

A major source of low self-esteem was the trauma of birth, in which you were squeezed almost to death and ejected from the womb, into the harshness of the outer world. Not only is this traumatic first experience of the world recorded in your Subconscious Mind, but it may be *interpreted* as punishment, not for something you have done but for what you are—unworthy. So your very first self-image was one of unworthiness, and this still sits deep in your Subconscious, ready to be called up and reinforced whenever you do something dumb as an adult.

What's the solution? Water birth! A tank of body-temperature water into which the baby slips, for a comfortable transition to the outside world. And mothers really appreciate it, too, because flotation greatly eases labor. However, it's too late now for you to benefit from that.

Another major source of screwed up beliefs is organized religion that in the West has made a fortune out of convincing you of your own low self-worth, and having exclusive rights on the means of your salvation, which they sell to you every Sunday morning. Religions also teach that self-love is narcissistic, and that self-effacing martyrdom is 'saintly.'

The communion service in the Church of England (my early brainwashers) has the congregation saying, "We are not worthy of picking up the crumbs from under Thy table, O Lord." "Oh, Lord" is right. There's no way the all-loving Supreme Source would want its creator-gods-in-training being such sniveling self-flagellators, for heaven's sake.

According to the Michael entity, the number one human fear is, "Would other people still love me if they found out who I really am?" That is, if they see through the flimsy ego-facade that I hold up as the idealized cardboard cut-out figure of myself that I want the world to think is me. Well, who really cares about the interface called ego? And if anyone does care, their opinion is their problem and not yours. For example, I meet people at nudist clubs who go to great lengths to prevent their 'textile' friends from knowing where they go at weekends. To me, this is hypocrisy. The nudist lifestyle is wholesome, healthy and a lot of fun. And the people are (mostly) free of hang-ups, so rather than be ashamed, I joyfully announce it to the world.

Incidentally, the #2 and #3 fears are public speaking and being nude in public when everyone else is clothed. I once gave a talk at a nudist club that was 'clothing optional' and most of the audience was 'textiled.' Of course, I wasn't, which was an interesting experience. I did have one problem, however … nowhere to clip the microphone!

So, examine your fears; they're yours, and only you can choose to deep-six them. And know they are not reality but just your parents' and grandparents' opinions about reality. *And* they are all that's stopping you from being the love you already are, so just get out of the way. I know, easy for me to say. I agree, but if it takes five years and you *don't* start now, you'll still be blocking love in five years' time.

Listening to Yourself

We've already seen how those who pray to God are really begging their higher self to make changes in their life. But before we even do that, though, we must realize we are thinking our life into being, moment-by-moment from our belief system. Of course, our collective higher selves are doing most of the work by organizing all the energy coming to the physical plane into subatomic particles to create the substance of 3-D, but our beliefs strongly influence the local reality we create around ourselves and experience as life.

Now here's The Big Secret from another angle. Local reality—your daily life—is intended to mirror your beliefs to you. Yes, your life is meant to be a mirror of your beliefs. Most of us have it backwards: we form our beliefs from our experiences, not realizing our experiences flow from our beliefs. Reality follows belief, and not the other way round. (Getting my mind around that one took a couple of years.)

Low self-esteem will show up in ways that reflect your own self-worth back at you, such as abusive relationships, car troubles, meaningless jobs, financial woes—everything you expect life to be, because that's all you're worth. High self-esteem tells the universe you are worthy of the finest things in live—healthy relationships, a reliable car, a great job where your creativity is given free rein, and material abundance.

So, before you pray, "O Lord, won't you give me a Mercedes-Benz," do you feel worthy of having one? Is your 'havingness quotient' (or HQ) high enough? With a low HQ, even if you got the car, it wouldn't be in your life long. That's why many big lottery winners are bankrupt within five years; their HQ is too low to accommodate great wealth so they lose their fortune and slip back into their comfort zone.

Take a good hard look at every area of your life, asking, "Does my HQ allow for abundance in this area? Do I feel worthy of abundance?" If not, change your beliefs about who you are. Read books about abundance (and if you can't afford them, go to the public library), talk to rich people about their self-image, and ask your guides and higher self to help you change your beliefs. (Living in Las Vegas, I love to walk through the Bellagio or Venetian and inhale the energy of luxury and prosperity, saying, "Yes, I deserve this. I am worthy of this." Try it some time.)

What is material abundance, anyway? It's the universe's way of showing love and support for you and the bravery with which you're tackling the goals your soul set up. Many spiritual people have hang-ups about money, but remember, it's simply one form of love that the universe and your soul have for you. This may sound weird but try it anyway … take a wad of bills of any or all denominations and smell them. Inhale deeply the smell of the ink and paper. You'll find it's a musky scent that after a while actually grows on you. (It can even become an aphrodisiac.)

In addition to seeing money as Spirit's way of loving you, appreciate it for the power it gives you to do things, such as publish books that change the world. But primarily enjoy it for what it is—a physical manifestation of Spirit's love for you. And your soul wants you to have as much as you can allow in, because that leads to different and more varied experiences, which leads to more growth … which is why you're here, after all.

And when you pay for something, see the payment as passing on Spirit's love for you to the next person, or to all the folks at, say, the phone company. Do not see the payment as diminishing what you have but as flowing out that love so that it can return to you.

During the period of examining and changing your beliefs, avoid hanging out with people who share your old beliefs. When they see you attempting to 'break out of belief prison,' they will get scared and try to drag you back down. That way, they are not shamed by not doing this work themselves and can stay wallowing in victimhood. Instead, find an abundance workshop, listen to Tony Robbins' tapes, or mingle with other high self-esteemers.

One last word. We're told at length to not judge the life path taken by others, because we can't possibly know their souls' intentions. Severe challenges may indicate an old soul trying to cram as much growth as possible into its last lifetime before graduating completely out of the incarnation game ... we just never know. However, this good advice also applies to *you* and *your life*. Very few of us know the details of the flight plan *we* filed before coming here, so we absolutely must not judge ourselves. Honor the Challenges that you built into this lifetime, and thank them for the growth they bring. They are never punishment but a sign of soul strength. Laugh at adversity as your friend and ally in the growth game. The value of adversity lies in how much growth you can wring out of it. Remember the old saying, "What doesn't kill you makes you stronger." And remember also, those on the higher dimensions regard those on planet Earth as heroes, for only the bravest dare come down here.

Just as love for others really begins at home with self-love, so does compassion for those working through Challenges. Begin by having compassion for yourself, the courageous soul who thought it would accelerate its growth by bravely incarnating one more time even though it knew, "it's gonna be hell down there but I'm going in anyway." New Agers are quick to cut slack for everyone else but ride hard on themselves so, if you're one of those, lighten up and cut yourself some, too. Apart from acts done with malicious intent (which earn you big black marks) or constantly thinking about suicide, you're doing great by just being here and getting through the day.

Once you've turned around your old beliefs about yourself and love your magnificent self, it's time to really work with guides and higher self. You talk to them all the time with your thoughts. Now most people's 'monkey minds' (a Zen term) are just an electromagnetic clutter of random thoughtforms, so clarify your thinking. Train yourself to become aware of all the monkey chatter going on. If you can hold one thought for 20 seconds, you're home free, for that's how long it takes to impress that thought onto reality. However, try it to see how difficult it is. Hold one thought to the exclusion of all others for 20 seconds. Practice until you can do it. But be careful about what that one thought is, however, because it *will* reprogram reality—the universe doesn't know you're only practicing, and will take you seriously.

Listening to Spirit

After laying out any changes in how you want your life to be, the next step is 'listening,' and there are three main ways. The first involves finding a peaceful place and getting your mind quiet for about 20 minutes. Again, not easy in today's world, which is why so few people enjoy spirit guidance. But dropping thoughts into our empty mind is a major way Spirit[1] talks to us. (If the term 'meditating' sounds too Eastern, call it 'just listening.')

Before a listening session, say something such as, "I surround myself with white light that allows in only that which is in the highest and best interests of all involved." This blocks any stray thoughts floating around the neighborhood and tells the universe, including your own Superconscious and Subconscious Minds, that you're serious about your listening.

The second listening technique uses your Emotional Guidance System. This is a highly tuned feedback system used by your body and by Spirit. Suppose you have been offered a good job in another city. This major career step comes at a price, however—relocation and dislocation of your life: new town, new schools for the kids, your spouse giving up his or her job, etc. What to do?

Now you have only a fraction of the information you need to make a fully informed decision. You don't know whether your new employer will still be in business in five years, what with corporate scandals, take-overs, mergers, downsizing and outsourcing. So, sit down, relax and take a few deep breaths. Now, become aware of your chest area, specifically your heart chakra. Visualize being in that new job in the new city. Do you get a tight, closed feeling in your chest? Or an open, expansive sensation?

Next, visualize staying put in your current job. Open or closed? The sensations are input from your guides and higher self, who exist free of the timeline and can easily pop five years into the future and tell you how things *could* turn out. ('Could' is italicized because the universe and everyone in it have free will.) Open means yes; closed means no.

I use a variation of this—my first waking thought. (The sleep/wake boundary is called the hypnogogic state.) Before going to sleep, I tell Spirit what the options are in a current decision, and ask for my first waking feeling or thought the next day to show me the option with the most love for all concerned. It never fails. Once I was contemplating a move to another city and had even found a house there. On the day I was due to put down a deposit, I awoke in almost

---

[1]   When capitalized, 'Spirit' refers to the community of your spirit, your guides, guardian angels, and whoever influences you for your highest good.

panic, doubled over with gut-wrenching pain. A no-brainer! So, if listening with your heart doesn't work, try listening to your gut.

The third means of listening is to closely observe the world around you for signs and clues. These can come unbidden, as when three different people independently tell you about the same book. Heads up! Two could be coincidence, but three is called synchronicity, or 'guided coincidence" (see below).

You can also ask for a sign that is not common, such as, "Show me a white bird." If you see an albino pigeon later in the day, it probably is a sign. Just acknowledge what it took to get that rare white bird to show up in your life.

If you have a digital clock on your coffeemaker, how often do the minutes read '11'? As confirmation of something, Spirit often has me go to the machine when it just 'happens' to be reading: 11:33—my life number.

(See Volume Two, Chapter 9 for using dowsing to divine the truth.)

Synchronicity

Appreciating synchronicity requires an openness and willingness to explore the connections between apparently unconnected events and the significance of that connection to our lives. Searching for its meaning reveals purpose behind the *apparent* randomness of our lives.

Jung first coined the term and defined it as: "The simultaneous occurrence of two meaningfully but not causally connected events."

So it involves two or more unusual and apparently unrelated but connected events that have a deep significance in your life. Let's look at this. First is 'unusual.' If a friend calls me and asks what I'm doing, I might say, "Sitting on my patio drinking a cup of coffee." He might reply, "That's a coincidence. So am I." Big deal! I spend most of my non-computer time out there and we're both prodigious coffee-drinkers. But suppose I say, "I'm in the coffee shop at the Luxor," and he says, "So am I." We both put our cell phones down and realize we're just a few feet apart, separated by a large, potted palm. Now *that's* unusual because it's the first time in there for both of us.

'Apparently unrelated but connected' means that to the world out there, the events seem unrelated. When you think about a person and the phone rings, there's no apparent relation. But when the caller is the *same person* you were thinking about, there's the connection.

'Deep significance' means something changes in your life that otherwise would not have happened. Perhaps you pay more attention to the reason your friend called, and end up going somewhere that you otherwise would have missed ... and that's where you meet your twin flame.

Synchronicity is 'meaningful' because it impacts your life. As a fiction writer, I have fun with the characters in the books I write or edit, and strive for tight story lines where, say, the hero enters a room *just in time* to hear two bad guys plotting something evil. A second later would have been too late, and there's no story. If my characters were able to talk to me, they would probably tell me their lives are full of such meaningful coincidences. It's true ... they are because I put them there to move the plot along and make things interesting.

Now, pull the camera back a little and look at your life. Are you sure you're not a character in a larger story? If you were, who would be the author, and what synchronicities would he or she write into your life story? And how would you-the-character interpret them? Would you even notice them? Or would you just dismiss them? Big shame if you do because they are a major way Spirit uses to 'move your life along.'

Other characteristics of synchronicity are that it is unique and unrepeatable— true one-in-a-million freaks of circumstance that tell you you're not the author of your life story, and there's a larger Author writing little subplots into the story. For example, this is a true story, but the names have been changed:

Mike and Jenny meet at a party near San Francisco and are immediately drawn to each other, but they are both in relationships, so the attraction goes no further. Jenny moves with her boyfriend to Texas, hoping he will commit and propose marriage. Over the years, she thinks often of Mike and the strong connection she felt with him. After eight years, her boyfriend still won't commit, so she leaves Texas and drives back to California.

Meanwhile, Mike often thinks of Jenny but knows she moved east some-where, and has probably married her boyfriend. One day, he has to go to Las Vegas to attend his grandmother's funeral but doesn't really want to. SF airport is fogged in so he sets out on the 12-hour drive. Late that night, driving through a 'blink and you miss it' town, his car starts acting up, so he checks into a motel, hoping the town mechanic can fix the car in the morning. He is astute enough to realize his car trouble is due to his lack of wholehearted commitment to his Las Vegas trip.

While Mike is in the motel office checking in, Jenny walks in, also intending to spend the night there on her way to California. Both see the synchronicity, and begin a relationship on the spot, to which Mike has no trouble committing be-cause that's the issue that was up for him.

Coincidence or synchronicity? Well, the two apparently unrelated events of the pair both separately checking into the same motel had deep personal significance to them. They were unusual 'once in a lifetime' events in that neither of them had ever been to that town before ... and it was impeccable timing—a few minutes either way and they could have missed each other—so they were unique and unrepeatable. You be the judge—guided or not?

But look at what their guides had to pull off:

1. This all had to be orchestrated around Mike's grandmother's funeral.
2. San Francisco airport had to be fogged in.
3. Mike had to take *that* particular route to Las Vegas out of all possible routes.
4. His car had to be 'tampered with' so he'd spend the night in *that* town.
5. He had to choose *that* motel, and exactly at *that* time, just as Jenny entered.

Similarly, Jenny's itinerary had to be meticulously managed so that she, too, would end up in the motel office at exactly the same time as Mike. Not a bad job, eh?

In another story, during the Vietnam War, John was in the Air Force, based in Thailand, where he fell in love with a young Thai woman and fathered a baby. When John was rotated back home, he was refused permission to take his new family. The mother subsequently married another American, who returned all John's letters, so John completely lost touch with his son. Several years later, John was driving on I-25 in Colorado and suddenly had the impulse to buy gas even though his tank was still half full. Of all the gas stations at the freeway interchange, oddly, he chose one brand he never normally used. Then, totally out of character for him, he wrote a check rather than pay cash. When the cashier saw the name on his check and ID, the young man asked John if he had ever been in the Air Force. Then, had he ever been in Thailand. And fathered a son while there. When John said he had, the cashier informed him he was that son.

Again, look at how hard John's guides had to work to bring these two together:

1. Make him buy gas when he didn't need it
2. Choose a different brand of gas than usual
3. Write a check instead of paying cash.

This one actually happened to me. In 1989, before I left California to live in Mexico for two years, I gave out a dozen or so copies of the manuscript of *An Ascension Handbook*. On my return in 1991, I ended up in Denver and began attending a regular weekly channeling evening. One night, three new people showed up from a nearby town and, in conversation, asked me if I'd ever heard of a Tony Stubbs who used to live in California and wrote a book called *An Ascension Handbook*. Apparently, their copy of the manuscript was about a tenth-generation photocopy and was incomplete, which was driving them crazy. Sure that this was a joke, I played along, but then I realized they were not joking, and told them who I was. Well, I ended up in a long and fruitful relationship with one of them, in which we both grew enormously.

Coincidence or synchronicity? To me, that was obviously a Spirit set-up, one that took enormous choreography on the part of all our guides. Even the story of how they came to hear of the event to begin with was major synchronicity in its own right.

When something 'spooky' happens such as the two stories above, immediately do a heads-up and ask, "What does this mean?" At one level, Mike meets Jenny and I meet a soulmate, and long relationships ensue. At another level, we can take comfort from knowing a larger Author is busy writing our life script. In fact, you-the-soul write all this before you're born, and it's up to your guides to keep you on track so that you play your agreed part. Your life plan has certain lessons built into it, but how you learn these lessons is up to you (free will). For instance, if you want to learn to drive a car, you can choose to learn on a busy freeway during rush hour or you can go to an abandoned airfield and learn on miles of empty runway.

You must, however, be open to the 'spirit nudges' to be in the right place and time … and that's a matter of balance between you the character and you the Author, with your ego flexible enough to step aside and let events unfold.

Synchronicity adds value to an otherwise apparently random universe, and reveals the Author of your life story. When ego meets synchronicity, ego always learns … if only that there *is* an Author. Synchronicity stories make our lives fuller and more meaningful, such as the tale of a man who catches a fish. While preparing the fish for dinner, his wife finds, inside the fish, the wedding ring she lost in the lake ten years earlier. Coincidence? Not to that couple, who went on to renew their wedding vows with the newfound ring. And the odds of *that* fisherman catching *that* fish with *that* ring? Astronomically low.

My favorite is the story of the rich nobleman whose son falls into a Scottish peat bog and is rescued by a poor local farmer and his son. The farmer refuses a reward for himself but agrees to have his son's college education paid for. The son, Alexander Fleming, goes on to discover penicillin. Years later, the rescued son contracts pneumonia and his life is saved … of course, by penicillin. His name?

Winston Churchill. Now a cynic would readily blow that story apart, but most of us get a warm glow from it.

One of the main problems people have with life is that it is apparently meaningless. They find themselves in a human body and struggle through, getting an education and then devoting themselves to keeping a roof over their head, marrying, and raising children. All of this is a great distraction from the real question, Why am I here? If we turn this around and assume life *is* meaningful, then apparent coincidences along the way are like the trail of bread crumbs intended to lead Hansel and Gretel out of the forest by pointing out the things that are truly important. So-called synchronicities are the bread crumbs that are meant to guide us to the people and situations that are important. The assumption that life is meaningful puts us into explorer mode, whereby we actively interrogate events and situations for their meaning, much as we use road signs to guide us when we are driving in unknown territory. Native Americans, for example, live by this assumption and constantly question events, such as looking for the meaning of a hawk circling overhead three times. Living your life on the assumption that it *is* meaningful turns things around completely.

Before you incarnated, you set up an intricate plan, which has been guiding your life since before birth, although you didn't know it. All the twists and turns your life has taken were carefully scripted *by you*, so you have been unknowingly following the trail of bread crumbs through the forest you put there for you to find. Think how much more effective you might have been if you had known this all along. But that's all changed. You *do* know this and from now on will be actively interrogating your life for meaning, asking each bread crumb: What are you trying to tell me?

Intuition and synchronicity work closely together, in that intuition divines the meaning of a particular bread crumb and presents that meaning to the left brain to be acted upon. Therefore it is important that your right brain intuition always be on and operating. And as with any endeavor, the more you practice, the better you get. So, have fun with synchronicity for it really is a window into the higher realms of the morphic field.

My life, and the lives of many I know, have been and still are so full of amazing 'coincidences,' clearly someone has 'a hand on the tiller,' guiding events, usually to my advantage but always to my education. Spirit guides, guardian angels, and higher self all have their part to play. But something else is involved—a phenomenon known as the morphogenetic field, or M-field, first defined by a scientist named Rupert Sheldrake. Suppose a friend calls out of the blue at the same time you're thinking of him. Did he call *because* you were thinking about him? Or were you thinking about him *because* he was about to dial your number? Or both? And if so, what's the actual medium for the connection? According to Sheldrake, we are all connected by the M-field, so let's take a look at it.

The Morphogenetic Field

The 'morphogenetic field' is an invisible field much like that of gravity and the Earth's magnetic field, only this field encompasses and connects social groups of animals (including humans) and other groupings such as families and their pets, all at the level of their intuition and higher self, so it exists in the 4th dimension.

When a herd of antelope, a flock of starlings, or a school of fish turns, they all turn at *exactly* the same time, so it's not a case of follow-the-leader. But how? Well, they are all connected by the M-field, or a kind of group consciousness. The field explains why the family dog will howl uncontrollably when a family member is hurt or dies, even an entire continent away.

It also explains why, in countless rigorous tests, a family pet will go to the front door and wait for its owner, at the *exact* moment when the owner sets his or her *intent* to come home. So the dog picks up on the thought, not the actual act of getting in the car, i.e., when you first *think* of heading home, regardless of distance. It even works, for example, when servicemen in distant countries go on leave and head home even though the journey may take several days.

Sheldrake set up an experiment to test his anecdotal observation of the phenomenon. For 45 days, he paged the dog owner to return home at random times and videotaped her dog to find out when the dog went to the window to await the owner's actual return. The results were that on *some* days, the correlation was spot on and the dog reacted exactly when the owner answered the pager. However, on *other* days, the dog completely failed to anticipate the owner's return. These days were marked by exceptionally high geomagnetic activity, sunspot fluxes and thunderstorms, plus more mundane things such as playing with other household pets. Bottom line: If you want to do any M-field work, such as creative visualization, isolate yourself and set your intent to be unaffected by the world around you. If lightning is impressive in the physical world, imagine what its M-field blueprint is like!

The M-field also seems to involve locations, for a dog accidentally left behind on a trip will often find its way home through hundreds of miles of unfamiliar territory. (Of course, it might also be homing on its humans' energy.)

Have you ever stared at someone from behind? How long does it take that person to detect the stare and turn round? Not long, but how did they know? What's going on here? Dr. Gary Schwartz of the University of Arizona (the researcher who tested John Edward and George Anderson) actually tested this phenomenon. He divided graduate students into two groups, with one group to act as the 'starer,' and the other to detect the stare. For a few seconds, they were directed to do one of three things: (1) stare at the back of a detector's head; (2) close their eyes but *think* about staring; (3) do nothing.

At the end of the short time period, detectors were asked if they had felt a stare. The law of chance says they would be right 50% of the time and wrong 50% of the time. In fact, they rightly detected an open-eye stare 56% of the time and a closed-eye *intended* stare 60% of the time. These better-than-chance results suggests that we imprint the M-field more strongly with our *intent* than with our *deeds*. Score one for visualization—your Subconscious Mind is more impressed by you *thinking* about doing something than by you actually doing it!

Students of metaphysics might see detecting a stare as an 'aura connection.' We know the aura around any living thing is stronger closer in and becomes less pronounced at a distance, but it never stops altogether, stretching out to infinity. So if someone you love is far away, your auras 'reach out' to each other through the M-field to form an energetic thread between you, conducting love and thoughts. This also explains how you often know who's on the phone when it rings and, of course, how your dog or cat knows when you're coming home. In other words, your aura precedes you via the M-field.

Let's look at working with this field, because we can also use it to *cause* things to happen rather than just wait around until they do. You can, of course, hammer away at changing 3-D, making phone calls, running around town to meetings, or getting mad at people. Or you can sit in your favorite chair and impress your desires and needs on to the M-field ... and *then* make your calls. In fact, until you *do* make an impression on the M-field, it's highly unlikely that *anything* will happen, despite all your running around.

You visualize what you want, form the image of the desired situation in your mind, and hold it there for 20 seconds. This broadcasts it into the M-field, where the aura of anyone else involved with the situation picks it up. Then, their higher self may filter your request down into their awareness, so they'll call you. If you visualized changing your job, say, a friend may call out of the blue with, "Listen, I've just had an idea. How would you like to come to work for me?"

Or their higher self may just leave your request in the person's aura, so when you call, that person is already predisposed to help you.

The M-field is also omni-directional, so it's important to know you're also open to incoming calls. Suppose your friend David needs another computer, so he visualizes one coming to him and broadcasts his vision into the M-field. You've just bought a new computer and want to get rid of your old one. Suddenly, you think: I'll call David. Maybe he knows someone looking for a cheap used computer. So you call him, and you're both happy.

However, be careful what you send. Use this technique to program the M-field ONLY for the highest and best interests of all involved. Anything less invites unpleasant karmic consequences.

Also, do not negate yourself by adding a PS to your vision, saying, "Probably no one will reply," because no one probably will. The M-field is a medium for transmitting awareness, so your *energy* and *intent* when you broadcast into it are crucial. And clarity is essential, because the field won't try to figure out what you mean; it will take you literally.

Suppose you're looking for a relationship and broadcast the image of your perfect mate, but with the energy of, "Why would someone like you bother with someone like me?" Well, you've just blown it. All the possible dream mates out there will pick up on your energy and hit the cosmic delete key.

So spend 20 seconds beaming out what you want in a mate, job, home, etc., followed by 20 seconds of what you can offer as a mate, employee, renter, etc. Then, keep this in the back of your mind as you reach for the phone.

The M-field exists independent of space, so you can pick up from anyone, any-where. But because it's also omni-*dimensional*, you can use it to send to and receive from those already crossed over or not yet born, confident you will be heard.

If you think about your deceased granny for 20 seconds with loving energy, your 'call' hits the M-field, and she is alerted to someone calling her. She follows the thread to its source—you—and she's there with you.

So, what's the practical use of knowing about the M-field? This is best answered by the example of Findhorn, a magnificent garden on wind-blown sand dunes in Scotland. Started by Peter and Eileen Caddy when Peter lost his job in 1963, it began as a cooperative venture between humans and the devic[2] world, channeled by Eileen and others.

---

[2] Devas are generally accepted as part of the angelic realms, each deva holding the blueprint for a par-ticular type of plant or tree, and working with the spirits of individual members of that type. Other members of the angelic realm over-light geographical areas, and 'elementals' are the spirits of wind, fire, water, etc.

Guided by the deva of each type of fruit and vegetable, the humans did their part, pouring love into the ground. Then devas, via the M-field, poured life force energy into the growing plants. The results were breathtaking and, within two years, the garden was supplying produce to local stores. Devas explained they can compensate for the poor soil and even enrich it with what they need, and that the use of artificial fertilizers and weed-killers actually confounds their work. And after being ignored for so long, they are eager to work with humans. Findhorn is a perfect example of working *with* the forces present in the M-field rather than *against* them, and what man and nature can accomplish together. As a bonus, because the food they grew was jammed full of life force energy, their bodies absorbed this, too.

Today, Findhorn has grown from a tiny garden in a trailer park into a large community, a spiritual foundation, a retreat center and a publishing company ... all because they listened to a pea deva, who said, "While the vegetable kingdom holds no grudge against those it feeds, man takes what he can as a matter of course, giving no thanks. This makes us strangely hostile." Another deva told them, "We know that if humanity could get the feel of our realms, life on Earth would be completely changed." (See *www.findhorn.org* for more information.)

Plants Have Feelings, Too

In 1966, an American expert on use of lie detectors accidentally discovered that plants have high-level emotional activities similar to those of human beings and are connected to their environment via the M-field. One day, he connected a lie detector to the leaves of a 'dragon tree' to see how long it would take for the leaves to react when he poured water on the plant's roots. He expected the plant to increase its conductivity and decrease its leaf resistance after it absorbed the water, but the opposite happened, showing the plant seemed 'happy' when it drank water.

Next, he decided to burn a leaf and the lie detector graph went crazy, as if the plant was reacting to the mere *intention*. When he returned with a match, the graph peaked again. When he merely *pretended* to burn a leaf, the plant had no reaction.

In another experiment, the plant was hooked up and a subject in the room was asked a series of questions; the plant could tell whether or not the person was lying. When the subject was asked to answer questions incorrectly, the graph reflected the incorrect answers.

To test whether a plant can recognize people, six subjects were blindfolded and asked to draw lots from a hat. One of the seven drew the instruction to uproot a second plant in the room and stomp on it. No one except the 'murderer' knew the culprit's identity. Each subject was asked to approach the plant, and the graph went crazy for just one person, proving that plants can identify a person who causes harm to them.

When the researcher went on a trip, all his plants registered a reaction at the moment when he *decided* to return home even though he was in another state. Plants also reacted negatively when brine shrimp were dropped into boiling water via an automatic mechanism, the timer of which did not involve human decision. Comparing someone's IQ to that of a houseplant doesn't make as much sense now.

(If you think this talk of the M-field is fanciful, two other prominent scientists, Karl Pribram and David Bohm, have come up with almost identical scenarios. See Appendix C for a discussion of their findings.)

Homeopathy

Homeopathy is the practice of treating illness and disease with minute concentrations of healing agents in solution, often so dilute that only the molecular memory of the active ingredient is present. What confounds researchers into why and how it works is that rarely can two practitioners duplicate each other's results, as must happen in pharmaceutical drug trials where the active ingredient is the causal agent. To find out what's going on, we must look behind the scenes.

In homeopathy, no one takes illness or disease at face value (as do allotropic doctors); it's seen as the *result* of an energy pattern in the M-field interacting with the energy field of the patient's body. (Carving away at the patient's organs does nothing to resolve the disease's energy pattern.) Now when a homeopathic solution, such as a flower essence, is prepared, it's as if magic is being performed in that the process is almost a ritual. The resulting energy structure in the M-field is part flower, part solution and part *preparer*. This explains why a flower essence prepared by two people can yield different results—the M-field blueprints are different. (To some extent, the patient's mindset also affects the outcome, which opens up the field to charges that the *placebo effect* is the real healing agent.)

Bottom line: However homeopathy works, the featured ingredient is *not* the causal agent working upon the patient's physical body; healing comes about when the two energy patterns interact in the M-field.

To close this topic, in one Navajo healing ritual, if someone is sick, the medicine man prepares the appropriate herbal mush but does *not* give it to the sick person. Instead, he gives it to the person's relations, the principle being that this puts the cure into the M-field, and the relations' love for the sick person conveys the cure to him or her. Looks like the Navajos are centuries ahead of the game.

Radionics

Radionics is a methodology for detecting and manipulating subtle energies linked to physical animal, vegetable or mineral matter, and even broadcasts healing vibrations to a single subject. The instrument can also detect specific elements in mineral samples, or dowse for mineral veins using an aerial photograph or map. When considered from the viewpoint of modern science, this looks like magic, but not once we understand the relationship between matter and energy.

At one level, radionics instruments consist of circuitries of resistors, coils and capacitors, which provide a range of 'rates' that are dialed in to set the instrument for various organs or disease patterns. At another level, however, they generate energies in the M-field, outside of the electromagnetic spectrum, in ways that are beyond the modern scientific worldview. Radionics operates in the M-field realm of life force energy much like dowsing, and aids the investigator in detecting and identifying subtle vibrations associated with water, oil or a buried pipe. The dowser holds in mind the sought-after goal and their body reacts, with the pendulum amplifying the reactions.

Radionics started in the early 1900s, when Albert Abrams, an American physician discovered that an energy field existed around the human body that varied in frequency and intensity over individual organs. He also found similar energy associated with a patient's blood sample. Between the 1930s and early 1960s, Ruth Drown, a chiropractor, experimented and worked out a vast range of rates for specific conditions. She also found she could diagnose and treat her patients *in absentia*, simply by using their blood crystal she kept on file.

The rates allow us to identify and treat conditions, even remotely, as each condition is associated with an organized field of energy. Users tune in their intuitive mind and radionic instrument to the patient, calling upon their ESP to determine the underlying cause of a disease condition. A radionic diagnosis develops a health profile of the patient, including the rates for all organ systems and energy imbalances. This can be done remotely using a drop of blood or a hair. A radionic diagnosis may not coincide with a medical diagnosis, but that's because the two fields use totally different models of reality. One of the advantages of radionics is that it can discover potentially serious conditions at an early stage and, by appropriate treatment, prevent the condition from becoming a health problem.

Then one can determine the energy pattern that will eliminate this cause. Treatment projects healing energy patterns back to the patient. Modern research has proved that humans, plants and animals respond to projected thought patterns, regardless of the distance between sender and receiver. Unlike allopathic medicine, radionic treatment is non-physical and non-invasive, so cannot cause harm or produce any unwanted side effects.

Modern units operate with the Ruth Drown rate system, but can work with any other system, including the waveforms of flower essences, essential oils, homeopathic remedies, patterned energy, or anything else you wish to broadcast. Units cost between $500 – $3,000 but be warned: In the U.S., anything other than experimentation is illegal.

Techniques for Talking with Spirit

Mirror Technique

Of course, holding a thought for 20 seconds, or even 20 years, won't work if that thought conflicts with the image of you and your life that you hold in your Subconscious Mind. If, before the age of seven, you were told, "You're a worthless piece of trash who won't ever amount to anything," then that's the image you hold of yourself at the deepest level … even if you're the head of your own successful company—you're just trying to prove 'them' wrong.

One highly effective way to reprogram your Subconscious Mind is the mirror technique. In complete privacy so you don't feel self-conscious (you will anyway in the beginning), look deeply into your own eyes in a mirror and repeat your affirmations, such as, "I am an attractive and worthy person and deserve an equally worthy mate," or, "I am the best person for that new job and deserve to get it." All the rules for affirmations apply, i.e., present tense ("I am …," not, "I will ….") and positive ("I am keeping my job," not, "I won't get fired.")

You can practice speeches in the mirror, tell yourself you're lovable and deserve love, that you're competent and deserve a raise, or that you already have that next contract or client in the bag, etc. There's no limit.

How does this work? The eyes are the direct line to the soul, so it's *got* to pay attention, which includes the Subconscious and Superconscious Minds—the sources of your daily reality as it manifests from the 4th dimension. And repetition is the key, so say things aloud and often.

Why isn't this technique more widely known? How do you know it isn't? Since it's done in strict privacy, how do you know you're not the only one *not* doing it? Throughout history (or at least since we've had mirrors), movers and shakers have talked themselves to ever greater heights, so it's about time you knew how they do it, and level the playing field.

Frameworks 1 & 2

The Seth entity, who brought in about 20 books through Jane Roberts (see Jane Roberts' Seth books for more information) calls the M-field 'Framework–2.' Framework–1 is our everyday world, which many people think 'just happens,' but it doesn't; it flows every microsecond from Framework–2. The two Frameworks are separated by a quantum veil, across which flows an enormous volume of aware energy that manifests on our side as subatomic particles, which then agglomerate to form atoms.

Framework–2 contains an exact duplicate of Framework–1, although, of course, nonphysical in our terms. There, our spirits and guides try out situations and events before they come barreling across the veil for us to experience. We tap into this process whenever we have pre-cognitive dreams, when we catch glimpses of the rehearsals in the Framework–2 'reality factory.'

One of the most famous examples of this occurred in 1898, when writer Morgan Robertson wrote a book titled *The Wreck of the Titan*. Via automatic writing, the 'other side' author told the story of the *Titan*, a 70,000-ton luxury liner, hailed as 'unsinkable,' driven by triple screws at up to 25 knots, that hit an iceberg and sank on its maiden voyage from Southampton to New York, with great loss of life because it had only 24 lifeboats. Of course, 14 years later, in 1912, the 'real' *Titanic* played out the drama perfectly, except she had only 20 lifeboats. We'll never know how many people did not sign up for her maiden voyage because of Robertson's book. However, one passenger, newspaper editor W.T. Stead, was warned by two psychics that he would die on that voyage. He even wrote an editorial claiming that: "This is exactly what might take place if liners are sent to sea short of lifeboats." However, he didn't heed his own warning and died.

Because events and situations are more fluid in Framework–2 before they 'harden' as they cross the veil, we can influence them with our own thoughts. Again, for this to work, those thoughts must be (1) clear, (2) consistent, and (3) fueled by emotion.

Because dreaming is a major communication channel between spirit and personality, let's take a deeper look at this phenomenon. In fact, your waking mind is only half of the story.

Dreams

Researchers find the human sleep cycle to be well organized and predictable. Starting in the *beta* state of normal waking consciousness (14 − 20 Hz), we drop through the *hypnogogic* state (13 Hz) as our mind switches from waking mode to sleeping mode, and is open to visits from deceased loved ones.

We quickly drop through *alpha* (8 − 12 Hz) and *theta* (5 − 7 Hz) into deep *delta* sleep (0 − 4 Hz) where healing and regeneration take place. Delta state encounters can include healing and meeting your guides and other visits, which we usually don't remember unless we wake up abruptly. These delta visitors may give us information or guidance about challenges we face in life. We often then weave this into a dream during the next alpha spike.

Every 90 minutes, the mind comes back up to alpha and dreams for between 5 − 45 minutes. Dreaming is accompanied by rapid eye movement (REM), muscle twitching, variations in blood pressure, heart rate, breathing, and emotional arousal. The Subconscious Mind cannot distinguish dreams from waking reality, and the imagery can be intense enough to actually wake us up. Because dreams happen in a higher dimension and bypass the physical brain, the details are not in your short-term memory, so they fade as quickly on waking, and the dream content is not consciously retained. However, if the dreaming self wants to get a message to the waking self, the content will be retained.

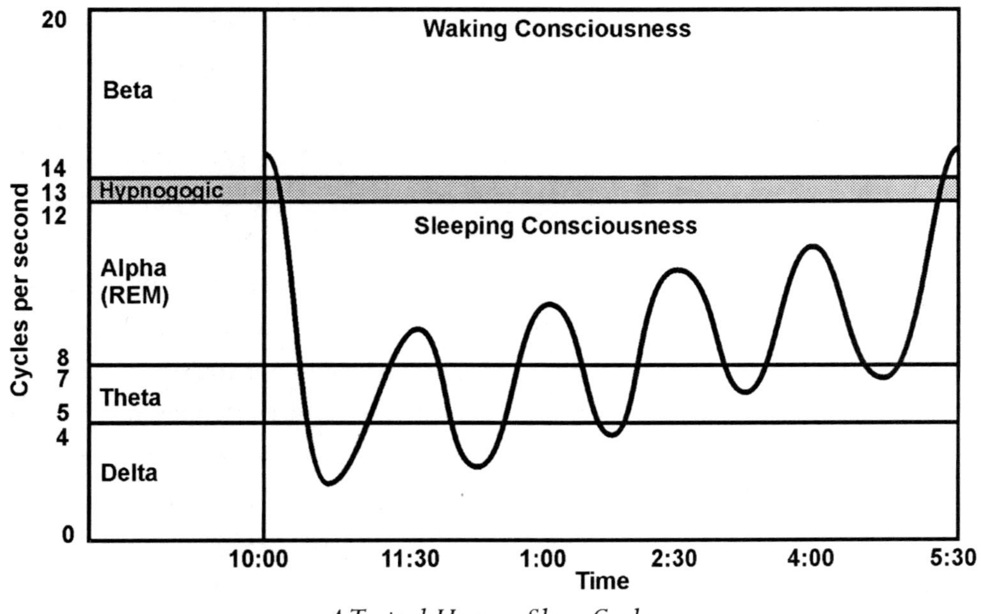

A Typical Human Sleep Cycle

Between REM periods, when in delta, we may have psychic visits from Earth plane beings who are astral projecting, and beings from the soul plane or higher. These visits have a different quality than ordinary dreams, and can be so much more vivid, they shouldn't really be called 'dreams.' Also, they are rarely casual but may convey important information that can be independently verified afterwards. On some unknown inner signal, or if woken, the mind climbs through the hypnogogic state, maybe glimpsing a fragment of the most recent dream activity or psychic visits, which we remember on waking.

In the Framework–2 reality factory, our souls meet nightly for planning sessions about what will happen next in our lives. Committees of involved souls hammer out the realities their incarnations will experience on the Earth plane. The waking mind switches off while your body sleeps, but suppose it peeks through the window at a planning session. What does it make of the experience, especially as, on its return, it must process what it saw and heard through the mind's substrate—your linear brain?

This is one source of dreams, but there is another that is far more practical for our survival.

Dreaming as Course Correction

Fantastical images and weird events involving people you may or may not know in your life all jumble together as you lie in bed trying to sort it out. What does it all mean? "Why was my dead mother riding a dragon? Who was that person I had that argument with, and what were we arguing about?" It's a great loss, however, to conclude that dreams are meaningless jumbles of chaotic nonsense simply because their content does not correspond to our limited waking reality. Dreams break all the rules of our time/space, cause-and-effect waking reality of daily life, because to our dreaming self, there *are* no rules. So what's going on?

To the conscious mind, dreams are apparently spontaneous, hazy, meaningless and often chaotic, mental activity below the level of the conscious mind. In fact, they are well-crafted, whole, meaningful, and coherent activities at the level of mind they are created. Dreams bypass our nice and tidy causal time-space framework by compressing past and future, instead presenting us with a framework based on emotional distance; i.e., aspects of our lives that are *emotionally* linked will seem closer together.

Our waking mind is continually evaluating the world around us and dealing with ever-changing events and situations. To do this, we must group together many of life's variables, try to discern patterns, and then make the choices that best ensure our survival. In doing so, the waking mind misses many hidden connections that lurk in the background, behind the foreground that waking consciousness focuses on.

Dreaming consciousness, on the other hand, reverses foreground and background. (It's similar to the drawing of the old crone and young woman in a hat. You can see one or the other, but not both at the same time.) Using emotional symbolism, the dream presents unmade connections between different areas of your waking life—opportunities missed, skills left unhoned, how today's events mirror childhood events. Because the connections are emotional rather than intellectual, figuring them out takes time and effort on our part, and symbols are rarely to be taken at face value, but mined for what they *represent* to you. Your mother riding a dragon is really about whatever your mother represents to you, guiding whatever dragons represent to you.

Dream interpretation is such an enormous topic, usually it has its own section in the bookstores. Subconscious-driven dreams reveal underlying issues and missed connections, usually symbolically. Recurring dreams are always a signal that you haven't got the point yet and really need to attend to an issue before it becomes a problem. In addition to personal symbols, dreams also use universal symbols, such as the ocean as the subconscious, drowning as fear of being swamped by subconscious drives, your house for your ego personality, being nude in dreams as spiritual emergence or openness, and being chased as part of your needing integration. The list is endless, and many great dream dictionaries are available.

An invaluable aspect of dreams is that they are always honest. Your waking mind is notorious for deluding itself and presenting an edited image to itself. But your dreaming mind shows you who you *really* are, not who you would *like* to be or how you would like to be seen by others. Not facing the truth, waking mind can run afoul of the law of unintended consequences by taking a risk without knowing all the background connections. So the dreaming self sets out to remedy that with the antidote to self-delusion. Also, if waking self is engaging in some shady dealing, dreaming self reveals your moral compass and how you're off course so you can make required course corrections. Of course, again it's all cloaked in emotional symbols.

An interesting aspect of dreams is that the dream is like going to a play where the dreaming self is both cast and audience. The curtain rises and the play unfolds, but the dreaming self is soon involuntarily drawn up onto the stage to interact with the cast in metaphors that explore the connections hidden in the background of your life.

Another source of input to our dreams are scenarios woven together by our soul and guides to explore possible options that we may or may not choose to experience on the Earth plane. If you do choose to manifest a scenario in waking life, you may experience *déjà vu* when it actually happens.

Dream Programming

In *dream programming*, just before going to sleep, you can instruct your subconscious mind to:

1. Root out and process any limiting aspects of your self-image or belief system.
2. Bring to your conscious awareness any helpful hints or pointers to promote health of your ego and its ability to cope with daily life, especially those hidden connections that your waking mind is missing.
3. Ask for solutions to a specific problem to be delivered either in the dream or as an intuitive flash the next day.
4. Ask for a physical body condition to be healed during sleep.
5. Ask for a visitation from those on the other side to help with a specific problem. Do this by focusing on the person's energy and then stating the problem as clearly as you can. This is ideal for inventors whose research has hit a snag, because you can be sure the problem has already been solved over there. The best example of this is the scientist who was trying to figure out the benzene molecule but couldn't. He dozed off and dreamed of a snake swallowing its own tail. On waking, he realized the benzene molecule is actually circular.

Lucid dreaming is a special dream in which you know you're dreaming and have full waking consciousness. You can influence the dream, change outcomes and, within limits, probe the contents of your subconscious mind.

IDEAL Manifesting

The Big Secret involves reality and how your thoughts create that reality … whether you know it or not. We've seen how today's reality flows from yesterday's thoughts; today's thoughts birth tomorrow's reality. Those who don't know this can create some horrible realities *and* miss out on valuable feedback as to the content of their minds. Soul allows this to happen as a learning tool for its incarnations to realize that the world they create for themselves is a far better mirror to their thoughts than a mirror is to their physical bodies.

To help you harness and channel your thoughts into productive avenues, here's a suggested way of formalizing the reality creation process. You can use this technique to bring anything into being, such as a new car, new mate, new job or new living space. If you're reading this, you're probably dedicated to bringing more of your soul's vibration into your life, so let's apply it to that, but again, this is a universal technique.

Hinging on the word IDEAL as a mnemonic, the five-step process involves:

- **Intention:** Clarify what you intend to have happen, for muddled thinking leads to a muddled life ... and we see plenty of people living those. Formulate your goals, such as becoming more sensitive to the urgings and whispers of soul in your life. Use your imagination to en*vision* how that would feel. (Imagination is the most powerful tool on the planet, so use it wisely.) Talk to and read books by people who are already there. Immerse yourself in your intention. Be careful to specify only *what* you want to happen, and not *how*; give the universe plenty of leeway about how the new reality shows up. Finally, be sure that your intention is in the highest and best interest of everyone involved. Of course, becoming more spiritual cannot break the Golden Rule (treat everyone as you would be treated), but some intentions could generate subtle karma, which I define as limiting the sovereign reality of any other being, be it human, animal, or even plant. And loving intention always manifests more quickly because it goes with the grain of our loving universe.

- **Desire:** While you are immersing yourself in your intended outcome, really want it to come about. Imagine how happy and joyful you will be once the vision happens. Fantasize about it, daydream it and enjoy yourself feeling good about it. (If your vision is the direction, your desire is the fuel that will propel it into reality.) And have no fear around it not happening, because that's the surest way to kill it dead.

- **Energy:** Check your physical, mental, emotional, and spiritual energies for any blocks or downside to this envisioned reality. Make sure all four energies are aligned around the vision and its outcome, just as a chair must have four legs all the same length. Be particularly alert for fear in your emotional body, for fear about something in your current reality is not a valid foundation for creating a new one. Far better to deal with the fear first and *then* choose to move on. In fact, your soul will perpetuate the existing situation *until* you've dealt with the fear.

- **Action:** Take at least one positive action step towards achieving the outcome. This could be a trip to a metaphysical bookstore, or a seminar or workshop on how to channel. Or just a day at the beach or a hike, during which you reflect deeply on the outcome. Better yet, begin a program of regular meditation. (If prayer is asking, meditation is listening for answers.)

- **Love:** Bathe the whole situation in love for yourself, for anyone else involved, and for your respective selves at the spirit level. Also pour gratitude over the entire venture. It has already manifested in a higher dimension—otherwise you couldn't even be doing the exercise—so give thanks for it there, and use a tractor beam to pull it gently into daily reality. Also, express gratitude for being sufficiently spiritually aware already to even be doing this—you're already halfway there.

Now you can relax. It's up to the universe to reorient itself around your vision and deliver the outcome to your life. Just go about your business, remaining on the alert for dreams and synchronous events that reveal the inner workings of the 'reality factory.' Within hours or days, you should be receiving 'feedback' from the universe.

But what if nothing happens? Did you do it wrong? Probably not. Chances are, your intention is not aligned with Divine Intention and somehow you're out of step with the larger beat. Take a good, hard look at why that desired situation isn't already in your life. Is there anything to learn from the current situation that would be lost once the new reality came along? Would the new situation mask any fear present in the old one that your soul first wants you to clear? Is there any victim energy around the existing situation? Any lack of personal accountability? (You can't change what you don't first own.) And unearth any limiting thoughts because these build a prison around you rather than a palace.

Regardless of what the actual intent is that is not happening, you can ask your soul to show you any blocks to manifesting. Ask for dreams, synchronicities, chance remarks from friends, and then be hyper-alert for clues dropped in your path. Once you clear a block or pour light into a fear, try IDEALing again.

Or maybe it's a timing issue. Perhaps there are things for you to do that wouldn't get done once the new reality showed up to distract you. Or you may be waiting for other people involved to catch up. If *they* still have fears, blocks or outstanding issues, their souls will put things on hold until they are clear. Take a good look at everyone in the loop in case the hold-up is there.

Once all the blocks are cleared and everything is in Divine Alignment, the new reality is inevitable. (There is much more in later chapters about Divine Alignment and manifestation.) Happy manifesting!

Think Yourself Bigger

The universe is a faithful mirror of our beliefs and rearranges itself to accommodate our pictures of reality. So, if we believe we are helpless victims, that is exactly what we will experience. The task, therefore, is to switch from being reality's victim-reactor to being its master-creator, and from an isolated 'doing' to a unified 'being.'

This does not entail changing *who you are*, but only who you *perceive* you are. The left-brained rational thinker will want evidence before it changes its perception, but there isn't any evidence until you change your way of looking at things. This Catch-22 says, "I'll believe it when I see it," but you can't see it *until* you believe it.

The right-brained intuitive thinker, however, goes on hunches, gut-feelings about things, and doesn't need evidence. To switch from reactor to creator, intuition needs to open itself to this truth and play, "Just for now, let's pretend it's true. Then how would that change how I feel about me?" Call it 'suspension of belief,' or 'fake it until you make it,' but for an hour or a day, the intuition is given free rein. The higher self will use this opening to reinforce the intuitive truth of reality mastery, and confirm it as a knowing. We can go further than just opening to the truth, by setting the *intention* of this to become a certainty, manifesting in our experience.

Graphic Is Good

Why do affirmations pale into nothing compared with visualization? Because for most people, the Subconscious Mind has the reasoning power of the three-year-old. Up until age three or so, it ran the show, but then the rational, reasoning Conscious Mind began to take over, leaving the Subconscious Mind behind in the shadows, not to progress any further.

However, if for some reason, the Conscious Mind is overwhelmed and is paralyzed in indecision, not knowing what to do, the Subconscious Mind takes over, often with disastrous consequences. Suppose someone comes unglued at you and erupts for no apparent reason. Your Conscious Mind hasn't a clue what to do, so your Subconscious Mind retaliates with a barbed comment that only makes things worse. Knowing that when people come unglued on you is *never* about you but always about them, you could keep your cool and step in with your rational Conscious Mind, saying, "Wow, you're having a bad day. Can I do anything to help?"

At this point, he may break down and tell you his beloved four-year-old daughter has just been diagnosed with leukemia, and it doesn't look good. Or that he's just been diagnosed with prostate cancer and is faced with chemo and/or impotence. Or that the wife he loves has just left him—it could be anything … except about you.

Why is the Subconscious Mind like this? In the early years, it simply recorded verbatim every piece of input it received, often misinterpreting that input. If a little boy is touching his penis (as they all do) and his mother says, "You should be ashamed of yourself. If you don't stop that, I'm going to cut it off," that input is recorded and sticks deep in his Subconscious Mind, completely unedited. Many years later, when a woman (who reminds him a little of his mother) makes a remark during sex that pulls that memory to the surface, he suddenly finds himself deeply ashamed and impotent … without knowing why.

Because most adults were hopeless as child-raisers when we were young, the contents of our Subconscious Mind rarely support us as adults. (Today, parents in the know play New Age music to the fetus by placing a speaker on the mother's abdomen, and speak encouraging words.) So the task facing us is to bring the Subconscious Mind forward to the age of about seven, and giving it new input that aligns with our rational Conscious Mind's decision-making agenda. The problem is that three-year-olds are not good with words, so affirmations are ineffective. However, at that age, we responded well to images—movies, TV, posters and pictures in books.

From any applicable image source—women's magazines, girlie magazines, automobile brochures—cut out images that portray someone's needs being met, and surround yourself with them. Once a day, go into relaxation mode and repeat your affirmation, such as, "I have the perfect relationship." As you do, look at a photo of two people obviously in love and enjoying each other's company. Keep looking and repeating for 30 seconds or so. Then go on to the next thing—maybe the perfect vehicle, job or body. Your Subconscious Mind doesn't have any physical senses of its own, so doesn't know the difference between actual experience and that image. It believes and remembers whatever it's told because that's its job.

Suppose you're a woman boss with several men working for you who often challenge your authority. If, as a little girl, your brothers always got the neat stuff and you were told, "You're just a girl," those challenges will cause you great stress because your Subconscious Mind memories are undermining your Conscious Mind's agenda. So find an image of a powerful-looking woman standing at the head of a conference table, addressing a roomful of men who look at her with respect and deference. As you gaze at this image and project on to the woman, say, "I am powerful, respected and admired."

At this point, your Conscious Mind may be saying, "C'mon, gimme a break," but do you *really* know what's in your Subconscious Mind? If you don't, it will cost you only a couple of minutes a day to find out. Do this for 21 days, and see what happens. And again, how do you know that everyone else but you isn't doing it, so at least level the playing field. So if you want to be richer, healthier, sexier, more popular, or a better lover, driver, artist, give it a whirl.

As for developing the age of your Subconscious Mind from three to seven, find an image of a teacher you respect, addressing a roomful of rapt students and say, "Every day, I become wiser and more spiritual," as you gaze at the image and project yourself onto him.

Reactors vs. Creators

Yesterday is full of facts about things that happened and that we can all agree on; tomorrow is full of possibilities about things that might happen. Reactors project yesterday into tomorrow and see no possible change; creators see only the possibilities in the unwritten tomorrow. Facts were once only possibilities, and possibilities are potential future facts. Creators see beyond what is there, to what *could* be there.

We can grasp possibilities only with right-brained intuition, because there's no factual evidence to make the left brain happy. The creator sees the entire world as possibility: conceive – believe – receive.

Once we begin acting as a creator rather than a reactor, we place ourselves at the *cause* of life rather than as its *effect*. When we become the cause, the effects line up according to our *intent*. One or two minor, reality-creation successes show the way, and the dam bursts, unleashing your creativity. You move from victim-reactor to master-creator, in line with *the* creator Source.

Moving from reactor to creator involves three things:

1. Accepting that the future is pure possibility, and an unwritten book.
2. As the universe unfolds reality minute-by-minute, it looks to your beliefs for source material. How will those beliefs program your reality? Do they include your worthiness for the perfect mate, job, house, relationships? Or the opposite? Root out any beliefs that will program reality for less than the highest and best outcome for all concerned.
3. Tell the universe that:

- *You* now know what's going on and are the creator of your life, not a reactor to it.
- You look to your higher self for the grandest expression of who you could become—and already are.

Stop Recycling

How do you end the cycle of taking today's beliefs into tomorrow, and write new ones instead? Accept, at a very deep level, that tomorrow's events flow inexorably from today's beliefs, as surely as a railroad train follows the tracks. The universe has to work that way ... or life would be chaotic, with train wrecks everywhere.

Do you regard your beliefs as sacred cows, to be protected at all costs ... or as arbitrary opinions that can be discarded and replaced? Across the many lifetimes your soul has fashioned, all those ego-personalities have held every conceivable belief; what's so special about yours in this lifetime? Nothing! They're just temporary opinions you have borrowed about the way things are, and really have nothing to do with who you *really* are, and how things *really* are.

As a soul, you believe everything ... and nothing. Everything is potentially true; so is nothing. Therefore, you are free to explore every possibility once you dump all the old baggage and adopt the wisdom of uncertainty.

Once you declare that you believe something, you have closed the door on the blank canvas of uncertainty. If you keep that canvas clear, then your higher self can paint a higher truth for you. To paint a new life portrait, you must begin with a blank canvas, free of any beliefs you currently hold, for these limit your inner artist's freedom of creativity, so let them all go—they're just old baggage.

The Parasite

Don Miguel Ruiz, author of *The Four Agreements*, calls this baggage 'The Parasite,' which consists of three parts:

1. *The Book of Law*, or the belief system that rules your life. It's the basis for all your judgments of self and others, even those that harm or limit you.
2. *The Judge*, who is constantly evaluating you against your Book of Law, finding you guilty, and sentencing you to punishment.
3. *The Victim*, or that part of you that receives the verdict, accepts the blame, carries the shame, feels guilty and serves the sentence. No matter what

the Victim does to please the Judge, the verdict is always the same: GUILTY!

Ruiz calls this happy triad *The Parasite* because it constantly siphons off your Life Force, sucking you dry, feeding on the fear it causes, while offering nothing in return but more fear. Like all parasitic relationships, it's strictly one way, a mosquito sucking your life's blood, even killing you through suicide and self-destructive drug use.

You inherited your Parasite from your early imprinters, who cloned theirs and passed it on, like a communicable disease. From early childhood, this living, growing entity has been gnawing at you, eroding your self-esteem, feasting on your fears. Nice!

One of the nastiest little agreements in your Book of Law is that you need the approval of others to be okay, and that you will compromise yourself, even martyr yourself, in order to get that approval. It also contains everything you agreed with, in your early years. So if someone said, "You'll never amount to anything," and you agreed with that, then every time you screw up, the Judge says, "Just what I expected." If you succeed in something, the Judge reminds you that you're breaking your own law, so you will find some way to self-sabotage.

Stop reading for a moment and reflect on all the ways your Parasite currently feeds off you by judging you, berating you, making you feel guilty and ashamed. Nasty little critter, eh? Other people feed it, too, whenever you accept their limiting beliefs about you and life in general, or they pass on their fears. Every time, this voracious monster that prowls your mind gets bigger and more powerful. But it gets worse. We know you are broadcasting your self-image out into the M-field, so others receive your Book of Law telepathically and therefore know subconsciously what buttons to push to manipulate you through guilt and shame. And you thought your beliefs were your friends. On the contrary, they are betraying you.

Wouldn't it be better to make your beliefs your ally and not your enemy? To have a symbiotic relationship, where you mutually support each other? Of course it would. The good news is that it's *your* Parasite, which you choose to keep around … every time you pass judgment, criticize, limit, etc. And it feels oh so familiar, so the prospect of not having it could be scary. Rather than take some strong medicine to kill it, therefore, begin changing it a little at a time each day. Challenge its hold on you; wrest control from it. How? By drilling holes in it. Or pulling at its threads. Imagine your beliefs are pieces of string, and they are all tangled up into a ball. If you find a loose end, pull it and that piece will come out. Start with an easy one such as: The dead can't communicate with the living. Then watch *Crossing Over with John Edward* and you will see what a silly belief that is. One piece of string down. As you remove each piece of the Parasite, love the piece and the Parasite, and fill the hole with spirit.

First, stop feeding it. Run away from negative people, gossips, fear-mongers, etc. Get divorced if need be; a bad marriage is worse than none because the abuse feeds the Parasite. Turn off the TV news and be selective about newspapers.

Second, resolve to flush the Parasite from your system by loving it to death. And laugh at it, for they hate not being taken seriously. As you beam love and light into this dark, ugly critter, and forgive yourself for even having it, it will begin to transform before your eyes. Within weeks, you'll be amazed at how much joy and peace fill your life. People will begin remarking on how much you have changed, and asking how you did it.

Third, read only uplifting stories and associate with uplifting people. If you don't know any, go to the library or bookstore and get some *Chicken Soup* books to read. Your Parasite will hate you for that, because those books are powerful antidotes that will weaken it.

Fourth, keep reading this chapter … if your Parasite will let you. It may tell you all this personal growth nonsense is bunk and that you can never change. Dying Parasites can get quite nasty, so don't listen. Or you could strike a deal with it: "Just for today, I will live as if every word in this book is true, so shut up for 24 hours. Then, if you're right, I'll start listening to you again tomorrow. Okay?" Now see what happens.

A major tool of the Judge is *guilt*, which sits in your Subconscious Mind, eating away at your self-esteem like termites eating a home's foundation. But once you realize your purpose here is not to be perfect but to experience, learn and grow, most guilt evaporates. And when you realize that the Source and the universe love you anyway, the remaining guilt also evaporates.

One great source of guilt is our 'perceived' separation from whatever we conceive of as our Source. We feel that we have somehow 'fallen from Grace,' and are therefore less worthy. Of course, such separation is impossible, so you need to work on the *perception* of separation, not actual separation. So get over yourself and stop indulging in needless guilt.

Many of Edgar Cayce's readings reveal the only real sin as *selfishness*. Our spiritual nature is essentially self-less, but when we elevate the self above others, put our needs over those of others, and take advantage of them, then we're in deep trouble. We usually do this out of fear of being inadequate and getting found out. (However, this does *not* mean becoming a self-effacing wimp.)

The key to dispelling fear is remembering who you *really* are—not some ego-personality in a physical body trying to get through life, but a vast, multi-dimensional being, well-disguised and playing hide-and-seek with itself. Honor yourself for such a clever disguise—you're doing a great job, and the clincher is feeling separate from All That Is. Not an easy accomplishment!

We then compound the disguise by feeling guilty about not living up to our 'ideal' of who we think we should be, in order to make others accept us and approve of us. Healing this guilt is a four-step process:

1. Accept that: (1) life is not a 'pass-fail' enterprise but a process of learning, growing and evolving, and that: (2) making mistakes (or 'missing the mark') is a vital part of that process. As long as you keep trying, *you haven't failed*.

2. By the same token, do not condemn others. They, too, are learning and growing, so do not hold grudges, resentments or blame. Instead, forgive, forgive and forgive.

3. Take action to live up to your ideal. Begin to take positive steps—write a letter, call to tell someone you love them, or mend a broken fence, for *the lack of loving actions is second only to hurtful actions*.

4. Drop any notion that you are being deemed guilty by some outside authority—God, Source or whatever—for there is no authority greater than your soul. You are valued as a creator-probe into the Earth plane to explore and discover. You only fail when you give up.

Joy and Fear

Joy and fear are our two greatest teachers, but they cannot co-exist, and humans seem more open to fear than joy. Why? Joy is our natural state on the soul plane, and fear is unknown there, but when we incarnate, our early caregivers program our ego-personality to learn from fear, worry, anxiety and insecurity, as do our elders.

Fear (**F**alse **E**vidence **A**ppearing **R**eal) is simply not knowing the outcome of a situation, an outcome that you have already filed in your flight plan for the greatest growth. But while you're worrying about that outcome, joy flies out the window.

Also, be your authentic self, for nothing kills joy faster than playing the role of someone you would *like* to be in order to win approval from others. And don't put it off with, "I'll be joyful when _______" because there will always be another 'when' condition. Let joy happen in the moment, and accept that it may be fleeting, but know that more moments will come, longer moments that one day may all join up. So start with a moment—a cat's purr or a sunset—and go from there.

Probably the biggest joy-killers are other people—the 'sky is falling' kind. If you can't avoid them, at least wall them off by pulling your aura in tight and covering it with gold mesh, or if you're up for it, expand your aura to embrace them and flood them with white light.

Intending a New You

Once you have begun to erode your Parasite, and redefined yourself and your life as a blank canvas (easy for me to say), how *do* you let your higher self paint a new life portrait? By simply declaring your *intention* that this shall be done. By total commitment and total faith. Half measures won't cut it. Trapeze artists can't change their mind in mid-flight; once they commit, they must follow through. Until you are a master creator, you're still a victim reactor. Mastery is not a dimmer switch—it's either on or off. Even when life slaps master creators in the face, they are still master creators, incapable of blaming any outside force. Either you accept that you create it *all*, despite any and all evidence to the contrary ... or you're still a reactor.

The essence of mastery is expansion. Under pressure, reactors contract—they tense up, hold their breath and close their heart chakra. This locks the situation into their fields. Creators, on the other hand, expand—they loosen up, relax, take deep breaths, and open their heart chakra. Contracting lowers your frequency and makes you resist the challenge; expansion raises your frequency and allows you to embrace the challenge.

This seems to contradict the Serenity Prayer: "Give me the courage to change what I can change, the serenity to accept what I can't change, and the wisdom to know the difference." So how do we reconcile being a master creator with 'having the serenity to accept what I can't change'? There is no conflict once you see that, at the soul level, you orchestrated 'what you can't change' as a Challenge to summon up the Resources to accept it. Any inability to accept is pure ego-personality resistance. Of course, your flight plan lists some things that you *intended* to change—right some wrongs, help others, etc., so the wisdom to know what battles to fight is paramount. Good warriors know you just don't even tackle some battles ... at least not head on. You either go around it or live to fight another day. Remember *wu wei* in Taoism.

This brings us to a huge question: "How *do* I accept what I cannot change?" Again, think yourself bigger. Step out of your little ego-personality and see who you truly are—a vast soul on Earth with a mission. Live by the Golden Rule, and do what you can, where you can, to serve humanity while learning and growing in the process. And remember: "This too shall pass." It's only one lifetime out of hundreds, so view it through soul's eyes.

A friend of mine was wrongly convicted of a crime he did not commit and ended up in jail. Reactors would fall victim to such a circumstance, but he was a creator, so he started holding meditation classes for the other inmates and wrote a book, mailing out a few pages at a time. He also worked in the prison library and solicited publishers to donate spiritual books to the collection. Rather than living with resentment, he said to himself, "Well, spirit, I reckon it's in the plan that I'm here for a few years, or it wouldn't have happened," so he lived a life of service to those most in need of a shot of spirituality. But it wasn't *what* he did that really mattered; it was *who* he was—an exemplary role model to others.

This brings us to an even bigger question: "What is your life mission?"

Life Mission

"What am I supposed to be doing with my life?"

First, ask yourself why you want to know. Is it self-aggrandizement and self-indulgence? Or the deep sense of peace and fulfillment that comes from partnering with your soul? This is important because once you know, you will be driven, and will feel bad if you don't follow through. So, once you know, are you prepared to go for it?

One indication of your mission is what brings you joy. As Kryon and others remind us: "You're on mission when you follow your bliss." Turning a mess of words into beautiful prose that uplifts the spirit brings me incredible joy, so I guess writing and editing metaphysical books is a large part of my mission. But what brings *you* joy? And if you're not fully engaged with it, why not? Is it art, photography, music, rock-climbing, hot-air ballooning? And it doesn't have to be spiritual; the point is to relate to self and others with unconditional love ... and you can do this running a daycare center as well as (or better maybe even than) writing New Age books. The important thing is to make the Golden Rule your moral compass. Then you always know where 'north' is, so in any decision-making, you choose the option with the most love—love for self, for others and All That Is. And that love also includes forgiveness, compassion and gratitude. At the end of the day, when you cross over, those qualities are all you get to take with you. He who strives to 'win the most toys' leaves them behind for others to play with; you get to keep only the love.

Bottom line: *what* you do is less important than *how* you do it—with love or fear? Having said that, though, there are many concrete things you can do to uncover your mission. First, set your intent for this to happen. Then inform Spirit of your determination to know. (Of course, your guides already know this and may actually have dropped into your thinking, the notion of you asking. But you must go through the exercise; otherwise they can't interfere.)

Next, having asked the question (possibly using the Mirror Technique), you must listen, and the best way to do that is meditation. Keeping a still mind for 20 minutes allows Spirit to drop inspiration into it. You can also ask for signs, as in synchronicity. If you get two independent signs, heads up. On the third sign, *really* pay attention. The signs may be subtle or a blatant 2-by-4, and you can ask for signs to confirm that something really was a sign. Make it a game between you and your guides; tell them to be creative, outrageous even.

Don't feel guilty about putting your guides to work. How would you feel as a guide if those you were guiding never asked for your help, listened to you or even knew you existed? Like a spare groom at a wedding! So put them to work … it's the only way they can grow, and they really *want* to play with you.

You can also use divination tools, such as Tarot, the I Ching or a pendulum. These won't tell you what to do but they will reveal the prevailing issues and energies around a subject, which may clarify things for you. (More about these tools in Chapter 8.)

If you can find a good psychic who can read your flight plan, great, but be careful. If your soul doesn't want it read at this point in your life, the psychic may feel pressured to make something up. In this case, 'no advice' is better than 'bad advice.' And finally, regression hypnosis is a powerful investigation tool.

Amid all this talk of your guides, this is so important as to bear repeating. Your soul belongs to a soul group, a bunch of several hundred to a few thousand souls who interact closely with each other across eternity. We've seen that when you incarnate, many of these souls incarnate with you, and you all meet up as friends, mates, colleagues, even antagonists. A dozen or so souls who do not incarnate still agree to work with you, although not in physical bodies. These are your guides, and just as you and your physical buddies have agendas and objectives, you and your guides are just as much a team. They have agreed to help you meet your goals and keep you on track, so you can regard them as 'coaches.' Also, because they still operate in the higher realms, they can watch out for you there, managing energies that you're less aware of, since your focus is the physical plane.

Your guides try to nudge you into compliance with your flight plan, although they have no mandate to coerce you; your compliance is strictly voluntary. This means you must listen and remain open to their promptings by meditating and not dismissing new ideas that are dropped into your mind. When something odd happens in your life, ask them, "Why did that happen?" and then remain open for an idea to be delivered. Another way they communicate is by synchronicity, whereby the information comes to you via a roundabout way—a newspaper headline, a song on the radio, or a casual remark overheard.

The important thing to remember is that you're all a team by pre-life agreement, and one of you just happens to be in a physical body—you. None of you is 'better' than the others, and pretty soon, you will be a spirit guide to one of them when he or she 'draws the short straw.'

When working with guides or any spiritual being, protection is essential, and Chapter 14 offers my favorite technique for avoiding an STD (spiritually transmitted darkforces).

The Four Agreements

Don Miguel Ruiz also offers four covenants we can make with ourselves to replace the thousands of agreements that were imposed on us during childhood, such as, "Lie to be popular," and, "Do whatever you must in order to win the approval of others." Together, the Four Agreements are the prescription for self-esteem, self-love and mastery. Write them on a piece of paper and secure them to your refrigerator and/or bathroom mirror. Try to apply them for a day. Then, re-commit to them tomorrow ... and the next day. Pretty soon, they'll be habits.

As we've seen, before the age of seven, you had little or no choice about what to believe, for your very survival depended on your *agreement* with what you were told ... or at least you *thought* it did. You had *faith* in the adults around you, believed in their infallibility and accepted what they said as the way things were, i.e., you surrendered to their worldviews.

Ruiz calls this process 'human domestication,' and it is almost identical to domesticating a pet, using rewards for good behavior and punishments for bad. Because rewards (attention, affection, acceptance, and treats) felt good, you soon learned to please your adults, even if it meant being what and who you were not. And you mistook these rewards for love.

This compliance became so habitual, you became 'self-policing,' praising or beating yourself up if you behaved in ways you thought would displease your domesticators. You made 'agreements' with yourself, and your Inner Judge chastised you if you broke them. But unlike the justice system, where once your debt is paid, you're free to go, you punish yourself endlessly for the rest of your life because your 'sins' are buried in the Subconscious Mind.

Why don't we see this and discard the beliefs that no longer work for us? Because we trust that what we believe is the TRUTH, and we will defend it to the death. During our domestication, we also formed a perfect image of who to be, that would please our adults so they would accept and reward us. But, because we can't live up to that image, we reject ourselves, berate ourselves, and cannot forgive ourselves for our lack of perfection. So we continue to pretend, even to ourselves, and wear false masks. We deny who we are in favor of wearing masks to please others, and then beat ourselves up for doing it. We lie when we mess up, and then feel bad. This leads to physical ailments such as hives, shingles, gastric distress and cancer. And one day, in mid-life, it all crashes down in a crisis, and we totally freak out.

The antidote? Self-love. The prescription? The Four Agreements to countermand the thousands of agreements you made with yourself before age seven. The Agreements are:

1. Be impeccable with your word

Your word is your power to create reality, to express, to think. It can create dreams … or nightmares, free you … or enslave you. Thoughts are seeds that grow into words; words are seeds that grow into actions. You grew yourself from your self-image, which your parents gave you before age seven when you began to know better—and it still rules you today.

Impeccable means 'without sin,' and sin means 'missing the mark,' so impeccable really means 'hitting the mark.' Thus this Agreement means 'using your power to hit the mark,' or 'use it wisely, in love and for truth.'

The trouble is, we're taught to lie to both others and ourselves, to think one thing, say another, and do a third. This Agreement means that all three modes must be in alignment. It also means we should not listen to or repeat gossip, because others may not have made this agreement with themselves, and we should therefore weigh their opinions in that light.

When you are impeccable with your word, you feel good, love yourself and want to share that love with others.

2. Do not take anything personally

You can only take insults personally if you agree with them. Personal importance comes only from thinking that things are about *you*, whereas what others say and do is about *them* and their worldview. And your opinions of others are really about *you*, not *them*.

The degree to which you take personally the things that others say, depends on your need for their acceptance and approval, and the openness of your wounds. But really, what others think about you is *their* problem, not yours. About *their* fears, hurts and pains, not yours.

Self-love and self-esteem are your shields against the weapons they unleash. Of course, this also applies to your own self-chatter, by which your Parasite launches endless tirades against you.

Now, some people believe they are unworthy and must suffer, so they look for abusers to help. Simply deny them their 'pain fix.' Others will lie to you because they are afraid of being less perfect than you—again it's about them. So live in the bliss of being transpersonal.

3. Don't make assumptions

When we make assumptions, we believe them to be true, when in fact they are merely our *opinions* about things. Then, since they are *our* opinions, we take them personally. Worse, our assumptions are emotional poison, and gossip spreads it around.

We rarely see 'what is' but are afraid to ask for clarification, so we misinterpret our perceptions, take them for real, and then become defensive about them.

Assumptions in relationships can doom them, as you *assume* that the other sees things the way you see them, thinks as you think, feels as you feel, and wants what you want. Assumptions lead to unmet expectations ... and that leads to trouble. When we assume that others know what we mean or want—but they really don't know—then our feelings get hurt.

Assumptions stem from laziness over communication, which takes time to do properly. So we make assumptions to avoid the need for communication.

Most of us also make assumptions about ourselves—under- or over-estimations—because we don't take the time to really think things through. We also go into relationships assuming we can change the other person—we can't.

Bottom line: have the courage to ask questions.

4. Always do your best

Doing more than your best will exhaust you; doing less will instill guilt and self-judgment. Strike a balance between work, self, family and community … then take *action* because *you love what you're doing*, not for other rewards.

Those who work just to pay the rent do not do their best; *they do only enough to earn a paycheck*. When you love what you do and do what you love, it's not work but expression … and you do your best. This is life force in motion, an expression of spirit-in-flesh.

Though worthy of aspiring to for their own value, the Four Agreements also help us break the stranglehold of the hundreds of dysfunctional agreements we've made with ourselves since childhood. Those agreements feed the nasty beast Ruiz terms 'The Parasite,' which we've already met. The Judge and his or her Book of Law ensure that we are constantly reminded of our guilt. Worse, we've become so used to being judged, we regard this as *normal*.

Ruiz lays out three steps of Mastery for overthrowing the Parasite and claiming our freedom:

1. *Mastery of Awareness*. We must be aware that we're not free in order to become free. You cannot change what you don't know. This also involves becoming aware of who you really are, and how your beliefs control you. But these beliefs are just something you inherited and have no real basis.

2. *Mastery of Transformation*, or knowing how to change, how to throw off your domestication.

3. *Master of Intent*, or having the self-love necessary to fuel Step #2.

At this point, we see two choices: (1) we can continue letting the Parasite rule us, while sucking us dry; or (2) we can rebel and say "No!" If we choose the latter, and begin to dismantle all our dysfunctional agreements, we will need new agreements to fill the void. Enter the Four Agreements.

Suppose someone told you, "You're such a klutz," and you agreed; you have just made an agreement with yourself and will behave like one. But, because that is a lie, you are not being impeccable with your word. So break that limiting agreement and banish the spell it has on you. Feeling good about doing this will empower you to move to the next limiting agreement, replacing it with one of the Four Agreements.

It's vital not to blame yourself about having your Parasite, or your imprinters for infecting you with it, for they were just passing it on unknowingly. They brought you up the best they knew how, so forgive them and forgive yourself, and let your healing begin. And when negative emotions surface, learn to be a warrior. Do not let them control you; instead, control them.

Ruiz wraps up *The Four Agreements* by invoking our imagination to create a new dream to replace the dream that most people are sleep-walking around in:

- Imagine that it's okay to be happy and free of conflict.
- Imagine changing your life to the way you want it.
- Imagine living without fear of being judged or what others think about you.
- Imagine not needing to be loved and accepted, yet able to say, "I love you" without being afraid of getting hurt.
- Imagine not being afraid to risk, to live, to love, and to die.
- Imagine loving yourself exactly as you are, knowing you are a perfect expression of Source, right now.

All this is quite possible just by choosing it. Pain and suffering are choices, and we choose them because they are familiar. But joy and bliss are also just choices … so it's really up to you.

Lucid Living

We've all heard about lucid dreaming, where you are fully conscious in the dream and can change events, symbols and outcomes. But what about lucid *living*, where you are fully conscious while *awake?* It's surprising how many are not.

Lucid living involves being aware of the myriad nuances of life, with people, places, things and situations … and then acting on the fullness of all that. It also involves being totally aware of your own state, and the steady stream of self-chatter. And then trapping and reversing any thought about limitation, lack, weakness, failure, and any other negativity, i.e., any time you break one of the Agreements. But be careful not to beat yourself up when you catch one.

Essentially, applying the Four Agreements helps you to reprogram your Subconscious Mind. Now this critter in the basement has enormous influence on your life, organizing and retrieving beliefs, memories and emotions governing what you perceive about the world (see diagram below). Having limited you to seeing only certain aspects of a situation, your assumptions then govern how you interpret those perceptions. Most people are living on autopilot, letting their Subconscious Mind make their decisions for them. And often, the 'beast in the basement' will sabotage the efforts of your Conscious Mind unless you reprogram it to aid in your success. How do you do that?

First, you have been programming it all your life by what you tell yourself and what others tell you that you let in. For example, as a little girl, a woman was told by her grandfather that he'd survived starvation in World War II by being obese and drawing on stored fat. Her Subconscious Mind interpreted this as: "If I'm fat, I'm safe," and she ballooned up like a blimp, completely unable to lose weight regardless of what she did. If you are impeccable with your word and don't take things personally, you reduce the chances of faulty programming.

This programming doesn't just happen. It takes hundreds of repetitions over several years, so your reprogramming will need lots of repetition, which means affirmations, and notes on the bathroom mirror and fridge door. Always use positive, in-the-now statements. "I will not smoke more than one pack a day for the next year" is useless; try "I am a light smoker." Also, the Subconscious Mind cannot 'see' the outside world, so it has to believe what you tell it. If you keep repeating, with passion, "I have fifty thousand dollars in the bank, and am rich, prosperous and abundant," it doesn't know any different, so it helps deliver that into your reality.

The Subconscious Mind harbors negativity, so if you're harshly critical of others, it stores that negativity and reuses it whenever it can. If you habitually judge others, become conscious of it and stop; as Ruiz says, "Don't gossip for it's not impeccable."

Since the Subconscious Mind plays a huge role in creating our reality, having a healthy subconscious is essential to creating a healthy reality. Feed the beast with nourishing, light-filled meals of uplifting, inspirational truths rather than downers such as: "Life's a bitch, then you die." And, of course, the most nourishing meal of all is love … whatever *that* is.

Dr. Candace Pert's Molecules of Emotion

In *Molecules of Emotion*, Candace Pert, Ph.D. reveals the extent to which we are managed and regulated by the soup of neuropeptides constantly coursing through our bodies. They control our emotions, immune system, sex and hunger drives and whether a sensory stimulus will be perceived.

Neuropeptides and their respective receptors weave the body's organs into one miraculously orchestrated, non-conscious mind, with individual peptides being the notes on a musical score. Why is this important? Because once we know about it, we can influence it.

Neuropeptides are important because when a molecule locks on to a receptor on the surface of a cell, it triggers a brain cell response, as when an endorphin makes you feel happy. Dr. Pert also discovered that the body's immune system cells have receptors for neuropeptides, meaning the brain can fire up the immune system, too.

Going further, she found that the brain had receptors for immunopeptides such as interleukins, so the immune system can trigger brain cells. This finding gave the scientific basis behind the emerging medical field of psychoneuroimmunology, or PNI.

From there, Dr. Pert went on to discover that some cancer cells are actually mutated immune system cells called macrophages, and that they produce the very peptide that promotes their own cell division; which is why they multiply out of control. Toxicity in the environment and our body worries Dr. Pert, especially heavy metals which mimic estrogen, land on receptors, and may trigger breast cancer, as does natural estrogen.

Discovering over 50 peptides and their receptors in the brain, endocrine and immune systems led Pert to dub them 'molecules of emotion.'

The immune system consists of mobile white cells produced in bone marrow that roam the body looking for alien invaders, consuming them, carting away debris, and repairing damaged tissue. Although these cells are coordinated by peptides, they also make peptides themselves. This is akin to dozens of people sitting at their computers, sending out a bulk e-mail to everyone in their address book. Then recipients send out another e-mail to their list and so on. Soon thousands of sites have received e-mails. Some won't have receptors for a message and will ignore it, but others will fly into action. If you cut your finger, the news flashes around your body network, so that every node knows about it. Your digestive system won't care, but your immune system will galvanize into action.

Going further, Pert says the conscious mind can influence this body-mind network. For example, Lamaze breathing releases endorphins that block pain receptors during childbirth. And emotions trigger release of peptides that occupy receptors in other parts of the body to influence health. For example, the common cold virus enters a cell by sitting on the endorphin receptor but, if that receptor is already occupied, the virus is shut out. Hence the legend that happy people seem to catch fewer colds. So, hundreds of peptides and trillions of receptors turn the body into a huge information network, with consciousness as both observer and participant.

As with many brilliant researchers, when Pert and team discovered a peptide that prevented AIDS in 1985, her work at NIH was shut down by the 'big boys,' who were carving up tens of millions of dollars to develop the highly toxic AZT.

A simple little peptide that blocked the virus from even infecting the body in the first place was *not* what the medical establishment wanted to hear about. They wanted a *cure*, not *prevention*. Also, a simple nontoxic peptide did not fit the profile of the answer to the modern-day plague.

Pert is dismayed at the widespread use of antidepressant drugs that work by blocking the body's ability to reabsorb excess serotonin, which is left to flood the body and make us feel artificially happy. The excess serotonin triggers receptors throughout the body, with unanticipated results, such as gastric disorders.

Pert sees a vicious cycle of stress triggering the hypothalamus to release cortical releasing factor, or CRF, which then tells the pituitary gland to secrete another peptide that prompts the adrenal glands to pump out adrenaline and corticosterone, a steroid. This latter disrupts the entire feedback loop that normally signals 'enough,' but under ongoing stress, the cycle keeps running and the resulting steroid overdose causes massive depression and even more stress. Pert holds that the way to break the cycle is not more drugs but other interventions such as massage, hands-on healing and lots of hugs.

When Pert talks about health, she focuses on *emotional* health because our *emotions* are how we can contribute to the millions of conversations going on in our body at any moment. First, she says, we must *own* our emotions—all of them including fear, anger and grief. With anger, we define our boundaries; with grief, we cope with loss; and fear keeps us safe from danger. If we deny these, we suffer toxic emotional buildup that distorts or inhibits the peptide conversations.

Dr. Pert offers eight things we can do towards better health:

1. *Become conscious.* (We've just called this *Lucid Living.*) Get to know your body's processes, and learn techniques such as acupuncture, visualization and meditation. It doesn't have to cost much—public libraries and the Internet are full of the information resources you need.

2. *Tap into your body's network.* Own and release emotions that do not serve you. (We translate this as practicing the Second Agreement, "Do not take things personally" and developing the Buddhist's nonattachment.) This lowers your stress and frees you from the past, so you can become aware of and join in the chatter going on in your body's network *right now.*

3. *Honor your dreams.* Dr. Pert advises that some dreams are the psyche's way of bringing denied motions to the surface so you can feel, deal, and heal.

4. *Know your body.* The spine, skin and chakras are your ports of entry into the body's conversations, so get massages, touch and hugs as often as you can. And find time for a brisk walk every day.

5. *Reduce stress.* The fastest and easiest way to do this is meditation. Also, focusing on your breathing releases many peptides that bring the body's many systems into harmony. Dr. Pert also finds that 'self-honesty' lowers stress (the First Agreement). If you think one thing, say another, do a third, and feel a fourth, your systems run at cross-purposes. Far better is to declare your intent to yourself and then mobilize everything around that, the way a dog-sled team must all pull in the same direction.

6. *Exercise.* A good, brisk walk releases lots of endorphins and gets the blood carrying oxygen and nutrients to all organs.

7. *Eat wisely.* The digestive system is a huge source of peptide messengers, so work with them. Eat only when you're hungry and stop when full. Do not eat when stressed, depressed or angry—go for a walk instead. And Dr. Pert warns to avoid sugar. The body readily makes glucose, which fuels the brain, but ingesting sugar interferes with this natural process by flooding receptors in the liver.

8. *No substance abuse.* Tobacco, alcohol and recreational drugs mimic the body's own peptide messengers, which shuts down many of its natural conversations.

Dr. Pert closes her book by asking, if the body is a complex network of millions of peptide conversations happening in every moment, where is the *intelligence* that manages all this? There must be a higher-order, non-physical system running the show. Emotions release peptides, which then cause other emotions in a spectacular choreography. But who is the choreographer?

Although I would like to have seen more on the role of self-love in manifesting health, reading this book by Dr. Pert took me to a whole new appreciation of the human body. Delving deeply into the world of science ended up taking her into the realm of spirit. Go deeply enough into Creation and you will see the handiwork of the Source. Once again, I am impressed by the concept of Intelligent Design and even more sure that this magnificent thing we call our body simply could not have come about through natural selection during the few short millennia that took us from *Homo erectus* to *Home sapiens* … if that's what really happened, and there's strong evidence that it didn't. Far more empowering is the story that our entire species was taken hostage by the Anunnaki. Either way, did you ever see a tornado go through a scrap yard and create a Boeing 747?

Belief System Rework

Less important than what you believe is why you believe it. As for 'why,' we've seen in this book how, during the innocent first seven years of your life, you were a mental sponge, eagerly soaking up answers to life's Big Four questions. Unfortunately, you probably trusted your elders to tell you the Absolute Truth about the way things are, and you probably accepted that the values they conveyed to you were Absolute Values.[3] Equally unfortunate is the fact that many people do not revisit the validity of those truths and values, and go through life believing what they were told when they were seven. So, why you believe what you do is a function of geography (country of birth) and who you picked as early imprinters—you believed what those around you believed. Only later can you say, "Wait a minute. My beliefs no longer serve me." Although not Absolute Truth, this book has presented a worldview that has hopefully triggered a little belief reevaluation.

While on the quest for truth, it is vital to trust yourself and your soul, and to believe nothing … for once you believe one answer to a question, you close yourself off to other answers. (While walking my dogs in the park one morning, I was approached by two Jehovah's Witnesses, who asked me if I believed the Bible is the living word of God. They were not particularly thrilled at my equating God with Santa Claus, and soon left. (By the way, I said what I did because *they* approached *me;* I don't start such conversations.) Accept that with our limited minds, the closest we can get to truth is a working approximation. This book has presented a model of reality that may help you go forward with your own exploration, beginning with who you think you are.

It's guaranteed that who you think you are is not even close to the truth … but that's an intentional part of the game, because if you knew the truth coming in, there would be no point in being here. Earth lives are about *discovery*, not *knowing*. Therefore, soul carefully picked your early imprinters to dump a bunch of nonsense in your young head so you would have the fun of figuring it out.

It was an interesting game of hide-and-seek but now it's over … at least for you, because you know too much. You can no longer harbor limiting beliefs about who you are. Without getting puffed up about it, you now accept your own magnificence as normal, and just go about your life quietly loving everyone and everything unconditionally, even while striving to promote improvements.

[3] A 2004 study of youth and religion, funded by the Lillie Endowment foundation, surveyed 3,000 teenagers and found that 75 percent had the religious views of their parents, a typical comment being, "To believe differently would be a betrayal." In only about 10 percent were beliefs different.

You now have several techniques for dumping any old, limiting beliefs about yourself. Foremost is visualization. Suppose you're terrified by the thought of public speaking but find yourself locked into presenting a project to an audience of several hundred people. Or suppose you discover your new flame is a nudist and wants to take you to a nudist club … and the thought terrifies you. In both cases, you really *want* to do the thing that terrifies you, but you're hampered by, "I could never do that!"

Ask yourself two questions:

1. Who is the 'I' that is saying that? It's only your ego-personality, and that's not who you really are, so question the sway it has over the larger you.
2. Why is it saying that? What limiting childhood belief are you running (or is running you)? That people will laugh at you? Or they will eagerly await you making a fool of yourself?

As you answer the questions, you will realize how foolish your answers are against the backdrop of your soul's magnificence. (If you're still not convinced of that magnificence, reread this book.) Or, for 10 minutes or so, close your eyes and walk through doing whatever it is that terrifies you. See yourself standing on the podium as your audience applauds your wonderful presentation. See yourself walking around that nudist club, surrounded by lots of naked people, laughing and joking with them, and totally unconcerned with your own nudity. Visualize every aspect—sights, sounds, smells, the feel of the podium under your hands or the ground under your feet. Try to find time to rehearse your success like this a few times a day.

If you think that such rehearsal sounds dumb, here's a little secret. Successful people are already doing it; that's why they're successful. So why not you? Most successful sportspeople visualize their next stroke, swing, dive, jump or run.

How does it work? Your subconscious mind has *no idea* that it's not real; it only knows what the conscious mind tells it, which is that you have just pulled off a great feat … and it wasn't scary at all. This is not 'cheating' but simply reprogramming the patterns your early imprinters gave you. And the real kicker is that if you want to be soul having a human experience, then first visualize it … and this book has revealed enough about how that looks. Knowing you can rescript your beliefs about *everything*—you, God, the universe—is incredibly freeing. Even if you're locked up in jail, you're still free to decide what to think and believe.

If, during childhood, you were told you were 'not good enough' and you bought into that lie, that belief still drives you as an adult. As a result, your every action is geared to winning approval from those around you. Those folks will soon tire of you sucking up to them, and end up rejecting you, which confirms your worst fears—you're still not good enough.

Maybe one day, at your wit's end, you say, "Wait a minute. I'm no worse than anyone else. I'm a perfect incarnation of a perfect soul, and I don't need anyone else's approval—just from the person in the mirror. My worth does not depend on how I please others but on the love in my heart." If you can't say that sincerely, then *visualize* yourself saying that until it's true for you.

Of course, you may not paint as well as Michelangelo or compose music as well as Mozart, but it doesn't matter; you do not need fixing 'cause you're not broken. What *does* matter is how well you love.

Because you're not broken, attempts to fix perceived damage are destined to fail … and worse, those attempts simply confirm your erroneous beliefs about being broken (what you resist persists). All you really need to do is dump the erroneous beliefs you inherited during childhood. Just accept that your imprinters had no idea what they were doing or thinking.

If you accept that you really are the magnificent entity we've read about in this book, self-esteem and self-love are inevitable. So are joy, ecstasy, bliss and abundance. Immerse yourself in books such as this and surround yourself with like-minded people, and new empowering beliefs will wash away any old, limiting beliefs.

To sum up:

- You were born perfect.
- Because you were never broken, you don't need fixing, so don't even try. Accept yourself as perfect and open to becoming more perfect.
- Any guilt, shame, self-judgment or limitation was learned from those who knew no better, but you now own it and *only* you can erase it.
- It's okay to trust yourself and your feelings. A feeling may hurt but it can't kill you, so examine it and defuse it.
- Defusing old emotional 'bombs' allows for harmonious integration of your four aspects—physical, emotional, mental and spiritual.
- Harmony opens you up to influxes of love and insights from you-the-soul, which will ripple out from you like a stone dropped in a pond, and affect whomever and whatever is around you. Now, *that's* living with soul.

Let's look more deeply at how human behavior works.

1. Something happens that you perceive. Wrong, you perceive only a *fraction* of it, as many psychological tests have proved, depending on what strikes you as important about it.

2. Lightning fast, you consult your belief system for any relevant previous experience.

3. You interpret your perceived fragments according to your beliefs, as to whether there's danger, say, or cause to celebrate. Because you don't have all the data, you fill in the blanks with assumptions.

4. Based on your interpretation and assumptions, you respond in some way.

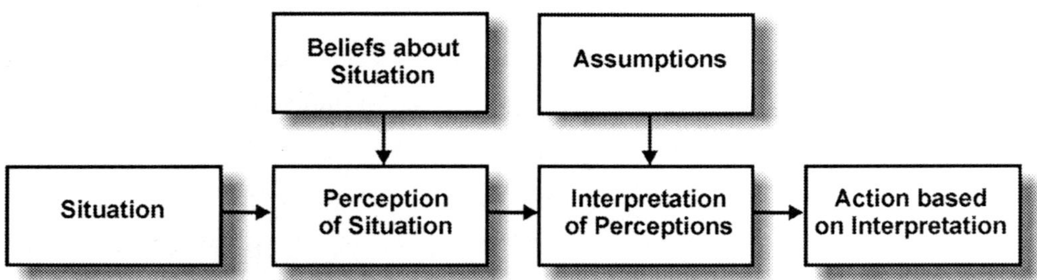

Interaction of Beliefs, Perception, Assumptions and Interpretation

Soul Age and the Subconscious Mind

Knowing and applying the material in this section can give younger soul ages the appearance and effect of being an older soul age than they actually are, which will help you-the-soul in your maturation.

One of the main factors to do with Soul Age is the amount of experience in your Subconscious mind *that is available to you*. Now you can't do much about the amount of experience your soul has accumulated over its lifetimes because that's fixed, but you *can* do something about making that wisdom available to you as personality. This is a matter of training and insight—things you can work on.

From birth, the Subconscious mind matures, and in most people stops developing at about age three, when the Conscious mind kicks in. This means that much of the wisdom of the Subconscious mind is trapped and not available. The task is to 'age' the Subconscious mind to at least age five, ideally age seven, where one is totally self-aware.

The Subconscious mind's maturation in terms of age in years goes as follows:

1. Instinctive, sensual, sexual, body-conscious, entirely dependent, nonexistent self-awareness

2. Affectionate and emotional, very dependent, very limited self-awareness
3. Basic skills and social awareness, occasional self-awareness
4. Advanced skills and creativity, dependent, self-aware about half the time
5. Basic ethics, some self-responsibility and regard for others, better social skills, increasingly independent with elevated self-awareness
6. Totally responsible for self and partially for others, largely independent, acutely self-aware
7. Leadership and social skills, full access to past memories in solving problems, utterly independent, completely self-aware.

In the first year of life, we are completely dependent on others, and have almost no self-awareness. How we were treated was faithfully recorded in the Subconscious mind as either "the world supports me and fulfills my needs," or "the world does not support me or fulfill my needs." This impression drives you for the rest of your life, if not examined.

At age two, you were still dependent, but a little more aware of self as separate from others. Again, how you were treated was locked in. By age three, you had some basic social skills and odd flashes of self-awareness. And that's pretty much where your Conscious mind took over, leaving the Subconscious mind's contents unexamined.

Why is this important? Because most people operate from their Subconscious mind most of the time. When the ego is presented with a novel situation, it turns to the Subconscious mind for how to behave. But it knows nothing of the Four Agreements, so ego breaks them all—it is not impeccable with its word, it takes things personally, it makes assumptions, and it doesn't do its best. So if you're in an argument with someone also arrested at age three, you're actually two three-year-old brats fighting. Scary thought!

At a minimum, you must 'age-progress' your Subconscious mind to at least age 5, but how? By being on the spiritual path, which is where you are if you're reading this book. On the path, your Subconscious mind learns about the larger you, about self-responsibility, and about self-esteem. This means you no longer *need* the approval of others, and do not manipulate them to get it.

At Subconscious age 5, you do something because it's the right thing to do, and not because you won't be caught. You don't blame others for any misfortune, but accept responsibility for your role. You also hold others responsible for their actions. And you're aware of yourself in relation to others. Because your Subconscious and Conscious minds are operating in tandem, you no longer live in ignorance and confusion, and you practice lucid living.

Ideally, you would continue age-progressing your Subconscious mind through age 6, and possibly even age 7, although the latter is rare. Such people are highly creative, resourceful, natural leaders, very cooperative, and outstanding problem-solvers.

Most people's reliance on the Subconscious mind means they're not focusing on their consciousness, and are not harnessing their most amazing attribute. For example, almost all illness originates from emotional activity in the Subconscious mind. Therefore it can only be treated by removing the cause from the Subconscious mind. Yes, you're sick and in pain, but those are only *symptoms*. Taking drugs or having surgery to address those symptoms, but failing to treat the *true cause*, is simply masking them, and they will reemerge later. All the research in the world will not find the cure for cancer, but a good hypnotherapist can rip cancer out of your Subconscious mind by the roots in an hour. Using your consciousness to examine the contents of your Subconscious mind will repair health, relationships, and your connection with All That Is.

The even better news is that just having read this section has placed this knowledge in both your minds, and progressed your Subconscious mind by about three months. Now just carry on the good work.

Talking of focusing on your consciousness, the next section gives us a technique for quantifying the usually vague concept.

Hawkins' Map of Consciousness

We close this chapter with a glimpse at the fascinating work of Dr. David Hawkins, who found a way to calibrate the M-field using kinesiology, or muscle-testing. In his book *Power vs. Force*, he reveals that all things are therefore knowable, given a means of discerning that truth independently of what the questioner *wants* to be true.

In kinesiology, hold your arm out and get someone to use two fingers to push down on the back of your wrist, while you try to resist. If your mind/body is in the presence of truth or life-affirming energy, you will be able to resist. Suppose you make the statement, "My name is _______," and you use your real name, you can resist, for that is truth, i.e., you test strong. On the other hand, if you say, "My name is [another name]," you test weak and your tester can easily push your arm down.

Holistic health practitioners have long used this tool to diagnose bodily conditions and dosages for supplements, etc. Hawkins went further and applied these infallible Yes/No responses to world events, for example, "Politician X is telling the truth."

The trick here is to turn your question into a statement that can be tested as True or False. However, how people respond to the truth depends on their level of consciousness, or how evolved they are. This led to Hawkins' Map of Consciousness. He devised an arbitrary scale of 1 – 1,000, where 1 represents 'barely conscious' and 1,000, the awareness of great planetary teachers such as Buddha and Krishna. Using thousands of subjects over 20 years, he applied kinesiology to map human states of consciousness. The diagram is a gross simplification; the real table is much more complex, and you really need to read at least Hawkins' first book.

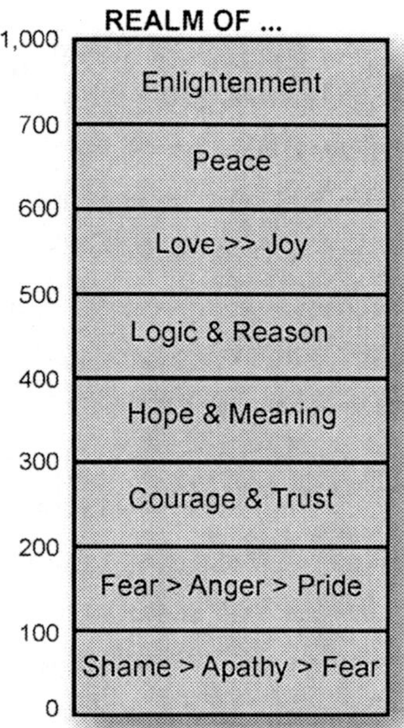

Hawkins' Scale of Consciousness

This is a logarithmic scale, like the Richter earthquake scale where a level 6 shaker is 10 times more powerful than a level 5, so, if you progress from 200 to 201, your consciousness has expanded tenfold. According to Hawkins, most people advance only a few points in each lifetime, and some actually regress.

Only one in 10,000,000 people calibrates at 600 and above, for this is the level where self-realization kicks in, and those folks certainly don't need this book. And above 700, you may be too blissed out to even read.

Anyone below 100 wouldn't be reading this either, because they would be too apathetic (50) to change, too sad (75) to reach out, or too fearful (100) of the consequences. Those in Desire (125) might read it if they thought it would make them richer or sexier, but they simply would not resonate with the technique because it calibrates at 600 itself. Same with Anger at 150, but around 160, this could mutate into righteous rage. People in Pride (175) predominate in the U.S., when war fosters fervent nationalism. This is encouraged in the U.S., where the Marine Corps is held up as all that is good about America. Pride looks and feels good when looked at from below, but from above, we see the arrogance behind it—a Young Soul trait.

Hawkins identifies 200 as the level of Integrity on his scale, a major pivot point below which lie life-negating states of consciousness that seek to destroy and bring others down. Above 200 are life-affirming states of consciousness that seek beauty and fulfillment. A staggering 85% of humanity lies below this point, but the 15%

of the population above 200 brings the average global consciousness to 207. Before 1986 (i.e., pre-Harmonic Convergence), the average was 195, so humanity was borderline destructive.

Courage and personal power emerge at 200, leading to the potential for growth by trying new things and contributing back to society. Hawkins calls 250 the level of Neutrality because you begin to see beyond the black-and-white, right-and-wrong of duality, and explore shades of gray and paradoxes. This is also the level of consciousness where you begin to lose attachment to rules (i.e., as in Baby Soul age), material things (i.e., as in Young Soul age), and drama (i.e., as in Mature Soul age), so 250 is analogous to the beginning of the Old Soul age, in which you throw off judgment and the need to control. You also cease to take things personally, and live and let live.

An opening occurs around 300, where we strive to do our best, and society recognizes and rewards our willingness to make a contribution. Another opening comes at 350 (Acceptance) when you realize you create your own reality, and that love comes from within. You see yourself as a balance between soul and personality, so judgment gives way to tolerance, and you become accepting of others who are still mired in the illusion.

According to Hawkins, because of the logarithmic scale, one person at 300 counterbalances 90,000 people below 200, and one at 700 balances 70 million, although there are only 22 people in the 700s on the planet.

The 400s are the arena of reason, where we take thinking as far as we can to perfect our understanding of the material world. For example, Einstein calibrated at 499.

Just as older souls understand younger souls but not vice versa, those who calibrate higher, understand those people and concepts that calibrate lower on Hawkins' map. For example, someone at 500 understands the acceptance of 350, and are merciful and forgiving towards level 350, unlike someone at 205, who sees compassion as weakness.

Crossing the 500 mark is a major event because it bridges from the head to the heart, opening us up to forgiveness, deeper paradoxes and the realization of our spiritual path. We rise into unconditional love at 540, where we no longer confuse 'the sin' with 'the sinner.' We know that people often act in the absence of the full facts, which doesn't make them 'bad,' just ill-informed.

The 600 mark brings the realization that we are spiritual beings having human experiences, and that the soul is eternal. Thus fear of death falls away in the 600s. We see the big picture and know that all exists within the vastness of the Source.

We also surrender to, and trust fully, our soul as the real 'mover and shaker' in our lives, and whatever happens is *precisely* what our soul intends. We see that 'self' is an illusion and that 'Self' is the only reality.

Because 700 is such a huge watershed, many Lightworkers today calibrate in the 680s and 690s, ready for self-realization in the 700s, where we get kinesthetically that Self and All That Is are one and the same, and all is in perfect harmony. (In the 600s, we just 'knew' this; now we *are* this.)

Whether those between 700 – 1,000 sit in a cave and meditate or teach in an ashram makes little difference, for they are working with the M-field and the many grids surrounding the planet. When 78% of humanity calibrates below 200 and only 4% (10 million) at 540 or higher, each loving thought counts and is vastly more powerful than hateful or fearful thoughts.

(The chart itself is best studied along with Dr. Hawkins' narrative, so you are encouraged to read his three books written about the Scale of Consciousness.)

Where do you calibrate in Hawkins' Scale of Consciousness? Kinesiology gives you an objective way to find out, a way that bypasses your conscious mind. To fully trust the results, have your tester silently ask the questions while testing your arm, so you don't know the questions. For example, suppose John is testing Sue. John silently says, "On the Hawkins scale, Sue calibrates at over 200." John then presses down on Sue's arm. If the statement is true, she tests strong and resists. If false, her arm falls.

John begins increasing the number in hundreds until Sue's arm tests weak, say at 500. So John falls back to 450, where Sue still tests strong. She is still strong at 460, 470 and 480, but at 490, she turns weak. This means she calibrates between 480 – 490, so John repeats the process, this time in single digits, and Sue turns weak at 486, which pegs her at 485.

The elegance and power of this technique is that all testers will arrive at the same figure because they are testing *truth* as it exists in the M-field. Similarly, Sue can be confident in her calibration, sure that it's unsullied by what she or John want to be true. And it can be used on children as soon as they can understand what the instruction 'Resist' means.

Once you know the technique, you can test anything and everything. For example, hold a packet of artificial sweetener to your solar plexus and get someone to test your arm. Almost everyone tests weak if it contains the neurotoxin aspartame.[4] Then try with vitamin C powder.

---

[4]   If you don't know about the harmful effects of aspartame, see www.dorway.com ... and put that diet soda down, right now! It could save your life, for the FDA has listed 92 serious symptoms associated with aspartame, including death! On September 15, 2004, a $350 million class action lawsuit was filed in United

Before joining a spiritual group or signing up under a spiritual teacher, for example, if their calibration is below 540, you know their foundation is not unconditional love. With Christianity, for example, the original teachings of Jeshua ben Joseph calibrated at 1,000. According to Hawkins, that dropped to 930 as the message became politicized around 200 AD, and to 540 after the Council of Nicea and Rome built the Roman Catholic Church around the teachings and used them as a means to control the masses. During the Crusades, it fell below 500, to 498, which meant it was no longer based on love. After centuries of the Inquisition at below 20, Christianity is still just below 500, except for special groups, such as those focused on *A Course in Miracles*, that can calibrate at 600 ... so choose wisely. But at least now you have a tool to compensate for the human mind's greatest weakness — ***that humans cannot distinguish truth from falsehood.***

The problem is that the worldview being poured into a child's mind during the process that Ruiz calls 'domestication' cannot be tested for truth, and an innocent mind naively accepts whatever it is told. Because 78 percent of the population calibrates below 200 on the Map of Consciousness, we might say that three-quarters of that input is flawed, either out of ignorance or because of the imprinter's agenda, as when a warped adult tells a child, "You'll never amount to anything."

As we've seen, your early imprinting was a cloned copy of what your imprinters believed, and that depended on their social class, religion, etc., with no regard to whether their worldview bore any relation to Truth. (In fact, we humans cannot know Truth because the process of knowing anything involves: (1) initial perception; (2) interpretation based on what is already known; (3) acceptance or rejection, also based on what has been previously accepted; and (4) integration with whatever has already been accepted. (So it's a purely subjective reality, which may have little to do with Truth and Reality.) And once you accept this Parasite, you own it and will fight vigorously to defend it, even if it can be proven erroneous.

However, a pair of five-year-olds can practice muscle-testing, and systematically test for the truth of everything they are told. Many adults will find that unsettling, especially those in the legal field who are responsible for guilty/innocent decisions. As witnesses are sworn in during a trial, even a five-year-old could determine whether they really do intend to tell the truth.

States District Court in San Francisco, naming NutraSweet Corporation and American Diabetes Association, claiming racketeering over how deadly this sweetener is when consumed by humans. The lawsuit claims that current Secretary of Defense, Donald Rumsfeld, used his political clout to push aspartame through the FDA back in the 1980s when CEO of Serle, despite objections by the FDA, who knew of its deadly effects on human health. As a result of all the negative publicity, the sweetener industry is switching to Splenda, a reputed carcinogen. In October 2005, the state of New Mexico announced it would hold hearings in summer 2006 into whether to impose a statewide ban on aspartame.

Muscle-testing works because consciousness responds positively to truth and life-affirming situations, and that response allows the body's muscles to resist when a tester tries to push your arm down. In the absence of truth and in life-negating situations, the muscles go weak and cannot resist.

When a light switch is turned on, the flow of current causes the bulb to glow. Similarly, the flow of truth energy in the M-field causes the muscles to 'be strong.' and to test weak when the energy does not flow. It's not that a lie is a tangible thing; it's more that the absence of truth is a weakness in the M-field that is reflected in the body, which is bathed in the M-field.

Testing has some limitations. First, it cannot predict the future, as in, "Event X will happen," because there are too many variables. However, you might test, "Event X happening is consistent with my soul's intent."

Second, according to Hawkins, both tester and subject should calibrate at over 200 for the results to be reliable. This means the technique cannot be misused by someone lacking in personal integrity. It also means the mind/body may be free of the adverse effects of mind control grid programming in place around the planet.

Interestingly, the book on which Christianity is founded is a mixed bag. Overall, the Old Testament calibrates at 190 according to Hawkins, but without Genesis (at 660), Psalms (650) and Proverbs (350), the rest falls to just 125. This is because the rest concerns the antics of the *YHVHs*, the Anunnaki overlords who ran our planet for almost half a million years. These angry technocrats gave us our 'gods,' one of which became mentor to the Hebrews and got written up as the one 'god' in the Old Testament (see Chapter 3).

Most readers of Genesis do not realize that it recounts the Nephilim (aka Anunnaki) genetic engineering of the human race as a slave species, and how, "The sons of the gods looked upon the daughters of men and found them pleasing." I'm sure they did, after long shifts as mine supervisors. Incidentally, the 'God' of the Old Testament calibrates at around 200.

The New Testament calibrates at 640, which rises to 790 if we exclude The Book of Revelation, which is a scary glimpse into the lower Astral Plane, a nasty place indeed.

The Source of All That Is cannot be calibrated on Hawkins' 1 – 1,000 scale, which pertains to *human* consciousness. Of course, each dimension has its own scale, stacked on top of the one beneath it, like octaves on a piano, but each scale is *one thousand* times more potent and expansive than the one below, something that's way beyond my ability to imagine, but I figure the Source calibrates in the trillions.

After the 1987 Harmonic Convergence took humanity from 185 to 207, we now see phenomena such as the global debate before the U.S. launched the March 2003 military action in Iraq. Although the general population of the U.S. as a whole calibrates at 431, the Bush Administration is at 175 (Pride), exactly the level of the British Empire when Gandhi (at 700) led India to freedom from colonial tyranny. Thus it is vital that the more aware American citizens 'hold the high ground' in relation to the colonial empire-building aspirations of their leaders, so that Revenge and Pride take back seats to Understanding, Compassion and Forgiveness.

On the plus side, before Saddam Hussein took power in Iraq, the population calibrated at 86, just worse than the level of Fear as a way of life. During Saddam's 'reign,' this sank to 54, or Apathy, with poverty and despair the norm, where 1% of the population consumed 90% of the resources. After Saddam was deposed, the population's calibration rose to 154, or Anger. This is a major improvement over Apathy and can be positive, creating great social change that sweeps the population to 200 in one generation. Or, as in Somalia, Anger can take a country back into the Stone Age. However, it's unlikely that the U.S. will let that happen in Iraq.

Until Hawkins mapped human consciousness, science could get no handle on it and tried to write it off as too chaotic; courage, valor, loyalty, compassion and hope were all lumped together as 'feelings.' However, being able to calibrate nations, organizations and individuals allows us to predict how they will react in various situations. For example, Nazi Germany and Japan (both 185 – 190, or Pride) were predictable, as were the responses of England (225) and America (200).

Although Hawkins' research reveals that most people advance maybe 5 points per lifetime, just knowing and practicing what you have read in the last few pages can trigger a 35-point jump. This is also because readers are already into self-improvement, whereas others may put a lower priority on being the highest expression of who they could be.

One final word: Because this technique itself calibrates at 600, if you calibrate much below this, you may think this is all pure garbage *or* that it's a great tool for controlling people. Either way, it won't work for you and may even backfire, because you're tapping into the M-field. This tool can only be used for the highest and best interests of all concerned. As with *any* contact with the M-field, protect yourself, ask if such contact is appropriate, invoke everyone's highest and best interests ... and give gratitude afterwards.

In the end, keep in mind that when you are calibrating people, nations, etc. (anything other than states of consciousness), you are actually calibrating an illusion. The self who I think I am is an illusion that Self projects into an illusion. And it's so convincing because Self is very good at doing it.

Chapter 8

Soulful Relationships

Love

Everyone talks about it, but how many of us really know what it is? Love is the key characteristic of the Source, and hence percolates down through the dimensions, imbuing the Earth plane with the need to affiliate with, nurture and care for each other. For an idea of unconditional love, we need look no further than the Wedding Vows, where we see such words as: 'cherish, honor, in sickness and in health, and for richer or poorer.' Nothing there about possession, holding on, or denying another's sovereignty or free will … which is how many relationships end up.

The basis of spiritual love is the knowledge, sense and feeling that, because we are all thoughts of the Source, we are all part of the One. Hence, it's natural to care for and nurture the other parts of ourselves. And anything less than the Golden Rule is unthinkable. Love is a way of relating to the world with the desire to make people feel better about themselves. Love naturally wants to serve without thought of reward, which brings joy. Love seeks to help others be the grandest expression of who they are, and in doing so, finds its highest expression. Love does not possess but liberates; it lets go but is always there when needed.

This state of being is, unfortunately, rare because most of us focus on our own wants, needs and fears, and not on those of others. Love is, however, all around us, if we can but see it. Love causes the flower to bloom, the cat to purr, and the dog to wag its tail. And the perception of this leads only to gratitude and humility for living in such a love-filled world … which, of course, naturally brings more love.

There are many forms of love:
- Erotic, which fuels the libido
- Platonic, or brotherly/sisterly love
- Parental
- Agape, or unconditional love.

A new relationship usually incorporates a high level of Eros, which may slowly fade, so the couple had better have the platonic and agape in place as back-ups if it does.

Also important is our love for our own soul—our personal creator—that in turn loves, nurtures and supports us … if we'll let it. For this, getting out of the way is vital; most people block this love with fears and prejudices. Letting love in is just a matter of getting out of the way.

Love of soul naturally spills over to love of who you are in this incarnation, your hopes and aspirations, your fears, and your quirks of personality. And if there's any part you cannot love, then you've got some work to do, because what's not to love?

Unconditional Love

There's no middle ground with this—love is either unconditional or conditional, where the latter is simply bartering attention to get something you want.

If I love you unconditionally, you do not need to earn it, pass any tests, win any contests, or in any way deserve it. If you *did* need to prove your worth, you have tenure only until someone more worthy comes along—bluer eyes, whiter teeth, better cook, etc.

Unconditional love says, "You can be who you *really* are, and share your deepest thoughts, fears and feelings in absolute surety that I won't judge you or stop loving you. We may agree to disagree on things but I will never reject you, for I am committed to your well-being and growth."

When it comes to growth, how can one person support another? By criticizing, nit-picking, and pointing out flaws? Obviously not, but that's how most parents approach child-rearing; "Eat all your greens or mommy won't love you." That's flat-out manipulation but we carry that into adulthood, with 'love' as a reward for a well-prepared meal or a promotion.

Many people use 'love' to coerce a mate into conforming to their opinion of how the mate should be (just watch a few movies on the Lifetime Channel). Such 'love' forces the mate to contract and shrink into a little box, often with the justification, "I love you and want only what's best for you." This really means: "… what's best for me." On the other hand, unconditional love encourages expansion and growth, which brings us to how love really works.

1. Love Allows

First, love allows itself to flow. Love isn't a 'doing' thing, but an allowing thing. Imagine love as water, and you're a hose. How big a hose are you? A tiny tube used in an irrigation drip-watering system? A standard garden hose? A fireman's hose? Or a huge pipeline? This obviously determines how much love can flow through you, which increases with practice. Next, are there any kinks or blockages stopping the flow? As an adult, your flow rate depends on how you were loved in the womb and then as a child. If, in those early years, you picked up some kinks and blockages, you have some work to do, as we saw earlier.

Love also allows the beloved to be they are, without seeking to change them, except for encouraging growth. We all know it's impossible to change others; only *they* can change themselves but plenty of people do try … and end up exhausted and frustrated. It's about as pointless as mud-wrestling a pig—it's too slippery and besides, the pig *likes* it.

2. Love Cares

Love cares about the happiness of the beloved and constantly reminds them of how special and important they are to you. Love says, "You are valuable to me; I care about you and will do whatever I can to ensure your happiness."

3. Love Respects

When you respect those you love, you honor them, are honest with them, let them be who they are without trying to change them, and want what is in their highest and best interest.

4. Love Forgives

All of us incarnate to learn, grow and explore, and we inevitably screw up somewhere along the way and hurt someone else. If someone harms you, you have two options: (1) you can hold a grudge, or (2) you can forgive. Clearly, the first harms you further and gives all your power to the very person who harmed you, allowing that person to determine how you will feel.

The second option allows you to move on, free of other people's energy, knowing they will get theirs in their life review. You'll also live longer and healthier. However, the other person doesn't just walk away. They must be made to understand how you were harmed by their actions, offer a sincere apology and promise it won't happen again. If they are spiritual, they will be eager to learn the consequences of a hurtful word or deed … otherwise there's always the court system. And if that deed stemmed from malicious intent rather than an innocent accident, the apology had better be good.

If you're the miscreant, it's essential to own the deed, without finger-pointing or blame. Fess up and accept the consequences of your actions. And preferably apologize *before* you're found out. Suppose a friend confides a secret in you and you have too much to drink and blurt it out. Apologize before word gets back to your friend, who may then still have some respect for you.

5. Love Encourages

Most of us have untapped strengths and potentials, and only discover these when slammed by some major Life Challenge. And if we run around 'fixing' things for our friends and loved ones, we're simply enabling their victim-ness. Instead, love encourages others to find the strength and courage to tap their own potential for confidence and abilities to grasp life by the horns. Love en-*courages* others to explore the grandest expression of who they can be. And rather than nay-saying, love says, "Go for it! You can do it!"

6. Love Challenges

Love's final gift is to challenge the other to rise and stretch to achieve a goal or blast through a self-limitation, and thereby grow. Love's encouragement reveals the strength or ability; love's challenge calls it into action. Love says, "You have the *vision* of your grandest expression, so now *become* that expression."

Given that love allows, cares, respects, forgives, encourages and challenges, the trick is to blend these ingredients in just the right proportion, or things won't balance. And the best way to avoid imbalance is communication. Ask, "How does it make you feel when I encourage you to find a better job?" or, "How does it make you feel when I dare you to _______?" Finding the right mixture of allowing, caring, encouraging and challenging is not easy, and both partners must communicate openly and frequently … for that, too, is part of growth.

Love and Sacrifice

Some people fear that loving means selling yourself short and playing doormat. This fear is one of the major blocks to intimacy and unconditional love: "I'm terrified of my own 'me-ness' dissolving into an amorphous 'us-ness.'"

However, love never requires you to surrender your me-ness, for that would be a very unloving act towards yourself. In fact, you *cannot* love another *until* you love yourself. The degree to which your mate or parents love you is limited by the degree to which they love themselves. So a self-loathing mate who claims, "I love you," has no idea what those words mean.

Of course, we all get a little needy at times, and seek some extra attention, but this should never escalate to requiring others to abdicate their own identity on our behalf. Love says, "I'll be there for you until you're back on your feet." It never says, "Let me carry you on my back for the rest of your life." That's *martyrdom*.

Personal Will vs. Divine Will

A mighty river may twist and turn, but it *will* get to the ocean someday. Similarly, Creation unfolds according to some vast plan, of which you are a part. The degree to which you are aligned with that plan determines how much you are in the flow of life, or the Tao.

Some of us chose to swim upstream instead, expending huge amounts of energy and getting hit by floating debris. That's okay, of course. Deciding to do that is what free will is all about, and the Source learns more about itself from our detours and bruises, so nothing is wasted. As long as the detours are done with unconditional love and without fear, side-trips can be fun.

At the soul level, you are free to engage in countless projects on the soul plane, and you periodically incarnate on the Earth plane to speed your learning or pass on your understanding to others. So, at the same time, you are both part of the big river flowing to the ocean *and* a self-willed individual consciousness within it. The Earth plane is the *only* place we can go to explore this unique paradox.

Free will allows us to explore being separate from the flow as self-willed, autonomous beings rather than loved-based automatons. But, it also allows us to *choose* to align with Divine Flow and be one with the Tao … or not.

Know that every thought, word and deed is a free will choice to align with your soul's will … or not. But it is always a *choice*. You can try to blame things on astrology, the weather, etc., but it always comes down to your will to align with—or fight—the flow. One way gets you peace, joy and harmony; the other gets you strife, pain and misery. Your choice!

So how *do* we align with our soul's will? Given possible courses of action in a particular situation in your life, hold each course in mind and explore all aspects of doing it and not doing it, using your rational mind. You might draw up 'pro and con' lists for each. Then meditate on both sides of each option, checking on whether your heart chakra opens or closes. This Emotion Guidance System points you to the option with the highest 'love quotient' (or LQ) for *all* concerned, not necessarily just for you.

Once you have your answer, let it incubate for a while and then repeat the meditation. If the answer is still the same, then *that* is the path that is most in alignment with your soul's will. Or you could try *dowsing* as we'll see in Vol. II, Chapter 9.

Soulmates

Before getting into relationships with others, let's look at the issue of soulmates. When two souls incarnate together and have a relationship (business, romantic, friendship, etc.), those two souls form a special bond. When they next incarnate into the same timeframe as each other but in new bodies and those two people meet, they sense that special soulmate bond, usually as an instant liking and trust. Or it can be dislike and mistrust, depending on what happened before.

Obviously the meeting is no coincidence, but what did your souls intend when they planned all this? It all depends; are the two of you a cash-strapped inventor and someone seeking to invest a few million? Or a man and woman both recently out of relationships and ready for the next?

When you first meet a soulmate, being able to recognize him or her is vital. Next comes figuring out what roles you are to play in each other's lives—this is the fun part of being spiritually aware. The soulmate relationship operates via all four of the bodies:

1. It begins in the spiritual body on reaching the point in your flight plans when you both had planned to meet. You're triggered by cues you had embedded in your fields, and the 'heads up' alarm tells you this other person is significant and important to you. (In one case, two souls embedded the cue that she would wear an odd-shaped pendant that he would subconsciously recognize and begin a conversation about it.)

2. Next, your mental bodies engage with similar and consistent world views. This is because the souls in your soul group (from which the other is drawn) are of similar Soul Age, so have broadly similar world views, while differing on the small stuff.

3. Emotionally, the two of you hit it off from the start, with a feeling of 'we've known each other before.' This affinity quickly deepens to unconditional love.

4. At the physical level, because of the deep trust, lovemaking is ecstatic, with each partner delighting in finding new ways to please the other.

Because we've had hundreds of lifetimes in which we've had meaningful relationships with thousands of people, our souls may plan a rich tapestry of dozens of soulmate relationships in our life, some at the same time. For example, you may be married to one, business partners with two others, and seeing a fourth as a shrink. And when you meet a soul mate, the immediate trust and familiarity quickly allow you both to get on with your joint mission.

Soul mates are not to be confused with twin souls. A soul can incarnate twice into the same timeframe, and when the incarnations meet up, the effect is 'soul mate-squared.' Or early in its existence, a soul may divide its energy into two, with each part going off to gather experience and then pool it at some distant point in the future. If incarnations of these two soul partitions were to meet, the effect would be similar—instant and total love, caring, bonding, trusting, etc. The plan may or may not call for a romantic relationship, but whatever these two do together is unstoppable and a force to be reckoned with.

Where Do Souls Come From?

Remote viewer[1] Bruce Moen asked this question and was taken to a very high dimension where he saw what seemed to be a 'wall of undifferentiated consciousness.' Out of this wall, bubbles of consciousness seemed to emerge, in a process that Moen 'knew' was controlled by a much higher intelligence, which he could not see. He also 'knew' this being was able to look far into the future to see what 'soul mix' would be needed across billions of years, and was configuring the bubbles of consciousness with whatever 'I-awareness' was deemed necessary for these new souls. He was also told these souls would incubate 'for a very long time' to perfect their I-awareness before incarnating.

Incidentally, Bruce Moen's website (www.afterlife-knowledge.com) is a treasure trove of information about the afterlife. In his out-of-body journeys, he has identified a number of afterlife levels:

- Focus 1 — physical waking consciousness in which we experience the everyday reality of the physical world.
- Focus 3 — the level of awareness when using the Hemi-Sync®, a device that synchronizes the left and right hemispheres.

---

[1]   A technique by which viewers dislocate part of their consciousness and send it to a designated location and timeframe. (See Vol. II, Chapter 12 for more information.)

- Focus 10 — the level at which the physical body is asleep but the mind is awake and alert. The Monroe Institute has developed tools to use in this state to reduce anxiety and tension, for healing, for remote viewing and for establishing resonance with other individuals. Focus 10 also seems to be the level of lucid dreaming.
- Focus 12 — consciousness is expanded beyond the limits of the physical body for exploring nonphysical realities, making complex decisions and enhanced creative expression.
- Focus 15 — enjoys a state of 'No Time,' which offers vast opportunities for self-exploration outside of time and space.
- Focus 21 — enables one to explore other realities and energy systems beyond our time/space continuum.
- Focus 22 — Within Focus 22 we often find those perhaps still physically alive who are in an unconscious state. These include people in comas, in drug induced states, who are dreaming, who are insane or deranged. This is a very chaotic level.
- Focus 23 — the astral plane, occupied by the deceased who have become trapped for some reason, often related to circumstances of their death or habitual patterns of thinking prior to death. (Dannion Brinkley briefly passed through this realm on his second NDE, and calls it 'the blue-gray place.') Often occupants are confused about or unaware of their death, and try to contact those still in the physical world around familiar people or places, i.e., *ghosts.* They are typically alone and completely isolated from communication with other humans, and are frequently the targets of Moen's rescue missions.
- Focus 24, 25 and 26 — what Moen calls the 'belief system territories.' These correspond to firmly held beliefs about the afterlife in the minds of those who cross over. Inhabitants are stuck like those in Focus 23, but are not isolated from contact with others. Some of these areas have characteristics of heavens and hells, and are rigidly structured around the inhabitants' beliefs. For example, a fundamentalist bible-thumping minister could give endless fire-and-brimstone sermons to avid congregations for centuries in Earth years. Moen also attempts rescues there, but finds it difficult to move people from this area to areas of greater free will choices.
- Focus 27 —the true soul plane of greatest free will choice. Often resembling physical earth environments, Focus 27 supports open contact and

communication between all inhabitants. Highly organized and structured, this realm has centers of activity to provide for our needs as we continue our growth in the afterlife. In his explorations, he's come across centers for orienting and rehabilitating new arrivals, education, life review, health and rejuvenation, planning and scheduling. These centers also coordinate Earth plane human activities to assist in human development.

Moen conducts what he calls 'Exploring the Afterlife' workshops in which he teaches people to go beyond the boundaries of their fear of death, and to explore the soul plane. "Not so many years ago most people believed the earth was flat. No one holding that belief ventured too far out to sea for fear of sailing off the edge and falling into the great abyss of death," he says. "Most people lived lives limited by the beliefs held by the culture of their time. Curiosity drove a few to sail beyond the horizon to discover that the edge most everyone feared only existed within their beliefs."

Because direct experience of the soul plane proves that it exists, he actually takes people there. "When I first began exploring the Afterlife, I was convinced I was making it all up in my own mind. The hardest thing is to believe you are doing it," which is exactly what I said when I first learned to channel.

When remote viewing the higher dimensions, we must remember we're being shown a representation, or model, of what's really happening, and not get too hung up on the details. For example, when he asked about how synchronicities are orchestrated, Moen was shown what looked like the huge display panel for controlling a subway system, with the tracks as people's life plans and the people as dots, like trains moving along the tracks. Thousands of 'controllers' sat at an infinitely long console, arranging for people to be in the right place at the right time for synchronous events to occur. Which brings us to the next question ...

How Do I Meet a Soul Mate?

By now, we know the answer. You program the M-field by imposing your intent to do just that. Of course, the meeting will only happen if and when it's in your flight plane to happen, but you can help solidify it into your reality.

Any self-hypnosis method will work, such as visualizing yourself at the top of a flight of ten stairs. Take a few deep breaths and relax every muscle in your body. Then descend the stairs, counting from nine down to one, becoming more relaxed with each step. At the foot of the stairs is a door that opens to reveal a breathtakingly beautiful scene. (You can have fun designing this place and coming back to it often.)

In the far distance of your paradise stands a person waiting for you, and you *know* it is a soul mate. As you approach, his or her features become clearer, revealing exquisite beauty. And the love you feel for each other is off the scale.

As you embrace, kiss or whatever, the energy between you sparkles and crackles, and you feel complete. At some point, you will need to count back up to ten and return to the outside world, but until then … have fun.

Why Isn't My Soulmate Perfect?

Different people are just that … different. Roles, Soul Ages, Goals, Modes, Attitudes and Challenges all make life interesting … and bumpy. Also, two people have differing hopes and aspirations, and old baggage from previous relationships, so it's amazing that *any* relationship works at all!

Once the first flush of Eros fades and reality sets in, making the relationship work begins … and it can be work. Eventually the work may outweigh the joys, and you must decide whether you're still learning and growing … or if it's time to move on.

Some relationships are not *meant* to last. The Michael entity talks about *pivotal facilitators*, where someone, possibly a soul mate, comes into your life, turns everything upside down, and just as quickly leaves, having facilitated a pivotal event in your life, such as being the rebound relationship before you meet a soul mate.

Suppose your spouse of many years died a while ago and you're unsure you'll ever love again. Suddenly, a person shows up in your life and you have a whirlwind relationship that restores your faith … and then he or she is gone just as quickly. Or you may be going through a divorce and are comparing the uncertainty of your future with the plodding, boring security of your old marriage. The whirlwind affair convinces you to go forward, not backward, despite the uncertainty.

If things are not perfect, you can always walk away … unless you have a karmic contract, in which case, you may have toe-to-toe, eyeball-to-eyeball confrontation until the lesson is done. Or you can call on your higher self to reveal the lesson without the combat, then call on the energy of Grace to dissolve the contract, and go your separate ways. But make sure you both *really* get the lesson, through deep reflection.

Relationships with Others

Once you are loving yourself, allowing love in and receiving it, you're ready to love others. Until you love yourself, however, you cannot love others or accept love from them—you're just bartering attention to ease your insecurities. It's a common arrangement; after all, only one in 20 people are really self-loving, so the other 19 must play the barter game to get the approval and validation their ego needs to feel secure and good about itself.

Assuming you're the one in 20 and are fully self-approving and self-validating, and do not look for your self-worth anywhere other than in your own heart and mind, let's look at the role that relationships play in our lives. Our relationships serve to help us know ourselves better, because sharing worldviews with others clarifies our own, including our self-image.

Why we believe something is just as important as *what* we believe. In fact, the 'what' is relatively unimportant because it's guaranteed wrong, for we cannot comprehend Truth through our limited, linear brains, nor express it in any human language. *Why* we believe what we do is revealing. It is usually because it's what our early imprinters told us, and we've never bothered to reevaluate it. Even experience is not the best source, for, as we have seen, we are selective about our perceptions and then we even interpret them by consulting our beliefs and applying assumptions. So what we believe has nothing to do with Truth.

The only reliable source for beliefs is our own higher self. So read widely and debate the nature of reality with an open mind. Then test what you hear against your truth sense, i.e., ask your higher self to guide you via your emotions, by making you feel good and expanded when you hear truth, and closed and compacted when you hear falsehood. After a little practice, you can actually feel your heart chakra open and close.

Relationships are an excellent arena for exploring fear, something that doesn't exist on the soul plane. We have already seen that fears are blocks to love, so if you are trying to let love in from someone, fear gets in the way. For example, we all have a fear of abandonment to some degree because we're down here on the Earth plane, feeling cut off from our soul, God or whatever. This fear can drive us towards other people, so we become overly dependent, or away from them, making us overly *independent*. Either way, it's not love.

True love is unconditional and flows from the soul. Only the ego-personality imposes conditions on love, or can feel hurt or slighted. Souls often build Challenges into the flight plan with which the ego-personality must deal; or the ego-personality builds them in itself. Either way they are blocks to the flow of love, put there to be explored and dispelled as the Source learns more about itself and its Resources through its many parts, including you.

As we've seen, fear of abandonment or being hurt are common blocks to love. Of course there are risks that your loved one will leave or die, and these risks prevent many people from even opening to love in the first place. But their leaving or dying was all scripted in your respective flight plans as a Challenge from which to grow. Believing 'if I open up to love, I will be hurt' can be cemented in the Subconscious Mind at an early age by, say, the arrival of a new sibling, which demands attention away from you, the older child, who interprets this as love being withdrawn; so you feel unloved. And the way you may come to terms with this is to redefine yourself as unlovable, which haunts you throughout adult life.

Another way we block love is by finding closeness scary because it might mean the loss of identity or self. This can happen if the parents did not give the child a good role model of intimacy, or if one partner is afraid of what the other partner might find. The trick is to set healthy boundaries to balance the need for closeness and separateness.

An anonymous piece circulating the Internet points out that people come into our lives for a *reason*, a *season*, or a *lifetime*, and when we figure out which it is, we know exactly what to do:

- When someone is in your life for a *reason*, it is usually to meet a need you have expressed outwardly or inwardly. They have come to assist you through a difficulty, to provide you with guidance and support, to aid you physically, emotionally or spiritually. They may seem like a godsend, and they are. They are there for the reason you need them to be. Then, without any wrongdoing on your part, this person will say or do something to bring the relationship to an end. Sometimes they die. Sometimes they walk away. Sometimes they act up or out and force you to take a stand. What you must realize is that your need has been met, your desire is fulfilled and their work is done. The prayer you sent up has been answered and it is now time to move on.

- When people come into your life for a *season*, it is because your turn has come to share, grow, or learn. They may bring you an experience of peace or make you laugh. They may teach you something you have never done. They usually give you an unbelievable amount of joy … but only for a season.

- *Lifetime* relationships teach you lifetime lessons; those things you must build upon in order to have a solid emotional foundation. Your job is to accept the lesson, love the person/people (anyway); and put to use what you have learned, in all other relationships and areas of your life.

Remembering that we are probes, exploring the nature of Creation on behalf of the Source, where do we begin? With self, of course, and the question, "Who am I?"

Suppose you were marooned on a desert island as a baby. You would grow up feral, with no idea of who or what you were. Without a mirror, you wouldn't even know what you looked like. The character played by Tom Hanks in *Castaway* was marooned for four years and, as an adult, he missed human company because he knew what he was missing. But what *was* that really? Mirrors! He had a physical mirror of sorts (the blade of an ice-skate), but he missed the mirroring effect that relationships provide in our search to know who we are. We learn more about ourselves in intimate relationships with others than from any other source, which is the main reason we do it (apart from the sex, of course, but that, too, is just a mirror).

As with the Source (in Chapter 1), our castaway was so lonely, he created a companion by painting a face on a volleyball and became so attached to it, he risked his life when a storm carried it away. So we're all playing the role of Wilson to each other.

Our richly textured lives offer countless mirrors that reflect clearly (hopefully) who we are. But, of course, these are living mirrors with their own agendas, which often include manipulation in order to control. Hence such chilling remarks as, "I always knew you wouldn't amount to anything." An accurate mirror? Hardly. More like someone's attempt to feel better at another's expense. (That's why I enjoy my two Labrador dogs so much. Their agendas are simple—food and walks; everything else is pure love. I once saw a bumper sticker that read: The more people I meet, the more I like my dog.)

When you look at someone else (friend, relative, lover, etc.), look beyond what you see, and visualize a brave soul taking on dozens, hundreds even, of grueling lifetimes, and trying to figure out the rules as they go along. You will have compassion for their confusion, anxiety and fear, and you will share their joys and triumphs. Also, do the same for yourself in the mirror.

Until you understand karma, you will be caught on a carousel, endlessly repeating dramas. You know you're in a karmic relationship, or KR, if one or more of the following happens:

- You are bonded to someone else despite abuse or pain in the relationship.
- If you keep breaking up and then going back.
- If the person keeps pulling you back in, against your better judgment.

Now being in a KR isn't too bad if you know what's happening, but it's hell if you don't. KRs are soul's way of getting your attention and focusing it on another person with whom you have a spirit agreement. KRs only become a problem if you don't seize the buried treasure of understanding and move on. But many people spend decades in a KR, endlessly repeating the same behaviors, hoping somehow to 'make it work.' Meanwhile, they become frustrated and worn down.

Even if they do end a KR but haven't yet gained the understanding, they jump into another one and play out the same old dramas, hoping 'this is the one.' But if you are emotionally needy and require constant attention, say, you will attract a string of emotionally unavailable partners from whom you try to elicit what you need … without success.

For example, suppose in a past life, a husband flies into a jealous rage and kills his wife whom he believes is having an affair, when she is actually innocent. When they meet up again in a new lifetime and form the inevitable KR as husband and wife, all manner of wounds open up. The alleged betrayal makes the husband unable to trust his wife, so he remains aloof. And she cannot open up to him, with the anger over her murder still deep in her subconscious. So even though they both want intimacy, it eludes them. The solution? Regression, which would reveal the buried wounds and bring up these emotional scars for healing.

Anger over some past-life transgression is one of the main blocks between two people whose souls co-incarnate again to heal the wounds. Anger wounds are often a fear that history will repeat itself, so you either refuse to be vulnerable or you 'come out swinging,' to get the first blow in.

If you are suspicious, unable to forgive or apologize, are quick to criticize or easily fly into a rage, you probably have an anger that needs healing. Or you may have gone the other way and feel fearful around someone, but are really suppressing anger.

When you find yourself suddenly angry or fearful of another person, whether your mate, boss or the cop writing you a traffic ticket, say to yourself, "This incident is not the cause. It is merely triggering a much older and deeper wound, so I am not going to react blindly." Then set about healing the wound via regression.

Another major cause of wounds between people is past-life abandonment. Given how often men have marched off to war, leaving wives and children behind, or how many women have died in childbirth throughout history, we've had lots of opportunities to be wounded this way. And when we co-incarnate with the same soul who abandoned us before, these wounds make trust and intimacy difficult, as in: "I'm not going to let *that* happen again!" But, of course, we must if we are to heal the wound. Again, regression is the fastest and most effective way to do that.

If you found you were successful with the Soul's Life Gallery technique, you can return to the gallery and ask to visit the relationship section. There you will see portraits of your soul's incarnations beside your soul mates. What do you see? Two soldiers in Vietnam who die side-by-side, or an American soldier and the Viet Cong guerilla who kills him? Two Marines fighting beside each other on Guam? Or the two sisters who both lose their husbands to the fighting and console each other? A husband and wife team, slogging through the frontier, dodging Native American war parties and rattlesnakes? Two Sioux braves or two brothers-in-arms at the Little Big Horn? The combinations are endless, because we have dozens of soul mates in each lifetime.

Ask your guides to light up the portrait where your soul incurred an emotional wound that you can heal in this current lifetime. Watch it come to life and reveal how the wound happened. After the movie ends but before coming back to normality, ask for insights about the wound and how you can best heal it.

Going deeper into relationships, let's start with the mother lode—romantic relationships.

Romantic Relationships

As souls, we've been exploring love since the dawn of everything, so down here on the Earth plane, the only variables come from blocking that love and seeing what happens. So, intimate relationships are actually exercises in 'block and watch.' And the more stress in our lives, the more blocks we erect.

We show our 'bright, shining self' to friends and colleagues, and only in intimate relationships can we see and explore our 'shadow self,' our blocks and old baggage collected during childhood and from prior relationships.

As creator probes, romantic relationships are fertile ground for examining our 'probe-ness' through the Challenges we built into our personality and belief system. As mirrors for each other, we get to see who our personalities really are, what we want them to become, how to achieve that, and how much soul they can embrace … and mates are the ones who hopefully help us get there, assuming we can get past *their* assumptions and agendas.

A common problem in the 'becoming business' is that exploring the highest and grandest expression of who we could be, and then becoming that, involves change, and some partners resist our changes, fearing where those changes may take us. But, life is about the Source exploring its Creation, and if nothing changes, nothing is learned. So change is a mandatory part of incarnating here, otherwise we're just a waste of skin.

An interesting sidelight is that a woman often marries a man believing she can change him … but she can't; a man, on the other hand, often marries a woman hoping that she won't change … and she does.

People often talk of 'failed' relationships, but the only failed relationship is one where nothing changes. As long as both parties are changing and growing, nothing fails. And if the parties change and grow in different and incompatible directions and split up, so be it. They can continue to grow alone or with someone else. Nothing is lost, nothing is wasted, and the Source learns and grows. The only real failure comes when a couple really *should* separate to continue their growth but do not, and stagnate instead, the relationship becoming either a comfortable habit or a familiar battle-ground. A twenty-year relationship can actually be a one-year relationship repeated twenty times … little is learned and glorious opportunities for expressing soul are wasted.

When a couple can no longer support each others' growth for whatever reason, it's time to move on with no hard feelings, for the relationship is over. Spiritual folks and hopefully their families will realize that splitting up was all filed in everyone's flight plans and that everything is on course. (Even though it might have been in their flight plans, they still had free will. Again, the lessons are pre-planned, but not how we go about learning them.)

Couples often stay together 'for the children,' but that's a compromise, because what does that teach the children? To stifle self-exploration, to martyr freedom for someone else's sake. Before they incarnated, they knew their parents would likely divorce, but came in anyway for the Challenge to stimulate their Resources, so even parental divorce was factored into their flight plan. Of course, this is a hotly debated subject. Some radio talk show hosts would dismiss these parents as self-indulgent in wanting to leave a non-loving marriage, thereby denying the kids two full-time parents. While that's true, the real issue is, what's best for the children? To live with constant bickering, as the parents conduct running battles designed to erode each other's self-esteem, and maybe use the kids as hostages of war? Or to go through an amicable separation, with mutual respect, where everyone honors everyone else? If only it was that clear cut …

Spiritual parents would, of course, pass worldviews on to their children that would ensure the kids' self-esteem and tell them, "As souls, we all love one another to eternity and back but, at the ego-personality level, Mom and Dad need to live apart even though they both love you." All just the Source challenging itself to explore its Resources.

Just as we individually must learn to balance our spiritual and human parts, relationships should also strive for that balance. For example, sex can be both a transcendental Tantric experience or a lusty animal romp … and the ideal is perfect balance.

Spiritual lovemaking involves knowing about how energy flows in the body, and consciously working with that flow. Understanding the chakra system is important, too, because these energy centers are where true connection is made. When a couple sits face-to-face and 'hooks up' their chakras like rungs on a ladder, the depth and height of lovemaking goes off the scale. Fortunately, the bookstores are full of invaluable reading on the subject of Tantra.

Beyond the physical attraction and sexual compatibility, it is important that the couple are best friends and, just like best friends, share similar worldviews and will do anything to help the other explore the grandest expression of soul. There is no co-dependency here, where one partner 'needs' anything of the other; both are sovereign individuals, strong, self-contained, and spiritually oriented. They are together to draw the strengths out of each other, not criticize the weaknesses. It's a true partnership, with each partner looking out for the other, a synergy where the whole is greater than the sum of the parts. And whether it lasts a year or a lifetime doesn't matter, for the beauty of it is recorded in both partners' souls.

Now if the relationship does come to a natural end, spiritual partners will recognize that it's run its course and be grateful for the gift of the experience. Then, after a suitable recalibration as a single person, they move on to the next Challenge/Resource cycle.

If conflict does come into a spiritual romantic relationship, neither party is egocentric enough to take it personally, and instead both immediately go *transpersonal*. That is, they transcend the personality and look for the highest resolution that offers the most loving outcome for all involved.

Transpersonal psychology does not see the human personality as an end in itself. Personality traits, tendencies, and attributes are seen as just 'clothing' for our transpersonal essence and the vehicle that enables the soul and spirit to navigate through the world. Thus, the proper role of the personality is to be a semi-transparent window on the soul within, which goes back to the sheets of colored plastic of Chapter 5.

Spiritual Relationships

Many 'love' relationships never leave the mushy, adolescent, puppy-love stage, where two people (A and B) sacrifice their sovereignty and smush together as one symbiotic unit. Such submersion in each other can be an unhealthy loss of identity in which the parties do not grow as individuals. It is also *ego-centric* in that both parties do not feel whole within themselves, and believe, "My mate

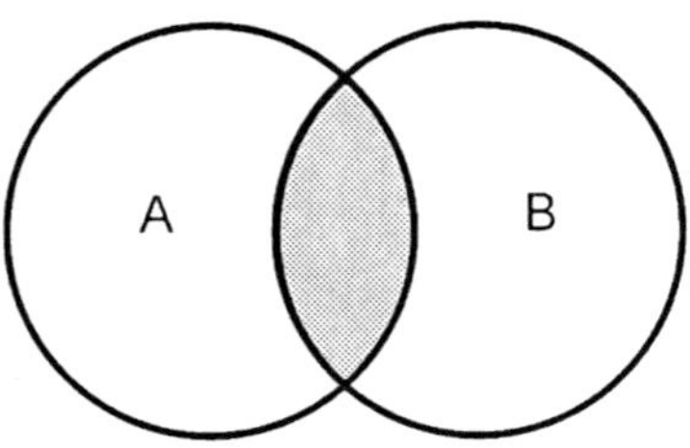

Ego-centric Relationships

completes me." This means that a break-up devastates one or both partners.

In a spiritual society, relationships will be *soul-centric*, in that both partners honor that their primary relationship is their soul connection—both their individual connection with soul and their connection *within* soul. They know they prearranged the relationship before either of them incarnated, with the goal of their mutual growth. It's then up to them to figure out *how* they intended to do that. As with all spiritual matters, you can meditate to listen to soul, or ask your guides to show you via synchronicity. Be careful about consulting psychics, however, because their ego agenda can color the information.

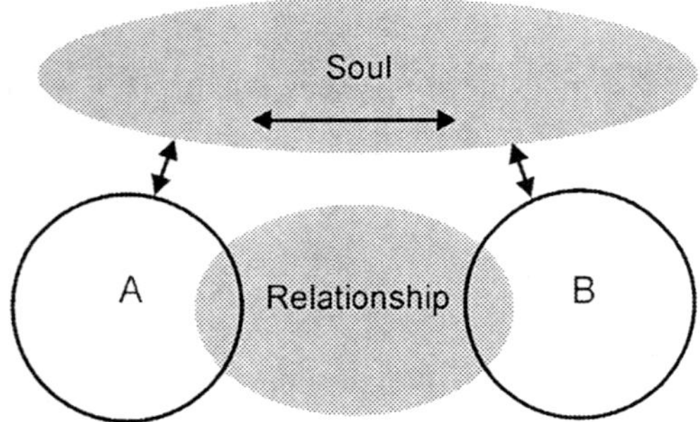

Soul-centric Relationships

The partners are very aware that the relationship down at the ego level exists in the space between them, and that 'to love' really means 'allowing soul to play in that space with them.' Both parties treat this space as 'hallowed ground' and rigorously apply the Four Agreements to their interaction with it, and hence with each other:

> #1—They are *impeccable* with their word, in that they put only their highest expression into this sacred space. Both know that so-called 'constructive criticism' is really saying, "There's something wrong with you and I'm going to fix it." Being impeccable means, in the words of John Edward, 'honoring, appreciating and validating' your partner, and *not* trying to fix him or her. One absolute agreement underpinning the relationship should be truth. Relationships can weather many storms but none has room for deceit, for when trust breaks down, what else is left?

#2—Whatever enters the sacred space, neither party takes it *personally*, for both know that as soul's playground, whatever enters is a mirror for growth. Your partner's infidelity, say, is not seen as a stab through your heart but as your partner's sexual expression outside the relationship. Whether you previously agreed to this brings us to ...

#3—Neither partner makes *assumptions* about what happens in their sacred space, and everything is discussed and agreed going in, including outcomes for transgression. For example, if both agree to have an 'open relationship,' there can be no sanctions against sex outside the relationship. But if both agree on monogamy, then outside sex would be a problem the parties must deal with. There can be no, "But I assumed you'd know how I'd feel."

#4—Both parties automatically do their *best* to nurture the relationship and the other person; doing less is unthinkable, as is presenting your best self to the outside world while trashing your partner in private.

In a spiritual relationship, therefore, the parties are careful about what they put into their sacred space and what they take out. The rule is 'no personal baggage,' which means old relationships are healed before starting a new one, and any new baggage is dealt with outside, and not 'dumped' into the relationship for the other person to fix. Of course, your partner can be compassionate about your plight, but it's not his or her job to fix you or your problems.

If conflict arises in the sacred space, the parties must take time to resolve it, otherwise it will fester like an open wound. With true listening, each partner has five minutes to explain, "I feel X when you do Y." The other listens without interrupting, and then mirrors with, "So when I do Y, you feel X. Is that accurate?" This ensures that both are really hearing each other, without distortion and assumptions. Resolution should then follow swiftly.

If one or both parties feel the relationship is no longer supporting their grandest expression of spirit, both can look for ways to remedy this. However, people change and the time may come when the sacred space no longer serves and should be dissolved. Without recrimination, both agree that it's time to move on and seek expression with another partner or alone. Life's too short for any ''til death us do part' nonsense. This way, the ex-partners leave with fond, loving memories of each other, plus the knowledge that another spirit agreement has been successfully completed and growth accomplished.

So the next time you look into the eyes of your beloved, be aware of the sacred space between you ... and treasure and nurture it.

Images and Projections

If only it were that easy. Suppose two people, a man and a woman, are in the very early stages of a potential relationship. There are just the two of them, right? No, there are eight altogether. First comes who they *really* are (M-1 and W-1 in the diagram), followed by who they each *think* they are (M-2 and W-2), which is usually a very different thing due to layers of denial and internal self-talk. Next, the partners project idealized images of themselves to each other (M-3 and W-3) that emphasize what they each value about themselves and what they think the other values in them, while downplaying what they perceive as the negatives. So each party has three selves: real self, perceived self and idealized self.

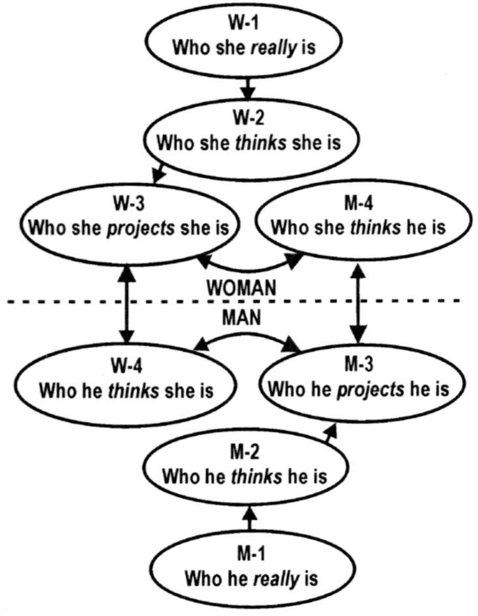

Images at Play in a Relationship

Now it gets tricky, for we also have in play the being who each perceives the other to be (M-4 and W-4). The latter are complex because the W-4 image perceived by the man is a collage of image-pieces of every woman he has ever known, especially his mother, superimposed on the woman's W-3. So, although she's projecting W-3, he's interacting with W-4, which is a combination of W-3 and his own superimposed image of her. In W-4, he exaggerates what he likes about her personality and body, and downplays what he doesn't like. Similarly, the woman is busy generating M-4 based on the men she's known, especially her father, and her preferences.

So within the woman's psyche, W-3 (her idealized projection to him) interacts with M-4 (who she thinks he is). In the male's psyche, his M-3 (his idealized projection to her) responds to his W-4 (his image of her). And this is assuming both parties are playing straight with each other. If one of them is hiding something (a drug or drinking problem, say), then it gets complex. And we're assuming these are psychologically healthy people; if one or both has sub-personalities that pop up on occasion, it gets *really* complex to the point where meaningful communication is probably impossible.

Now, because we're not a fully telepathic species, his M-3 doesn't know much about M-4 (how she sees him) because that's locked up in her heart and mind. The best he can do is guess about her M-4 based on whatever feedback she gives him. But even the feedback may be a ploy to make her W-3 look good rather than reveal her M-4 to him.

In this scenario, both parties break the First Agreement by projecting false, idealized M-3/W-3 images, and both break the Third Agreement by making assumptions about each other when they create M-4 and W-4, respectively. Worse, when the other party fails to live up to the M-4/W-4 image, the expectant party feels let down, takes it personally, and breaks the Second Agreement.

Also, living up to M-3 or W-3 images becomes a trap, a prison of their own making. Because M-3 and W-3 are so different from M-1 and W-1, both people feel great inner pain and self-rejection, which makes them try harder to bolster up M-3 or W-3, a process that is stressful and exhausting. And because M-3 and W-3 are not authentic, both people must remember all the lies that make up these projected images. The greater the gap between our #2 and #3 images, the more we may despise #2, resulting in zero self-love. Oh boy, what a world!

So what can our couple do? They can start by 86ing the M-4 and W-4 images created by both parties' assumptions and expectations of the other. By following the Third Agreement and seeing each other's M-3/W-3 image instead of concocting the #4 fantasy images; they can accept what is being presented. And if either doesn't like what they see, they can either live with it or move on. What you *cannot* do is change that person. You can only help people change what they do in terms of behavior, but you cannot change who they are because that's a matter of what they *believe* about themselves. Only they can do that … and even then only if they really *want* to change.

Next, dump M-3 or W-3 by projecting yourself as honestly as possible. Be as authentic as you can rather than project what you want the other person to see you as. (And if that's not good enough, maybe this is not the relationship for you, but at least you are basing a decision on the truth.) This will also let the other person relax into being who he or she is.

The final—and scariest—step is to drop M-2/W-2 by stripping away any pretenses and denials you have about yourself and allowing more of your soul to shine through the layers of ego. Work to accept and love who you *really* are, which will make it easier for your partner to love and accept you.

If either of you cannot love who the other really is, then walk away—there are still a few billion other people on the planet. However, you'll find the rewards are worth the risks of being authentic.

Expectations in Relationships

Reasonable expectations in a healthy relationship are basic support, affection, equal partnership, and encouragement for the other's growth and well-being, plus honesty and integrity. Without these, we don't even *have* a relationship. It is *unreasonable* to expect our partner to be our parent, solving all our problems for us.

Optional expectations, such as sexual fidelity, should be honestly discussed and negotiated, and then honored. If this negotiation is not done explicitly, then it is not reasonable for either side to assume anything. (Remember the Third Agreement about not making assumptions.)

If you feel good and secure about yourself, you will accept your partner as-is, and not try to mold him or her into someone *you* want them to be; it's better to look for someone else who already *is* that. However, if you don't feel secure, your expectation for change could easily become unrealistic. (Another common unreasonable expectation occurs when an insecure partner constantly seeks validation from the other. Cherishing each other is reasonable, but propping up a partner's self-worth is not.)

One of the greatest sources of friction in relationships between men and women stems from something that neither can do anything about, since it's hormonal. Over millions of generations, males have evolved with higher levels of testosterone than women, to give them the edge in 'flight or fight' situations. Because of their primary role in child-bearing, suckling and caring, women have evolved with higher levels of oxytocin, the so-called 'cuddle and huddle' hormone that fosters bonding between mothers and offspring, and between women gathering around to protect their children. This unchangeable fact of nature explains why 'men are from Mars and women from Venus,' and to expect any different is simply a waste of time and energy.

This has enormous implications for affinity bonding, or the ability and desire to be close with someone else. Imagine an 'Affinity Scale' ranging from totally separate on the left to totally unified on the right, and figure out where you lie on the scale. Because of oxytocin, women invariably fall to the right of men, and tend to exhibit smaller deviations from their comfort zone.

Affinity Scale

In addition to testosterone, society also encourages men to fall more to the left. And men may believe that society expects more of them than women so, feeling more challenged, they compete with other men rather than cooperate, which further separates them. They also display a wider movement on the scale, sliding to the right during intimate moments but then retreating to 'get some breathing room.'

Given this fact of life, for either gender to expect the other to slide permanently sideways on the Affinity Scale is pointless. So each partner can only accept the other's affinity position and comfort zone. It is particularly hard for women to accept that where their mate is on the scale is where he will probably stay all his life. But, barring oxytocin shots or pills, 'he is what he is.' Men can try to fake a shift to the right but both partners should accept 'what is as what is.'

It is also a man's position on the Affinity Scale that partly determines whether he can commit in a relationship and form a true partnership with his mate. Of course, commitment phobia is a book in its own right, and has psychological roots buried deep within the Subconscious Mind that would take therapy or past-life regression to resolve … given an intense desire to do so.

A pernicious aspect of unrealistic expectations is that if a man simply cannot meet them, even if excessive, such as, "Try to be more open to intimacy," he can plummet into feelings of inadequacy, and then has to work hard at covering up the resentment he feels towards his accuser.

So how does a woman adapt to a man who is way left-of-center on the Affinity Scale? First, accept that it's not about you; the pattern results from his chemistry and childhood. Next, since you can't change him, can you live with it? If not, maybe move on. If you can, invite him to make forays right-of-center, and accept it when he gets uneasy and retreats to his comfort zone, possibly even making light jest of his Martian origins.

Above all, remember, this is just a personality thing, and you're best buddies on the soul plane. As always, go into your higher self and ask for signs about whether you're supposed to be together, and for guidance about whether your expectations of your mate are reasonable. Then remain open to those signs, such as bumping into an old friend who just happens to be a couple's counselor.

Know there are several problems with trying to change others to meet your expectations:

1. It is not your right or responsibility to do so, and is karmic. Hopefully, others are who their soul intends, but if not, getting back on track is *their* responsibility, because change can come only from within.

2. It suggests you know what's 'best' for others, which implies judgment on your part, and maybe even self-righteousness.
3. You're overlooking the Mars/Venus thing, which will lead only to frustration and grief. Far easier on yourself is accepting the difference and deciding whether you can live with it.

The greatest stumbling blocks to intimacy are the fantasies we weave into our M-4 and W-4 views of our idealized mate. We fantasize about the perfect man or woman, project that on to our mate, and are disappointed when he or she doesn't measure up. For intimacy to develop and love to bloom, we must abandon our M-4 and W-4 projections.

The inherent problem in finding love in a relationship is our motivation for seeking it, which is usually the need for *meaning*, *validation* and a sense of *'being alive'*:
- Many of us find *meaning* as solitary beings but, as essentially social animals, most of us also seek meaning in relating to each other, usually as a couple, or team of two.
- Again, many find self-esteem from within (we approve of, even love, who we are), but many others also look outside for *validation* from others to bolster their own flagging self-esteem, a pattern laid down in childhood and hard to change. So, not only does one partner look for this in the other, but also believes that being well-mated will also win societal approval—the 'I am nothing without a man/woman' syndrome.
- Relationships are almost inevitably an emotional roller-coaster, and the ensuing thrills and spills make us *feel alive*, sometimes to the point of addiction, where if things are running smoothly, one of the parties introduces 'a little drama to spice things up.'

These three needs underpinning relationships propel us into them, but can also scramble the purity of whatever love emerges, as it streams from our soul, through us, and out to our partner. So how do these needs color the three stages of love?

Stage 1: Infatuation. Romantic relationships often begin with head-over-heels falling in love, where each partner savors the other with all five senses on overdrive ... and often *overload* while reality takes a hike and love really is blind. This stage can take three months in a non-soulmate relationship, where the two souls have not previously interacted, but only days when two soulmates meet up.

Stage 2: Adjustment. Over the next year (for non-soulmates), the initial fool's rush gives way to reality, and the partners see each other for who they really project what they are, i.e., M-4/W-4 moves closer to M-3/W-3. This revelation is either the basis for a healthy reality-based partnership in which the couple can open to each other and work towards unity, or the 'kiss of death' to the relationship, where the partners get defensive when their needs are not met and withdraw to get 'breathing room.' The quality of the sex is the best barometer of the passion in a relationship, and either becomes better or spirals down into a habit. Both partners should strive to stay fully aware as they move through this transition stage towards the third stage.

In a soulmate relationship, the couple could move through this stage in weeks or months rather than a year, because trust comes more readily and the couple doesn't need the usual protective defensive walls.

Stage 3: Maturity. Driven by the memory of Stage 1's highs, relationships that survive the tumultuous Stage 2 allow the partners to move into greater intimacy. Also, the relationship becomes the third entity in the equation and is nurtured as such. The three 'me-first' needs give way to 'us-first,' and each partner tends as much to the needs of the other as to their own. They look out for and 'vote for' one another based on honest appreciation for who the other *truly* is, i.e., M-2/W-2.

This stage is marked by deep surrender into the relationship, while the partners retain their own identities. Thus the 'taking from' of Stage 1 gracefully transitions to 'giving to,' as the partners see through ego-personality into each other's souls, i.e., M-1/W-1. This blossoms into true commitment, wherein lies the courage to be vulnerable, loyalty and mutual honoring. The bedrock on which this happens is the deep inner security, self-esteem and self-love that both parties have for themselves.

A possible problem here is that men and women tend to go through the three stages at different rates. Being more intuitive and in touch with their feelings than men, women sense earlier when they've found 'a keeper.' Men, on the other hand, often take longer 'just to be sure.' A woman ready for Stage 3 may find her man still mired in Stage 2—uncomfortable for both and a source of friction. Men may compound the problem by being less demonstrative of their feelings, especially when in the company of other men.

Finally, arriving at Stage 3 isn't an event but the beginning of a life-long (well, the life of the relationship) process, and the biggest blunder is complacency and failure to make the daily investment in the relationship. As with any living thing, it must be regularly nurtured (but without getting self-conscious about it).

Acceptance

Testosterone outpictures in men as a drive for autonomy, freedom, independence and a sense of being effective, of making a difference in the world. From boyhood, courage in the face of fear is rewarded and extolled. Role models are portrayed in countless movies, whether set in boardrooms, battlefields, submarines or boxing rings, where being 'strong' isn't a choice but a *necessity*. The mottos 'winning is everything' and 'failure is not an option' sum up the male drive, and the specter of screwing up makes men go the extra mile. From boyhood, they are measured and judged, whether it's being picked for the team or locker room ribbing about penis size. Men are engrained with being heroes but, aside from war, are denied the opportunity for heroism.

On top of these pressures, add the need to be gentle, open and caring around women, without being dubbed a 'girly-man' and you have a powerful mix of conflicting demands. A woman who can truly *accept* a man as-is will be well-rewarded with a loyal partner and best friend.

So who is this 'as-is' person? Who we are psychologically is an amalgam of three things: (1) personality (e.g., the Michael attributes); (2) imprinting from our earliest moments in the womb; and (3) soul influence.

Many people are Type A, where the role of soul is not acknowledged, sought after, honored or valued. Personality is who they are, and imprinting dictates how they act. The only way soul and spirit guides can make themselves known is by arranging notable events such as car accidents to get attention, and prompt remarks such as, "Maybe there's something I'm not getting here."

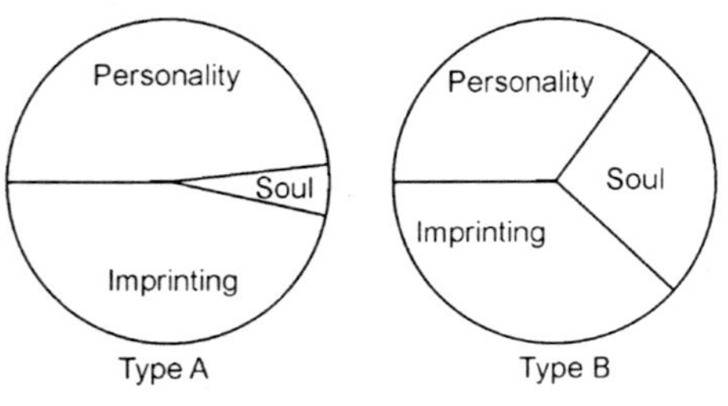

Personality and Imprinting

Type B folks turn this around completely and see personality as a tool crafted by soul, with imprinting as just a challenging starting point. Type Bs elicit input from soul and guides at every turn, and are ever-vigilant for signs and synchronicities. Their credo is, "Soul, thy will be done," because they know they are an emissary of soul, but also know enough to know they don't know enough about soul's agenda to go it alone.

Sub-personalities

The previous section talked about personality as if it were a monolithic whole. However, psychologists know well that we don't have just a personality, but are actually made up of many different *sub-personalities,* where each sub-personality has its own identity and individuality. (This has nothing to do with split personality disorder, which is a clinical pathology. All healthy people have their collection of sub-personalities.) You call upon the different sub-personalities in your make-up to interact with your children, your parents, your boss, your mate, your friends, and the cop who writes you a speeding ticket.

Due to their upbringing, most people get locked into and limited by a small group of these sub-personalities, called *primary selves.* Other selves of which the primary selves disapprove are relegated to the background, and are called *disowned selves.* Your primary selves form a committee that runs your life, and the disowned selves are a silenced, dissenting voice.

Whether or not you are aware of them, the small group of primary sub-personalities creates your whole life experience, including your patterns in relationship, your inner feelings, your recreation, your career, and your finances, health and creativity. If any part of your life is not working, don't look for an outside cause; instead, try to figure out which sub-personalities are responsible.

Getting to know your sub-personalities is a source of great personal growth because you widen your repertoire and can express more and more of your 'selves.' You will be able to connect with other people at a deeper level, which will imbue your relationships with more intimacy and love. The alternative is stagnation, as you live in the narrow but deep rut to which your primary selves confine you.

The process of creating sub-personalities begins in the crib, where you soon learn you must rely on others for everything, and your Vulnerable Child sub-personality emerges. Then you learn that some behaviors bring rewards and cuddles if you please adults, so with repetition, your Pleaser sub-personality forms and joins your 'ego-committee.' When younger siblings come along, a Controller sub-personality may develop to try to run their lives. Or, if you're the youngest, a Protector may emerge to deal with any bullying.

If you're a dominant, assertive type, you may add a Driver sub-personality to organize your playmates that rules your adult life, too. Or a picky person may develop a Perfectionist sub-personality that also stays around for a lifetime.

How your parents treat you is a major factor. Even if their criticism of you is well-meaning, you will develop an Inner Critic that will be constantly on your case, much like Ruiz' Parasite.

Each of the primary selves that make up your ego-committee will eschew its opposite qualities and disown that self with those qualities. For example, your Perfectionist will disown your Sloppy Self, and your Inner Critic will disown your Rebel sub-personality. By disowning these sub-personalities, their behavioral responses are not available to you, so you will not be able to kick back and relax, or stand up to authority. This can cause inner conflict and stress.

Also, it means that neither you nor those around you know 'the real you' but only your masks. You present a different sub-personality to the various people in your life, as if you have dozens of masks and you keep slipping one off and another on. However, these primary sub-personalities, developed to protect you as a child, become barriers to intimacy in your adult relationships, so it is vital that you get to know who these selves are.

As a couple, thoughtful, loving dialog will help reveal much about your respective sub-personalities. Interaction between the two of you is actually between two sub-personalities in your primary selves. For example, one partner's Driver may evoke his partner's Pleaser, or an Inner Parent may evoke the other's Inner Child. Then the two sub-personalities interact in a narrow, limited bonding pattern where none of the partners' larger needs get met.

If these two people become familiar with their primary and disowned selves, their interpersonal repertoire is dramatically widened, and much personal growth happens. This also breaks down many barriers to soul, so their love can evolve from erotic to agape, or unconditional love.

One Wants to Leave; the Other Doesn't

Once one wants to leave, the relationship is over. Even if the partner stays, it is with less than 100 percent commitment, which is no partnership. So, rather than hanging on and becoming bitter enemies, split while you're still friends. Parting with dignity, respect and honor allows you to lick your wounds and move on. And don't fall into the trap of saying, "There will never be another relationship like this, so I'm doomed." You're half right; there *will* never be another one like this ... but the next may be better!

Healthy relationships don't just happen, even between soul mates; they take constant maintenance by thought, word and deed. Keeping the fires of love burning requires a steady supply of new kindling. Take each other for granted and even soul cannot keep things hot.

Also, keep the flow of communication going. Once a barrier goes up over some unvoiced gripe, you're doomed and, without intense remedial action, it's only a matter of time.

Following a major transgression, such as infidelity within agreed monogamy, you can: (1) follow Agreement #2, not take it personally and forgive; (2) strike back in revenge; (3) simply leave. Just as parents impose *consequences* for certain behaviors, a couple must have talked things through in advance. If you agree on mutual monogamy, then what consequence does infidelity carry? You can't just break Agreement #3, and assume anything.

Ten Commandments for Soulful Relationships

1. *Nurture nature.* Your guides bring you together, nature handles the chemistry, but you must nurture the outcome. This means learning what makes your mate happy … and unhappy, then acting accordingly. And as the years roll by, stay on top of this, for it's easy to become complacent.

2. *Honor the Second Agreement.* If something happens in the relationship to put your ego out of joint, don't let pride get in the way. Unless done out of spite, misunderstandings do happen, so call on your higher self for some perspective and to remind you of the love you both once felt for each other.

3. *Fix you yourself.* Your mate is not your therapist, so if you need to work on your own issues, do so outside the relationship. Do not pollute the sacred space between you by dumping your stuff into it, or subsume yourself so completely into the relationship that you don't have the space to do the work.

4. *Leave your mate alone.* You are not your mate's therapist and have no right to try to change him or her, apart from encouraging growth. Love is about acceptance and remembering the Mars/Venus thing.

5. *Honor the Third Agreement.* Do not assume you know your mate's mind or that your mate knows yours. Assumptions lead to unmet expectations, which lead to trouble, so avoid them.

6. *Honor the First Agreement.* It's tempting in a mated relationship to try to manipulate your mate or twist the truth to make you look better or to even downright lie. However, anything less than the honest truth dishonors your mate.

7. *That goes for actions, too.* Being impeccable also applies to what you do, so weave the Golden Rule into every action you take. Honor and loyalty are two cornerstones of a relationship, and any deceitful action dishonors your mate because you know something he or she doesn't, which violates integrity.

8. *Encourage growth.* Accept that over the years, you will both change. You can choose to find this threatening or, with a solid foundation, you can savor and enjoy each other's personal growth and evolution.

9. *Clean up your own messes.* Your mate is not your parent. Scapegoating your mate is tempting when things go wrong, but there's only one person responsible for your life—you.

10. *Cultivate a 'gratitude attitude.'* If you're in a relationship that brings you joy, you are blessed indeed, so thank soul, your guides, and your mate. Nurture your gratitude within and express it frequently. Show it with spontaneous acts of kindness and gift-giving. And be appreciative when your mate reciprocates.

Sex, Lies and DNA

When we talk of balancing the spiritual with the physical, we must be aware of a deep, hidden drive within the physical that gets us into incredible trouble, especially involving men and young women, by which men lose all reason and risk going to jail, losing their jobs and their families. But what unknown force makes men lose their senses? It's called the biological imperative—or the power of DNA.

Buried deep within every cell in your body are two tiny strands of amino acids in a pattern that is uniquely yours. The one thing that all DNA shares, however, is the drive to propagate itself, a drive that is hardwired into your cells, way beneath the level of your conscious awareness. And there's nothing you can do about it except acknowledge it and strive to balance it with the spiritual side of your psyche. It was there when our forebears were swinging from trees, and it's still there today, pretty much unchanged except for some ET interference. In fact, it's the very reason we *are* here at all.

This fascinating DNA imperative to propagate shows up differently in men and women, all because the female has the womb in which to carry a fetus in her body and the breasts to suckle it for a couple of years. This means that a pregnant female (of most live-bearing species) needs good nourishment, a safe place to live, adequate resources, and protection from predators for months, even years. Her biological imperative drives her to obtain and hang onto these things so that her DNA will propagate into the next generation and beyond. But how does she get these things? By attracting and keeping a strong male to build a house or fight for a cave, hunt for food, and protect her and her offspring until they are self-sufficient, able to mate and pass on her DNA to their children. She would find the most suitable male to be the strongest, most powerful and resourceful, and owning the most territory. Appearance is less important, except in so far as it denotes health. This is why we see gorgeous young women on the arms of older, richer, more powerful men, but who are less attractive than the women. Physical attraction plays a smaller role in the 'package deal' that women seek; without realizing it, she has other priorities.

Males are driven to supply these things, because their children carry his DNA, too, but he must be sure that it's *his* DNA that impregnates the female(s) whom he supports; hence the fighting off of other males so they cannot impregnate his female(s). Successfully fighting off other males also ensures that only *his* DNA is passed on, which keeps the species healthy.

So the imperative shows up in males as a twofold drive: First, he is genetically driven to impregnate as many healthy young females as possible, to maximize the chances that *his* DNA will be what goes into future generations. Second, he is driven to keep other males away from his female once they have mated, to make sure she is not also impregnated by another male. (This explains why, when a new lion takes over a pride, he often kills all the cubs sired by the ousted male. They are not his DNA and he will expend no resources to protect another male's genetic legacy.)

The main drive in the female is to ensure the ongoing protection of her offspring, and her biggest worry is that the male will abandon the family and go off to start a new one with a younger, more attractive female … and double his DNA propagation chances.

This deep biological drive explains much human behavior. Even though our social patterns have changed greatly in the last few millennia, primate species (which is where we evolved from, plus a little extraterrestrial DNA) go back 25 million years, and a strong genetic drive has been built into our cells. So this applies to *all* primates, even though we might prefer that it didn't.

For example, when a husband admits to being unfaithful, his wife's first question is often, "Do you love her?" rather than, "Did you have sex with her?" Biologically, she fears abandonment more than her husband's DNA getting spread around. If he doesn't love the other woman, he is less likely to go off with her to begin a new family.

The man's first question to his wife, however, is often, "Did you have sex with him?" because this raises the specter of another male's DNA impregnating his mate. He would then be raising another male's offspring and not *his*. Biologically, he is less worried about his mate loving another man than he is about not expending resources on protecting another male's DNA.

This also explains the double-standard in many Third World countries that are heavily patriarchal, where there's no real penalty for male adultery. For women, however, it's public stoning in the village square. The culture condones men sowing their DNA widely but reacts sharply when a woman risks impregnation by other than her husband's DNA.

In September 2003, the newspapers were reporting that a Nigerian woman faced being stoned to death, not for adultery but for just having sex out of wedlock. Her accusers planned to dig a big hole, bury the poor woman up to her neck and then throw rocks at her head. Nice. And her alleged lover? He was acquitted for lack of evidence. Fortunately, due to the international outcry, an Islamic panel of five judges voted 4-1 for a less cruel penalty, but it's horrifying that even *one* judge wanted the woman's head used for target practice by a rock-throwing mob.

Like it or not, we supposedly civilized humans are still driven by our biology, which explains why men are irresistibly drawn to healthy, attractive young women and seek sex with them, even to the point of crossing the age of consent and risking jail. This drive throws the spiritual/human balance out of kilter, unless the male is fully conscious and rational, and can say, "My role is to protect and nurture the younger members of my tribe, and not violate them." However, the fact that, biologically, women aged 14 – 16 are in their child-bearing prime makes that very difficult, as many male schoolteachers have learned the hard way … from a jail cell. (In the summer of 2004, over a dozen male teachers in Clark County, NV were in jail, arrested for having sex with female students, aged from 12 to 16. Pity they didn't read this first.)

Women, too, are still driven by their biological imperative. When choosing a mate, her main concern is, "Has he got his act together? Good job, nice place to live, skills, resources?" Even though she may have her own house, good job, healthy bank account and not want children, biologically she is still driven to find a powerful man. Of course, exceptions occur all the time. An older woman takes a young drifter as a lover because he looks good in tight blue jeans. Or the young go-getting male falls for the older woman. But other factors are at work here, such as the young man's need to heal the relationship with his mother.

The biological imperative reveals an often overlooked piece of the human equation, and knowing about it should help us balance the spiritual with the physical. Of course, the imperative is overlaid with cultural and societal conventions that differ around the world, but is itself deeply unchanging. When it comes to humans, the biological imperative knows nothing about contraception, religion, or pornography laws. It is what it is … and it's still alive and kicking.

I've known about this for 20 years, but was pleased when David P. Schmitt, an evolutionary psychologist at Bradley University in Peoria, Ill, published a report in August 2003, saying, "This study provides the largest and most comprehensive test yet conducted on whether the sexes differ in the desire for sexual variety. The results are strong and conclusive—the sexes differ, and these differences appear to be universal." This study caused a firestorm in academic circles, and the hordes descended on poor David. Scholars who assert the primacy of culture in shaping human behavior charged him with practicing not science but 'wishful thinking' and justifying his own male urges. Sociologists claim that differences in sexuality stem from a double standard in male-dominated societies, where female sexuality is tightly controlled. I just ask, "Where did that double standard come from in the first place? Don't confuse basic biology with superimposed sociology."

Soul Age and Relationships

One of the most important aspects of romantic relationships is harmony between the couple's belief systems and approaches to life. And because soul age influences beliefs so heavily, it is probable that both parties are the same soul age. As a memory jogger, the soul ages again are:

- *Infant:* Figuring out the Earth plane rules.
- *Baby:* Learning, following and enforcing the rules.
- *Young:* Breaking the rules with, 'he who dies with the most toys wins,' where the toys could be money, power, territory, trophy wife, or any other status symbol.
- *Mature:* Going inward with emotional exploration, or 'life in a soap opera,' full of drama and karma.
- *Old:* 'Been there, done that,' cosmic boredom, and teaching others what you know.

To form a healthy mated relationship (except for karmic relationships, where two people are compelled by soul to be together with little choice in the matter), the parties must 'get along' on many levels, including compatible world views, which depend highly on soul age wisdom. A Baby Soul male may be appalled at his Young Soul girlfriend's disregard of the 'rules,' and a Mature Soul wife may get frustrated with her Old Soul husband's lack of emotional intensity. Old Souls just look at everyone else busily running around like headless chickens, and shake their heads. So, except at the boundaries (such as Late Young and Early Mature), different ages may simply not get along well enough to even make it through dating and courtship.

However, souls can freely explore the clash of soul age understanding in family relationships, which are another goldmine of Challenges.

Family Relationships

After romantic relationships, families are our greatest source of both joy and pain. But remember, at the soul level, we carefully choose our family members to bring us the specific Challenges we need to test our Resources. Even the soul whose incarnation is violated by an incestuous uncle knew this may happen. Of course, this in no way justifies such callous treatment of someone younger and more innocent, for the scars inflicted may never heal, and will color the rest of the child's life.

Apart from the aberration of incest, family members are usually only too happy to give you a piece of their mind, so they make excellent Wilsons once we compensate for any distortions in them. Some families are veritable Halls of Mirrors, however, reflecting back distorted images of distorted interpretations of distorted perceptions expressed using our limited language. (No wonder we see people screaming at each other on the Jerry Springer and Maury Povich shows.)

Soul Ages in Family Relationships

Not only do soul age conflicts occur naturally here, but the incoming soul actually sets up conflicts to present Challenges in which to explore unconditional love and the ways in which ego-personality blocks it.

Conflicts in belief always underpin conflicts in behavior, for behavior always follows belief. That is, no matter how bizarre people's behavior is, they always act consistently according to their beliefs. Ted Bundy felt perfectly justified in killing upwards of 50 young women, Jim Jones felt perfectly justified in getting 900 people to drink cyanide-laced Kool-Aid, and Jeffery Dalmer felt perfectly justified in killing scores of young men and eating their flesh.

For example, suppose a Baby Soul couple living in a small town have a happy routine, he as police chief and she as chairwoman of the Kiwanis. They attend their civic lunches and church functions, cozy in their little lives. At least until along comes a Young Soul son. He is aggressive, competitive and can't stand their blind, unquestioning adherence to the Bible and their faith in the country's leaders. Being a Young Soul, he sees clearly the greed and corruption in Washington and in the boardrooms across America because that is exactly what he would do if he were there. When he grows up, he launches into a life fueled by greed and thirst for power at any price, which horrifies his Baby Soul parents. Then, rather than face a lengthy jail sentence for embezzlement, he blows his brains out with his father's service revolver. The family and whole town are devastated, not realizing they've just witnessed the effect of Soul Age clash. All just the Source finding out more about itself … and no one really dies—they just go Home early.

Two Mature Souls locked in deep emotional intensity may find their Old Soul daughter curiously aloof from their soap opera lives, and interpret her behavior as unloving or uncaring. The conflict lies in what she cares about—the plight of whales and dolphins, say—while her mother's alcoholism and her father's mistresses are unimportant to her.

The scenarios are endless and, although soul age doesn't explain everything, it is one parameter for evaluating conflict in families. But what can you do if it *is* the cause? Live with it … because you can't change it. An incarnation is limited by the wisdom and understanding of its soul fragment. Although a Baby Soul incarnation living in the Bible Belt is intellectually capable of reading any New Age book ever written, would its ego-personality even *want* to? Unlikely, because it may not have the desire, understanding and soul experience to transcend its fundamental Christian beliefs.

It's vital to emphasize that such a lifetime is not 'lesser' than that of, say, a spiritual master, just as a first grader in school is not 'lesser' than a high school graduate. They are just at different points on the timeline, and for a New Ager to look down on a Bible-Belter would be the height of arrogance, not to mention a source of self-karma. Unfortunately, Bible-Belters are not so charitable to New Agers.

Families and Soul Groups

Another major factor in family relationships is whether you have incarnated with family members before. If relationships are intense, for better or worse, it is probable that you have done lifetimes before with incarnations of the same soul. Depending on your 'history' with them, you will form either loving, trusting relationships, or ones of mutual antagonism. If you are relatively indifferent to parents and siblings, chances are, this is your first time with them. You chose your parents for the DNA, imprinting and circumstances they provided, and not to have in-depth relationships with them. This happens particularly among Old Souls, who are here for the Shift (see Chapter 14) and not to play karmic games in a family setting.

Old Souls who wonder why they don't have the close family relationships that their friends do should find it reassuring to know that this wasn't their reason for being here. Instead, they have a mission, and intense family karmas would simply be a distraction. So, they leave home early, seldom write or call, and visit rarely, if ever. If you are one of these, do not feel guilty, and parents, do not feel slighted. Family interaction just wasn't part of the deal. Your parents and siblings are not part of your soul group and you did not come together to have a 'Brady Bunch' experience or spit nails at each other on Jerry Springer.

Relationships with Children

Within families, the relationship between parents and children is second only to mated relationships in impact. The relationship between the generations is important because it is only here that the cycle of spiritual myopia can be broken and humanity be pulled out of its nose dive.

All problems within humanity stem from low self-esteem. People who do not see themselves as magnificent sovereign souls with high self-esteem do not see others as magnificent sovereign souls, so they trample on each other's sovereignty. If children are taught they are just ego-personalities, and not yet very mature ones, then that is how they will act.

Every single block to love and self-love that we adults have was put there before the age of seven by someone we trusted and thought 'they had it figured out.' As children, we saw adults as perfect, powerful and infallible, so we took their criticism of us as proof that we were flawed and unworthy of love. As a result, only one in a thousand of us is not a 'recovering child of parents.' Because parents go through no training for that role, most really botch up the job horribly, leaving scarred and damaged children who grow up not loving themselves, and are therefore unable to love or be loved. Then *they* in turn become parents … and so it goes on.

A nasty outcome from parental blundering can be the condition known as Borderline Personality Disorder, or BPD. The DSM-IV states that BPDs display instability in interpersonal relationships and self-image due to unstable childhoods. This results in desperate efforts to avoid real or imagined abandonment, flip-flopping between idealizing and debasing their intimate partner. They are also impulsive with such activities as spending, sex, substance abuse, reckless driving, and binge eating, and suffer from intense mood swings, irritability, or anxiety. BPDs also have difficulty controlling anger and outbreaks of physical violence. Mature Souls may choose such intense self-karma in order for Spirit to study it, but heaven help the partner of a BPD.

A particularly unfortunate form of BPD is Narcissistic BPD, where a lack of psychological awareness leads to problems in handling intimate relationships. Narcissists see everything as having to do with them, and are hypersensitive to any slights or imagined insults. The DSM-IV lists indicators as feelings of grandiosity and self-importance, obsession with fantasies of fame and power, conviction of being special, requiring constant admiration and adulation, expecting priority treatment and full compliance with their demands, and arrogance coupled with rage when frustrated, contradicted, or confronted. NBPDs are hell to be in a relationship with, but to the rest of the world, they are poised, affable, witty and charming.

In *Breaking Free from Boomerang Love*, Lynn Melville recounts being in love with a man with NBPD and, even though she knew the relationship was destroying her, every time she left, he pleaded for her to return, which, just like a boomerang, she did … until she got smart and got out for good.

Children need a stable, consistent structure, firm boundaries, and clear consequences for infractions that are enforced with compassion, or even tough love. They do not want their parents to be their 'best friends,' but they *do* want to feel respected, through being listened to and having quality time spent with them.

With the responsibility of parenting comes the authority and obligation to set the boundaries and enforce consequences. Of course, kids will rebel, for how else can they grow, but when they push too far, they expect the world to push back; if it doesn't, they feel unloved and unsupported. Better to learn this at home than in the Criminal Justice system … for *that* pushes back *really* hard, and you don't want your parenting to be limited only to jail visits.

Not being a child psychologist or even a parent, I cannot stick my neck out any further other than to point to those children born after 1982. Many of them have remarkable spiritual gifts and understanding. Given a variety of names—Indigo Children, Crystal Children and Star Children—they are unmistakably different, and some adults find them unsettling. They come into the world sensing they are 'on mission' and have a problem with anything that gets in the way of that mission. They despise senseless rules, have a high level of creativity, and are frustrated with a school system that does not challenge their creativity in any way. This can result in Attention Deficit Disorder, and if left unchallenged, their creativity may be expressed through outlets such as school violence. They have their own inner self-esteem, so they do not need to appease anyone in order to win external validation and approval, which can make them appear antisocial. In reality, they are just dancing to their own drum, and not society's.

For example, here's what one Japanese Crystal Child recently said to James Twyman when he was on tour there:

"If we can spread love, we will have peace. All children wish for peace, so just wait for the new children who are coming into the world now! These children are all really serious about love. Children, including me, are more open about expressing love than grown-ups, so you see, it's not really a role; it's our natural state. We don't think of it as a role. That's why it's easier for children to spread love. Don't worry, we will spread the message of love no matter what. Each of us has love in our hearts, and if we can spread it, such a wonderful new love will be born. This love has already started, and we'll see more and more love in the coming days. Joyous days are waiting for us."

These Old Souls in young bodies are humanity's salvation. They took Earth lives not to learn, grow and face Challenges, but to be in place to move Earth though the Shift around 2012, and to be the new leaders, teachers, and healers of the post-Shift world. It will be up to the 'old guard' to recognize their role and defer to them. As it happens, most of the old guard in the West lived through the liberating Sixties (even if they didn't inhale), and will be more flexible than the previous generation. Already, the more aware Indigo Children are serving as spiritual teachers to the adults around them, and do so with rare purity and innocence. (More in Chapter 15.)

Relationships with Friends, Colleagues, etc.

"You choose your friends but not your family," the old saying goes, but only at the ego-personality level. At the soul level, you choose your family specifically to create/discharge karma, to serve as mirrors for each other's soul growth, or just for entry to the Earth plane.

But, apart from karmic binding where you are under soul contract to interact, you do consciously choose friends, colleagues and acquaintances. Why one person and not another? Basically you choose people who make you feel good, usually based on similar beliefs, worldviews and ego-personality compatibility. Or your choice is in your flight plan because of a shared mission.

It is likely that your close friends are fragments of souls from your own soul group, with whom your soul has co-incarnated before. This explains the initial mutual ease and trust when you meet, which serves as the bedrock of a lifetime friendship or even a business partnership. When you meet a soul that is new to you, that 'old buddy' energy isn't there, and establishing it can take a while. However, when new fragments of your respective souls meet up in other lifetimes, they will click right into 'old buddy' gear, thanks to the work you have done.

Relationships with Animals

The first thing to note about animals is the similarity in the reincarnation process to humans. Almost everything we have said about the soul's process in selecting a historical period, gender, body type, and circumstances is also true for animals. But the aspect that predominates at the soul level is that *they choose us* after a careful period of observation. My Old Soul black Labrador and I go way back, and we're old buddies. (By the way, his mission in this lifetime is to balance exercising free will within boundaries.)

Animal souls do have an advantage that we do not, in that they can incarnate in bodies of different species. However, once a soul has experienced a lifetime of closeness with humans, future incarnations will probably also involve human interaction because of the richness and growth that this offers, so this will limit the soul to domesticated species such as dogs, cats and horses. It is vital that we know our pets choose us from the soul plane for our mutual growth, joy and sharing of love. And they are wonderful teachers of unconditional love. Pets are also excellent 'health aids' for children, the elderly and the housebound.

Controversy often rages when dogs attack humans. Dogs are descended from wolves, and are territorial pack animals that will only attack if they feel threatened or someone trespasses on their territory. Two breeds receive particularly bad press—the pit bull and the rottweiler. These breeds are especially empathic, and sense and mirror the emotions of their human companions, so 'mean people' have mean dogs, while loving people have loving dogs. Many pit bulls have most loving temperaments … but their people are loving, too.

On a final note, we humans are not the pinnacle of spirituality on this planet. That honor goes to the cetaceans, who do not have the same veil between soul and incarnations that we do. They are fully aware and here on missions, as we are. To talk of 'quotas' for killing them for food is as abominable as the United Nations deciding how many citizens of each country can be culled and eaten each year.

When it comes to whaling, certain nations on this planet are still barbarians and the odious practice must stop before we can even think of calling our species anything other than spiritually primitive.

Relationships with the Deceased

*"Appreciate, validate and communicate with those in your life today
so that a medium like me doesn't have to do it for you."*

— John Edward, *Crossing Over*

On November 23, 2004, The Associated Press wire reported: "Las Vegas resident Lance Cpl. _________ was laid to rest Monday … in a ceremony that relatives said would have made him proud." There are only two things wrong with that sentence: (1) Putting a body in the ground does not lay anyone to rest; and (2) the young Marine probably *was* proud, as he stood there in full dress uniform for any psychic to see. We've still got a ways to go.

In another story reported in February 2005, the bodies of over 1,100 of those who crossed over in the World Trade Center cannot be identified from DNA because the technology isn't here yet. This leaves a lot of relatives in the position of having nothing to bury. One young widow said, "The emptiness of not taking someone home is beyond being able to explain. But you get the point of what are you going to get back? A fragment of a person? Is that my husband?" Again, we see the pain caused by identifying too closely with a physical body. The relatives of another person filled a casket with memorabilia and buried that so they would have a focal point for their grief when they visited the cemetery. It is sad that they are missing out by not knowing their loved ones are all around them but just on a higher dimension.

"My son's death five years ago left me devastated and I've stopped living" is heard all too often from those whom John Edward and James Van Praagh read on their shows. This actually compounds the tragedy of a loved one's death for several reasons. First, to be the cause of such pain is not what those who have crossed over want. In fact, our grief mars what, for them, is a time to celebrate arriving Home. They still love us and do not want to see us suffer in this way.

Second, although we factor grief into our planning for an Earth life (in fact, the Earth plane is the only plane where we even *can* study grief), it's only one facet of life. Admittedly, grief is to be explored thoroughly but, once done, it's done and we should move forward according to our life plan. Of course, remember the joy of being together but let go the pain of separation, for you'll be reunited in a few short years. So rather than focus on what you've lost, focus on what you had, still have and will continue to have.

I recently met someone who was very sad. He told me, "I've just come from a funeral. We buried my brother." He was a staunch Catholic so I didn't correct him but, in truth, they had just put in the ground an empty husk that his brother no longer needed … *not* his brother. His brother was probably standing right beside him with a hand on the guy's shoulder, and checking out who came to his funeral. However, his etheric body was vibrating a little too quickly for most people to see him. To those with their sixth sense operating, however, such as mediums, dogs and cats, and some children, he would have been quite visible.

Those who cross over don't actually go anywhere. Nor do the so-called 'deceased' cease. They are right here among us, listening to us, watching us, laughing and playing with us. Ask them for a sign, and the lights in your house may flicker, or the TV may change channels—two very easy things for them to do, whereas levitating the family dog may take a little more effort, not to mention scaring the hell out of the dog.

Ignore psychiatrists who tell you that talking to them is morbidly codependent and a refusal to accept reality. Feel free to chatter away about your daily life, for they enjoy being included. The time will come when you talk less and less as you move on through life, but know that just thinking of them brings them right to you, even after many years.

How do they talk to us? Any way they can, such as through our senses (a touch like a breeze, a characteristic scent or aroma, audible words, visually by materializing, feeling a presence, dropping thoughts into your mind, and so on). They love arranging synchronicities in our lives, and watching out for our safety and well-being. (The literature is full of cases in which a deceased loved one shows up to give a warning of impending danger.) They also manipulate the world around us, such as by having an exotic butterfly appear out of season. Whenever you get one of these after-death communications (ADC), it's vital to thank them for the sign they've given. Without your gratitude, they may quit bothering.

Recently, a friend was driving from Las Vegas to Sacramento, CA. In Barstow, he did something totally stupid—he put his transmission into PARK while the car was still moving, causing a truly horrible sound. He nursed the car to a repair shop, where he learned the bell housing was cracked. The cost to repair ($800 plus labor) was more than the car was worth, so it was a write-off. Waiting for a friend to come to get him, he asked Spirit why this had happened. His deceased wife, plus guides, showed up and told him, "There's a serious problem with the front end, and soon you would have lost steering and brakes, so we had to kill the car before it killed you. We wiped your mind momentarily so you would mess up the transmission."

Contemplating what would have happened if the front end had collapsed at freeway speeds, my friend was extremely grateful to Spirit for their intervention. And he got to complete his journey in a brand new rental car. Nice to know our loved ones watch over us, eh?

Dream Visitations

Of the three kinds of dream (psychic, symbolic and visitation, all discussed later), *visitation dreams* are pure ADCs and must be taken seriously. During sleep, our Superconscious Mind is free to roam the astral and soul planes, and meet up with those on the other side. As the Conscious Mind looks on and listens in, you think you're 'just dreaming,' when in fact you're *having a meeting*. Visitation dreams usually seem far more vivid, and when you wake up, you're convinced you actually were meeting with your loved one.

Of course, it's easy for skeptics to dismiss these dreams as 'wishful thinking,' but many people report dreams in which the visitor tells them something they didn't know, which later turns out to be true, so that explanation falls apart. Further, the dreamer often doesn't even know the visitor was ill, or had just died in an accident. In fact, moment-of-death dream visits are very common and seem to reassure the dreamer of the ongoing existence of the person crossing over. Visitors also show up on anniversaries, birthdays, or other special occasions.

Third-party visitations are also common, where the visitor has a message for someone other than the dreamer. This dream should be conveyed to the requested recipient, even though the message doesn't make sense to you; it will make sense to the intended recipient.

Skeptics will be quick to ridicule you and your claim of contact, but ADC is a well-proven fact, so do not let some knee-jerk debunker rob you of the joy that it brings. Our loved ones on the other side of the veil work hard to let us know they are still around, so accept their success with gratitude. And no, it's not just your wishful thinking—their presence has been objectively proven.

When you watch programs such as *Crossing Over with John Edward* or *Beyond with James Van Praagh*, note the people in the audience who have readings that put beyond doubt the reality of contact. Also, note that these people are not 'special' but are just ordinary folks. So what is true for them is also true for you. Just as their deceased parents, children, siblings, uncles and aunts are around them, *so are yours*. Just because they are on TV and get read by the medium does not make them different, and does not make their love stronger than yours. You, too, are surrounded by a sea of loved ones who have crossed over, so keep the lines of communication open.

Death-Related Visions

There are countless accounts in the many books dealing with After-Death Communications of our deceased loved ones appearing while the person visited was wide awake. These usually come at moments of great stress. Perhaps the best example is one reported by Melvin Morse, MD, in his book *Parting Visions*. Martha is the mother of four young children, and lives next door to her mother, who takes care of the children during the day while Martha is at work. One day, the mother dies unexpectedly of a heart attack, and Martha is heartbroken but holds herself together. A short while later, Martha's two youngest children die in a car wreck, and Martha continues to keep her act together.

The day before the funeral, Martha is at the funeral home, dressing the bodies of the dead children for the next day. Suddenly, all the grief over losing her mother and two children overwhelms her and she breaks down sobbing. Suddenly, she notices her mother standing beside her, smiling. The mother says, "It's okay. They are here with me now. I'll take care of them."

In a moment, Martha's grief was transformed. She suddenly saw the beauty of the grand scheme of things and her place in it. As a result, Martha went into nursing, but not just any nursing. She went into geriatric nursing, where she deals with death and dying every day.

In his book, Morse observes that such visions reveal to us that our lives are significant, important and meaningful. More than that, however, is the change that can occur in people who just read about them. In one study, the carefully selected subjects were given a psychological death-anxiety test to elicit their level of fear about death. Then they were given a package of information to read of other people's death-related visions, such as Martha's story above; and again they were tested. The study found that 87 percent of subjects had an increased belief in life after death, and a correspondingly reduced fear of death. They were also more determined to love others in their life unconditionally.

Another study involved those who had failed in their first suicide attempt. One half of the group was chosen as the control, and the other half was given a packet of death-related vision case studies to read. Both groups were then monitored. Among failed first-time suicides, the chance of a second attempt is up to *100 times greater* than for society as a whole, and the control group was no exception. But the repeat rate for the study group was practically zero.

Morse concludes that hearing about other people's death-related visions helps us all in many ways. For example, reading the studies:

- Validates our own intuition and prevents us from dismissing our own visions as not real.
- Reveals that we use only a tiny part of our brain and that we do not understand the mind/brain connection, freeing us up to being open to spiritual matters.
- Reassures us that there is a larger, meaningful pattern to the cosmos which we do not normally see, and that we too are part of that pattern. This erodes our fear of death, which allows us to LIVE with more gusto.

Grief and the Illusion of Death

It's vital that you fully grasp that death is an illusion *before* you or a loved one comes face-to-face with it. If you don't, the shock may throw you for such a loop, you won't be able to think rationally, and you will engage in the anger-denial-pity cycle rather than say, "Wow, you're about to go home. Wish I could, too."

Before I moved to Mexico for two years, I read dozens of books about the country's history, culture, people, etiquette, etc., to prepare myself. I emphasize *before* because once you're there, culture shock can make the rational absorption of information difficult, if not impossible. It's the same with going to the soul plane—learn all you can *before* the trip. Then, if you get slammed in a fatal car wreck, you're not hovering around, looking at your mangled body and wondering what to do. Instead, you're looking for the tunnel and ready for the grand adventure.

If it's a loved one about to cross over, there would be no grief. Of course, you'll miss the person's immediate physical presence but *there can be no grief.* How could you deny them their grand adventure? And you'll be together again in a few short years anyway, so what's the problem? Just remember, no one gets annihilated, erased or zeroed out, but just changes frequency slightly. They can still see everything in your daily life and are with you for all important occasions ... it's just that *you* can't see *them.*

Absolutely do not associate your loved ones with the bodies they once occupied. At death, what were once vital focal points become empty shells ... health hazards to be disposed of hygienically. They don't need them where they're going. To me, visiting cemeteries is gruesome and grizzly; remember them in life, not death.

Of course, you'll feel sad. That's only natural, as when your best friend moves away to take a new job or attend college. Change is an inevitable part of life, but no need to put your *life* on hold because a loved one has moved away. Look at things from the soul perspective and you will see how it was all carefully planned long before your respective births. And by whom? You, of course. You planned every last detail, so how can you grieve over your own agenda? No one took your loved one from you—it's all part of your impeccable plan!

Remember that on the back of every birth certificate is a death certificate, with the time and cause of death left blank. Life doesn't come with a written lease but a day-by-day rental agreement, and spirit can up and leave at a moment's notice, so let your loved ones know they are just that—loved.

Grief is just the other side of the coin stamped: Love. You can't have one side without the other. It's unavoidable; if you love, you will grieve, unless you and your beloved plan at the soul level to 'go out together.' What people in grief can't see is that their grief is 'love backing up.' All the love they had for the person who crossed over suddenly has nowhere to go, and backs up. Of course, having read so far, we know the person who crossed is still around and would really appreciate that love still directed towards them, so ideally, we call that person into our presence and pour our love out to them while thanking them profusely for our time together.

In my work, I edit many books about grief, usually by authors who were unprepared. Sometimes the loved one was ejected instantly from the body; others have a few months' notice of eviction. Either way, the usual response is, "Why me? Why now? Why?"

The only true response is: "Why not?" The fine print on the back of the flight plan you filed during Phase 1 (Pre-Life Planning phase) says you won't remember the time and means of return. (Phase 2 is the physical plane phase, and Phase 3 is the return to continue whatever you were doing on the soul plane before Phase 1.) The fine print does not say your mate, son, daughter, mother, father, brother or sister will all do Phase 3 together. That would leave the joy-sadness equation unbalanced … and that's not growth.

For most of us, we're guaranteed that one or more loved ones will do Phase 3 before us, so it's smart to be prepared. But you can't read books about grieving while you're grieving because your head's too messed up, so prepare while you can still rationally process a thought. That way, you'll still miss your loved one but you won't be plunged into a bottomless pit of grief.

Even if it's too late and you are grieving a 'loss,' what about grief support groups? Be careful about hanging out with people who reinforce the annihilation myth. ('Annihilation' comes from the Greek *nihil*, or 'nothing,' which we know is simply not what's happened. Consciousness is eternal and can *never* become 'nothing.')

Even knowing all this, however, it's tough to watch someone you love disintegrate daily. But it's vital to remember that the body in the bed, drooling or slurring its words, is *not* the person you love. It's just what they've been driving around in for a few decades and is a little worse for wear. To confuse your loved one with that battered body is a tremendous mistake, for your beloved is strong and whole in spirit. The body is just a visible focal point that's necessary for interacting on the physical plane, but it's not who you love. Your beloved (human or animal) is soul, spirit, mental body (mind), emotional body, and etheric body. The physical body is just a parking place for a few years, on a much longer journey that includes many such parking places of different genders, colors, races and even ET species.

When all those other bodies pull back, the physical body is just an empty shell, even though a lucrative industry has built up around it, giving it a lavish, ritual-laden burial costing thousands of dollars.

People might object to this section, saying, "But it's normal to grieve." That's only true when you don't know what's going on when your loved one crosses over. Grieving denies the natural cycle of birth-death-rebirth. And remember, no one really dies; we just graduate to Phase 3 and end up in much better digs than the ones down here. And death doesn't hurt ... in fact, it's blissful.

If by now you're calling me an insensitive monster, please remember, I'm an Old Soul and appreciate that other soul ages, Mature in particular, have grief in their flight plan. But if it hurts too much, just ask your soul for an Old Soul perspective, and it won't hurt so much. A young woman I heard of grieved so much when her fiancé died that she contemplated suicide. Never an option.

So what *is* the Old Soul perspective? Six things:

1. We all planned everything that happens.
2. The separation is only a temporary illusion.
3. Your loved one is still around and may not appreciate the tethering effect of grief.
4. Sack-cloth and ashes don't become you.
5. The love is still there.
6. Life comes with no guarantees.

The last point leads to the huge topic of *gratitude*. In this country of extremes, earthquakes, floods, tornados, tsunamis, wild fires and hurricanes can strip any of us of everything at any time, even our lives, so the *only* stance is one of gratitude that you're not in the middle of a natural disaster *right now*. Also, you're probably not being mugged, raped or murdered *right now*. So be grateful, *right now*.

If you're reading this to a terminally ill loved one, *right now* stop to express appreciation for their role in your life. *Right now!*

Stages of Grief

Grief usually has four stages, and the only variable may be how quickly one works through the transitions:

1. *Disbelief, denial and 'busyness.'* Immediately following the crossing of a loved one either suddenly or after a brief illness, there is much to do—hospitals and coroners, maybe a police investigation, medical and life insurance, memorial services, funeral arrangements may all need to be taken care of. We attend to these things in a numb, almost fugue state, often forgetting to eat or sleep until forced to. We manage to stave off accepting the reality of our loss, but when the dust settles, reality sets in.

2. *The Crevasse.* As we begin to accept that our loss is permanent and that we won't see that person again, we can feel as if we've fallen into a deep crevasse in a glacier and the gap has closed up over our head. We can see other people moving around up on the surface, but we're engulfed by depression, helplessness and hopelessness. The latter can be particularly hard, especially in the case of loss of a child or mate, where we had been expecting a life with them in it, growing old together or watching a child grow up. We had *hope* for that relationship, and now that hope has been dashed. You will *not* be walking hand-in-hand along a beach again. Or you will never again wash the mud out of that soccer uniform. The loss of hope can be devastating, and it can feel as if there's no point to anything, even your next breath.

3. *Acceptance.* Due to a miracle akin to new buds sprouting in early spring, you finally accept your loss and a ray of hope filters down into your crevasse. Maybe you *can* go on with your life and achieve something with it. Maybe you *weren't* to blame for the accident. Maybe you feel *less guilty* for being the survivor.

4. *Balance.* Although life will never be 'normal' again, slowly a new normal develops as you emerge from your crevasse into the sunlight on the surface. You can say to the world, "My mate/son/daughter crossed over and I really miss them greatly, but I'm okay now." You can face the world with-

out worrying about being hurt again, and you go on, seeing the beauty all around you, giving gratitude for having had that special person in your life, however briefly.

The progression through the stages is not linear, and you can slip backwards, only to pick yourself up again and keep going. The timing is entirely individual, depending largely on your beliefs.

If you take life personally and believe in a vengeful God, you can be in grief, guilt, anger and blame for decades, even for the rest of your life. But if your worldview is similar to that presented in this book, your progression can take only a few months.

Yes, as souls you all planned this, long before incarnating, to offer learning and growth to all concerned. Maybe the rugged individualist wanted to learn the dependency of being cared for during illness and death, or maybe the child sought to bring the parents closer. Only the souls involved know, and you may not find out until you yourself cross over. If you're impatient, you can consult a reputable psychic medium and ask, "What was *that* all about?" Or you may already know in your heart; living with soul can do that. And, of course, those on the soul plane are busy pumping energy to you, especially during dreams.

If you know someone working through the stages of grief, you have the opportunity for compassion and consolation. Rather than letting that person struggle with what they have lost, you can point out what was shared while both were alive. Even a baby who lives only minutes has already given great gifts to the parents, and its soul will happily wait until they conceive again. It is important to remember that the baby's soul is a vast spiritual entity on its own journey of growth and learning, and it got a lot out of the lead-up and birth itself.

If the griever's mate has returned to the soul plane, the mate will be working from across the veil, sending energy and loving support, and it is vital that grief not be allowed to block this, for that makes it so much harder for souls to be supportive.

Remember that love must keep moving, otherwise it backs up as grief, so encourage your friend or relative to keep the love flowing towards the loved one—that does them both immeasurable good. Ask the crossover to send unmistakable signs of continued presence in the life of the griever, and encourage the griever to keep on the lookout for them, such as one or more butterflies, or a favorite piece of music on the radio. Our loved ones can be *very* inventive when it comes to reassuring us of their continued existence.

One man whose father had died from a sudden illness was consumed by grief that exhausted him so much, he had to take frequent naps. During one nap, he received a full-blown visitation by his father, who said, "I came back for one very particular reason—to stop you from grieving my so-called 'death.' I wasn't sure I'd be able to get through to you, but now that you see how alive I am, you can understand how pointless it is to grieve—it really makes it harder for us to do what we're meant to do. Just remember from now on that we're not only still alive but more alive than we ever were before. So when you think about me, I want you to be happy for me, not mournful."

The hardest part of recovery may be forgiveness if a third party was involved—the drunk driver who killed your child or the bungling car-jacker who killed your mate, say. Again, none of this is random but plays out according to everyone's flight plan on file. However, can you bring yourself to forgive that person? Not condone, but forgive? If you cannot, but instead hold blame and hatred in your aura, you are the second victim. For any spiritual growth in this lifetime, you *must* forgive.

Grief is the 'great leveler,' because whether you're the chairman of the board or the janitor, it hits you the same. If both men lost their sons in the same accident, both men would grieve as fathers and as human beings. And this is one of grief's gifts—that of giving us a uniquely human experience. After all, you cannot experience grief on the soul plane because no one dies; soul is eternal.

Suppose you were worrying about whether the color of the new couch matched that of the drapes, and there's a knock at the door. "I'm from the coroner's office and have some bad news. There's been an accident. Perhaps you should sit down." Would you still be worrying about color coordination? I don't think so.

Grief can only happen if you believe someone you love has been taken from you *permanently*. So grief stems from us having forgotten that this does not happen. Grief therefore arises from not knowing the truth, and the *perception* of loss rather than an *actual* loss. If you expand your worldview to include soul, then *no one ever dies*.

From soul's perspective, earth lives are about growth and learning through challenge and intensity, and grief brings both of those. It calls upon us to summon our finest resources to deal with it—strength, compassion, forgiveness—and in doing so, we are truly living with soul.

Inspirational Words from Ptaah

Ptaah is an ancient being who channels through Jani King (*www.ptaah.com*), and has some inspirational words on the subject:

"If you are feeling sad that you did not have time to say the words you would have said, we say to you, say them now! You will be heard. Your heart is known and if you think there is any forgiveness required, it is only for you to be kind and compassionate to you. In the after-death, the heart is truly known and there is not anything to forgive.

"We say to you that truly it is more fitting that you celebrate the passing of your people with great gusto. Celebrate their lives. Celebrate the gift they have been to you. Focus on the wondrousness that was their lives, and the joy and vitality that is their now life, in the after-death. When you may do it thusly, you will find that truly the grief is replaced by a quiet contentment in the knowing that as each of you creates your birthing and life, so indeed you do, at a very deep level, create your circumstances of dying and death. To come again into the all knowing, the wholeness, and new choice points in your eternal game of being the Source experiencing Itself, however, wherever, and whenever It may.

"I love and honor you eternally in your eternal games.

"Namasté."

Living Will

Finally, even though you might be quite ready to return home rather than remain a vegetable on life-support, how do you convey that if you're brain-dead? That's where a living will comes in, but watch the wording, for the medical/legal world can be a minefield. If a living will specifies, "no extraordinary resuscitative measures to be taken," but an Alzheimer patient gets some food stuck in the throat, is the Heimlich Maneuver extraordinary, or just commonsense First Aid? Or how about an antibiotic in the case of pneumonia?

A Google search on 'living will' yields over a half-million sites, and you can download a template for your state for under $10. Around $50 will buy you some paralegal help, and for $350, an attorney will do it for you. It makes sense for you and your loved ones to make your wishes known while you still have all your mental faculties. And leave copies with doctors, lawyers and any relatives who might be party to a possible 'Do Not Resuscitate' decision in the event that the three standards are met: (1) mental incapacity to make a DNR decision; (2) inability to communicate that decision; and (3) recovery is very unlikely. Doing so will bring you great peace-of-mind.

Teamwork across the Veil

Sometimes two people will incarnate together with the express life plan of having a relationship and then one of them crosses over, so the relationship continues across the veil.

For example, Tom and Walda Woods had been married for 25 years, and on Labor Day 1996, at a New England neighborhood barbecue, Tom suffers a massive heart attack and is rushed to the hospital. He crosses over a few days later, and the signs of his continued presence in Walda's life begin almost immediately—lights going on and off, the TV jumping from a movie to the sports channel, etc.

Walda, already a spiritual student, picks up her studies and becomes a medium. Soon, she and Tom are having lengthy talks, which Walda transcribes on her computer. The compilation grows and becomes a fascinating book, *Conversations with Tom* that talks about life on the other side. In it, Tom also coaches us on how we can all become mediums.

The story jumps to October 2001 and 2,000 miles west to Salt Lake City, Utah, where Joe and Jen, a highly spiritual couple, plan to start a healing/retreat center called Sol Sanctuary. However, Joe is diagnosed with cancer and crosses over in April 2002. Jen is in shock and goes through the full grief cycle of anger, depression and finally acceptance. In the midst of this, she has a thought telling her to go to a particular bookstore. As she is walking down an aisle, wondering why she is there, she notices a book on the floor—*Conversations with Tom*. Realizing this is an obvious set-up, she buys the book, which helps her enormously, so much so that after finishing it, she sends an email to Walda. However, she doubts ever receiving a reply from 'such a famous person as a published author.'

Meanwhile, back in New England, Walda is going through her own crisis. Following a serious illness, she is advised by Tom to sell the house, which she does, and is wondering, "What next?" All she knows is that she has to leave New England, which is feeling less and less like home.

Into this uncertainty comes Jen's email, and the two women become 'email buddies and phone pals.' It soon dawns on Walda what she has to do, so she loads her three cats and a couple of suitcases into her car, and drives the 2,000 miles to Salt Lake City and a new friendship.

Both now mediums, they contact their respective husbands, only to find that they, too, are good friends on the other side, and the force behind Walda's move. The four are now collaborating on a book, and Walda has joined forces with Jen to make the retreat center a reality, with the help of Tom and Joe, of course. (This was also confirmed through two third-party mediums. With Walda's kind permission, Volume II, Chapter 13 features excerpts from her book.)

So, the crossing over of a loved one is never an end but just a redefinition of your relationship. Anyone can do what Walda and Jen have done, if it is in your soul's flight plan. And if it isn't, at least keep in contact and get on with your life.

Finally, there's nothing wrong with asking your deceased mate to help you find a new one. He or she would be pleased to help, for all possessiveness and jealousy fall away once you're free of the Earth plane, and your happiness is their main concern.

Resources

Rather than offer a reading list, this section lists authors whose works have influenced the worldview presented in this book. Anything from these authors is worthy of time and energy, and an AOL, Google or Yahoo Internet search on their names will reveal all you ever wanted to know about them and their works:

- After-death communication: George Anderson, Anthony Borgia, John Edward, Judy and Bill Guggenheim, Melvin Morse MD, Suzane Northrop, James Van Praagh, Walda Woods
- Ancient history: Gregg Braden, Drunvalo Melchizedek, Zechariah Sitchin
- Billy Meier: www.billymeier.com (duh)
- Conversations with God: Neale Donald Walsch
- Enneagram: Enneagram Institute (for tests and articles), Thomas Chou, Enneagram Central (for a 55-module online class). (Entering 'enneagram' into a Google search returns over 7,500 URLs ... have fun!)
- Four Agreements: Don Miguel Ruiz
- Map of Human Consciousness: Dr. David Hawkins
- Michael Teachings: JP Van Hulle of the Michael Education Foundation, Emily Baumbach, Steve Cocconi, Holly Coleman, Shepherd Hoodwin and Joya Pope
- Near-death experiences: Dannion Brinkley, Betty Eadie, Dr. Raymond Moody, Dr. Melvin Morse, Dr. Kenneth Ring
- Reincarnation: Morey Bernstein, Allen Eastman, Dr. Michael Newton, Marge Rieder, Walter Semkiw, Dr. Ian Stevenson
- Seth Material: Jane Roberts

Appendix A: Nibiru and the Birth of Planet Earth

Five thousand years ago, the priests of ancient Sumeria (present day Iraq) committed to clay tablets a remarkable story, proof of which is slowly filtering out of the scientific community. The story begins with a description of the solar system that lists the planets *from the outside in*, as if told by spacefarers arriving rather than departing. The account includes the outer planets of Pluto and Neptune, whose existence would not become known again for five millennia, when modern astronomy would finally catch up.

We owe this ancient knowledge to Zecharia Sitchin, who translated the tablets' ancient Sumerian and Akkadian accounts and published his work in *The Earth Chronicles* series, beginning with *The 12th Planet* in 1976.

The tablets record what the Sumerians were told by visiting extraterrestrials calling themselves Anunnaki, and named Nephilim and Elohim by the Sumerians. In addition to the remarkable story the ET visitors told, and documented in Chapter 3, they also told of a cataclysmic event that occurred about 4 billion years ago, which resulted in the formation of our planet.

Apparently, at one time, no planet existed between Venus and Mars, but a large planet named Tiamat, about the size of Uranus, lay in orbit between Mars and Jupiter. Also, a wandering planet or brown dwarf star had been captured by our Sun, possibly with the help of an outer planet. This wanderer carves a huge elliptical orbit around the sun, taking about 3,600 earth years and going as far away as 4 billion kilometers from the sun.

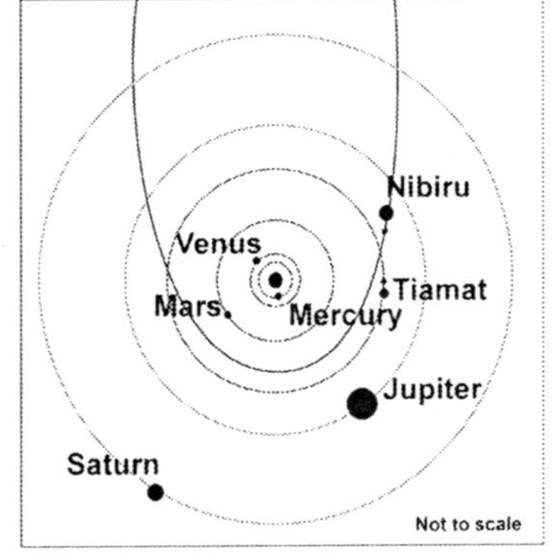

Pre-collision Solar System

During one of its passes around the sun (maybe the first after its capture by the Sun), Nibiru approached Tiamat on a collision course. As first the moons and then these two enormous bodies themselves slammed into each other, Nibiru, being the larger, inflicted more damage. About half of Tiamat's bulk was ripped away from what is now the Pacific Ocean, and was smashed into small pieces that began orbiting the Sun to form what we call today the Asteroid Belt between Mars and Jupiter, and what the Sumerians called 'The Hammered Out Bracelet.' (The passage of Nibiru also tilted Uranus on its side, and dislodged one of the 30 moons of Saturn to become what we now call Pluto.)

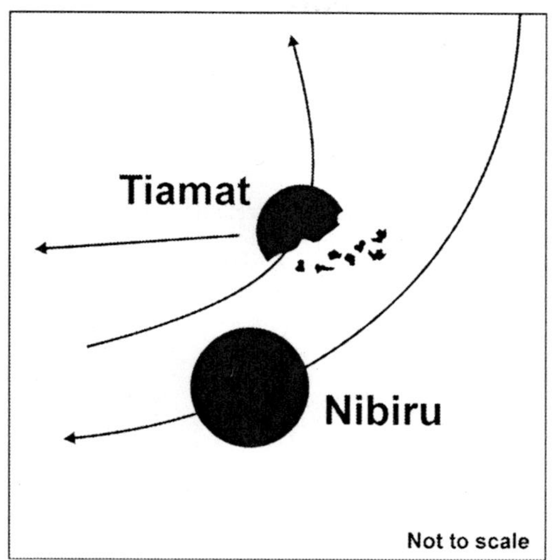

Tiamat-Nibiru Collision

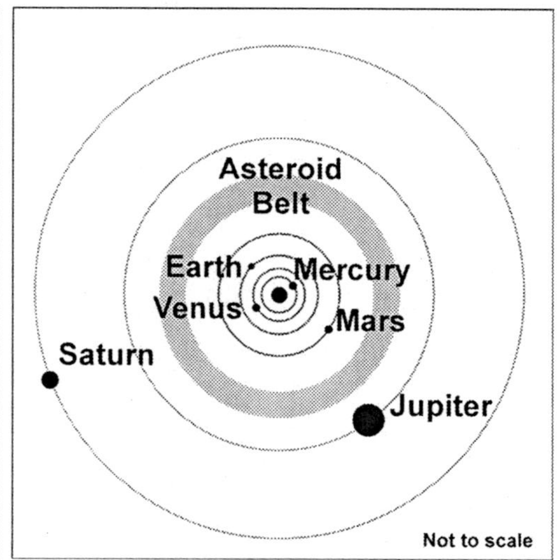

Post-collision Solar System

The remainder of Tiamat reeled with the impact and became a molten blob of rock, still weighing a massive 6,580 trillion trillion tons. She would take millions of years to cool down again, and even today her molten iron core is still over 8,000°F. Along with her moon, the remnants of Tiamat were knocked out of orbit and moved inwards toward the Sun. Eventually, they found a stable orbit 91.8 million miles from the Sun, between Mars and Venus, which is where we are today.

Remarkable as this story is, even more remarkable is that evidence is coming forward that it is true, that something catastrophic really did happen almost 4 billion years ago. In 1996, NASA launched a craft called NEAR to enter the asteroid belt and orbit a large asteroid named Eros, which it did on February 14, 2000. Four days later, NASA held a press conference to announce that Eros has a heavily pockmarked surface and appears to have a layered structure. NASA chief project scientist, Dr. Andrew Cheng, explained that such stratification could only have happened if the asteroid had been melted while part of a planet.

Further, a report appearing in *Science News* (April 7, 2001) revealed that a team of astronomers had discovered a celestial body, dubbed 2000CR/105, orbiting the Sun on a vast, elliptical, 3,300-year path that takes it 4.5 billion km out into space and then back in for a close pass around our Sun. Harold Levinson of the Southwest Research Institute of Boulder, CO told the magazine, "Something massive knocked the hell out of the Belt. The question is whether it is still there now."

This was also reported in the *Journal of Science* in April 6, 2001, where the lead paragraph of an article said, "A supercomet following an unexpected far-flung path around the sun suggests that an unidentified planet once lurked in the outermost reaches of the solar system. What's more, the mysterious object may still be there."

And finally, the April 7, 2001 issue of *New Scientist* carried an article that read, "There is new evidence that a sudden barrage of deadly debris crashed against the Earth and the Moon 3.9 billion years ago. What triggered this onslaught? Something in the structure of the solar system must have changed."

That something was Nibiru.

Robert Harrington and Planet X

As lead scientist at the US Naval Observatory, Robert Harrington was curious about unexplained anomalies in the orbit of Uranus. He concluded that its motion cannot be adequately represented within the present gravitational model of the solar system, and suggested the possibility of at least one undetected planet in our solar system. His ideas were published in a paper titled "The Location of Planet X," published in *The Astronomical Journal* (October 1988).

Harrington analyzed positional observations for Uranus back to 1833 and found perturbations in the orbit that could only have been produced by the presence of an unknown Planet X, which had a wildly elliptical orbit around the Sun. (He used 'X' to mean both 'unknown' and the number 10.) He derived a formula to describe the interaction between Planet X and Uranus and Neptune, and began the tedious task of plugging in a variety of values for Planet X's mass and orbital vector (speed, angle to the ecliptic, elongation of orbit, etc.), to see if any combinations would account for the actual observations. He succeeded after a grand total of over a third of a million trials … and all on the slow computers of the day. The best fit for Planet X's mass was 4 Earth Masses, in an orbit inclined at $32°$ to the ecliptic (the plane of orbit of most of the other planets). (Interestingly the existence of Pluto had been predicted mathematically long before it was actually found.)

Harrington's computations resulted in a nominal position where astronomers can look for Planet X. Because its orbit is mainly below the ecliptic, it can only be seen from the Southern Hemisphere, so Harrington used the Navy's observatory in New Zealand. Sadly, after three years of searching, he died of cancer in 1993, aged 51. Even more sadly, no one else seems anxious to pick up the trail.

Pangaea

About a billion years ago, the Earth's continents formed one huge landmass we've named *Pangaea*, with the rest of the surface under one gigantic ocean named *Panthalassa*.

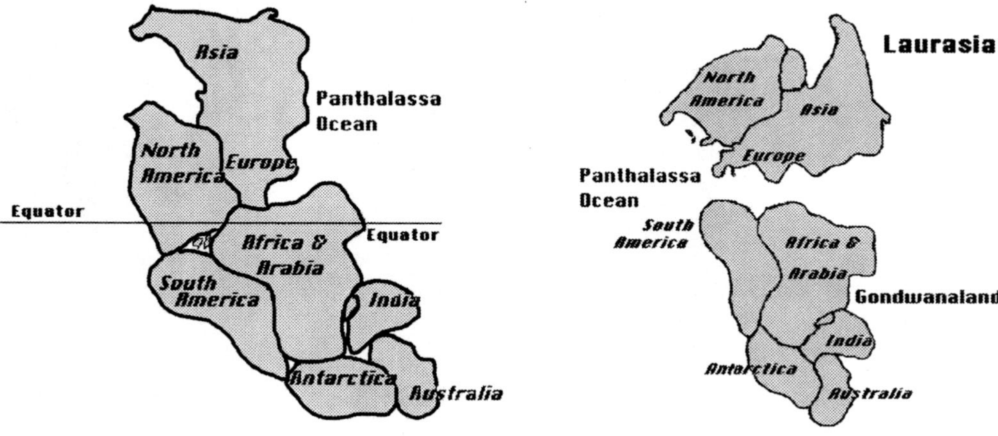

Pangaea 250 million years ago   *Pangaea 180 million years ago*

Then about 200 million years ago, just before the days of the dinosaurs, the supercontinent began to break up, caused by convection currents in the magma of the upper mantle. This movement caused the plates to move slowly across the surface of the Earth. First, Pangaea broke into:

- *Laurasia*, made of the present day continents of North America, Greenland, Europe, and Asia
- *Gondwanaland*, made of the present day continents of Antarctica, Australia, South America, and the subcontinent of India.

About 135 million years ago, Laurasia broke up further into the continents of North America (which started to drift west), Europe and Asia (Eurasian plate).

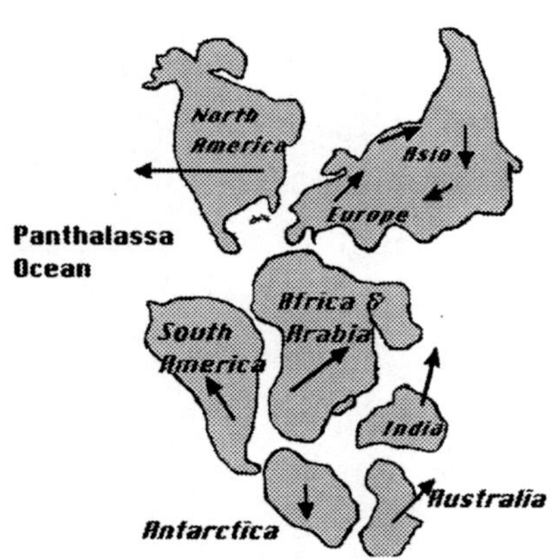

Gondwanaland broke up into the continents of Africa (headed north-east), Antarctica (south), Australia, South America (north-west), and the subcontinent of India (north). Arabia started to separate from Africa as the Red Sea opened up.

The arrows indicate the direction of the continental movements. The Indian subcontinent has moved hundreds of miles in 135 million years at a whopping 4 inches per year, crashing into the Eurasian plate with such

Pangaea 135 million years ago

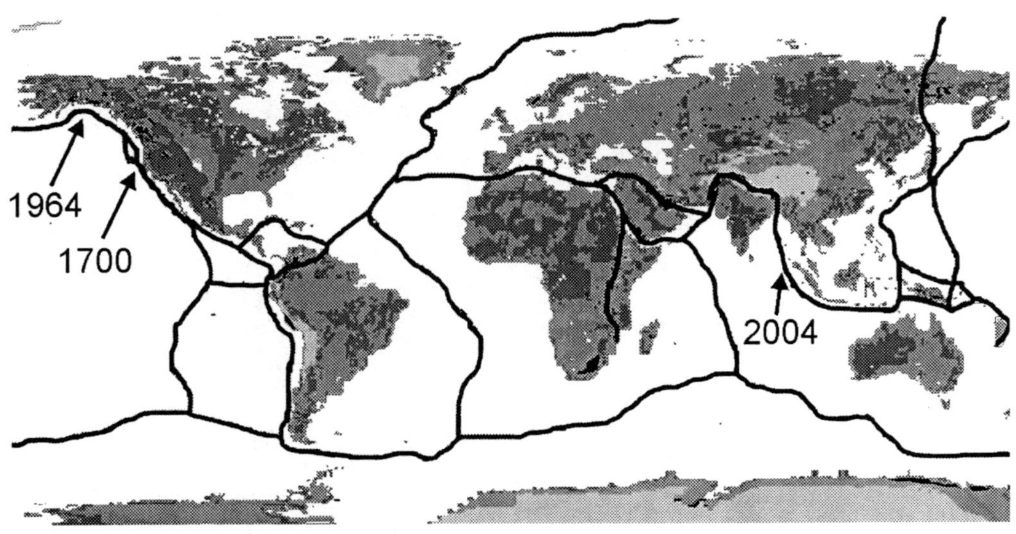

Pangaea now

force that the impact created the Himalayas. Today, we are left with a number of major plates, with ongoing tectonic shift still forming the Himalayas and Rocky Mountains. Those plates have bumped and ground against each other throughout history. For example, in 1700, they produced an estimated magnitude 9.0 earthquake and tsunami off the Puget Sound, and on Good Friday, 1964, a 9.2 quake and wave destroyed Anchorage, AK.

On December 26, 2004, a series of about a dozen major subduction events (the release of stresses developed as the India plate ground below the overriding Burma plate in a sudden drop of many feet) measuring up to magnitude 9.0 occurred within a half-hour off the coast of Sumatra, and two hours later, a series of massive tsunami waves swept up to a mile inland in 10 countries, killing at least 250,000 people and making five million homeless. In this case, the tsunamis surges we saw on the TV news were just 50 feet high and went no more than three miles inland; imagine 500 foot surges going over 10 miles inland. This happened in 10,800 BCE, at a time when 90 percent of the population lived at or near sea level. No wonder the Great Deluge was almost total extinction for humanity! And one can only wonder about the massive triage on the soul plane when hundreds of thousands cross over simultaneously. Thanks to today's satellite imaging, we see before-and-after images such as the following at Phuket.

Similar events occurred in Hawaii in 1946 and 1960 and killed many thousands. Even today, devastated cities are still open parkland. How can we live our lives in any security when images such as this show how everything we have—and even are—can be swept away in seconds? The only way is to know that you

Before and after satellite images show the total devastation following the tsunami

planned your return to the soul plane long before you incarnated, and that it is immutable. You can't outrun your destiny, so don't even try. In the meantime, live to the fullest and dance as if no one is watching.

On the subject of monster tsunamis, this may be why the Anunnaki finally left the planet.

What Happened in 1650 BCE? Earth's Dark Age

This short section really has nothing to do with living with soul, but ties up a loose end as to why the Anunnaki may have finally left Earth. Having lost everything about 10,000 years earlier and rebuilt the colonies from scratch, it happened again, probably really ticking them off, and making them wonder if it was really worth it.

Around the year 1650 BCE, several of the world's major civilizations mysteriously vanished:

- Egypt's Middle Kingdom fell to nomadic Asiatic plunderers called the Hyksos and remained under the conquerors until the New Kingdom asserted itself and restored control about 1550 BCE. What happened that rendered the Egyptians vulnerable to attack? And why were no documentation or records kept for that missing century?

- Bands of Indo-Europeans named Hittites swept down through Asia Minor, conquering and settling a vast area, from which they attacked the powerful Babylonian empire, ending the great Hammurabi Dynasty and plunging the region into a Dark Age that lasted until 1500 BCE.

- The sophisticated Harappan civilization, dating back to 3100 BCE, in the lush Indus Valley was wiped out by bands of marauding Arians, sweeping down from Europe. All cities were either destroyed or abandoned, but no record exists of the Arian occupation—another Dark Age.

- The highly advance Minoan civilization, based on the island of Crete collapsed and vanished almost immediately, leaving few traces that it had ever existed.

Three other mysteries also hinge in this landmark date:

- In China, the powerful Xia Dynasty suddenly fell for reasons unknown, and the Shang Dynasty took control.
- In England, the huge monoliths of Stonehenge were regularly adjusted to remain in synch with the sun's position, but this activity mysteriously stopped around 1650 BCE.
- Across the Atlantic, the city of Caral had been occupied since 3000 BCE, as a religious and administrative center, and was mysteriously abandoned around 1650 BCE, leaving the way open for the rise of the Inca.

What single major planetary event could have plunged Earth's civilizations into chaos, making them vulnerable to invasion? In August 1883, the eruption of Krakatoa, Indonesia, ejected more than six cubic miles of rock, ash and pumice, and generated the loudest sound ever recorded by human beings, being heard up to 3,000 miles distant across the Indian Ocean. Ash fell as far away as 5,000 miles and created such spectacular atmospheric vivid red sunsets that people in U.S. routinely called out the fire department. It also lowered global temperatures by over one degree for five years. Tsunamis of about 120 feet high killed over 36,000 people and wiped out 165 coastal villages. Traveling at over 300 mph, the wave reached Aden in 12 hours, a distance of 3,800 miles. The air pressure wave circled the planet for five days after the explosion, going around as many as seven times. The volcano spewed rafts of floating pumice, thick enough to support men and animals, which crossed the Indian Ocean in 10 months, and were still afloat two years after the eruption. However, this pales in comparison with the explosion in 1650 BCE of the island of Thera (today named Santorini) in the eastern Mediterranean Sea.

Thera, about 10 miles in diameter, was a major seaport of the vast, thriving, sea-going Minoan civilization, based on the island of Crete just to the south. That year, in the eruption of Thera's volcano, almost the entire island exploded in one of the largest events in the last 10,000 years. The blast ejected about 7 cubic miles of magma as high as 25 miles. Ash fell over the eastern Mediterranean and Turkey, and remained in the atmosphere long enough to cause a global climate change. But, as with Krakatoa, that was just the beginning.

The ejection of such a large volume of magma caused the volcano to implode into its own caldera. Billions of tons of sea water poured into the huge opening, which the remaining magma turned to steam. The resulting explosion created a huge tsunami, which devastated the entire Mediterranean region, especially the Greek Islands, ending the Minoan civilization.

To the north, tsunamis 500 – 1,000 feet high (*ten to twenty times* the waves in 2004's S.E. Asia event) raced up the Aegean Sea, wiping out hundreds of coastal villages and reaching far up into the mountains of Turkey and Greece. They may even have crashed over the land bridge into the Black Sea.

To the east, the waves traveled unimpeded over Cyprus, to the coasts of today's Syria, Lebanon and Israel, going far inland to swamp the Jordan Valley and down behind the Sinai Peninsula.

To the south, Crete was destroyed almost immediately, and the waves then had a clear shot of the coasts of Libya and Egypt, overrunning the low-lying Nile

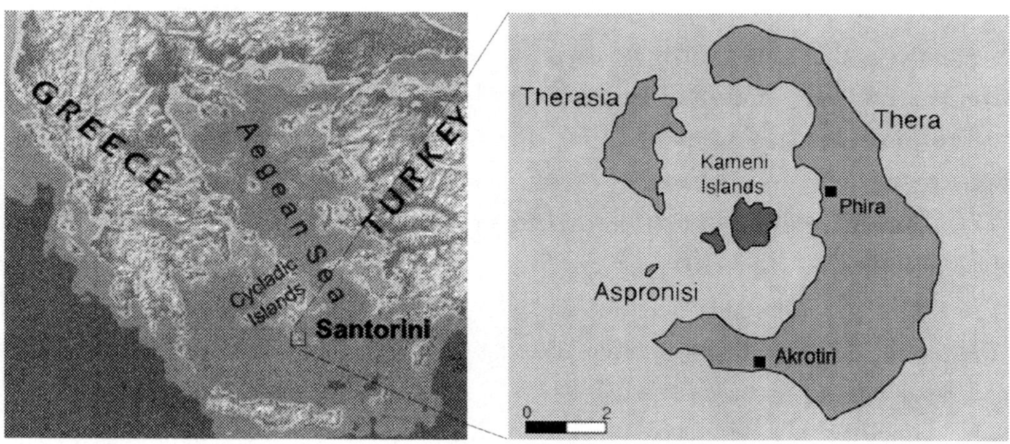

Santorini, the remains of ancient Thera

Tsunami waves from the Thera eruption

Delta, along with Alexandria, hitting up against the mountains of the Sinai Peninsula, meeting up with the flood waters coming down the Jordan Valley.

To the west, they roared unimpeded into Sicily and the toe of Italy, and swamped Tunisia's coastline. Then on to Corsica and Sardinia, and finally expending themselves against the mountains of Spain and France. Whether they managed to get out into the Atlantic is unknown.

All told, this disaster could have wiped out half the world's population of the day, the Mediterranean being the planet's most heavily populated area. The volcanic winter would have resulted in crop failure for several years, leading to massive numbers of deaths due to starvation.

In the midst of all this, the Anunnaki may have felt it was time to leave for good, and let humanity pick up the pieces by itself. Their departure, plus the chaos following the tsunami, would have left a huge vacuum in the defenses of all major civilizations, that could easily be exploited by hordes of invaders from the north, who had not been impacted by the immediate catastrophe. History records that the invasions actually happened, but why is not well-documented because there was no one left to document it, certainly not the illiterate invaders themselves. (The Roman Empire, scrupulous documenters of everything, would not come about for another thousand years.)

How could the planet have started its existence with just one huge landmass and one huge ocean? It doesn't make sense … at least not until we realize that it's only half a planet, with the other half still orbiting outside Mars in 10-mile wide pieces. As Tiamat, the land may have been evenly distributed, albeit under miles of ice, but the new orbit resulted in the ice melting, leaving a sea level such that most of the land above ice ended up covering less than 25 percent of the surface. Today, the Pacific Ocean covers the huge collision scar to a depth of 38,000 feet, or a staggering seven miles.

"Uranus and Neptune are both greenish-blue watery planets, with molten cores of up to 8,000°F that compensate for their vast distance from the Sun." This wasn't discovered in 1986 when Voyagers I and II flew by those planets; it was recorded on ancient Sumerian tablets in 4000 BCE. So modern science only *re*-discovered what was known 6,000 years ago … and forgotten. In fact, modern science didn't even know Neptune existed until 1846, following the discovery of Uranus in 1781. (With Uranus and Neptune about 2 billion and 3 billion miles from the Sun respectively, we can see neither with the naked eye.)

~ ~ ~

More confirmation of what the Anunakki told the Sumerians comes from Bode's Law, established in 1772, which predicts the orbits of planets in a system such as ours. There are two significant problems, however: (1) Earth should not be where it is, and (2) a planet is missing from between Mars and Jupiter. In the following table, column 2 shows in AUs (Astronomical Units, or the distance of the Earth from the Sun) where *predicted* planetary obits should lie if the solar system had formed naturally and had not been disturbed in some way. Column 3 shows the ratio of a planet's orbit to the planet orbiting just inside it. The table shows that this ratio should be 1.7 – 2.0. Columns 4 and 5 show *actual* orbits and ratios. Column 6 shows the percentage difference between the predicted and the actual.

	Bode's Law Distance	Ratio	Actual Distance	Ratio	% Error
Mercury	0.4	–	0.4	–	0
Venus	0.7	1.7	0.7	1.7	0
Earth	–	–	1.0	1.4	∞
Mars	1.6	2.2	1.6	1.6	0
Tiamat	2.8	1.7	2.8	1.7	0
Jupiter	5.2	1.9	5.2	1.8	0
Saturn	10.0	1.9	9.5	1.8	5.0
Uranus	19.6	1.9	19.2	2.0	2.1
Neptune	38.8	2.0	30.0	1.5	22.6
Pluto	–	–	39.4	1.3	∞
???	77.2	2.0	–	–	∞

Bode's Law predicting planetary orbits

Quite clear is the fact that no planet should exist where Earth does, yet there *should* be a planet between Mars and Jupiter where the Asteroid Belt now lies.

Equally obvious is that the orbits of the outer planets were perturbed by something catastrophic. Neptune should be 8.8 AUs further away from the Sun, and Pluto should not be there at all. (Pluto was a satellite of Saturn that was 'jostled' into an unnatural orbit.)

The vast distances have interesting implications that we rarely think about. At the equator, the circumference of the Earth is 29,935 miles, and a point on the equator that rotates in 24 hours is moving at the speed of 1039 miles/hour. But that's nothing. The Earth is 91.4 million miles from the sun, so has an orbit of 574 million miles, which our planet traverses in one year.

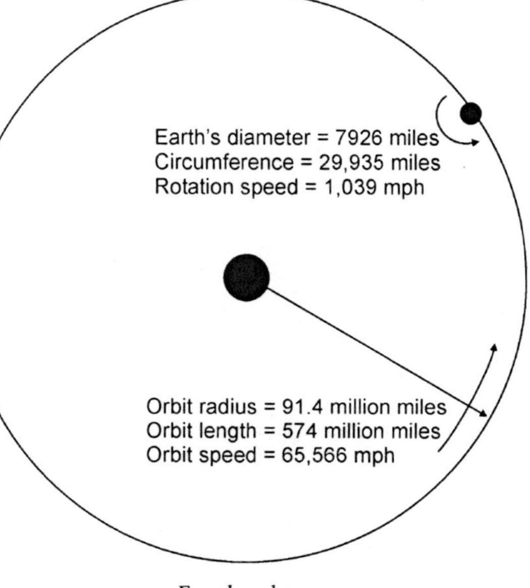

Earth orbits

Doing the math reveals that we are traveling through space at a dizzying 65,566 miles/hour, while rotating at over 1,000 mph. Phew!

Until Ceres was discovered in 1801, astronomers had no idea of the Asteroid Belt, but now we know of about 50,000 mile-wide asteroids making it up, plus billions of smaller space debris. However, the 'Hammered Bracelet' was well-known in Sumer 6,000 years ago.

A common criticism of the 'missing planet' theory is that the Asteroid Belt mass alone is not enough to account for the planet's estimated mass. Where did the rest go? You're standing on it.

Thanks to the Sumerian scribes, we know *we are a species that should not exist, living on a planet that should not be where it is.* Odd how things turn out, eh?

There is plenty of other evidence supporting the truth of Sitchin's translation of the Sumerian tablets:

- Ancient goldmines, dated as 100,000 years old, existed in Africa at *exactly* the location that mitochondrial DNA researchers point to as the origin of human life.
- An ancient gold processing plant on Mt. Sinai still shows traces of monoatomic gold, a recently discovered form of the metal that is a superconductor at room temperature.
- Several 1,000-ton stone blocks forming a huge 16-acre platform at ancient Heliopolis in Lebanon (today called Baalbek) that carries the ancient name 'Place of Landing.' Since this is far inland, the only landings could have been for space craft. This may have been built around 10,800 BCE,

Vast stone block at the Baalbeck quarry. dwarf the human figure.

when the previous landing zone on the Tigris was destroyed in the Great Deluge. The photo shows a huge slab still in the quarry, with the figure of a man beside it. It is 70 feet long, with sides 16 by 14 feet, and weighs more than 1,200 tons. How these blocks were moved, around the time of Noah's Flood, remains a mystery … unless, of course, you read the works of Sitchin. As a onetime 'abode of the gods,' the site was revered as holy by the ancient inhabitants, then by the Greeks, who renamed the site Heliopolis in honor of Zeus, their sun god. (The Egyptians also had a Heliopolis on the Nile in honor of their sun god, Ra. Much later, the Romans used the platform as the foundation for a temple complex in honor of Jupiter. (This artist's rendition of c. 1900 shows what the complex would have looked like at its height c. 400 BCE.)

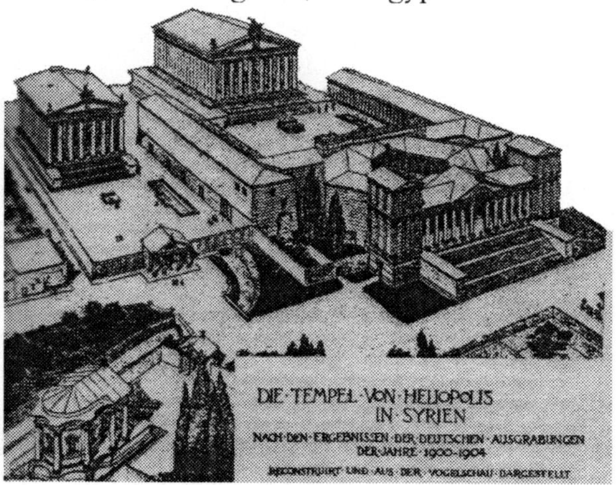

Ancient city of Heliopolis c. 400 BCE

Obviously space travel was vital to the Nefilim, and they went to elaborate measures to ensure safety and functionality. According to Sitchin, the earliest cities in Sumer were laid out to guide incoming spacefarers.

The cities of Eridu, Larsa and Nippur were on the edges of the glide path into the spaceport of Sippar, and ancient tablets at those sites show strange apparatus that look like radio navigation antenna, much the way our modern airports have ILS (Instrument Landing System) antenna. Eridu was the first city the Nefilim built, and the center line of the glide path lies directly over the ancient city of Ur.

Unfortunately, the Great Deluge wiped out the entire area, and the Nefilim had to start over with a new post-Diluvian spaceport to augment the pre-Diluvian site in Baalbeck in the Lebanon. The place chosen was a southern site in the central massif of the Sinai Peninsula.

After the Flood, approach to the Sinai spaceport began over Mount Ararat (the most prominent landmark in the area) and went southeast over the city of Jerusalem, whose ancient inscriptions mention the extensive communication facilities of this city ('stones that talk'), as one would expect of 'mission control.' The glide

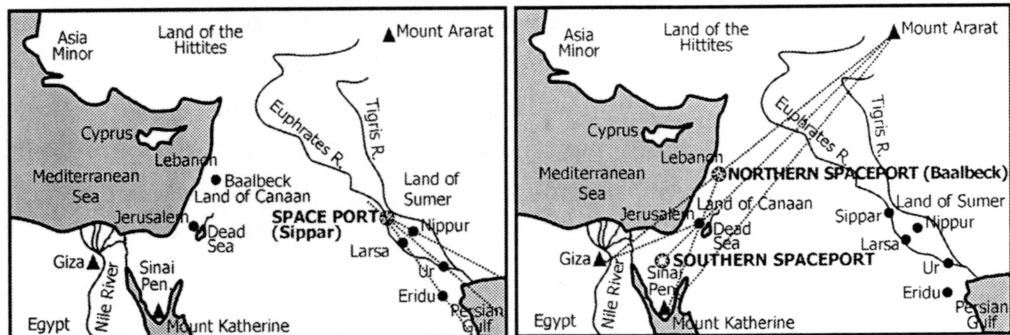

Anunnaki space ports before and after the Great Flood

path limits were Mount Katherine and an artificial landmark at Giza—the Great Pyramids. Of course, they had other uses, but Sitchin's work reveals that navigation and communications were part of their functions ... and we have no idea what was in the missing capstone—a powerful navigation beacon, perhaps.

The approach to Baalbeck in the Lebanon began in the southwest and went over either the Giza Pyramids in a straight line for Mount Ararat, or over Mount Katherine on a straight line beyond Jerusalem. Back in those days, the pyramids were covered by polished white casing stones, and the bright sunlight would have rendered them visible to pilots for hundreds of miles. Although all these sites used to lie in the realms of different Nefilim, they all had to cooperate in space travel because of the lengthy glide paths needed, much as NASA's shuttlecraft spends hours on its glide path approach.

Proof of the Pyramids' Antiquity

Before the Flood, about 20600 BCE, Enki retired from supervising mining operations and the genetic engineering projects and went to rule the area of what is now called Egypt. Under the name of Ptah, he began the history of Egypt in four great epochs:

1. *First Nefilim Dynasty*, or Epoch of the Gods that lasted 12,300 years (Ptah-Enki, 9,000 years; Marduk-Ra, 1,000; Shu, 700; Geb, 500; Osiris, 450; Seth, 350; and Horus, 300).

2. *Second Epoch of the Gods*, of 1,570 years, beginning with Thoth, for a total of 13,870 years of Nefilim rule.

3. *Epoch of the Demi-Gods*, under a series of hybrids (Nefilim-human rulers) who reigned for 3,650 years.

4. *The Pharaoic Dynasties* of purely human rulers, the First beginning with Menes c. 3100 BCE.

Ptah-Enki ruled c. 20600 – 11600 BCE, and Marduk-Ra ruled c. 11600 – 10800 BCE, his rule cut short by The Deluge. Ptah-Enki returned to Egypt to restore order and plan a massive system of dikes to drain the land and contain the Nile, which would give Egypt its old name of 'The Raised Place.' Ra and his son Shu (He who controls the skies) built the Sinai spaceport, and were followed by Geb (He who piles up the earth), who actually raised Egypt above the receding floodwaters, thus restoring Egypt to be habitable again after the Flood, taking about 1,000 years.

The Giza Pyramids and Sphinx had already been built as part of the Baalbeck spaceport navigation system, and show a water line consistent with having been flooded at some time. Also, the Sphinx shows damage consistent with prolonged, heavy rain, which historically has only occurred when the planet warmed up after the last Ice Age that ended c. 10800 BCE. This water damage proves the antiquity of the Giza site, because the area has been extremely arid for the last 5,000 years, so the landmarks were certainly not erected in 3750 BCE as Egyptologists claim.

That silly claim stems from the 1837 shenanigans of one Col. Vyse, an amateur British archeologist who was having a dismal campaign of fruitless exploration. His family threatened to cut off his funding unless he came up with something spectacular, so he decided to create something to discover. One night, he or a henchman painted some cartouches (a pharaoh's personal insignia) in a pyramid, which he 'discovered' the next morning. This tied the Great Pyramid to Khufu/ Cheops, an obscure 4th dynasty pharaoh who reigned c. 2600 BCE. Egyptians were delighted that this dated the structures so recently (good for tourism), and the timing has become an established part of Egyptology's folklore, despite its impossibility. What is less well-publicized is that the cartouches were hopeless, botched, inept frauds. Fundamental Christians also grab onto this date because it fits with their belief that the Earth was created in the year 4004 BCE. It's hard to maintain this belief when you've got artifacts going back to 10800 BCE.

As a footnote to this story, Sumerian texts report that the En-lil camp did not like this major spaceflight navigation aid being under the control of the En-ki legion, and a major war broke out over its possession. Fighting concluded c. 8670 BCE, with En-lil's son gaining control. He promptly stripped the site of all its navigation and communication equipment, including the 'radiant stones' (crystals) lining the inclined gallery, and smashed the capstone, leaving us with the enigmatic, empty hulk we puzzle over today. Thanks to the Sumerian scribes, the mystery is solved. A peace accord awarded stewardship of the site to Thoth, being of the lineage of both En-ki and En-lil, so acceptable to both sides. The Pyramids remained as visual navigation aids, and Ra built the communications center east, across the Nile, and named the site after himself, the Sun God—Heliopolis.

The existence of the Sinai spaceport, built after the Great Deluge, came to an abrupt halt in 2024 BCE, when a conflict between the descendents of En-ki and En-lil turned nasty with the use of seven atomic bombs. The bombed-out site is still visible in aerial photographs of the peninsula.

The enigmatic dark patch shows the extent of the blast that swept away the spaceport. Also, the area is littered with odd black, fused nodules, typical of what happens at 'ground-zero' of an atomic blast.

The anomaly on the Sinai Penninsula

In the same war, the cities of Sodom and Gomorrah, sitting south of the Dead Sea, were bombed, which created a huge crater into which the sea flowed, thus flooding the area and dropping the sea level. This area, too, shows the same fused nodules.

Worse was to follow, however. Westerly winds blowing off the Mediterranean carried a vast plume of deadly radioactivity eastward across Sumer and Mesopotamia, from which the Nefilim escaped by taking to the air and joining their orbiting craft. Their human subjects suffered a similar fate to those downwind of the Chernobyl disaster, sickening and dying in such vast numbers that the cradle of existence became a waste land, with no plants, animals or people in the area for about 70 years. References to the so-called 'Evil Wind' puzzled scholars until Sitchin realized that the weapons used, named the 'Great Brilliance,' were actually atomic or nuclear bombs. During the period of desolation, the Nefilim lost interest in Earth as an outpost, and never really returned. Slowly, humans straggled back into the area, but Sumer had seen its heyday and never regained its pinnacle of success of previous millennia.

To test the acoustics of the King's Chamber, sound engineers once generated a variety of frequencies in the chamber, and it went into resonance at 30 Hz, almost liquefying the engineers' bodies. Researcher Alan Alford suggests the Great Pyramid was built partly as an acoustic amplifier for natural Earth frequencies, using the huge airshafts as 'organ pipes.' The resulting hum would be audible for miles across the desert, possibly as part of a ceremony to celebrate life and rebirth. This would explain the seven massive granite layers forming the ceiling to the chamber, with the carefully carved grooves being the means to 'tune' the enclosure.

~ ~ ~

Why isn't this whole story of human history better known? Because scientists and the Church are holding the truth hostage for their own self-serving purposes. Science holds fast to Evolution and the Church holds on to Creationism and has now hijacked Intelligent Design (ID). Interventionism is not even on the horizon, and all three factions try to portray it as a crackpot notion. Academics who try to explore it soon lose their tenure and research grants, and few professors have the courage to admit to having taught a lie all their lives. Even Darwin never talked about evolution. One species cannot evolve into another because DNA doesn't allow it, so a T-Rex will always be a T-Rex. Species do adapt, however, and a T-Rex can get larger, faster, or grow hair during an Ice Age. Fortunately, Sitchin and a few other brave souls do have the courage to search for the truth and embrace Interventionism.

As for the Church, how could they possibly fess up to the Jesus and God myths? It was only in 1952 that Pope Pius II repealed the 1654 doctrine condemning the heresy of believing anything other than that the Earth was created in 4004 BCE —a little late for poor Jordano Bruno, who was burned at the stake in 1600 for believing Earth was not the only planet in the universe, and for Galileo, who actually saw the planets through his telescope and spent his last years under house arrest.

Nibiru Appearances

The passage of such a huge celestial object as Nibiru would not go unnoticed on Earth, and ancient reports claim that at perigee, it can be seen in broad daylight. Ancient inhabitants of the Middle East had hundreds of years to prepare, arrival being signaled first, depending on orbital position, by a possible conjunction with Mercury (point 'A'). Next would be with Jupiter at point 'B' and the major celebration held at the planet's closest point to Earth (point 'C'), when it would be at the perigee of its orbit ... and *very* bright in the sky.

Ancient texts described great excitement at the arrival of the Nibiru royal family during these close encounters, but also trepidation about possible geological and meteorological disturbances. In fact, the ancient records reveal that one pass around 13,000 years ago did trigger mas-

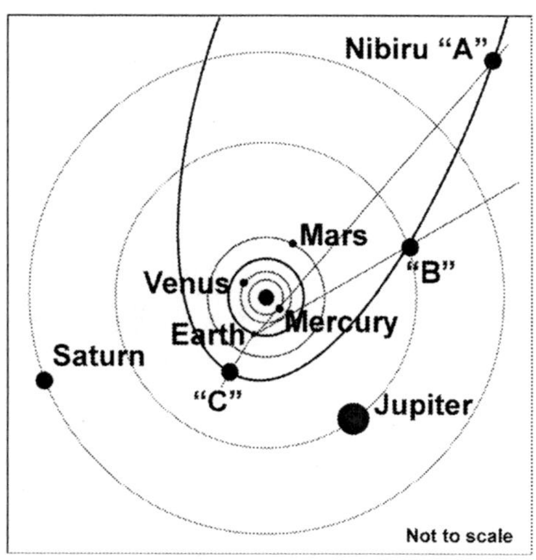

Eccentric orbit of Nibiru

sive seismic and volcanic disasters and caused a huge piece of the Antarctic ice-shelf to break off, resulting in a planetary tsunami, i.e., Noah's Flood. Zecharia Sitchin's *The 12th Planet* talks extensively about the impacts on Earth that result from Nibiru's crossing.

Core samples from Antarctica and the Earth's ocean beds reveal that Earth entered an Ice Age c. 75,000 years ago that ended abruptly 13,000 years ago, lasting 62,000 years. This was particularly brutal for its last 25,000 years, locking up most the planet's fresh water in the Antarctic ice mass, up to a mile thick. Science and ancient texts agree that billions of tons of this ice slipped off the massive ice shelf, creating a huge, global tsunami and raising sea levels by up to 600 feet, thus wiping out the majority of Earth's population, who of course, lived on the coasts and on river estuaries. When did this happen? One text places it in 'The Age of the Lion,' or 10860 – 8700 BCE, which coincides with a 'passing' of Nibiru, an event whose gravitational impact could easily have dislodged the ice. The four most recent passings have been 0 CE, 3600 BCE, 7200 BCE and 10800 BCE., and it is quite possible that the Hebrew sect that created the Jesus story wove in the 0 CE passing as the so-called Star of Bethlehem to give a cultural anchor.

Finally, ancient Sumerian records also mention an annual festival to honor the solar system's 12 planets, in which Earth is named as the *seventh* planet, and Pluto, Neptune and Uranus are first, second and third respectively, even though modern science did not 'discover' them until the 1930s. The Sumerian account can *only* be the perspective of people coming *to* Earth from outside, and not that of a resident counting out from the Sun. This lends much credence to the ancient records of a culture that knew about a 12th planet not currently familiar to many astronomers.

However, it is familiar to NASA, which in June 1987 issued a press release and followed it up with a press conference in July 1987. Jointly, the Jet Propulsion Laboratory, Ames Research Center and NASA HQ in Washington stunned the scientific community by admitting the presence of a *hitherto unknown* planet—obviously they don't read Sitchin's books—four times the mass of Earth on a 200 AU eccentric orbit, inclined at 30 degrees to the plane of the solar system (the ecliptic). Currently, it is far from the center of our system, but it *is* out there.

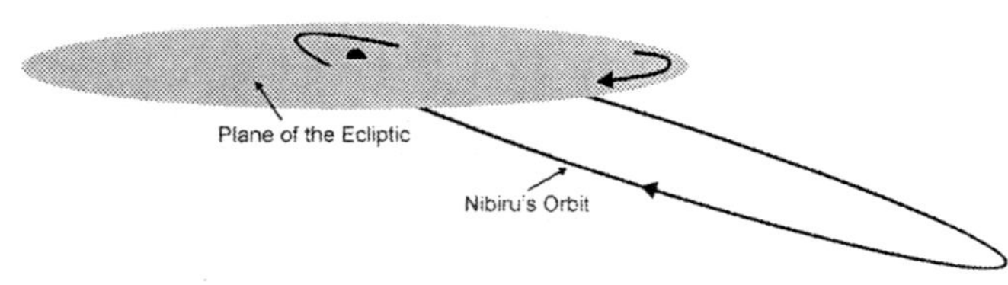

Zecharia Sitchin

Since Chapter 3 and this appendix are based on the translations by Zecharia Sitchin of ancient Sumerian, Akkadian and Babylonian texts, let's take a deeper look at his work. Many critics claim he has taken a few facts and woven a fantastic story around them to come up with his Earth Chronicles series, but such personal attacks come nowhere near to assaulting his impeccable scholarship, and are clearly motivated for other reasons, including, "Why didn't I think of that first?" and, "If he's right, everything I hold

Dr. Zecharia Sitchin

true is wrong." The latter comes from established historians who must rethink the entire worldview that got them tenure at their universities.

Another reason is self-interest, as with Dr. Zahi Hawass, the Director of Antiquities of Egypt's Giza Plateau, who, despite water erosion patterns and the laws of physics, steadfastly holds to the view that: "The pyramids were built by Egyptians around 2750 BCE as tombs for the pharaohs." Since the pyramids are the focal point of Egypt's tourism industry, an admission that they were built by an off-world race around 12,000 years ago is unthinkable.

Another argument of many scholars is that the Sumerian tablets depict ancient myths and not actual history as given by the Anunnaki to the Sumerian scribes. However, Sitchin has proven unequivocally that the Old Testament is a brief synopsis of thousands of much older tablets. But if the latter are telling mythological tales, so is the OT. Which is it? Both myth or both factual? The OT cannot be factual if it's based on myth.

To be fair, Sitchin admits that his translation and some of his observations could be off in a few places, but the sheer volume of material in the six books of the Earth Chronicles series plus two others, and hundreds of articles, presents a huge, unassailable, unified, and highly plausible explanation for our planet's ancient history.

Something very interesting happened in February 2003. The French scientific journal *Science &Vie* published an article based on an interview of French astronomer Alessandro Morbidelli by a staff writer. The astronomer asserted that around 3.9 billion years ago, a stray Mars-sized planet entered our solar system and collided with a planet orbiting between Mars and Jupiter. The ensuing destruction

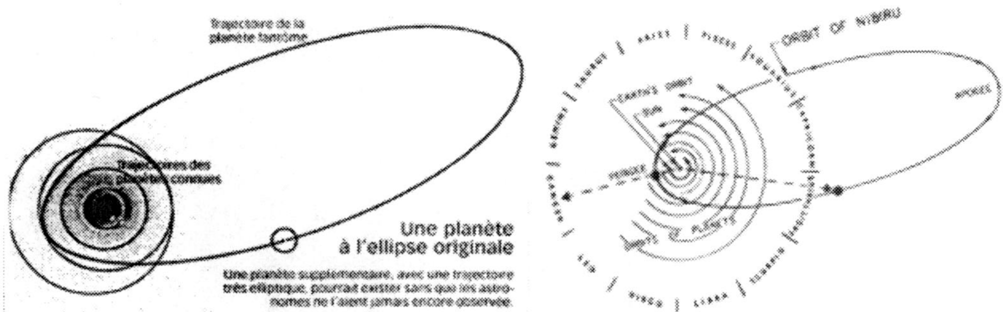

Left: French version of Nibiru orbit; right: Sitchin's version

resulted in what is now the asteroid belt. He went to say that the intruder has a huge, elliptical orbit of several thousand years, adding, "I expect that one day we will discover a new planet in our solar system."

The astronomer drew a diagram for the interviewer, explaining his theory. A reader of Sitchin's work saw the diagram (above left) and noted the similarity between it and Sitchin's own diagram from *The 12th Planet* (above right).

So far, Sitchin's efforts at contacting the astronomer have failed, but the scientific journal's staff told Sitchin it's unlikely that the scientist was familiar with Sitchin's work, which if true, independently corroborates the latter on *scientific* grounds rather than through translation of ancient texts. If the astronomer *had* in fact read Sitchin's work, plagiarized it, and presented it as scientific fact, that also adds much credence to Sitchin's writings.

Critics of Sitchin's account make the point that over the last 3.6 billion years, Nibiru has made about 10,000,000 passes around the Sun, so where is the evidence of its passing? Well, just four passes ago, its arrival coincided with the end of the last Ice Age, and its gravitational pull may have dislodged a huge part of the Antarctic ice shelf, causing billions, if not trillions, of tons of ice to crash into the ocean. At several hundred feet high, the resulting tsunami would have dwarfed the 2004 S.E. Asia tsunamis and wiped out 95% of the Earth's population, giving rise to the Great Deluge story in every aboriginal legend. And who knows how many other times Nibiru has had a catastrophic impact on Earth before man appeared on the scene.

Finally, to end the 'history versus mythology' debate, we have the anomalous Out-Of-Place Artifacts, or OOPARTS, which archeologists find so embarrassing, they strive to ignore them because they eviscerate every academic sacred cow. For example, a rock hound broke open a 500,000-year-old geode and found a white porcelain object surrounding a shiny metal shaft ending in a tiny spring, much like today's spark plug. How did it get there, and who made it? And then there's the gold artifact discovered in Central America believed to be over 1,000 years old yet depicting something very similar to today's space shuttle. What was the inspiration for the artist? (If you're ever bored, just enter "ooparts" into a Google search; you won't be bored for very long, I promise!)

For example, we have the oopart found in the sand at Saqqara in Egypt that is reminiscent of the space shuttle. What on Earth is *that* doing buried deep in the sand of an ancient pyramid site in the Egyptian desert?

In conclusion, Sitchin has given the world a tremendous gift—its real history—and he has left just about every conservative antiquities scholar dazed and confused. To put himself beyond the pale of academia took great courage, and I am delighted that, in return, his books shoot to the top of the bestseller lists in every country where they are published.

APPENDIX B: MEF'S MICHAEL ROLE QUIZ

Your role reflects your *soul's* personality, or who you are, in your most intimate values, abilities, and beingness. It can be somewhat obscured by cultural values as well as parental and social conditioning. Because of this you may appear to be just like your parents, but when you look through this layer of conditioning, your true nature emerges and your role becomes more apparent.

For this reason, your role becomes most noticeable after substantial life experience, usually by the mid-thirties.

Role Questionnaire Instructions:

Check as many statements as you closely identify with. You can check and uncheck as often as you need to. Your Role will probably be related to the group of questions with the highest number of checked statements. Sometimes people will have two Roles that they identify with closely. This is commonly due to parental influence. Read about both Roles and see which one you identify with most closely as your deepest self, and not your image. Or take the quiz on-line at the MEF website: *www.mef.to/seven_roles/the_roles.html*.

Role #1:

- ☐ I like to work behind the scenes making sure everything runs smoothly.
- ☐ Nurturing people is what inspires me most in life.
- ☐ Sometimes I feel trapped into a care taking role.
- ☐ I like to quietly arrange situations to make other people happy.
- ☐ I frequently perform little services that go unnoticed.
- ☐ I love to take care of people and see to it they are comfortable.
- ☐ I'd make someone a perfect wife or househusband.

Role #2:

- ☐ I often feel a strong urge to tell people what I see is best for them.
- ☐ My spiritual path is of higher importance to me than my relationships or material needs.
- ☐ Sometimes I get pretty zealous in my efforts to set others on the right path.
- ☐ I feel responsible for the spiritual guidance of my "flock," even if I am not a minister.
- ☐ I see where people are blocked and I have the urge to save them from themselves.
- ☐ Compassion is the force that motivates me to relate to the world.
- ☐ My friends consider me to be an inspiration to them, even if I'm not sure why.

Role #3:

- ☐ I am most stimulated by inventing and remodeling.
- ☐ I love to influence the mood or flavor of what is going on.
- ☐ If I can't express innovative ideas I feel blocked and frustrated.
- ☐ People see me as artistic and doing things with an unusual flair.
- ☐ I like to invent things in my mind that have never been thought of before.
- ☐ I am fascinated with how different elements combine to make a cohesive unit.
- ☐ I love to create new projects from old materials.

Role #4:

- ☐ I hate to have my communication misunderstood.
- ☐ I love to have the last word.
- ☐ I secretly (or not so secretly) love to be on stage and to be noticed.
- ☐ I often mentally correct others' communication, whether written or verbal.
- ☐ I have a little voice in my head that almost never shuts up.
- ☐ I am renowned for my wit and sense of humor.
- ☐ If there is some juicy new gossip around, I won't feel comfortable until I've heard the details.

Role #5:

- ☐ I like to get things organized.
- ☐ I don't mind taking charge of situations to get results.
- ☐ The one thing that really makes me furious is an attack on my principles.
- ☐ I get so focused in one direction that I sometimes do not see the side paths.
- ☐ When people irritate me they see my sword come out.
- ☐ I will quietly but relentlessly work toward something I know is right.
- ☐ I know I am basically a strong person and I am quick to defend the weak and innocent.

Role #6:

- ☐ I expect to be the person who is put in a leadership position or ultimately responsible.
- ☐ I like to grasp the big picture and then delegate chores.
- ☐ I don't stop until I've mastered what I'm attempting.
- ☐ I get frustrated if I cannot do something perfectly the first time.
- ☐ I am responsible for the action flowing smoothly in whatever situation I'm in.
- ☐ When things go wrong, the buck ultimately stops here.
- ☐ I am only interested in 'A' experiences; 'A minus' is not quite enough.

Role #7:

- ☐ I am innately curious and I love to study what interests me.
- ☐ I am known for being objective, and I make a good mediator.
- ☐ I pursue knowledge avidly.
- ☐ I don't like important information to slip away unrecorded.
- ☐ People value my opinion because they know that I can see any point of view objectively.
- ☐ I have an inner compulsion to experiment and risk for new knowledge.
- ☐ I like to research before deciding anything.

Role 1. Server

As a Server you get deep satisfaction from nurturing others. You are usually a friendly, approachable, modest person. People love you and are inspired by you because you are willing to think of their needs as well as your own.

You are very good at controlling from behind the scenes. For example, you can make a large dinner party look effortless. You specialize in close, one-on-one contact with others. You never lose touch with the needs of an individual loved one while you are trying to cater to the crowd. You are excellent at personal touches like serving hot cocoa on cold days or taking an hour out of your busy weekend to fix a friend's car.

On the other hand, you may neglect your own needs and become overly committed to others. You may have a tendency to become intrusive or smothering in your attempts to assist your loved ones. Remember to take good care of yourself or you'll be too frazzled to do anyone else much good. Also keep in mind that you deserve respect and high self-esteem for being such an inspirational and unselfish person.

Currently, countries such as China and India have a great number of Servers in their populations. We conjecture that at one time there were a great many more Servers in the United States. Recently with the move to a more creative, productive, and self-oriented society, the numbers have dwindled down to about ten per cent of the population. This apparent decrease in Servers has been paralleled by a corresponding increase in the divorce rate and the general dissolution of the family unit. Servers, then, are the glue that holds the fabric of society together. Servers are: Nurturers, helpmates, healers, caretakers.

Role 2. Priest

As a Priest you have a special talent for being able to recognize where people are most blocked in their development. You are usually an inspiring, motivating, dedicated person with a magnetic personality. You are very compassionate toward mankind in general and you hate to see someone lose their path. You are good at discussing personal difficulties with people gently but forcefully and are willing to nudge them toward a more enlightened experience.

Most Priests have a liking for large congregations of souls who look to them for some spiritual guidance. Even those of you who are more shy and quiet like to think of doing something for mankind as a whole, making a positive difference in the world during your lifetime. Be careful not to run roughshod over others as you attempt to improve them or the world. Even if you do have their best interests at heart. Friends don't always take kindly to having their lives rearranged.

We have observed the role of Priest is so specialized that there are not many of them in the population at large: only about three to five per cent. The world needs fewer shepherds than members of the flock. Recently, as many traditional and orthodox religions have begun to dwindle in numbers, the need for leadership by individual Priests has increased. Therefore, your presence is felt more in everyday life. Priests are: Preachers, consciences, goads.

Role 3. Artisan

As an Artisan, you are very aware of and affected by your environment. You tend to subtly create the mood wherever you are. For example, if you are happy, a party shines; if you are sad, it can be subdued, even if you are a wallflower and don't think you are participating. You are creative, innovative, visionary, and are usually one step ahead of the crowd. You have an unusual artistic, eccentric flair, and a style all your own. Whether you use it or not, you usually have a fair amount of artistic talent and interest in the arts.

On the other hand, you may be a daydreamer living in a world of your own creation, deceiving yourself about reality. You may find it difficult to make it in the material world. You can get so out of touch with objective reality, some of you forget who you really are. Try to remember that the simple truths in life are not complex. When you take things down to a minimum, you can feel more secure and less like the universe is one chaotic mess. You need to build bridges between your far-reaching visions and the mainstream realities of others, or you can feel quite cut off.

We have observed that since the 1960s, there has been more demand in United States society that people be in touch with their inner creativity. We believe this is accountable for the quiet subtle rise in the Artisan population; presently about 20%. Artisans are: Artists, innovators, trendsetters, inventors, eccentrics.

Role 4. Sage

As a Sage your job is to find out everything important there is to know and spread that knowledge to as many others as possible, through humor and entertainment. You are a lighthearted, wise, articulate individual. You hate to grow up or lose your childlike wonder towards the world. You excel verbally and make a great lecturer, communicator, or comedian. Most of you love being the center of attention and are the life of the party.

On the other hand, if you aren't careful, you can be loud, tasteless, or childish. You also have a tendency to be overly garrulous and talk the ears off your listeners. You need to avoid scandalous gossip which you tend to love. Juicy stories always grab your attention but when you spread them, you can become slanderous. It would be easier on your listeners if you give them just kernels of basic information.

We have observed that Sages have found their ways into the entertainment and media fields in large numbers, particularly since the advent of film, television, and radio. Even though these Sages are very visible, we have found that the percentage of Sages in the population as a whole is quite small, probably not more than 15%. Sages are: Communicators, entertainers, teachers and tricksters.

Role 5. Warrior

As a Warrior you are in charge of defending and protecting society. You are a productive, organized, persuasive individual always out to protect the underdog. You have an excellent head for business and are usually viewed by others as competent and powerful. You are the most focused of individuals, are good strategists, and you 'get the job done.' Under your tough exterior you are actually a tenderhearted individual. You tend to be patriotic to a cause or country and are monetarily conservative.

On the other hand, you can be overly coercive and argumentative. You are a pushover for a hard luck story and occasionally too naive for your own good. You are subject to tunnel vision in pursuit of your principles. You need to remember to look at the bigger picture and widen your focus. You can look scary and intimidating to those around you, so be gentle with them. Remember, be persuasive rather than coercive.

We have observed that the USA is rapidly becoming a predominantly Warrior culture. The presence of Warriors in the population has moved up to approximately 30% in recent years. With this kind of influence, even non-Warriors will be drawn into the productive, ambitious type of energy that Warriors represent. Warriors are: Strategists, advocates, organizers, business-people, Rocks-of-Gibraltar

Role 6. King

As a King you are a born leader. You may have a regal bearing and inspire great loyalty from others. You are never satisfied until you feel you have mastered whatever you are attempting to accomplish. You have a good grasp of the big picture and are excellent at orchestrating large complex projects. You are a natural delegator; you can see which person is best suited for each job, and charismatic enough to get them all to work together. You can be quite magnanimous and generous with your loyal followers when you are feeling good. You usually feel responsible for their well being and will take great efforts to provide for them. In fact you are willing to take the ultimate responsibility.

On the other hand, at your worst you can be tyrannical and overbearing. You have a strong tendency towards perfectionism and tend to apply your exacting standards to others. Remember, if you ease up on yourself and those who serve you, you will be able to lead more effectively. You do not want to inspire a mutiny.

We have observed that there are very few Kings in the population, one to two per cent, and often you are found in positions of power or authority. Kings are: Adepts, masters, leaders, orchestrators.

Role 7. Scholar

As a Scholar you are a natural observer, arbitrator, and born philosopher. You like to maintain a neutral perspective and you are very good at seeing all sides of an issue. You are a natural student with a high level of curiosity and a great willingness to risk, in order to satisfy your thirst for new knowledge. You love to experiment with things to find out, "What would happen if ...?" This makes you a good scientist if you wish to actualize this aspect of yourself. Often you have a love of books and like to take copious notes in order to learn something new. You are the most eclectic of all the roles, often having more than one profession as well as numerous hobbies. In addition you are visionary, adventurous, and usually have good judgment.

On the other hand, you can blend in too much with the wallpaper in your effort to maintain neutrality. You are often so busy assimilating what is going on around you that you don't share your vast experience and may even be considered dull company. The phrase 'absent-minded professor' was coined for you.

Watch out for your tendency to over-intellectualize. Theorizing isn't the same as being knowledgeable. You'd have a lot more fun and be more involved if you participate more noticeably.

We have observed that Scholars, although sprinkled throughout the population, tend to cluster in academic settings such as universities, scientific projects, and libraries. Nevertheless you may be found in almost any line of work.

Scholars are: Students, philosophers, adventurers, anthropologists.

APPENDIX C: THE NATURE OF REALITY

We've already encountered Sheldrake's M-field and Seth's Framework–2, but two other explanations come from the fields of holography and quantum physics.

First, what is a hologram? The word 'holography' comes from the Greek for 'complete writing,' meaning that every part of the recording contains information about the whole. A hologram is the image recorded on a photographic plate using a laser beam. When the hologram is illuminated by a laser beam, you see a realistic, three-dimensional representation of the original scene. If you cut up the photographic plate into small pieces, the whole image can still be extracted from any piece, although with some loss of clarity. In other words, the information is not localized (as with a photograph), but is distributed across the entire plate.

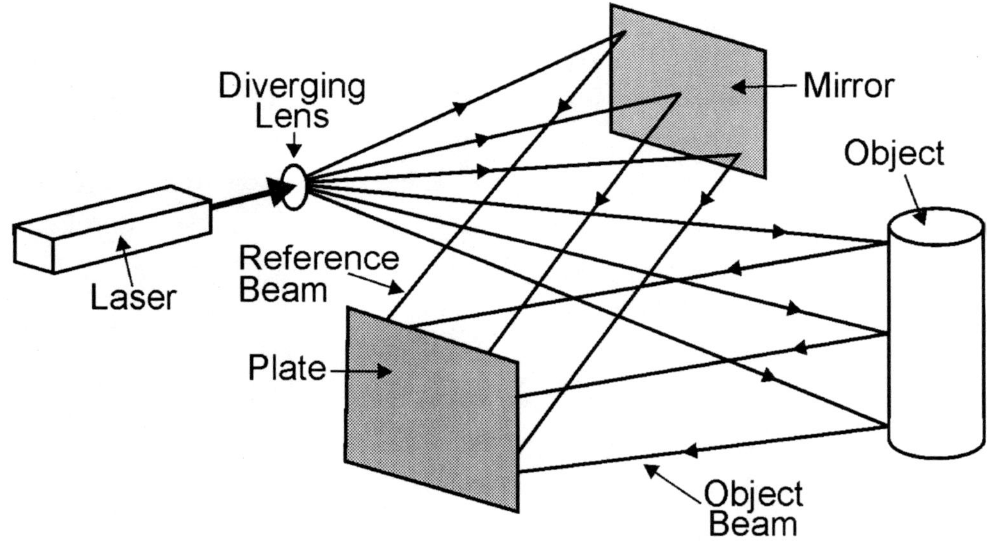

Creating a hologram

The above diagram shows that two laser beams, one reflected from a mirror and the other reflected off the target object, both impinge on the holographic plate, which records an interference pattern between the reflected laser light and the laser light scattered off the object. This is similar to the pattern made when two stones are dropped in a pond as the ripples interfere with each other. All parts of the interference pattern on the holographic plate contain information of the whole, because light bouncing off each point on the object spreads out to every location on the holographic plate.

To reproduce the image, laser light is shined through the holographic plate, picking up the holographic information from the plate, and impinging on the eye. The incoming light forms an image on the retina, which the brain's optical system interprets as coming from a virtual object, thus it 'creates' the image of the object in the mind, even though it's not actually there.

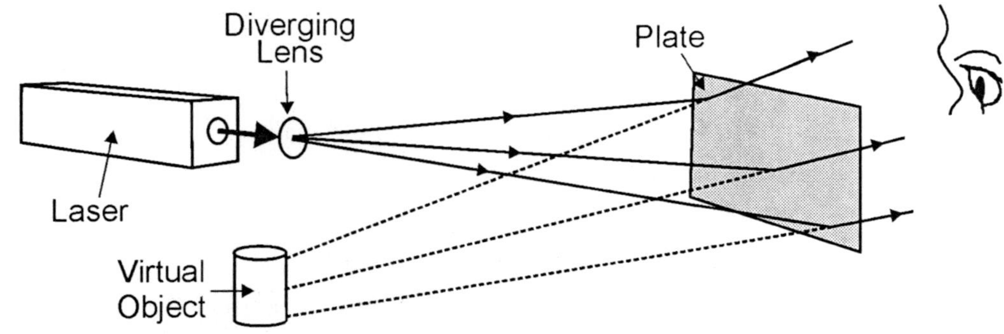

Creating a holographic image from a hologram

Karl Pribram, a neuro-specialist, was struck by the notion that the physical world could be a holographic image that our senses create from the true 'reality' of the interference pattern in some huge generator. At around the same time, physicist David Bohm was studying the paradox by which two sub-atomic particles flying apart at the speed of light could affect each other. This is clearly impossible, but happens nonetheless. Bohm proposed that the particles exist in an 'implicate order' in which their separateness is an illusion. This implicate order is the underlying source reality that flows across the quantum barrier to form the 'explicate order' that we experience as the world around us, much like the pattern on an audio CD yields actual sound and the pattern in a hologram yields our 3–D reality.

The left-brained objective mind picks up only the final projected image, but the right-brained subjective mind can, in some people, tap into Pribram's holographic image, Bohm's implicate order, Seth's Framework–2, or Sheldrake's M-field, depending on which model you use. So when psychics visit a crime scene and 'see' the crime being committed, some quirk in their mind is tapping into the timeless behind-the-scenes pattern, as do psychometrists and dowsers.

However, this is not a passive activity. Renowned medium Eileen Garrett referred to her 'inner condition of alertness that is *the* essential factor.' She entered into full and intimate engagement with events and did more than watch them; she *lived* them. From the age of four, she talked about the 'envelopes' around people (i.e., auras), and had conversations with people who had only envelopes and no bodies (i.e., invisible friends) who played in her garden.

This raises a question that strikes at the heart of the nature of reality. The two apples on the left are physical and seemingly separate. The hologram of them is one interference pattern between two laser beams, and when illuminated, produces the reconstituted image on the right. Which is more real? The holographic pattern, in which the apples are not separate, or the ghostly image on the right, where the apples are seemingly once more separate? Scaling up, which is more real—the reality you see around you, or the implicative M-field source from which all explicative order flows across the quantum veil?

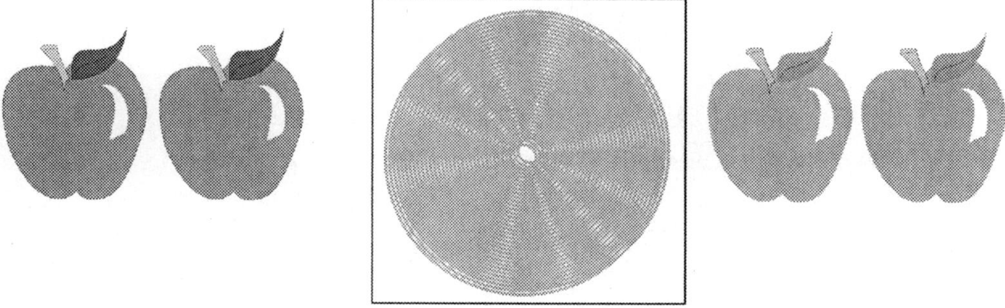

Real apples to hologram to holographic apples

I know many clairvoyants who see the source of reality superimposed on 3–D reality, which makes driving an interesting exercise, as the roads are filled with nonphysical entities. This can happen to 'ordinary' folks, who have spontaneous 'peak experiences' during relaxed moments, in which they see the perfection of creation and their intimate role within it as part of the Source. Unfortunately, these lucky folk cannot put their revelation into words since the experience is ineffable. However, they carry the memory of 'having seen the face of God,' as many describe it.

The important aspect of such peak experiences is that they are our normal state and represent the next level of evolution. Our species seems to be currently stuck on the evolutionary ladder, like a broken record that's been playing the same track for centuries. To the Indigo Children, it's their normal way of being, so through them we are watching evolution take place before our very eyes. Maybe in another generation or so, we won't be forcing Ritalin down their throats, and our species can blossom as intended.

About the Author

Born in Scarborough, England in 1947, Tony graduated from Liverpool University in 1969 with a Bachelor's degree in Electronic Engineering. He joined British Telecomms and also received a Master's degree in Computer Science from London University. After moving to the United States in 1979, he continued in the computer field, but also 'woke up' to metaphysics in 1980.

In 1988, he began cooperative writing with Ascended Master Serapis, one outcome of which was his first book *An Ascension Handbook*, which has enjoyed strong sales for 15 years. For many years, he maintained a close association with the members of Angelic Outreach organization run by Tashira Tachi-ren with whom he shares a great deal of enthusiasm and accord.

After living in Mexico for two years, Tony moved to Denver, Colorado in 1990 where he spent much of his time running a technical computer learning center and teaching computer classes at local universities.

In 1996, he joined Oughten House Publications as Editor-in-Chief, where he managed the production of many fine metaphysical books. When Oughten House closed in 1998, he became an independent publishing consultant so that he could continue to help metaphysical writers bring their messages to the world. It is from this interaction with hundreds of spiritual authors, plus his extensive reading, that *Living with Soul* has sprung.

Tony now lives in Las Vegas, Nev., and can be reached at: tjpublish@aol.com.

About the cover art

The **Flower of Life** is an arrangement of evenly-spaced, overlapping circles that form a flower-like pattern, wherein the center of each circle is on the circumference of six surrounding circles of the same diameter.

The oldest known example, dated to about 3000 BCE, can still be seen carved on the side of the Temple of Osiris at Abydos in Egypt. It is believed that the 90 *vesica piscis* shapes may represent the Eye of Ra. The symbol is considered to be sacred among many cultures around the world, because from it can be derived all the building blocks of the universe known in Sacred Geometry as the Platonic Solids. It therefore symbolizes the connectedness of all life and spirit within the universe.

Meditation on symbol opens one up to the nature of consciousness and awareness of All that Is and the unity within the creation of all things.

toll of the US Military in Iraq... "far more realistic than the government's current official number of 1,800-plus," according to data researcher Brian Harring. Also includes Russian daily military intelligence reports of the Iraqi War from March 17 – April 8, 2003. (ISBN 1-893302- 84-9)

America Speaks Out: Collected Essays From Dissident Writers John H. Brand, Meria Heller, John Kaminski, Norman D. Livergood, Wayne Madsen, Kurt Nimmo, Albert D. Pastore, Michael E. Salla, Sherman H. Skolnick & John Stanton... A collection of essays extracted from works recently published by Dandelion Books. (ISBN 1-893302-63-6)

America 2004: A Power But Not Super, by John Stanton [Foreword by Bev Conover, Editor - online-journal.com, Introduction by Karen Kwiatkowski, Lieutenant Colonel, USAF (Ret.)]... Stanton explains how Bush has adroitly fused state, religious (faith-based government) and business interests into one indistinguishable tyrannical mass... his explanation of how this has been accomplished is eye-opening. (ISBN 1-893302-26-1)

Exopolitics: Political Implications Of The Extraterrestrial Presence, by Michael E. Salla, Ph.D.... According to Dr. Michael Salla and many other experts in the field of ET research, for almost 70 years the US government has engaged in an extensive "official effort" of disinformation, intimidation and tampering with evidence in order to maintain a non-disclosure policy about extraterrestrial presence. (ISBN 1-893302-56-3)

Stranger than Fiction: An Independent Investigation Of The True Culprits Behind 9-11, by Albert D. Pastore, Ph.D... Twelve months of careful study, painstaking research, detailed analysis, source verification and logical deduction went into the writing of this book. In addition to the stories are approximately 300 detailed footnotes Pastore: "Only by sifting through huge amounts of news data on a daily basis was I able to catch many of these rare 'diamonds in the rough' and organize them into a coherent pattern and logical argument." (ISBN 1-893302-47-4)

Unshackled: A Survivor's Story of Mind Control, by Kathleen Sullivan... A non-fictional account of Kathleen Sullivan's experiences as part of a criminal network that includes Intelligence personnel, military personnel, doctors and mental health professionals contracted by the military and the CIA, criminal cult leaders and members, pedophiles, pornographers, drug dealers and Nazis. "I believe my story needs to be told so that more people will understand how 'Manchurian Candidate' style mind-control techniques can create alter-states in the minds of unwitting victims, causing them to perform deeds that are normally repugnant." (ISBN 1-893302-35-0)

Ahead Of The Parade: A Who's Who Of Treason and High Crimes – Exclusive Details Of Fraud And Corruption Of The Monopoly Press, The Banks, The Bench And The Bar, And The Secret Political Police, by Sherman H. Skolnick... One of America's foremost investigative reporters, speaks out on some of America's current crises. Included in this blockbuster book are the following articles: Big City Newspapers & the Mob, The Sucker Traps, Dirty Tricks of Finance and Brokerage, The Secret History of Airplane Sabotage, Wal-Mart and the Red Chinese Secret Police, The Chandra Levy Affair, The Japanese Mafia in the United States, The Secrets of Timothy McVeigh, and much more. (ISBN 1-893302-32-6)

Another Day in the Empire: Life in Neoconservative America, by Kurt Nimmo... A collection of articles by one of Counterpunch's most popular columnists. Included in this collection are: The Son of COINTELPRO; Clueless at the State Department; Bush Senior: Hating Saddam, Selling Him

Weapons; Corporate Media: Selling Dubya's Oil War; Iraq and the Vision of the Velociraptors: The Bleeding Edge of Islam; Condoleezza Rice at the Waldorf Astoria; Predators, Snipers and the Posse Comitatus Act, and many others. (ISBN 1-893302-75-X)

Palestine & The Middle East: Passion, Power & Politics, by Jaffer Ali… The Palestinian struggle is actually a human one that transcends Palestine… There is no longer a place for Zionism in the 20th century… Democracy in the Middle East is not safe for US interests as long as there is an atmosphere of hostility… Suicide bombings are acts of desperation and mean that a people have been pushed to the brink… failure to understand why they happen will make certain they will continue. Jaffer Ali is a Palestinian-American business man who has been writing on politics and business for over 25 years. (ISBN 1-893302-45-8)

Ben-Gurion's Scandals: How the Haganah and the Mossad Eliminated Jews, by Naeim Giladi… The painful truth about the Zionist rape of Palestine and deliberate planting of anti-Semitism in Iraqi Jewish communities during David Ben-Gurion's political career in order to persuade the Iraqi Jews to immigrate to Israel. (ISBN 1-893302-40-7)

America, Awake! We Must Take Back Our Country, by Norman D. Livergood… This book is intended as a wake-up call for Americans, as Paul Revere awakened the Lexington patriots to the British attack on April 18, 1775, and as Thomas Paine's *Common Sense* roused apathetic American colonists to recognize and struggle against British oppression. Our current situation is similar to that which American patriots faced in the 1770s: a country ruled by 'foreign' and 'domestic' plutocratic powers and a divided citizenry uncertain of their vital interests. (ISBN 1-893302-27-X)

America's Nightmare: The Presidency of George Bush II, by John Stanton & Wayne Madsen…Media & Language, War & Weapons, Internal Affairs and a variety of other issues pointing out the US "crisis without precedent" that was wrought by the US Presidential election of 2000 followed by 9/11. "Stanton & Madsen will challenge many of the things you've been told by CNN and Fox news. This book is dangerous." (ISBN 1-893302-29-6)

America's Autopsy Report, by John Kaminski…The false fabric of history is unraveling beneath an avalanche of pathological lies to justify endless war and Orwellian new laws that revoke the rights of Americans. While TV and newspapers glorify the dangerous ideas of perverted billionaires, the Internet has pulsated with outrage and provided a new and real forum for freedom among concerned people all over the world who are opposed to the mass murder and criminal exploitation of the defenseless victims of multinational corporate totalitarianism. John Kaminski's passionate essays give voice to those hopes and fears of humane people that are ignored by the big business shysters who rule the major media. (ISBN 1-893302-42-3)

Seeds of Fire: China and the Story behind the Attack on America, by Gordon Thomas… The inside story about China that no one can afford to ignore. Using his unsurpassed contacts in Israel, Washington, London and Europe, Gordon Thomas, internationally acclaimed best-selling author and investigative reporter for over a quarter-century, reveals information about China's intentions to use the current crisis to launch itself as a super-power and become America's new major enemy…*"This has been kept out of the news agenda because it does not suit certain business interests to have that truth emerge…Every patriotic American should buy and read this book… it is simply revelatory."* (Ray Flynn, Former U.S. Ambassador to the Vatican) (ISBN 1-893302-54-7)

Shaking the Foundations: Coming of Age in the Postmodern Era, by John H. Brand, D.Min., J.D.... Scientific discoveries in the Twentieth Century require the restructuring of our understanding the nature of Nature and of human beings. In simple language the author explains how significant implications of quantum mechanics, astronomy, biology and brain physiology form the foundation for new perspectives to comprehend the meaning of our lives. (ISBN 1-893302-25-3)

Rebuilding the Foundations: Forging a New and Just America, by John H. Brand, D.Min., J.D....Should we expect a learned scholar to warn us about our dangerous reptilian brains that are the real cause of today's evils? Although Brand is not without hope for rescuing America, he warns us to act fast—and now. Evil men intent on imposing their political, economic, and religious self-serving goals on America are not far from achieving their goal of mastery." (ISBN 1-893302-33-4)

The Last Days of Israel, by Barry Chamish... With the Middle East crisis ongoing, *The Last Days of Israel* takes on even greater significance as an important book of our age. Barry Chamish, investigative reporter who has the true story about Yitzak Rabin's assassination, tells it like it is. (ISBN 1-893302-16-4)

The Last Atlantis Book You'll Ever Have to Read! by Gene D. Matlock... More than 25,000 books, plus countless other articles have been written about a fabled confederation of city-states known as Atlantis. If it really did exist, where was it located? Does anyone have valid evidence of its existence — artifacts and other remnants? According to historian, archaeologist, educator and linguist Gene D. Matlock, both questions can easily be answered. (ISBN 1-893302-20-2)

Fiction:

Taboo: A Memoir — Confessions of a Forbidden Love, by Tom Hathaway... A brave and honest exploration of the primal lust of our psyches, *Taboo* points the way to a new sexual frontier. Women who want to know what men really want must read this erotic rhapsody. Th chronicle of a remarkable love affair between mother and son, Tom and Diane did what others only dream of. (ISBN 1-893302-87-3)

Drifters: The Final Testament, Volume One, by Michael Silverhawk... Within the DRIFTERS trilogy is a powerful secret, a key that unlocks our human potential! Can one man "make a difference" not only in his own life but for everyone else on the planet? Is it possible for a single human to transform chaos into order, darkness into light? (ISBN 1-893302-57-1)

Ticket to Paradise, by Yvonne Ridley... Judith Tempest, a British reporter, is searching for the Truth. But when it starts to spill out in her brilliant front page reportage of Middle East suicide bombing in retaliation for Israeli tanks mowing down innocent Palestinian women and children, both 'Tempest' and 'Truth' start to spell 'Trouble'-- with a capital 'T', joke her friends and colleagues. A non-stop mystery thriller that tears along at a reckless pace of passion, betrayal, adventure and espionage. (ISBN 1-893302-77-6)

Synchronicity Gates: An Anthology Of Stories And Poetry About People Transformed In Extraordinary Reality Beyond Experience, by Stephen Vernarelli... An inventive compilation of short stories that take the reader beyond mere science, fiction, or fantasy. Vernarelli introduces the reader to a new perception of reality; he imagines the best and makes it real. (ISBN 1-893302-38-5)

The Alley of Wishes, by Laurel Johnson... Despite the ravages of WWI on Paris and on the young American farm boy, Beck Sanow, and despite the abusive relationship that the chanteuse Cerise endures, the two share a bond that is unbreakable by time, war, loss of memory, loss of life and loss of youth. Beck and Cerise are both good people beset by constant tragedy. Yet it is tragedy that brings them together, and it is unconditional love that keeps them together. (ISBN 1-893302-46-6)

Freedom: Letting Go of Anxiety and Fear of the Unknown, by Jim Britt... Jeremy Carter, a fireman from Missouri who is in New York City for the day, decides to take a tour of the Trade Center, only to watch in shock, the attack on its twin towers from a block away. Afterward as he gazes at the pit of rubble and talks with many of the survivors, Jeremy starts to explore the inner depths of his soul, to ask questions he'd never asked before. This dialogue helps him learn who he is and what it takes to overcome the fear, anger, grief and anxiety this kind of tragedy brings. (ISBN 1-893302-74-1)

The Prince Must Die, by Gower Leconfield... breaks all taboos for mystery thrillers. After the "powers that be" suppressed the manuscripts of three major British writers, Dandelion Books breaks through with a thriller involving a plot to assassinate Prince Charles. *The Prince Must Die* brings to life a Britain of today that is on the edge with race riots, neo-Nazis, hard right backlash and neo-punk nihilists. Riveting entertainment... you won't be able to put it down. (ISBN 1-893302-72-5)

Waaaay Out There! Diggertown, Oklahoma, by Tuklo Nashoba...Adventures of constable Clint Mankiller and his deputy, Chad GhostWolf; Jim Bob and Bubba Johnson, Grandfather Ghost-Wolf, Cassie Snodgrass, Doc Jones, Judge Jenkins and the rest of the Diggertown, Oklahoma bunch in the first of a series of Big Foot-Sasquatch tall tales peppered with lots of good belly laughs and just as much fun. (ISBN 1-893302-44-X)

Come as You Are, by Sarah Daniels... "Tongue-in-cheek" entertainment at its wackiest—and most subtle. If anyone ever doubted that sex makes the world go around, author Sarah Daniels will put your mind, and body to test. Non-stop humor, humanness and wisdom are bundled together to deliver one of life's most important unheeded lessons: each of us has a unique destiny to discover, and until we find and embark on that destiny, life may be one bowl of cherry pits after another. Adult language and scenes. (ISBN 1-893302-15-6)

Unfinished Business, by Elizabeth Lucas Taylor... Lindsay Mayer knows something is amiss when her husband, Griffin, a college professor, starts spending too much time at his office and out-of-town. Shortly after the ugly truth surfaces, Griffin disappears altogether. Lindsay is shattered. Life without Griffin is life without life... One of the sexiest books you'll ever read! (ISBN 1-893302-68-7)

The Woman with Qualities, by Sarah Daniels... South Florida isn't exactly the Promised Land that forty-nine-year-old newly widowed Keri Anders had in mind when she transplanted herself here from the northeast... A tough action-packed novel that is far more than a love story. (ISBN 1-893302-11-3)

Adventure Capital, by John Rushing...South Florida adventure, crime and violence in a fiction story based on a true life experience. A book you will not want to put down until you reach the last page. (ISBN 1-893302-08-3)

A Mother's Journey: To Release Sorrow and Reap Joy, by Sharon Kay... A poignant account of Norah Ann Mason's life journey as a wife, mother and single parent. This book will have a powerful impact on anyone, female or male, who has experienced parental abuse, family separations, financial struggles and a desperate need to find the magic in life that others talk about that just doesn't seem to be there for them. (ISBN 1-893302-52-0)

Return to Masada, by Robert G. Makin... In a gripping account of the famous Battle of Masada, Robert G. Makin skillfully recaptures the blood and gore as well as the spiritual essence of this historic struggle for freedom and independence. (ISBN 1-893302-10-5)

Time Out of Mind, by Solara Vayanian... Atlantis had become a snake pit of intrigue teeming with factious groups vying for power and control. An unforgettable drama that tells of the breakdown of the priesthood, the hidden scientific experiments in genetic engineering which produced "things" -- part human and part animal -- and other atrocities; the infiltration by the dark lords of Orion; and the implantation of the human body with a device to fuel the Orion wars. (ISBN 1-893302-21-0)

The Thirteenth Disciple: The Life of Mary Magdalene, by Gordon Thomas... The closest of Jesus' followers, the name of Mary Magdalene conjures images of a woman both passionate and devoted, both sinner and saint. The first full-length biography for 13 centuries. (ISBN 1-893302-17-2)

ALL DANDELION BOOKS ARE AVAILABLE THROUGH

WWW.DANDELIONBOOKS.NET... ALWAYS.

NEW: TOLL-FREE ORDERS 1-800-861-7899 (U.S. & CANADA)

Astral experences seep
through consciousness uninvited

avoidea by maintaing "white
light protective shield"

LaVergne, TN USA
24 March 2011

221347LV00001B/41/A